CW01496867

LENKIEWICZ

The Life

'All Are Welcome'

Volume I: 1941–1979

Mark D. Price

LENKIEWICZ

The Life

'All Are Welcome'

Volume I: 1941–1979

Mark D. Price

WHITE
LANE
PRESS

First published 2021
© Mark D. Price 2021

White Lane Press, 39 New Street, Plymouth, PL1 2NA

All text, photographs and original works by Robert Lenkiewicz
copyright of The Lenkiewicz Foundation Trust

Mark D. Price has asserted his right to be identified
as the author of this work

ISBN 978-0-9568488-8-8

Official website of The Lenkiewicz Foundation:
www.robertlenkiewicz.org

info@whitelanepress.co.uk

'The lover embraces the world; the fascist embraces the individual.'

Robert Lenkiewicz, Diary, February 1990.

'It is only as an *aesthetic phenomenon* that existence and the world are eternally *justified.*'

Friedrich Nietzsche, The Case of Wagner (1888).

Contents

Acknowledgements

Generosity of spirit is contagious. Robert Lenkiewicz excelled in passing it on. The barest facts of Robert's life provide a colourful tale, but without the contributions of the interviewees this biography would be thinner and paler. For although Robert's projects, paintings, and diaries speak for themselves they were necessarily created from a unique Lenkocentric perspective. In hot pursuit of images worth making and tales worth telling, Robert often outran what we philosophers laughingly refer to as 'the truth'. The interviews are an essential counterbalance to some of his creative excesses. Robert's life and work was amazing, dizzying, courageous: and the same must be said about the generosity of the contributors: you are my co-authors.

Many questions were easy and people smiled and sang out memories of golden times, truly magical times. Others were altogether less easy and summoned memories of dark things. Sometimes I heard anger and frustration and exasperated laughter in one breathless answer: classic symptoms of profound friendship and true love. Robert's paramours, children, and friends are near-unanimous about his powers of *enchantment*. Even among those whose relationship to Robert was mainly commercial there was wonder and fascination. *How did he get away with it?* People I had never before met revealed how they teetered on the brink of bankruptcy or suicide. Others volunteered details of self-harm, murderous jealousy, contested paternities, sexual violence, long-hidden infidelities, and base criminality. But most of all I was gifted stories of adventure and joy. I am a man of many words but not enough to sufficiently thank everyone whose open hearts and minds made this research a transformative process for me. I hope my contribution is enough to conduct your magic to the readers.

In writing these acknowledgements I considered the long, long list of contributors. I tried to make a shortlist. This did not work. I juggled with the ideas of being unequally fair to everybody or equally unfair to most. It soon became clear that I should mention everybody and every institution by name – or none at all. But you know who you are, and you may at any time appear in a flash of red lightning and claim the soul of the book, and a seat at the round table, and a feast of gratitude from its so-called author. All are welcome!

Mark D. Price

The Barbican Mural

The 3,000 square foot mural next to Robert Lenkiewicz's studio in Basket Ope, Plymouth, completed in July 1972. Commonly known as the Barbican Mural, its formal title is *The Influence of Jewish Thought on Elizabethan Culture, 1580–1620*. The artist can be seen centre left next to his self-portrait under the semi-circular opening.

Foreword

After the painter Robert Oscar Lenkiewicz died on 5 August 2002 at the age of 60, it was not the first time his obituary had been published. His untimely death had first been announced on 3 February 1981 in *The Times*. Amongst those most interested in the shocking news, brought to him by his friend and patron Lord Eliot, at whose stately home the artist was concealed, was Lenkiewicz himself: 'I am officially dead', his diary notes. 'Started work on life-size self-portrait. Much thought on the sense of "being dead". A private, subtle feeling of absenteeism.'

Lenkiewicz, preparing an exhibition exploring contemporary attitudes towards death, had decided to observe public reaction to news of his own demise and add his own self-portrait to his paintings of terminally ill people, doctors, hospice staff, coroners, and morticians. 'One cannot know what it is like to be dead, only what it is like to be thought dead.' Intending to 'resurrect after three days', the absence of a body soon alerted the local press that something was amiss. The resulting media frenzy and the tone of the local letters pages suggested that the painter had gone too far. And so on 1 April he stood in penance on Plymouth's historic quayside, the Barbican, in front of his largest public mural, whose entire 3,000 square feet had been whitewashed over and replaced with an image of three flying ducks. Two collection boxes were set out; whichever box held the greatest amount at the end of the day would determine the public's preference for the old landmark or the new one.

The Barbican Mural, arguably still Lenkiewicz's best-known work, is a cipher for the transformative role of Jewish ideas during the English Enlightenment. It refers to alchemy, witchcraft, Cabala, ceremonial magic, science, art and literature, the cult of melancholy, and Fool symbolism. Elizabeth I presides over the chaotic scene, clutching a rainbow, symbol of peace and a firm hint that she is England's sun. At street level there is an image of the painter seemingly crushed beneath the weight of his own creation. One hand points to three gold coins in a begging-bowl, the other rests on a skull: a traditional reminder that death is imminent. The vast mural, covering the north-west elevation of a former gin bottling warehouse, was completed in July 1972. In the notes on the mural, Lenkiewicz foreshadowed the tension between the public's 'natural aggressions towards elitist culture' and the artist's desire to bridge 'an enormous gap that lies between what he thinks he is trying to communicate and the persons and circumstances he is trying to communicate with.'

Lenkiewicz's career as a painter after his arrival in Plymouth in the late 1960s can be seen as an attempt to address the simple fact of the visual illiteracy of his chosen audience without condescension. 'The truth is that I am very, very keen on the opinion of the ordinary person, the man in the street,' Lenkiewicz said in an interview in 1997.

As critic David Lee observed: 'Lenkiewicz's greatest gift was to show us that an artist could be genuinely concerned about social and domestic issues and attempt the difficult task of expressing this conscience through the deeply unfashionable medium of figurative painting. In that sense he was one of the few serious painters of contemporary history'.

Time and the weather have not been kind to the Barbican Mural, however. Exterior house paints with a 15-year lifespan cannot defy physics, and after the artist abandoned attempts to repair the painting in the 1990s it deteriorated inexorably into a faded, flaking ruin, partially obscured by wooden battens intended to hold a new mural, never started. But its meaning endures. In his notes on the mural, Lenkiewicz stated: 'it is intended that the Barbican mural should convey some of the feeling of the demoniac brilliance of the Elizabethan Age, a time of tremendous skills, flights of imagination, and great brutalities; a time very much like our own.'

Lenkiewicz's Polish-born Jewish father had been a horse trader in Saxony, before escaping to settle in London just as war broke out, while his mother was also a Jewish refugee from Nazi Germany. This background instilled in the young Lenkiewicz a fascination with the great figures of 19th-century German culture – Goethe and Schiller, Schubert, Wagner, and, in particular, the philosopher Friedrich Nietzsche.

As an art student, captivated by his painter heroes in London's National Gallery – Rembrandt, Caravaggio, Hals, Velázquez, and Courbet, among others – Lenkiewicz accumulated an encyclopaedic knowledge of the history of art (later reinforced by his 5000-volume library on art and art history). In that tradition, many of his paintings are tonally dramatic, battles of light and dark, invariably painted direct from life; his aim was to convey the 'plain fact' of his subject's existence in the belief that it was of more importance than an artist's canvas.

Although he worked almost entirely in isolation, outside of prevailing art fashions, Lenkiewicz was far from immune to what was happening around him in the new art and ideas of the 1960s. Influenced by his readings of radical counterculture thinkers such as R. D. Laing, Michel Foucault, and Ivan Illich, much of his earlier work concentrated on the outsiders and dispossessed of consumer society. At the same time, he was ruthlessly analysing his own personal relationships and, mainly in notebooks and works on paper termed 'aesthetic notes', developing a more private language to express them. The relationship between ethics and aesthetics had obsessed both Schiller and Nietzsche, and lies at the heart of Lenkiewicz's enquiries into the human condition. What was it, he wanted to know, that drove people to kill or die for a belief or point of view?

The 'Death Project' was the 15th in a series of 20, which the artist described as 'sociological and philosophical investigations into the human condition'. The first was titled: Vagrancy. Later ones included Old Age, Suicide, Jealousy, Education, and Addictive Behaviour. These were based on extensive research, often recording the sitters' own views, contained in 'Project notebooks' and backed up by an ever-growing library on these subjects, as well as art, metaphysics, and philosophy.

On Lenkiewicz's 'second' and final death, his vast archive of hand-written notebooks, private diaries and illustrated journals was bequeathed to The Lenkiewicz Foundation. The Foundation made it available to Dr Mark Price whom it commissioned to write this first, extraordinary biography of the artist.

Francis Mallett
The Lenkiewicz Foundation
October 2021

1.1 Alice Lenkiewicz holding Robert's non-identical twin Bernard with father Isaac holding Robert, *c.*1943.

1.2 The Lenkiewicz family in 1945. Johnny sits on Alice's lap.

1.3 Isaac Lenkiewicz, London *c.*1946.

1

Through the Gap Between Death's Front Teeth

Robert Lenkiewicz was fond of remarking that if we are seriously interested in somebody then we are also interested in their parents. His distant ancestors migrated via a series of adventures and persecutions from the Levant to a region of north-eastern Europe once known as the 'Paradise of the Jews': Poland. For many centuries Poland was the most remarkable centre of religious inclusion. From the 9th to the beginning of the 17th century its monarchs welcomed Jews fleeing Europe's forced conversions and pogroms. The kingdom supported a fertile mix of Ashkenazim Jews, Mizrahim from the Middle East, and Spanish, Turkish, and Italian Sephardic Jews. The office of Chief Rabbi was inaugurated by the Polish monarchy, which granted autonomy to the Qahal, the autonomous government of Ashkenazim, and trusted Jews to select their own judges, tax collectors, and other officials. It is estimated that during the 16th century almost three-quarters of the global Jewish population lived in Poland. But the Paradise hit a sharp decline in 1772 with the partition of the kingdom. Events worsened into outright persecution and genocide from outside forces: first Russia, then Prussia, then the German Reich and the disaster of Europe's mid-20th century.

The Romani scholar Ian Hancock uses the term 'O Porrajmos' – 'The Great Devouring' – to describe the mass murder of countless Gypsies under the Nazis. Wanderers without a written language or documentation, their history is harder to map onto numbered killings. By contrast the Nazis were great custodians of data for Jewish families. Documents of births, deaths, marriages, and presiding officials were preserved with the same rigour with which Jews and synagogues were destroyed. As Tracey Rich[1] notes, there are official Reich stamps on birth certificates going back to the 1840s: diligent desk clerks traced links between 'the parents and children, the rabbi, mohel, midwife, witnesses and so forth'. Then there are Sefer Yuchsin – family records, in some cases with deep and wide links, stretching back to Biblical Levites. 'Holocaust denial' is so far removed from the available facts that it became a source of fascination for Robert in his middle years, prompting him to make connections between such unlikely intellectual allies as the Marquis de Sade and Sigmund Freud, with whom he shared the opinion that what people believe has little to do with reality and much to do with satisfying their own desires. Polish census records and the Nazi's own documentation prove that upwards of three million non-Jewish Poles were murdered; and a population of almost three and a half million Jews was reduced to less than 300,000. One of these survivors was Robert's father, Isaac Lenkiewicz, and this is the story of how he slipped between the gap in death's front teeth and escaped Nazi Germany. The son of a horse trader, Isaac (Ajzyk) was born and raised in Grajewo, in north-east Poland, a middle-sized town on a windy agricultural plain with several beautiful lakes. He was devout in his youth and studied to become a rabbi. Along with his parents he emigrated to Germany aged 19. Like his father Reuven, Isaac became a trader in horses. He was a small man, with a cleft in his chin which he would later mythologise to his children as the wound where a horse kicked him. He was quietly spoken but fond of conversation. The family settled into their new house in Dresden, where Isaac and his father used the local Bierkeller as their office.

Anti-Semitism was rife and the Nazi Party was growing in power. During the early 1930s laws had been passed to ban Jews from public office, limit their access to education, and the 'de-naturalisation' laws stripped them and other 'undesirables' of citizenship and the most basic civil rights. The sociable and successful Isaac was betrayed to the Reich authorities for allegedly having a sexual relationship with a non-Jew. Slander or not, the 1935 Nuremberg Laws made this a potentially lethal accusation. This was a dire crime against German 'blood and honour' known as *Rassenschande* – racial defilement or biological fouling. The threat of degrading the 'pure' German race with *Mischlinge* – mixed ones, mongrels – was felt sharply enough to ensure that thousands of cross-mating men were convicted and sent to the camps. Many were simply murdered, without trial or conviction, on the basis of such accusations.

Isaac was removed to jail then acquitted by the Reich-Prosecutor but fearing further actions against him he fled to Paris: even without the racial sex-crime charges he would have had little chance of survival in Dresden. Twenty months after he left the city, a nation-sized pustule of hatred burst and the lethal intentions of the Nazi Party flowed freely during *Kristallnacht* – the night of broken glass. The Dresden synagogue was destroyed. Leading members of the community were assaulted, Jewish houses and shops were smashed by SA and SS men wearing ordinary clothes, partly assisted by mobs of ordinary German citizens. It was a co-ordinated action resulting in the destruction of over 7,000 Jewish businesses and almost every synagogue in Germany and Austria. Many were set alight. Those inconveniently close to 'Aryan' property were pulverised with sledgehammers, crowbars, and axes.

In all cases the archives were treated with respect and handed over to the Nazi *Sicherheitsdienst* as valuable leads to future murders. Far from being spontaneous riots prompted by the murder of a minor Nazi official, the *Kristallnacht* operations were obviously a product of state policy. Across Germany and Austria the police were ordered to arrest as many young Jewish men as the jails could accommodate. Had Isaac not been accused of racial mixing, he would likely have stayed in Dresden and almost certainly have been among the tens of thousands sent to Buchenwald, Dachau, or Sachsenhausen that November.

Isaac's three years in Paris could not have been happy ones. He would have been painfully aware of events unfolding in the lands he had left behind. Back in Dresden his father became seriously ill and died of natural causes in 1938. Isaac's mother, sister Leibe and several cousins were later deported to a transit ghetto and murdered at Auschwitz. Isaac was doubtless also aware that the threat to his own life had not been left behind in Dresden. The international ambitions of the Nazi Party were no secret. During Isaac's time in Paris, the Rhineland, Sudetenland, and Austria were annexed as German territory. France tried to create a defensive border along the Maginot Line, and in the summer of 1938 Hitler ordered a general mobilisation of the armed forces. Isaac pre-empted the German move into France and fled to England.

Here the immigration officials failed to appreciate that, as a Polish Jew escaping Germany, Isaac was highly likely to be more anti-German and certainly more anti-Nazi than any Englishman. The British tagged him as a 'suspect alien' and packed him off first to a Kitchener internment camp in Kent then on the Isle of Man. Many Polish Jews were held in the island's main town of Douglas, along with other German-speaking Jews in camp 'P', a long block of terraces on Hutchinson Road known as 'the artists' camp'. This included the Dada artist Kurt Schwitters, several internationally renowned musicians, university professors, and scientists. The few accounts of the Isle of Man camps we have present the situation as a miniature Germany: a heady mix of high culture and the threat of violence from armed agents of the state. Freddy Godshaw, speaking in the BBC 'People's War' archive tells us:

Very few of us even knew that there was an island in the Irish Sea and all sorts of rumours arose about our destination before we actually docked at Douglas on the Isle of Man. Armed guards escorted us with fixed bayonets to a square in the centre of Douglas. A double row of barbed wire had been erected around three streets. There were twelve houses each facing the lawned green square and the third row of houses backed on to one of the rows facing the square. All the houses were identical and were typical Edwardian houses built as boarding houses for the summer visitors. All rooms had double beds and with very little other furniture [...]. We soon made blackout curtains with our blankets, which could be taken down to use on our beds at night. We then scraped the blue paint from the windows. Some of the windows were left with amazing pictures of landscapes, flowers and also erotic shapes of the female figure where artists scraped away some of the blue paint but leaving those pictures for all to see. Unfortunately, none of these windows survived, as they really were quite spectacular, especially at night before the black-out curtains went up.[2]

Under the shadow of barbed wire and bayonets, with 30 men cramped in each house, culture bloomed:

There was no shortage of teachers as we had more than 50 professors amongst the 1200 internees. Every other person in the camp was a doctor of something or other. [...] Kurt Schwitters though was our main star. Not only was he a world-famous artist but he was also a most fascinating raconteur and could keep a full house entertained for hours. He wrote and recited a symphony in words.
It took weeks before we received any letters from our families and then they were all censored. We could only write one letter per week on special paper provided by the authorities and one was only allowed to write 24 lines. Again, they were all censored. The lack of letters etc. was really a real hardship as this was at the height of the Battle of Britain and a large number of the men in the camp had families in London.[3]

Isaac was befriended by a Mr Lemberger, a London German Jew who would become a lifeline, advisor, and matchmaker. The refugees had nothing but each other and their talents to fall back on. Therefore, they spent much of their time making links and plans and commitments to help each other should they be first out of the camp. In this sense they were surrounded by friends. But Isaac was also surrounded by armed guards and barbed wire, in a strange country, with an uncertain future, and no news of the dwindling numbers of his family and friends in Europe. News reaching the Isle of Man via every new inmate was bad: the Nazi programme of slaughter was accelerating, and anyone with kith or kin inside the Reich should fear the worst. Having lived in a state of high anxiety for many years it is hardly surprising that Isaac Lenkiewicz's heart broke into a series of irregular seizures. He may have briefly thought he was about to die, but probably fainted before he could berate himself for being 40 years old and single and childless and thus a failure as a Jewish man – unaware he was soon to encounter the formidable figure of his future wife, Alice von Schlossberg.

Alice was born in Frankfurt in 1900. Her family were genetically no more or less 'mongrel' than their Aryan neighbours, but the von Schlossbergs were the inheritors of a richly mixed heritage. Religiously Jewish and culturally German, Alice never wore the Yellow Star because she looked like a pure Teutonic Earth Goddess. The word most readily used to describe her – not exclusively but especially by her closest family – is *massive*. She sometimes bravely and foolishly spoke out about her affiliation. One day when sitting on a park bench she was joined by a mean German *hausfrau* bemoaning the number of Jews using the park, grumbling 'Ach, all of Palestine is here!' At this Alice pointed to the bench on which they sat, then pointed to her substantial self before replying 'Palestine is here, too.' Not only did Alice look like the Wagnerian ideal of Germanic womanhood, the ideal was in her blood. She identified with Weimar culture and 'Teutonic nobility' in a deep sense. Her father had been employed and, according to family legend, ennobled by Richard Wagner's saviour and patron, King Ludwig II of Bavaria.

Stories of King Ludwig's life, mental health, and death are many and divergent: Robert knew and retold most of them, though we can only guess at how Ludwig's generosity influenced him. It is still disputed whether Ludwig committed suicide or was assassinated. What is not in dispute is his huge expenditure on the arts, which his enemies interpreted as a sure sign of madness. Alice often told her sons how her father came into the employ of Ludwig to create murals and possibly also theatrical scene-paintings. She claimed the King was deeply impressed by a large mural depicting the four seasons and that their grandfather was rewarded with the title Baron von Schlossberg. Various members of the Lenkiewicz family have doubted this tale, and Robert was not entirely convinced by it. No mural matching Alice's description can be found at any of Ludwig's castles, and neither is there any evidence that it was Ludwig who ennobled him, although some evidence does exist that Alice's father was indeed a baron.

Alice's niece Erika has told a version of the story in which the title 'Baron' was bestowed on the painter by some impecunious nobleman. It would be very unusual for such a rank to be conferred by anybody except a reigning monarch, but it is interesting that it was not Alice alone who thought that her father held the title. More convincing evidence comes from Robert's younger brother Johnny. When visiting Germany to research his family, Johnny established that his grandfather had been recorded as one of the eminent Jewish citizens of Frankfurt. Johnny searched for the graves of his grandparents in the Jewish cemetery, which was fortunately one of the few not entirely smashed by the Nazis. This tallied somewhat with Alice's story: she had claimed her father was buried in an ornate tomb directly alongside Paul Ehrlich, the great scientist who gave us the first effective and humane cure for syphilis. No von Schlossberg tomb was found, but Johnny persevered and eventually found two near-identical and very modest stone squares, set some way apart, one of them face-down. The stone still standing belonged to Eugenia, Alice's mother. The fallen grave marker was that of his grandfather, with the inscription naming him 'My Beloved Husband Bernard von Schlossberg, Portrait Painter, Died 1907'. Despite him being neither a rich baron nor a famous painter, the gravestone records him as a von Schlossberg and a painter nonetheless. More important than any facts supporting the true social rank of Robert's grandfather is Alice's strength of feeling on this topic. She believed her father to be a cultural giant, and in later life she impressed the consequences of this view upon her sons in large but very unequal measures.

Most of the Lenkiewicz family remember Alice von Schlossberg as difficult company and certainly not the closest friend of truth. All – including Johnny – were amazed that her tales of her ennobled ancestry had any basis in fact. But the story Alice told concerning her escape from Germany is wonderfully dramatic, and Robert's frequently told version bears recounting.

While the jaws of death were closing in around all of Frankfurt's Jews, somehow it was arranged for Alice to stow away on a cargo freighter bound for safer lands. Under cover of darkness she was smuggled aboard and led to the hold, hiding among sacks of grain. Night turned to day, but the vessel remained in the docks. Then she heard voices barking orders. A search!

Soldiers of the Reich stomped aboard and were seeking evidence of stow-aways. Their voices came closer, closer, and soon they were bayoneting the sacks in the hold. Alice held her nerve and her breath and wondered if she could keep silent if a blade cost her a finger, an ear, or an eye. By sheer chance, *ein Glücksfall*, a roll of the dice, her steely resolve saw her through and the seeking blades failed to find her. The soldiers were called away from their Jew-hunt; the vessel was soon in motion on the sighing seas to freedom. Thus, Alice von Schlossberg arrived in England, imperforated, but also without possessions, without passport, and without a shred of corroborating evidence for this story, not even the name of the ship.

Alice's life was already stamped with tragedy: a younger sister, possibly congenitally insane, had conditioned her hair with paraffin then acciden-tally set herself alight and died in an institution; her father perished in 1907. In London her life may not have been constantly under threat, but it was far from what she had been used to. Her poverty, insecurity, and isolation were mitigated by the Jewish Welfare Office but her ability to make friends was self-limiting. Over half a century later one of Alice's sons relates an example:

> Sabine Ney-Hoch, a spinster all her life, a very sweet lady who abso-lutely *worshipped* Alice, but for some reason Alice thought Sabine was a bore. The Ney-Hochs later came to live with us in the Hotel Shemtov. Stella and Maria called her *Tante Sabine*. When Alice first came to London, she had to go to a Jewish Welfare Office where people would come for handouts. One day, when the name Alice von Schlossberg was called out, a voice from the back of the crowd shouted out '*Liska!*' I'm told Sabine literally ran with her arms open towards Alice. Alice sighed and said '*Scheisse*'. This is the story Ma told me. And Sabine worshipped her!
>
> She [Sabine] was a really lovely woman. She used to work in a bookstore in Germany and one day some Nazi official came in and started berating her, saying she had to wear the [Yellow] Star. Anyway, she gave him a load of backchat and it was only when he left she re-alised she might expect a good kicking or the shop burned down, but nothing happened. She had that same stupid courage as Alice. (Ber-nard Leigh, Interview, August 2017)

The British Government was not kind to penniless female refugees: they were tolerated only on harsh conditions. Alice was deemed trustworthy only with the most menial work in return for a roof and a very meagre allowance. Many of the Jewish women arriving in England were skilled workers but regardless of their experience and qualifications they had to possess two and only two attributes: to be under 39 years of age and do exactly as commanded without complaint. Disgruntled 'employers' held the power to hand troublesome women back to the authorities or might even tell malicious tales to get them incarcerated. Alice was powerless. She worked for a Mrs Stiebel, who liked to mock Alice and engage in light-hearted psychological torture. While Alice cleaned toilets and scrubbed floors, Mrs Stiebel would stand over her offering criticism, and on the rare days when post from Europe arrived made sure that any rays of joy were pre-dimmed: 'Ah, a letter. For Fräulein … who? Von? Von? *Von Schlossberg?*' she would say, dropping Alice's mail into the bucketful of suds. Obviously, Alice detested this back-breaking grind and humiliation and thought – somewhat less obviously – that marriage would be her best escape route.

Her future husband was still an intern. Isaac recovered from the heart attack but was at risk of becoming the kind of prisoner the authorities detest above all except escape-risks: an expensive invalid. Some of the old and unhealthy refugees had been released to fend for themselves in England's cities on condition they reported to the police on a regular basis. Mr Lemburg was already in London and willing to welcome Isaac. A travel pass was arranged, and Isaac delivered himself into the waiting arms of London's Jewish community, where shortly before Passover 1940 in a café in Golders Green he was introduced by Mr Lemburg to Alice von Schlossberg.

For more reasons than meeting his future wife, the accusation which forced Isaac's flight from Dresden had been an unusual stroke of fortune. By 1938 Jews of Polish citizenship resident in Germany had been deported to Poland where they had little chance of survival. Even if Robert's parents had been among the 20,000 or so Jews who lived in hiding in Germany during the war, they could just as easily have been killed by Allied bombing raids. The Lenkiewicz's house in Dresden was directly opposite the abattoir subsequently made famous by Kurt Vonnegut in his novel *Slaughterhouse Five*. As a prisoner of war, Vonnegut emerged from the cellar of the abattoir to a place 'like the surface of the moon':

Every day we walked into the city and dug into basements and shelters to get the corpses out, as a sanitary measure. [...] We went to work

24

through cordons of German soldiers. Civilians didn't get to see what we were up to. After a few days the city began to smell, and a new technique was invented. Necessity is the mother of invention. We would bust into the shelter, gather up valuables from people's laps without attempting identification, and turn the valuables over to guards. Then soldiers would come with a flame-thrower and stand in the door and cremate the people inside. Get the gold and jewellery out and then burn everybody inside.[4]

The destruction of Germany was not foreseen in 1940 and Robert's parents could not have known that after the war there would be nothing and nobody left to return to. As far as can be discovered, everybody from Isaac's family died in the transit ghettos or in Auschwitz. Alice's family fared little better, with one brother, Oscar, escaping to the United States. Her only blood relation in London was Erika, the illegitimate daughter of Elena, Alice's sister. Elena would be murdered by the Nazis along with all the rest of the extended family. Isaac and Alice's wedding plans must have amplified their anxieties for absent family and friends: all the news from Europe was bad, and there was no chance of their loved ones being allowed to leave the Reich.

The wedding was a swift civil ceremony. Although Alice was imperfectly religious, she was a 'devout hypocrite, and very much concerned with what others thought of her'. She was 'also devoutly anti-sexual and keen to let others know it' (Johnny Lenkiewicz, Interview, April 2018). Thus, on her first wedding night, and for many days and nights following, no sex was allowed; nor would it be until a second, 'proper' Jewish ceremony was conducted. The tale of Alice von Schlossberg's arrival in England may not be entirely accurate but it seems certain that she had the rare distinction of being a proud virgin on both of her wedding days. Nevertheless, she was pregnant with twins almost immediately after the second wedding. Her attempt to escape domestic drudgery via marriage was, as she herself was fond of saying, 'out of the frying pan into the fire'. The twins were born on the last day of 1941. They were non-identical, and Alice made a point of treating them so. The first born was named Bernard after Alice's father; the second arrived a quarter of an hour later and was named Reuven after Isaac's father. The name was soon anglicised to Robert.

2.1 Robert *(left)* aged four and a half years, his brother Johnny aged two years, and Robert's twin, Bernard *(right)*, in 1946.

2.2 Robert aged nine years.

2

Lessons in Pain and Experiments in Pleasure

Despite his hardships and losses, Isaac remained a sociable and softly spoken man. He made the best of his situation in London by cultivating friendships and business connections, advising on the sale and purchase of horses, wheeling and dealing as refugees often must. The twins grew healthily but in Alice's heart and mind they were far apart. The arrival of their third child John in 1944 did not re-tip the balance. The boys were all made acutely aware of Alice's judgement on this matter:

> Bernard hated my mother because she had a very partial relationship with him from the very start in that Robert was the Golden Boy. She was utterly in love with him – as much as one can be in love without having sexual fantasies about them. Maybe she did; I don't know.
>
> Bernard was *backwards* according to Ma. But he was the only one of us who had a living from the age of fifteen, fixing radios and televisions. He was fantastic with electronics, had his own income, his own car. A proper grown-up, in a way that neither of his brothers were. (Johnny Lenkiewicz, Interview, May 2017)

Bernard was dark, lean, and physically robust though small in comparison to Robert, who was from the outset a 'huge blonde blue-eyed beast'. For reasons which remain obscure – though more than one person in the Lenkiewicz family attribute this to a strange kind of Jewish anti-Semitism – Alice took appearances as sure signs of future realities. She decided that Robert was destined for greatness. She poured all available energy into making her diagnosis of 'child-genius' a reality, even when that involved blatant injustices to Bernard, Johnny, or anybody else.

During 1943/44 the Lenkiewiczs lived at 41 Howitt Road, directly opposite Belsize Park tube station. But even in leafy Hampstead the threat of annihilation was not distant. In spring 1945 the twins were out with Alice in an area called Whitestone Pond on Hampstead Heath when the air raid sirens sounded. Bernard Lenkiewicz (name later anglicised to 'Leigh') recalls:

I can remember seeing the searchlights there. I think it was a different time when I was very young. A bomb fell; I remember going to somewhere very dark, very quickly, and only later I figured out we had been taken down into Belsize Park station. We went down the steps in pitch blackness, many, many steps. The next station is one of the deepest tube stations in London, three hundred and something steps. That was my earliest memory.

Not every risk to the young brothers fell from the skies, however. Their mother had some very cruel ideas about their education:

I remember a party in the garden for the end of the war, with my father. In Belsize Park we had an anthracite heater and my mother said, 'Don't go near it, you will burn your fingers.' I don't know whether Johnny ignored her or not but she said, 'I will show ...' and she pushed his finger in to burn him. Made sure he learned the hard way. That was my mother. Johnny doesn't remember it, but I do. (Bernard Leigh, formerly Lenkiewicz, Interview, August 2017)

Alice and Isaac Lenkiewicz worked hard and built a strong enough reputation to secure a loan from a local businessman who ran a series of kosher butcher shops. They must have been exceptionally well trusted for the sum was large enough to buy a twin house in a good neighbourhood in the autumn of 1949. This became not only a home for the family but also a business, a refuge, and a community. It also became a hothouse of intellectual, artistic, and erotic possibilities for young Robert: the Hotel Shemtov.

Proprietress – Mrs A Lenkiewicz
Telephone – Gladstone 0515-0707
Hotel Shemtov
STRICTLY KOSHER
CENTRAL HEATING – HOT AND COLD WATER
IN ALL ROOMS
85–87 Fordwych Road,
London, N.W. 2

Curiously, the hotel stationery carried no mention of Isaac. The Lenkiewicz twins were nine years old when they moved to the Shemtov. Two decades later when Robert left London the Shemtov became – at least in his flexible and expansive memory – a 60-roomed mansion of insanity populated by 'a combination of rabbis and lunatics, [people] no longer in control. Mother was a sort of nursemaid to about thirty people who paid her a nominal weekly rent for board and lodging'.[5]

In reality it was a large Victorian double-house conversion 'with twenty-five or perhaps thirty rooms at most, if we include cellars, attics and broom cupboards' (Johnny Lenkiewicz, Interview, September 2017). The Ney-Hoch family – Axel, his English wife Gladys, and their daughters Ria and Stella – lived for a while in one set of attic rooms. Stella recalls, 'I don't think the residents of Shemtov were any more or less mad than any other group. They just inspired the imagination of an impressionable youth'. We must bear in mind that Stella was herself a resident and the daughter of Axel, whose influence upon Robert would be considerable.

The Hotel Shemtov building and its daily operation can be described in some detail. From the wide tree-lined pavement of Fordwych Road several steps rose to the garden and a path led to the central ground floor entrance. Beyond the large front door lay a tiled hallway with Alice's office to the right. Ahead was the dining room with eight or ten tables for the residents, and a pair of stone columns against which young Robert would test his strength by playing the blind Samson in the Temple of Baal. Either side of the dining room were large kitchens: one for dairy, the other for meat, with a *Kühlschrank* or refrigerator large enough to present the mortal danger of being locked inside.

Irish maids lived in the Shemtov as a solution to affordable labour and the strictures against working on the Sabbath. In 1950s London the Irish were recipients of British racism no less than Jews, but by all accounts they were treated well at the Shemtov as long as they were prepared to work as hard as Alice, and not steal. Laundry was constant, cooking was constant, and there was according to John 'a permanent *institutional* smell to the place'. There was a dumb-waiter to deliver food to all floors for those too invalided to reach the dining room; there were many carpets to be beaten, stairs to be swept, and several bathrooms to be kept clean. Alice was anything but a hands-off proprietress: Johnny and Bernard attest they hardly ever saw her sit down, and she took absolute responsibility for the kitchens. By all accounts she was an excellent kosher cook, so much so that non-residents and non-Jewish neighbours vied for places at her Sunday dinners.

The three Lenkiewicz boys slept in room 3 at the back of the house on the first floor. Bernard's and Robert's beds were close by the window and often cluttered by Robert's paints and easels. John's bed was on the other side of the room where he would often lie awake picking away at the plaster wall as if to tunnel an escape from the atrocious pea-green linoleum.

The building had previously been a maternity home. Many of the high ceilings were marked with grooves in the plaster where the rails and dividers of curtained cubicles had been. John recalls that one ancient resident had been born there, lived almost all her life there, and died there. At the very rear of the building was a coal-delivery trapdoor leading down to a deep, high-ceiling cellar, pitch black, vexed with complex pipes, and home to tribes of large spiders. In here a furnace burned almost constantly.

The social and chemical climate of London during the 1950s was not pleasant. Despite a post-war economic boom, rationing was worse than ever. London was an ugly and unhealthy city. Polio cases soared. Bomb-sites still pitted the city like ulcers. Transport systems were overcrowded, and the smog sometimes forced drivers to abandon their vehicles at noon: even the strongest headlights were useless. The infrastructure creaked as new workers were drawn to the city. Sewer gangs, or 'flushers', struggled to keep 13,000 miles of waste pipes clear: overflows were horribly frequent. The Shemtov was located far from the worst of London's squalor but poisoned air knows no postcodes. In December 1952 temperatures plummeted. For five windless sub-zero days and nights, the eight million people of London heaped extra coal on their fires. The air thickened with a lethal chemical brew which blotted out the sun. More than a tenth of a million people developed serious lung problems. Twelve thousand people died. Johnny's asthma was already life-threatening: 'He would turn blue during attacks, it was very, very, upsetting to watch' (Bernard Leigh, Interview, November 2107). The Lenkiewiczs were very lucky that he was not among the fatalities.

As dangerously unhealthy as London could be, the residents were well insulated from most of the city's problems. They had warm lodgings, decent food, no threats of eviction or violence, and virtual room service. It generated a treasure-trove of memories about its inhabitants. Bernard recalls an episode when he and Robert were not yet teens. The elderly Mrs Plotnik fell over naked and he was called to carry her to bed. 'She said "Bernard you must not tell anybody of this, you must not say you have seen my *grey* vagina". Well, it wasn't a delightful sight but here I am telling you. Her *grey* vagina. She was self-conscious but not about her nakedness: about her age, the signs of age'. Bernard, of course, straightaway told this to Robert, who demanded more details than Bernard had. Unbeknown to

Bernard until many years later, Robert had made a tiny peep-hole in the bathroom wall to spy on the women of the Shemtov whenever he got the chance: his favourite ogles were the Irish maids Mary and Eileen. A few years later the twins began their sexual education with these lusty, direct, often middle-aged Catholic women whose lives were closer to normality than any others in the Shemtov.

The wealthiest and thus – second only to Robert – the most cared-for inhabitant of the Shemtov was Mr Cyril Myers. He was 'always incredibly dapper, in permanent business clothing' (Johnny Lenkiewicz) but was so averse to parting with money that he had a nervous twitch and stutter, both specifically related to taking anything out of his pockets. His hands juddered violently, and he jabbered like a scratched record as if to prevent the painful extraction of a wallet or cheque book. This eccentricity was treated patiently and almost affectionately by Alice and the staff. Mr Myers's nervous affliction was a minor one compared to the resident who would sit half-paralysed and recite, 'There's a fly on the floor there's a fly there's a penny we're all going to die like flies in the hot summertime'. This was tolerated somewhat less affectionately. Mr Myers had his own large room with the only private bathroom in the Shemtov, instilling in Bernard and Johnny the lesson that while money might not buy love, it could be very helpful in securing day-to-day care and social respectability.

Contrary to Robert's frequently told version of the story, not many residents were the direct victims of Nazism but equally few were left entirely untouched. Robert learned early on the power of symbols, images, and numbers. Several of the residents had numbers tattooed on their arms – Isaac himself bore a number, though from which branch of Nazi officialdom is unclear. Mrs Bobek, the assistant cook, bore the serial numbers from two Polish camps. The Rabbinical-inclined residents – his father included – doubtless had much to say concerning the word-magic and number-magic of the Hasidic tradition as well as the administrative depravity of the Nazis. It is little surprise then that Robert would develop a life-long fascination with coded writings and the 'occult' properties of symbols. He was formed in an environment where people had first-hand experiences of the life-saving or life-denying attributes of a gold star (Jew) compared to a gold triangle (half-Jew) or a black triangle (vagrant or Gypsy). He heard stories of selections for mass-murder being made on the basis of odd or even numbers. Irrespective of their 'truth', systems of categorisation considered as creative ways of encoding and decoding the world would inform much of his later works. By his mid-20s he was amassing books on the Kabbalah, Gematria, and the philosophy of language and signs.

He also saw and heard death everywhere. Residents and Jewish neighbours related the fates of their families back in Europe, and Robert would re-tell their stories whenever the opportunity arose. For the young Lenkiewiczs, death was not merely an element of stories. Most residents were old and frail. Several shuffled off their mortal coil either 'peacefully, in their sleep' or with a great deal of mess and indiscretion. Mrs Plotnik suffered a brain haemorrhage in her room which Robert remembered as a particularly violent scene. Almost certainly amplifying the event in his memory and imagination, Robert recounted this episode as if Mrs Plotnik's head had exploded with 'blood all over the ceiling and running down the walls'. The boys carried the body to a bed to await the coroner while Alice and the maids cleaned up the gore. The volume of blood may be exaggerated but there is no doubt that the Lenkiewicz boys often witnessed the undignified or unquiet ends of the Shemtov's residents. As Bernard recalls, 'In the earlier days it was more cosmopolitan. People came and went. Then it became more like a care home: they were dropping like flies'.

Robert described it as 'a lunatic asylum really. I witnessed dementia, loneliness, quite significant packages of suffering from people who had survived horrendous things. There were survivors from Auschwitz and Belsen [but] life was just a constant creative indulgence'. Much encouraged by his mother, Robert was painting regularly by the age of eight. Alice idolised her father and his connections to King Ludwig, understandably so, since she lost him when still a child. Total war and genocide had not diminished her love of German culture. She talked enthusiastically of 'Novalis, Hölderlin, Heine and the German Romantics: Goethe and Schiller in particular. You had this curious sense quite early on that great things had happened in Germany, that here was one of the most phenomenal cultures ever known. And yet look what it had led to'. (Robert Lenkiewicz, *Paintings and Projects*, White Lane Press, p. 9). Both Alice and the man who would become an informal tutor to Robert, Axel Ney-Hoch, talked of the 'Old Country' like staunch nationalists, though it is unknown whether Alice agreed with Axel's opinion that German culture was so elevated that had he not been a Jew he would have supported the Nazis (Stella Ney-Hoch, Interview, June 2018).

From Isaac and Reuven, Robert inherited a love of horses and one of his earliest surviving paintings depicts a mare and foal in a pastoral setting. It dates from his first year in the Shemtov when he would have been eight, nine years old at most. The tones are generally flat and the anatomy somewhat muddled but considering that the artist had been on the planet for less than a hundred months it is an impressive piece.

Mrs Plotnik's son is often attributed with giving Robert his first truly valuable art lesson. There are several versions told by Robert but the basis of the story ran as follows. He was painting in the garden and blocking in the grass with a uniform green when Mr Plotnik appeared over his shoulder and said, 'Very good, very good, but vat colour iz ze grass?' – the European Jewish accent was always emphasised. 'Green,' Robert replied. 'Ya, ya, gut, but vat colour is ze grass?' At which Robert repeated 'Green.' 'Ya, but vat colour is ze graaaass, Robert?' Mr Plotnik's insistence was interpreted as another case of derangement by Robert, who was not yet in his teens and more familiar with mad old people than philosophical methods. Mr Plotnik was provoking him to think harder. After a long series of repetitions, Robert finally starts to give way: 'It's a kind of yellow-green.' 'Ya, und vat else?' 'It's ... a blue-green and yellowish-golden green, and blackish green ...' At which point the wise Mr Plotnik says, 'Ya, *all colours in all colours*,' and walks away, his knowledge finally imparted.

Whenever he retold the tale, which was frequently, Robert smiled. He sometimes added the coda: 'They say there's no fool like an old fool, but sometimes there's no fool like a young fool either.' On occasions the teacher was described only as 'an elderly rabbi', and the lesson took place indoors with the multi-hued green belonging to a glass bottle. The details may change but the profound point about human perception remains: what we can experience is often limited by what we think and how we name things.

Alice and Isaac completed British naturalisation certificates in 1950 and were granted official status in January 1951. Both were recorded as previously being 'of uncertain nationality'. They had been in limbo for almost a decade since the Nazis had determined that Jewishness was a bar to citizenship and Isaac's Polish homeland had become part of the Reich. It cannot be claimed that they were thus made into philosophers, but on several levels the Lenkiewicz family must have been aware that the seemingly abstract operation of categorisation can have life-altering consequences. The category 'Jew' had been the basis for the murder of their families in Europe and their presence in England.

As well as experimenting with paints, Robert was experimenting with a full spectrum of human emotions and feelings and could sometimes be rather inhumane in his studies, as his brothers attest. As one example, before the twins became bar mitzvah at the age of about 11 or 12, Robert had committed some trivial offence which Alice found out about. She wanted him to admit to it, simply to own up. Robert would not. So, she perversely decided that the best way for him to learn a lesson would be for her to punish Bernard, who she locked down in the spider-infested coal cellar with its infernal boiler. He was to remain there until Robert gave up his defiance of her authority and admitted his guilt. Robert decided to outwait her on that matter, and the test of wills began. Bernard recalls:

> I can't tell you if I was down there for half an hour or three, but it was a long time. When I came out he was smiling. He'd won. I asked him years later if he remembered that and he said, 'I never forget anything that gives me pleasure.' (Bernard Leigh, Interview, August 2017)

Young Robert was fascinated by Hasidic tales of levitation and had 'a mystical experience' in Room No. 3 after placing an armchair atop his bed to approximate the sensation of levitating. In a related experiment he used the most basic equipment: his brother Johnny, a scaffold plank, and the 12-foot drop from the bedroom window. To discover whether the human will could indeed counteract such basic physical forces as gravity, Robert set his brother on the plank and shoved him out of the window, pirate-style. If levitation was indeed possible then surely Johnny's will-to-live would tip the balance at least a little and lighten his weight. Robert pushed the plank and Johnny further and further from safety. His weight did not lessen. Fortunately, Robert was sufficiently strong and Johnny sufficiently cat-like to avoid a disastrous result and the terrified boy was eventually dragged back into the bedroom unhurt.

Amid the mayhem there were islands of normality such as cinema visits two or three times a week with Alice, who treated the boys equally on this score. Left to their own devices the twins would go exploring local bombsites, or spend time reading, listening to music, or watching television. Robert liked Clarke Gable, Disney movies, especially Pinocchio, and he liked to listen to Paul Robeson and Enrico Caruso. Most influential of all these ordinary pleasures was the Charles Laughton film of the life of Rembrandt, directed by Alexander Korda in 1936. Although far from factual, the film inspired Robert to bend to the will of Alice in at least this respect: to become more like his grandfather, the artist. In doing so, he made a kind of unspoken pact with his mother. He would not be expected to function like other boys of his age, he would not be expected to do much apart from paint. His formal schooling was seen as an irrelevance, for he was in all senses an exception to any norms.

The Lenkiewicz boys initially attended the Menorah School at the junction of Finchley and Golders Green Roads, NW11. Both Bernard and Johnny remember it as 'very sweet'. It is likely Robert felt the same, at least until shortly after his 11th birthday when he and Bernard took their presents to school to show their friends. The fateful items were common enough in the world of schoolboys – Bernard's pair of plimsolls and Robert's book *Robin Hood* by Howard Pyle. For some reason, Mr Shapiro the head teacher decided that the twins' display of their cultural riches was inappropriate. The 1950s were an austere time but it is unlikely any riots would have started over non-edible items in a primary school, so what happened next could have been avoided. Mr Shapiro took the plimsolls from Bernard, but when he tried to take the book from Robert, he met with considerable resistance. Robert was according to Bernard the size and weight of a grown man well before his bar mitzvah. The ensuing struggle was uneven. Mr Shapiro found his way down a staircase at a speed and angle most displeasing to him. It is not known whether Robert pushed him with malice or any intent apart from keeping hold of the book. Despite Bernard's non-involvement in the deed both boys were expelled from the school immediately and permanently. John says:

Mr Shapiro bounced the twins out after a fight occurred. Afterwards we played truant for ... I don't know how many weeks, *ages* ... but eventually my mother found out. She went straight to the school and told Mr Shapiro that as she was the proprietress of the only Kosher hotel in the district he should show much more respect to her and never dare to expel her boys. (Johnny Lenkiewicz, Interview, September 2017)

Alice's sense of 'Lenkiewicz exceptionalism' must have been high on that day but it was not shared by Mr Shapiro, who was not inclined to forgive or forget. Twenty years later, when Bernard's electronics and audio business flourished and he had long since changed the name Lenkiewicz to Leigh, he was called to install a sound-system in the school. This he did, and saw that it was good. The elderly headmaster thanked him kindly and was about to make payment when Bernard mentioned that he had been a pupil and wondered if Mr Shapiro remembered him:

'I don't recognise you, sorry. What is your name?'

'Lenkiewicz.'

'Take your equipment and get out of here!'

The boys were briefly relocated to the Beckford School, which displeased Alice in some unspecified way, for it was only a temporary waystation to somewhere far worse: the Harben School in Netherwood Street, Kilburn. This was anything but a sweet school. Bernard compared it to a prison. Few pupils took the trouble to learn to pronounce 'Lenkiewicz' when it was easier to say 'Jew-boy'.

The rupture in Robert's school idyll would produce an important learning event outside the formal curriculum. At the Menorah Primary School, Robert recalled rescuing the prettiest girl in the school, Gloria Tessler, from a bee and 'was made hero for a day', basking in the intoxicating attentions of the endangered damsel. Johnny disputes this version:

> That was *my* story – Robert was a great embellisher! Gloria Tessler later became a journalist and worked, I think, for The Jewish Chronicle. The true story is that we were standing in the playground of the Menorah Primary School one sunny day (I was about 6 or 7 at the time) and the bee came along and was buzzing around. I waved my arms around and somehow hit it and it fell to the ground. Robert dressed that story up and claimed it as his own. I don't know what Gloria Tessler's experience of it was, or the bee's, but certainly it was *me*. (Johnny, Interview with White Lane Press, 2008)

Nevertheless, at the Harben School, encountering his first anti-Semitic abuse, Robert noticed the 'same butterflies-in-the-stomach sensation'. This lesson, delivered by his own physical reactions to two oppositely charged events – one beautiful, one ugly – became the basis of a profound life principle: that experiences were a matter of taste, of whether they gave pleasure or anguish; they were neither 'good' or 'bad' in and of themselves but merely *different*.

Johnny explains the principle in the simplest possible terms:

> [Robert] noted that people had preferences – I like tea, I like coffee, I like him, I like her – and can become quite partisan about those preferences. And then people go further and say 'because I like X, X is *Good*'. Then they convert that preference into a 'what should be', and

because you do not like what I like therefore you are *morally wrong.*
(Johnny, Interview with White Lane Press, 2008)

As Robert explained in an interview in 1997, these twin events led him to a formula – 'The only difference is the difference … But that difference was *aesthetic'*. Aesthetic responses – matters of taste – were the true basis for ethical rules or moral laws.

Impatient to escape regular schooling and the Hotel Shemtov, Robert directed his energies to gaining a place at the Christopher Wren School. Without the dubious protection of the now permanently truanting Robert, Bernard made himself useful to his fellow inmates. Because of his height, skinny athleticism, and daring, Bernard alone could scale the eight-foot wall topped with shards of broken glass. He became the 'runner' for the local shop from which cigarettes and other contraband could be brought back during lunchtimes. Meanwhile Robert was busy with his independence: his days were spent wandering, painting, sketching, and visiting London's galleries. There is no evidence that either of his parents discouraged him in this regard, and it seems that Alice preferred her *Wunderkind* to be out of school painting or visiting galleries. Bernard says:

> Robert had to keep his hair short for school but as soon as he could get away with it, he let it grow long. When out of school he wore jeans and long jumpers, always covered in paint. He painted almost constantly from the age of eight. Johnny's asthma was getting worse and he was sent out of London to recuperate. I felt sorry for him, he missed out on a lot because of that. From the age of ten to twelve, Robert was very interested in painting horses. When we got close to our thirteenth birthday Rabbi Levi of Park Road synagogue prepared us for our Bar Mitzvah. I remember my friend Anthony going to the d'var torah and Robert reading the prayer book upside down, deliberately, as a kind of protest I think. (Bernard Leigh, Interview, November 2017)

So now the twins were men and expected to behave as men. But role models for grown-up behaviour were few and far between at the Shemtov. Isaac was content to stand outside smoking Du Maurier cigarettes rather than risk confronting – let alone trying to correct – his wife's unique style of parenting, according to Johnny Lenkiewicz. Alice may have been built like a 'four-seater Chesterfield sofa, with thicker skin and less sense of humour' but she was far from invulnerable. Unfortunately, when anything did touch her or move her in some significant way, she often reacted without any thought for the consequences. Gestures of affection or desire from Isaac were swatted away with the warning 'Ach, remember your heart condition!' Despite this anti-sensuality she took good care of her appearance and was acutely sensitive to Robert's perceptions of her:

> I suppose the turning point in my relationship with my mother was when I was about fifteen. I'd painted her and thought 'My goodness, this is rather good!' I took the painting upstairs and put it on my easel by the bed. I thought I would go downstairs and get a hot water bottle and some cocoa for bed, not look at the painting and then sit myself up comfortably in bed and finally look at the portrait and see what I thought of it. An hour later, would I think it was as good as I first thought? I believed it a significant turning point picture.[6]

There followed a scene resembling a horribly ironic retake on Oscar Wilde's *The Picture of Dorian Gray*:

> I did all that and got into bed, puffed up the pillows and prepared to look at it. Then this horrible sinking sensation – the whole portrait had been completely swirled and smudged and scraped in the most violent way. I knew instantly that while I had been down in the kitchen my mother had sneaked up and destroyed the image because she didn't like the way she looked in it [...] I tore down the stairs to her room and said 'Why did you do that?' She said '*Noh!* It vaz a terrible picture, a terrible picture!' I said 'You don't know what you've done. That was a stupid thing to do, I can't tell you how angry I am.'[7]

Nevertheless, Alice continued to love and approve of Robert as she always had. She denied him nothing. Her feelings may have been mixed with disappointment, moral judgement, and endless suggestions as to how he should improve his behaviour, but Johnny is adamant in his evaluation of his mother's relationship with the twins. Bernard could never do enough to win the slightest approval from her while Robert was a genius, whatever he did.

Soon after their bar mitzvah both Robert and Bernard were having emotional and sexual relationships with the Irish maids, who the boys recall fondly as uninhibited peasant types of a wide variety of ages and skills. Bernard recalls how he and Robert would busy themselves in the maids' rooms 'not having full sex, but it was all going in that direction' to joyful cries of 'Oh Jayzus!' while in the rooms below Alice bellowed at their father: 'Remember your heart condition!'

3.1 *(Left):* The Hotel Shemtov *c.*1951.

3.2 *(Right):* The former Hotel Shemtov in Fordwych Rd, London in 2012.

3.3 Robert, his non-identical twin Bernard, their mother Alice (seated in armchair), and Sabine Ney-Hoch *(right)* with staff of the Hotel Shemtov, *c.*1957.

3.4 Robert aged 16 seated in front of his painting of the Ney-Hoch sisters
    at the Hotel Shemtov, *c.*1957.

3.5 Axel Ney-Hoch, with photographs of revolutionary figures, 1950s.
3.6 Axel Ney-Hoch, 1960s.

3

A Wayward Education

The Shemtov residents were not the philosophical and aesthetic Titans which Robert conjured in his memories. Instead they were judged rather ordinary according to the testimony of eyewitnesses such as Johnny and Bernard and Stella Ney-Hoch. There was, however, a daily background noise, a constant and perhaps unnoticed atmosphere which German speakers call a '*Stimmung*', a kind of 'tuning' of the voices around them: more than a generalised mood but less than an objectively measurable collective trauma. The Lenkiewicz children overheard and engaged in conversations about dehumanisation, deportation, torture, and mass murder. Their parents, and on some occasions they themselves, were seen as social outsiders: odd people with odd accents, with traditions and habits alien to England. Almost everybody at the Shemtov had been touched by horror. This does not promote them all to intellectuals, but any European Jew living through the middle of the 20th century would doubtless be asking themselves and their peers some fundamental questions. If the mass murder of friends and family doesn't provoke thought, then nothing will.

Later, at the age of 20, when his friend Alex Donoghue asked Robert to list the thinkers he considered most important, Robert presented him with a large and detailed drawing made in his teens. It was titled *Philosophers Carving up the Corpse of Humanity* and showed a large group of the giants of Western Philosophy including Spinoza, Aristotle, Nietzsche, Freud, Moses Maimonides, and Schopenhauer, knives and forks at the ready, surrounding an agonised cadaver.

Robert talked freely about them, and their thoughts accompanied most of his mature work: his notebooks from the 1970s onwards are crammed with notes and quotes. Yet according to John and Bernard there were very few books in their room in the Shemtov and Robert spent little time in school or libraries. Thus, it seems most likely that Robert's early aesthetic and philosophical education came to him via the living voices around him.

Several sources – his brothers, his first wife Celia 'Mouse' Mills, and Stella Ney-Hoch – attest that during his teens Robert kept company with sharp-minded young writers such as Heathcote Williams and Colin Wilson. He also found his way into the company of mature and internationally renowned political and religious philosophers: he was a frequent guest at Bertrand Russell's house. Robert knew the Hungarian poet and anti-Nazi activist Alfred Reynolds well. What was the thread leading out of Room 3 of the Shemtov to the private rooms and thoughts of these high-flying intellectuals? The large answer to this question dwelt 20 feet above the Lenkiewicz boys' heads in the attic of the Shemtov: Axel Ney-Hoch.

Axel Ney-Hoch was a monster of strength and intellect. Fleeing Nazi Germany for England, his French stepfather and Russian Jewish mother got as far as Amsterdam. His daughter Stella explains:

> They were hiding in the same road as Anne Frank's house. They were found and sent to Auschwitz. Axel had been sent ahead to England along with his mother's sister Sabine – not together, separately. I don't know if he was sent to somebody. Terrible. He never mentioned an orphanage. He did mention a farm and living with different people in bed-and-breakfasts. He went out to work. (Stella Ney-Hoch, Interview, 2017)

Axel had an exceptional ability to learn by the slightest contact. He had no formal schooling beyond the age of ten but could by ear alone play any tune on any musical instrument and was fluent in several languages. French, Polish, German, Russian, and English he intoned with the precision and authority of a state-sponsored radio announcer. He took up any work he could to feed himself. As an agricultural and building labourer he rapidly learned to drive tractors and trucks, and then later turned his hand to piloting boats on the Thames. This physical intelligence was matched by brawn and endurance. Many of his labouring days were spent hoisting 36-gallon kegs and 112lb sacks of coal. Heathcote Williams devotes over 40 pages of his book *The Speakers* (1964) to Axel's political performances at Hyde Park Corner, where he is described as:

> the Zarathustra of the Latter Days [...] quarter German, quarter Jewish, quarter Russian, and the other quarter accounted for by places, times, or emotions. [...] I remember a Jewish friend coming up to Axel after a meeting and saying that Axel was the only German anti-fascist, Jewish anti-Semite and Russian anti-communist that he knew, and that he was quite pleased to know him. [8]

Robert's mother had been acquainted with the Ney-Hoch family back in Germany, and by sheer fortune the refugee Sabine had found Alice at the London Jewish Aid centre. Axel knew Robert and Bernard from birth and was often asked to babysit the twins at Howitt Road. He was a frequent visitor to the Shemtov before he and his family took up residence there. According to Bernard, Alice Lenkiewicz adored Axel, largely because Axel saw in Robert the same qualities of future greatness that Alice had seen since the day of his birth. Axel colluded with Alice and Robert to a very high degree, ensuring that Robert's time away from school was maximised. On weekdays Axel would take Robert to Kenwood House or the National Gallery, or introduce him to political and philosophical groups in café society. Axel had read the great philosophers, especially the Germans, and passed his interpretation of their works on to Robert.

Axel's influence intensified when Alice invited the Ney-Hoch family to live in the Shemtov in 1957 along with British wife Gladys and daughters Maria (Ria) and Stella. Not all shared his mother's admiration for the man. When Axel's name was raised in interviews for this book Bernard described him as 'not a nice man', 'a real *schmole*', and 'a nutter', although he added, 'he was good to me'. At first, hearing this may sound like a re-action caused by yet another adult elevating Robert to a boy-genius while Bernard himself was side-lined. But there is much evidence to suggest that Bernard's opinion of Axel is well-founded.

Axel talked with compelling reason and high drama to rapt audiences in lecture halls or from his stepladder at Speakers' Corner. He spoke of Hegel, Kant, Marx, and Nietzsche, Mozart and Mahler, anarchism and animal rights. His stand-up rhetoric and logic were fine-tuned in these public arenas. His charm and language skills built him an impressive net-work of contacts from the highest to the lowest orders of London society. Cultivating connections ranging from drug addicts and prostitutes to the lordly philosopher Bertrand Russell, Axel sometimes acted as a transla-tor and guide for visiting Russian VIPs and, despite his statelessness and avowed anarchism, allegedly had dealings with the British intelligence agencies. He introduced the young Robert to Hungarian émigré Alfred Reynolds (1903–1993), the anti-Soviet, anti-fascist poet and thinker who was certainly an 'international asset' of Her Majesty's Government. Rob-ert became so well acquainted with Reynolds that he at least on one oc-casion shared a bed with him, chastely, though he recalled that Reynold's impulses were otherwise.

Although Reynolds was never in fact a 'spy' or 'spook', he was a highly politicised intellectual. Born in Budapest to a mixed Jewish-Catholic family he was in his youth taken with the ideals of Communism but rapidly realised that the Soviet system had become a murderous tyranny. In 1934 he left the Hungarian Communist Party in protest at Stalin's programme of assassinating dissenters and was promptly imprisoned. Paroled, living under a dangerous cloud, and driven out of his university post, he fled Hungary in 1936 for London. He was called up for war service in 1940 and fortunately stationed in the safety of the Cotswolds in an administrative role. In 1944 he was sequestered to the Intelligence Corps. He possessed an acute understanding of the social and psychological mechanisms at work within fanatical belief systems, having experienced them at first hand in Hungary and broken free of them. Reynolds and a cohort of intelligence officers at the Kempton Park prisoner-of-war centre were assigned the knotty problem of how to 'de-Nazify' the most fanatical of German National Socialists. The Normandy landings were under way and the British Government was planning beyond the most obvious objectives of dismantling the Nazi war machine. Assuming a successful outcome to the war, measures were still needed to prevent a Nazi resistance movement or the ideology resurfacing in later years.

What Reynolds correctly recognised was that German fascism was not a matter of 'mass hypnosis' or 'brainwashing' by Hitler alone. It was not *caused* by the false beliefs of *Mein Kampf* – which some of the prisoners knew so poorly that Reynolds insisted they read it to see what they agreed or disagreed with. Hitler's mass-movement had, however, tapped into real sentiments, then made them meaningful in terms of dubious concepts such as 'race'. The dangerous feelings – of shame and of being 'betrayed' in the Great War, of thwarted superiority and destiny, of aggression to anybody who does not share those feelings – are genuine experiences which can be factory-farmed by any cynical state apparatus. The Nazi leadership had itself proved that feelings, even the most profound aesthetic experiences of loathing or loyalty, are not uneducable. Reynolds and his team apparently proved that even the worst beliefs can be changed by free discourse and critical thinking.

Reynold's anti-Nazi efforts continued throughout the period Robert knew him via 'The Bridge Circle'. This was in part an artistic and intellectual discussion group, and in part a kind of exchange visit programme enabling former enemies to develop their new-found alliances and friendships. Throughout the mid-1950s meetings of The Bridge Circle were attended by Robert and Axel and a group of young writers including Stuart Holroyd, Bill Hopkins, and Colin Wilson, all associated with the 'Angry Young Men' literary group. Robert was deeply impressed by Wilson's book *The Outsider* (1956), which informed the popular reception of existentialist ideas in England, and they became lifelong friends. In 1971 Wilson published the wide-ranging survey *The Occult: A History* which condensed many of the ideas and interests he and Robert had discussed throughout their friendship: magic, witchcraft, alchemy, and the 'latent powers' of the human being and the possibilities for their development hinted at by the alchemists, magi, and heretics.

Stella recalls her first meeting with Robert, when he gave her a box of paints and brushes for her eighth birthday. Robert would have been 16. She recalls that he was already very intense, constantly talking about Nietzsche and Freud and Goya and Michelangelo: 'I was a young girl, there was no romantic interest at that point, but we were both very interested in painting and horses, so we just got on well together'. She confirms Bernard's view that Alice and Axel were in close accord on Robert's exceptional status: 'My father liked intelligent people, tall people, blond people. Robert was for Axel the ideal person'. Sometimes in the dawn hours Robert and Stella would clamber down the drain-pipe to the flat roof 'to avoid Alice on guard at the front of the house' then climb over the garden fence and spend the morning sketching the work-horses stabled under the nearby railway arches. Axel talked constantly of Robert, and Robert of Axel. 'We went here, did that, and saw this painting, and talked to so-and-so.' Stella would often accompany them to Bertrand Russell's house where she was allowed to sit in the basement kitchen while upstairs the men dined and talked over the weightiest issues of their times.

It was Axel Ney-Hoch who also introduced Robert to Bertrand Russell, probably earlier but certainly no later than 1957. Russell was in his eighties when Robert was in his teens. As a public intellectual Russell was most famous for his pacifism during the First World War and later his commitment to the Campaign for Nuclear Disarmament. As a philosopher he is most famous for his contributions to logic and the analysis of language. One might have suspected that Russell's complex and dry philosophy of mathematical logic would leave no discernible impression on a teenage artist, but there is some evidence that Robert absorbed something of Russell's scientific approach to problem solving. He certainly thought it possible to find a harmonious pattern or *logos* behind the seeming chaos of the visible exterior and inner emotional worlds. The following passage, written by Robert in his late teens, may not be a result of direct influence from Russell but rather the result of a common denominator, Pythagoras:

> Apart from the original sensitive awareness, the creating of art – be it music, literature, sculpture, or painting – appears to me to be little short of a science: in the case of painting, the use and application of the materials or the choice of subject display emotion, indeed inevitably so. But all the applications on the canvas of the myriad intricacies entailed in hours of highly developed perception is [*sic*] surely mathematical. [9]

Whatever a philosopher might think of the use of 'surely' in this passage there is something more valuable than a logical argument at work in the pamphlet. Robert was fascinated with symbols, and here there is clearly a delight in the thought that the tone-values and colour-values of painting entered into wider circuits of exchange and higher levels of abstraction via number-values and operational signs. In the case of music, the Pythagoreans had demonstrated definite links between the vibrations of matter, harmony, number ratios, and the human passions stirred by music. Throughout his life Robert remained fascinated by this discovery. The geometry of sacred architecture, the tessellating intricacies of Islamic art, the 'golden ratio' in Classical and Renaissance art remained firmly to the fore in his mature thinking on aesthetics.

Despite the tantalising inchoate hints in the Velázquez essay caution should be exercised in attributing Robert's Pythagorean tendencies to Russell's influence: but what any participant must have absorbed from the discussions at Russell's house was the primacy of clear and critical thinking. When Robert was 18, he commented to his classmate Aury Shoa at St Martin's, 'I don't admire a thinker because I happen to agree with their conclusions. I admire a thinker because of the rigour of their thought and the elegance of their methods.' This attitude stayed with him for life and carried over into his painting practice. In later years Robert would advise his many informal students, 'Make every mark a thought, and every thought a clear one'.

As an aside, in what perhaps is a parallel rather than an influence, we might note that Russell was married four times and left a trail of discarded and sometimes pregnant mistresses in his wake. Russell's sex life has been described as a 'chaos of serious affairs, secret trysts and emotional tightrope acts that constantly threatened ruinous scandal'. Axel Ney-Hoch was similarly promiscuous, though his status as a role model is contestable, as we shall see. Had Alice known of such things, her disapproval would have been certain but she would probably have tolerated the trade-off of knowing that her brilliant son was conversing with a Nobel Prize-winning lord who co-wrote manifestos with Albert Einstein, and who had met Lenin but 'was not impressed'.

It is difficult to judge if Russell's famous advocacy of 'free love' made any changes to young Robert's perspectives or whether Russell was preaching to the converted. At the Shemtov, love was indeed 'free', at least of the risk of pregnancy with post-menopausal Irish maids.

Robert related this story about his parents at the Shemtov:

> I caught him [his father] once in a rather touching incident. I was in the office and I looked through the window and saw 'big Mary', a huge Irish maid, standing by the phone. My father, who was only five feet tall, was there with his tongue sticking out the side of his mouth [Laughs] reaching to grasp hold of her breasts. She slapped his hand and said, 'Don't be so silly, Mr Lenkiewicz!' Well, my *mother* walked out of the milk kitchen! She saw it all and went, 'Noh! *NOH!*' and walked past into the meat kitchen.

> Ma knew I was in love with the maids. There was one maid in particular with whom I'd fuck on the landing outside Mrs Kempner's room, who was stone deaf, so we could do it outside her front door and not worry! [10]

Robert retained a copy of Russell's *A History of Western Philosophy* in his library for life, and whenever asked about philosophy would recommend it as a starting place, despite Russell's glaring misrepresentations of some thinkers, most notably Nietzsche. What appealed to Robert about the book was its scale: read it *all*, he insisted, don't just skip to the moderns: you must get the largest possible overview first. In this respect Robert's admiration for Russell was akin to his admiration for Aristotle and Bacon, where the sheer ambition of a coherent system covering everything from cosmology to biology to aesthetics excused any number of merely factual errors.

The largest early and enduring influences admitted by Robert were Rembrandt, Albert Schweitzer, and Nietzsche, a trio of heavyweights he suspected may have 'deformed' his development. As mentioned previously, Robert credited Alexander Korda's 1936 biopic of Rembrandt as the decisive motivation for his early painting. The rags-to-riches fairy-tale of high moral purpose and painfully honest genius is melodramatically laughable in places and historically inaccurate, even if Charles Laughton's misty-eyed profundity is enthralling. 'Pure *schmaltz!*' Robert would later say of it, but the seed had been planted and his admiration for Rembrandt's art was lifelong and intense. On his frequent visits to Kenwood House with Axel, Robert viewed what many consider to be one of the world's finest self-portraits: Rembrandt in his years of age and poverty – solid, earthy, and dour, bringing the judgement of his wise but merciless gaze upon himself. This and many other of Rembrandt's works echo loudly through Robert's entire output.

Albert Schweitzer's influence is equally profound, if somewhat more oblique, on Robert's artistic practice. Schweitzer's fortunes were assured at a young age: he was one of the finest musicians in Europe and a re-storer of priceless cathedral organs. Yet Schweitzer came to believe that however beautiful and meaningful the works of Bach and Mozart may be as a response to the life of Christ, they were insufficient as works of true Christianity. In fact, all beliefs, arguments, and artworks were inadequate to the Christian mission: what Jesus's message demanded was not sung masses or theology compendia but effective and direct action. Thus, at the age of 30 and against the advice of all around him, Schweitzer reskilled as a medical doctor and set out for one of the most deprived places in the world: 200 miles up the Ogooue River in Gabon, where he established a small hospital at Lambaréné. There he treated flesh-eating boils, leprosy, and parasitic worms in a converted chicken-hut in a steaming jungle.

If Rembrandt and Schweitzer attracted Robert by their practical unifi-cation of aesthetics and ethics, then Nietzsche may well have been a nec-essary counterweight. Robert's understanding of Nietzsche certainly did not come via Russell, who interpreted the thinker as a surly proto-Nazi, preaching an aesthetic of pain. In Robert's teenage years Axel Ney-Hoch and Colin Wilson are by far the more likely fellow travellers in Nietzschean thought. Throughout his life, all available evidence from Robert's notes and public pronouncements show that he was in accord with Nietzsche's deep suspicion of any claims concerning a 'purely moral' judgement. All of Robert's work on his large projects involves a consciously Nietzschean attempt to examine and describe the world around him without the dis-torting lens of moral prejudice, and Robert openly described himself as 'the most amoral person I know. Not immoral: *a*-moral'. In this respect he was also influenced by Oscar Wilde's work, especially *The Critic as Artist*

(1891) and *Phrases and Philosophies for the Use of the Young* (1894). In the latter Wilde writes: 'Any preoccupation with ideas of what is right and wrong in conduct shows an arrested intellectual development. [...] Pleasure is the only thing one should live for. Nothing ages like happiness.'

4.1 Robert painting in Fellows Road, Swiss Cottage studio, c.1958.

4.2 Robert aged 17 photographed by brother Johnny, Fellows Road studio, 1958. The painting is on the theme of 'Lovers'.

4.3 Robert, aged 17, 1958.

4.4 Alice Lenkiewicz, the artist's mother, *c.*1960.
4.5 Ivorine McLaren, mother of Robert's son, Dorian, *c.*1960.

4

'You Would Not Last Five Minutes in the Real World!'

At the Shemtov, Robert was certainly exposed to a constant stream of Hebrew history and myth, Hasidic tales, and Jewish-European folklore. It's impossible to say precisely when he became aware of ideas and tales such as the special relationship of the Jews to God or the expectation of the Messiah, the story of the Wandering Jew, or even the day he adopted Hebrew strongman Samson, Pinocchio, Jesus, and the giant musketeer Porthos as his heroes. But all these stayed with him for life. Robert declared a near-total amnesia concerning his earliest years: 'I can only remember from about eleven years old, and I was painting quite prolifically then'.

One of his earliest self-portraits, *Self-Portrait in Room No. 3 at the Hotel Shemtov*, was painted in 1955 or 1956 when Robert was 14 or at most 15 years old. It depicts the artist gazing up into the world of reflected light. On the chair next to him are his modest materials – ten small pots of poster paints, a tumbler of water, a single brush, childish and delicate compared to his chunky Aran sweater, which accentuates his already sturdy chest and shoulders. Once the viewer has recovered from the horror of 1950s linoleum, the first thing they will notice is the complexity and careful balance of the composition. A harsh critic might point out the indecisive tone-work or curious anatomy of jaw and ear, but what sings out from this work is the intelligence and ambition of a teenage artist. Robert had at this time no formal art training beyond a few hours with another 30 pupils in the schools he sporadically attended. The level of thought informing the composition is outstanding for an artist of any age: it is a representation within a representation, of a painter painting, observing a mirror within a mirror.

If we see painting simply as an accurate or realistic representation of what the artist observes, then this work is obviously inaccurate. A 'realistically' finished painting should contain not the sketch on the easel, for example, but a miniature coloured version of the entire painting; and the upside-down painting-of-a-painting also on the easel would contain a further miniature repeated right-side-up in a visual infinite regress (known as the 'Droste Effect'). This fascination with moving forwards and backwards through time and light, the play of mirrors within mirrors, and inversions of inversions would stay with the artist throughout his life. The young Lenkiewicz is intentionally directing our attention to the *process* of image-making – it is a painting essentially about the act of painting.

Many other earlier paintings survive, often of rural scenes and horses. The earliest obviously pre-date his conversation with Mr Plotnik, for in these Robert has areas of grass in lurid green and block shadows of black. Many show promise and talent, but none come close to the thoughtfulness and controlled complexity of the self-portrait in Room No. 3. Though not entirely successful as a work of portraiture, it is a convincing blueprint for many of the masterful self-portraits and mirror studies he went on to create.

At the age of 14 Robert transferred from the Harben School in Kilburn to the Christopher Wren School in Finchley. The school had dedicated art teachers who fostered skills of obvious relevance to a young artist. They may not have spent any time on philosophy or aesthetics, but they taught the classical principles of draughtsmanship, technical drawing, and figure drawing. Thus, Robert's attendance improved somewhat, though he still took days out to revisit galleries and cafés and make introductions with Axel according to a curriculum of their own devising. Robert was especially fond of Kenwood House with its fine collection of Old Masters, endless lawns, and the ornamental pond which supported a life-sized painting of a bridge.

Encouraged by his teachers at the Wren and unfailingly supported by Alice, Robert began a portfolio of work which he hoped would gain him admission to an even more specialised institution: St Martin's School of Art. Returning to the Shemtov from the Wren one afternoon he spied the fresh corpse of a pigeon on Fordwych Road. Aware of the shortcomings of many of his horse paintings and correcting for this by a serious study of Joshua Reynolds's *Anatomy of the Horse*, Robert decided some first-hand investigations were in order. He hoisted the feathery cadaver from the gutter and took it home.

Perhaps what happened next was one of Robert's psychological experiments, perhaps the simple carelessness of adolescence. Fortunately, Johnny was away from London due to his bouts of asthma which could sometimes be terrifying in their severity and could hardly be improved by nasty shocks or dead animals. Bernard returned from an errand to find the disassembled pigeon spread over his bed, pillow, and blankets. 'We had a terrible row ... he'd dissected it on *my bed* – blood everywhere. [...]

He made some wonderful sketches though, and supposedly they got him into St Martin's.' Whether the decision was made by Alice for Bernard's benefit or to allow Robert more time and space for his studies we cannot say, but Bernard was relocated to the attic. And so, at the age of 15, for the first time in his life Robert had a room of his own, all thanks to the avian corpse.

The arrival of the Ney-Hoch sisters, Ria (nine) and Stella (eight), early in 1957 gave Robert a spellbound audience for such wonders and daring pranks and a welcome change from the elderly life-models at the Shemtov. Unfortunately, many of the life-size portraits of the sisters were made on paper and do not survive except in family photographs. The younger sister Stella was a keen horse rider and shared Robert's love of all things equestrian. Ria was an entirely new aesthetic experience for the young artist, just prior to the physical adventures with the hotel maids and older lovers whose beds he would soon share.

> Perhaps the single most significant event of my youth, apart from my one-way friendship with Leonardo da Vinci, was the unexpected arrival of a family [the Ney-Hochs] at my parents' hotel who were placed in the attic rooms. One of the daughters, Ria, haunted my mind intensely from the first glance. She was nine, I about fourteen. We used to meet clandestinely on staircases or exchange glances across rooms. I painted her, drew her, talked with her. It was my first and probably only 'theological' experience. I smile when I look back on it now, but it really was the most extraordinary situation. Do you know that film *The Summer of '42*? How adolescent events can be so poignant they haunt the mind forever? It was very much like that. [11]

After Robert read the proofs of the book *R.O. Lenkiewicz* in July 1997, he phoned the publisher to make a single change to the 140,000 word manuscript. 'Please insert the following where I speak about Ria Ney-Hoch at the Shemtov,' he asked: 'She stained my life a silver-gold colour as I moved between the two worlds of brutish schooling and the unhinged ravings of my parents' environment.' This paean to 'first love' was included on page 16 of the published version.

Many of the canvas paintings from this period are of a heavier character than the earliest surviving large works. *Self-Portrait with Punch Magazine* (1957) and *Self-Portrait with Letter* (1957) are simple and striking compositions with a fine command of tone and colour. Already Robert is tending towards large paintings: the canvases are roughly the size of a standard doorway, and one suspects they would be larger if the interior of the Shemtov allowed. He was certainly producing images compulsively and seemingly inexhaustibly. He began to carry a small wooden box of paints with him, and on any occasions without them would sketch in pencil or biro pen on the nearest available surface: napkins, paper bags, or café menus.

While at the Wren Robert was also continuing with his research into sexuality which placed its own demands upon his time and energies. Bernard recalls:

> Robert was an early starter [...] He seemed to go for slightly older women at that time, when he was in his teens he always liked women in their twenties [...] He began to go missing for hours on end. When he was fourteen, perhaps fifteen. Ma sent me out to find him [...] I knew exactly where he would be: Elsworthy Road, Swiss Cottage. Robert used to stay with a girlfriend there. Well, two. I had been sent by Ma to bring him home, she was most insistent I brought him back. I knocked on the door and said 'It's Bernie here,' and he called 'Come in' and there he was in bed, sheet up here [indicates his neck], with two women, both in their twenties, and I said 'Ma wants you to come home.' Bernard mimed Robert lifting the sheet, looking first to the right and then to the left, then smiling. Robert said, 'I think not.' So when I went home I had to tell my mother I couldn't find him.

In the autumn of 1957 Robert enrolled at St Martin's School of Art, a plain building on Charing Cross Road which despite poor funding was already becoming a hot-house for young artists, thanks largely to the practice of employing young working artists and sculptors as tutors. This policy was spearheaded by Frank Martin, whose sculpture department soon became one of the finest in the world. Robert was taught by Frederick Gore, who was head of painting, Vivian Pitchforth, Ken Morse, and Peter Blake, the pioneer of British pop art who was later to design the Beatles' *Sgt. Pepper's* album cover (Celia 'Mouse' Mills, Interview, May 2018). Mouse Mills enrolled two years after Robert, but her description of the creative atmosphere is enlightening:

> [St Martin's] is plain from the outside, but inside modernisation hadn't reared its ugly head. The stairs had that lovely old wooden tread feel,

and the donkeys (the easels where you sat on a little bench attached to them) were old and covered in years of paint. The place buzzed. We wanted to work, and nobody shirked. Peter Blake was my tutor: I was so lucky. It was art for art's sake, not money, for God's sake! We were idealists and dreamers and we wanted to achieve the highest and best. (Mouse Mills, Letter, August 2017)

Much of Robert's patchy schooling had been grim and boring. St Martin's was quite the converse. His teachers loved what they were doing, and most were lively, eccentric, and generous characters. Mr Gore, a skeletal man who sometimes entertained students with his acrobatic roller-skating, found Robert's work fascinating, and he provides us with an insight into how committed the tutors were to their students. In the months following Robert's departure from the Shemtov, Mr Gore by some chance conversation discovered that Robert was hard-pressed for money. 'The next day he left a large relief parcel of paints and brushes next to Robert's easel.' (Mouse Mills, Interview, May 2018)

Another teacher who was financially helpful to students was Alan Swainston Cooper, a musician with the jazz band *The Temperance Seven*, who sported an immense beard and kept a pet monkey which he would occasionally bring to work. Lectures were given on feminism and sexuality as well as art history. And each day, hour after hour, was spent at the easels, sometimes working on still lifes but more often the human figure. Listening to the testimony of Mouse Mills and Aury Shoa, one suspects that St Martin's somewhat resembled an anarchist commune. Robert was in his element.

Surprisingly, the one violent change which – as far as we know – went largely unremarked and entirely unpainted by Robert was the death of his father in September 1958. Isaac smoked filter-less Du Maurier cigarettes constantly, which doubtless worsened his emphysema and heart condition. There was no decline: the end came quickly. Johnny recalls:

I remember him the day before, talking outside the house. There was no saying goodbye, no preparation. A very sudden death. [...] My mother was not very private when it came to her private life, and Robert said she told him that on the morning of Isaac's death, Isaac had attempted to initiate sex: rebuffed, he rolled off the bed fell to the floor and died [...] at some point and she screamed for Robert and Bernard to pick him up and put him back on the bed. I slept through this until about nine. Then Eileen O'Sullivan, one of the maids, a very loyal Irish woman said, 'Yer father's not vary well.' As I looked in and saw his body lying under the pink counterpane Alice screamed, 'Your father has died!' (Johnny Lenkiewicz, Interview, May 2017)

The ambulance arrived but the crew refused to remove the body: the soul had already left the stable and what was needed was a death certificate, not a hospital. Before sunset of the next day Isaac Lenkiewicz was buried simply and swiftly according to Orthodox Jewish law in the International Jewish Cemetery at Bushey. Johnny and Bernard relate that Robert again held the prayer book conspicuously upside-down. Robert's final gesture of respect was aesthetic, not religious: he and his brothers had seen too much 'piety' to take it seriously. Alice was devastated but the boys were remarkably untroubled.

> And from that moment to this, I have not had a moment's grief, nothing. From that moment to this, I felt nothing. And I liked him! My mum was in bits for the rest of the year. She wore black constantly after that, which wasn't a Jewish thing. She was a hypocrite, especially when it came to religion. On Yom Kippur she would sit watching television with the sound turned down very low and have the prayer book on the side of her armchair in case there was a knock on the door. She would quickly switch off the telly and pretend to be reading, but it was usually *upside-down* [my emphasis] because she didn't know Hebrew. At Isaac's funeral Robert drew a small pencil sketch of a horse and laid it in the grave. (Johnny Lenkiewicz, Interview, April 2018)

In holding the prayer book upside-down, Robert was engaging in something more than mere clowning. It was a symbolic refusal of authority and tradition: serious clowning with a serious point. Humour – sometimes sharp to the point of perversity – would remain one of his best weapons. Like Schweitzer, he was demonstrating that a critique of piety is not something one argues about in words alone. One's actions are one's argument. The bar mitzvah and funeral episodes are small, dramatic preludes to his lifelong engagement with two archetypal and interlinked figures, that of the Philosopher and that of the Fool.

There is little to say as to whether Robert also took his father's death with 'philosophical' detachment, or was traumatically numbed by it, or if he genuinely did not feel very much at all. What must be remarked is that his relationship with his father was not characterised by the phrase 'cold and distant'. Johnny tells us that Robert and Isaac shared a deep love of horses and spent hours discussing the various breeds and temperaments while poring over a well-worn book from which Robert traced and copied illustrations (Johnny Lenkiewicz, Interview, April 2018). And by all accounts Isaac was a very sweet and gentle man, a living renunciation of the Freudian 'patriarchal tyrant'. Yet Robert's silence on this front is deafening. Neither Johnny nor Bernard can recall any emotional response from Robert. It seems he never discussed the matter. Nor did he make notes and artworks as he did quite extensively when his mother died. It is of course possible he had little or nothing to report, and that Isaac's influence was felt very lightly if at all due to the immense gravity of Alice, larger in every way. Robert was familiar with Nietzsche's *Ecce Homo* and one wonders if or how these words resonated:

> My father died in his thirty-sixth year: he was delicate, loveable and morbid, like one who is preordained to simply pay life a passing visit – a gracious reminder of life rather than life itself. [12]

Whatever Robert did or did not feel about Isaac, the remarkable fact is that of the dozens of people interviewed for this biography, few recall Robert even once mentioning his father – who was in many cases their grandfather. Tales of his escape from the Third Reich were not dramatically performed to listeners alongside those of Alice, and Isaac is as absent from Robert's diaries, personal letters, project notebooks, and artistic output as he ever was from Hotel Shemtov letter-heads and documents.

Johnny and Bernard recall that Alice was devastated. Cyril Myers stepped into the breach in an entirely Platonic and helpful way. Alice was not in the least grateful to him but always took his support and advice in financial matters. Robert was fond of saying that children need mothers throughout their early years but have no need of a father or father-figure until they reach their teens: precisely when Isaac died.

Did the obvious surrogate of Axel Ney-Hoch then become an exemplar or father-figure to Robert? Perhaps he did so in terms of intellectual and physical strength, though Axel was certainly no moral exemplar. He was in very large measures both a hypocrite and a sadist. His youngest daughter Stella has this as her earliest memory: 'He was very angry about something, angry at my mother, I don't know what, and I was in my pram and he picked it up and hurled it across the room at her.' What triggered these violent outbursts? Seemingly anything: 'He didn't want to go to work, he didn't like his job, the wind was blowing in the wrong direction. [...] Ria had worse treatment than me' (Stella Ney-Hoch, Interview, May 2018). Axel frequently threatened to kill the children, or to kill Gladys, her parents, or 'everyone' if she left him. Gladys committed suicide in December 1978.

> He used to speak at universities and publicly [...] He would talk for hours about animal rights in front of hundreds of people, keep them all enthralled, then come home and kick a puppy to death. His words didn't go anywhere with me. We had a puppy: he kicked it to death in a temper. So yes, so much for his commitment to animal rights. I was starving once, we didn't have very much apart from pasta, and I wouldn't eat pasta at all. He dumped me and my sister with somebody to do with politics who had a large apartment overlooking Hyde Park. I think [Axel] was going to visit one of his girlfriends, so we were abandoned for a couple of hours. This chap said to us 'would you like something to eat?' and he had this big roast chicken on the side. I took hold of the whole chicken and ate about half of it before giving it back and saying thank you. Anyway, he saw me a week later, I had two black eyes, a broken nose, split lip. He said, 'What happened to you?' I looked at him and said, 'Somebody told him.' (Stella Ney-Hoch, Interview, May 2018)

This was a rare slip: there was only one other incident where Axel allowed his violence to show so publicly. He beat one of his girls in the street and was checked by a passing woman who berated him: needless to say, he took the child home for more of the same treatment. He told his daughters that he regularly beat their mother in very painful ways which don't leave marks, and there seems little doubt that he drove his wife to suicide (Stella Ney-Hoch, Interview, May 2018). But Johnny, Bernard, Mouse, Aury, and Stella attest that Axel continued to play a major role as Robert's friend and mentor. It is a matter of conjecture as to how much he knew about Axel's propensity for high-grade domestic violence. Robert's portraits of Axel do not reveal any signs of adverse judgement such as were apparent in the early painting of Alex Donoghue, the powerfully built stunt man who he initially suspected to be a man of violence. On the other hand, Axel was expert at concealing his worst cruelties with a fine veneer of charm and intelligence (Stella Ney-Hoch, Letter, June 2018). And judging from his published pamphlets such as 'Stateless Persons and Terrorism', Axel was a first-rate thinker. From the philosophy of Schopenhauer he adopted a profound pessimism and an arsenal of principles concerning vegetarianism and animal rights. From Nietzsche he drew a philosophical critique of 'herd values' and a profound suspicion of authority, especially as it appears in the form of the state. This perhaps more than anything else was passed on to Robert (Aury Shoa, Interview, June 2018).

During his first year at St Martin's, Robert continued to live at the Shemtov but tensions with Alice were growing and there were many good reasons to be elsewhere. Galleries and cafés and time with Axel figured largely, and so did the pursuit of his researches into sexuality. Robert was involved in a complex series of relationships and affairs at St Martin's. Some were serious, some capricious, and some experimental (Aury Shoa, Interview, June 2018). Any such 'monkey-business' which came to Alice's attention 'was disapproved of in the strongest possible terms' (Bernard Leigh, Interview, August 2017).

Robert might be excused for not feeling that he was wrapped in the cotton wool of unconditional love at the Shemtov, but as Bernard pointed out, the Lenkiewicz boys had no acquaintance with the hunger and poverty – and beatings – which afflicted so many of their generation. Robert now wore a poncho he had made from an army blanket, but this was an aesthetic choice, not a necessary improvisation. Had he asked for a cashmere overcoat Alice would likely have bought it. Leaving the Shemtov would mean leaving a world of housemaids, hot baths, heated rooms, and some of the best cooking in North London, all laid on by Alice's and the maids' hard work and without a bill to pay. 'Robert left home very early because of my mother [...] she was a tyrant,' says Bernard, though it is hard not to suspect that there was a large measure of benevolence in Alice's tyranny.

Robert's account of how and why he left the Shemtov may not be entirely accurate – the claim that he did not return for a full nine months is a personal myth of rebirth – but his outrage at missing a reshowing of his favourite biopic rings true:

[Ma] was very, very upset when I left home. I was getting ready to see Charles Laughton in the film *Rembrandt* on the black and white television [...] and we had some sort of row and she said 'You would not last five minutes in the real world. What do you know about the real world?'

A philosophical question if ever there was one, but Alice and Robert's conversation was not tending towards the merits of Nietzsche or Plato:

> I said, 'I could walk out the front door, turn left or right, and I'd get on fine.'
> 'You think so? Then do it! Do it!' she shouted. So I did, then and there. I didn't come back for nine months. I had nowhere to stay. I walked all the way to Soho. I was at St Martin's, so it must have been when I was sixteen or seventeen. I slept on a doorstep. One thing led to another. I met an older woman and stayed with her for a while. I remember I left without any desire to inflict distress. I really was determined to be independent. I left quickly, my brothers didn't. I didn't go back, but I know that it upset her deeply. Obviously, as you get older you realise just how much. [13]

Contrary to Robert's story of leaving 'there and then' and remaining away for nine months we can weigh the memories of Bernard, Johnny, and Stella Ney-Hoch who all independently recall Axel helping Robert to load easels and canvasses into a van. This was not *en route* to the house of the 'older woman' he refers to but to Axel's council flat in Haringey near Highgate, where Robert slept on a sofa, not a doorstep, and was within walking distance of his well-loved social spaces such as Kenwood House, the Freud Museum, and the British Library.

The woman Robert refers to here was most likely Ivorine McLaren. She was born on 8 September 1938 to parents who had quit the valleys of Wales for north-west London. Her father was tall, handsome, athletic, and at one point Regimental Boxing Champion of the Welsh Guards. All these traits but not the title he passed on to his daughter (Dorian Lenkiewicz, Interview, May 2018). There are many reasons why Robert was attracted to Ivorine, but they can be condensed into the fact that she shared every characteristic of Alice Lenkiewicz, with two exceptions: Ivorine was as beautiful to behold as Alice was not, and she was anything but fanatically anti-sexual. For reasons entirely mysterious Robert nicknamed her 'Faggot'. She was 24 years old to Robert's 18, an artist who worked variously as a shop assistant and bus conductor.

There are many incompatible accounts of how they met, all given by Ivorine herself to her son Dorian, who was hesitant to recount them because Ivorine was even more in love with fabulation than Robert (Dorian Lenkiewicz, Interview, May 2018). One version has it that she worked in an art supplies shop and caught Robert in the act of stealing brushes and paints. He waxed apologetic and charming: she took pity on a young artist, they talked about painting, and romance instantly bloomed. On other occasions she claimed that she met Robert at a life-drawing session at St Martin's. A third equally plausible version has it that they simply met in the street. Ivorine lived in Oaklands Road, Cricklewood, a short walk from the Shemtov, and Robert already had a habit of approaching beautiful women to ask if he could paint them. Whichever tale is true – and Dorian laughingly said 'possibly none of the above' – both Ivorine and Robert were rapidly lost in a mist of passion, and neither worried about the inconvenient existence of her husband, Michael.

There is a very strong, simple, and beautiful painting of Ivorine from 1959. Dressed in white pyjamas she is half-reclining against a white sheet or duvet, arm extended. Robert was not yet 20, but the luminosity and cleanliness of his palette is remarkable. This was obviously painted quickly, possibly in a single sitting. The brushwork is lively but controlled, the draughtsmanship loose but wonderfully evocative. He seems to have captured Ivorine in a moment of thoughtful uncertainty, pausing before the moment of some weighty announcement. The clinical associations of her costume and setting might misdirect the viewer to musings on maternity, but this was painted long before she fell pregnant with Robert's first child. By all accounts Ivorine was as instantly and deeply in love with Robert as his mother was: that alone should give any woman plenty to think about.

Free of the Shemtov, Robert took his new-found independence seriously. True to his word he worked at a furious pace, though almost exclusively on his art. He did not stay with Axel for longer than he had to: a matter of days rather than weeks (Stella Ney-Hoch, Interview, May 2018). He paid several return visits to Alice and his brothers but these usually lasted minutes rather than hours (Bernard Leigh, Interview, November 2017). He certainly did not live with Ivorine at Oaklands Road, but it is possible they cohabited for a short time in 1959 or 1960 in one of Robert's odd and temporary spaces which he was – sometimes – funding by various odd and short-lived jobs. A nomadic decade was about to begin.

The addresses we know of from this time include King Henry's Road in Swiss Cottage, Regent's Park Road in Primrose Hill, and Steeles Road in Belsize Park, although there may have been many more. For preference he took large and semi-derelict properties with high ceilings and low rents. He occasionally invited himself into empty properties, thus avoiding all financial inconveniences. And with the derelict places came the derelict people: Robert's ramshackle studios were soon inhabited by minor tribes of outsiders and misfits. Johnny tells us, 'He lived around [Hampstead] for years [...] It was always tense when he came to visit Ma at the Hotel Shemtov. Neither enjoyed each other's company, because Alice knew she'd lost him' (Johnny Lenkiewicz, Interview, May 2017) for Robert remained the unhappy recipient of Alice's many judgements about how he should improve himself. He would deliberately instigate arguments with contrary views, some of which were sincere, others straightforwardly provocative.

For example, in May 1960, when Adolf Eichmann was kidnapped and held to account for his crimes against humanity, Robert was vocal in his assessment of Eichmann as a harmless old factory worker minding his own business. Bygones should be bygones, the man had surely suffered enough, etc., and this Robert announced in the dining room of the Shemtov. Alice and any sane person in earshot reacted with outrage. Johnny completed the story with the observation:

> There was an element of Robert which was a bit sick, from a feeling point of view. He would say things like 'Why should I treat my children more specially than any other children, when all I contributed was a teaspoon of spunk?' I don't know whether it was to gauge the effect on the listener, or for his own pleasure. (Johnny Lenkiewicz, Interview, September 2017)

Robert enjoyed psychologically manipulating Johnny. According to Robert, Ivorine was psychic and could accurately predict the future. Walking along any street she would guess at unexpected or unusual features of houses some way in advance of sight: that number 50 would have a stack of books next to the milk bottles on the step, or that the door of number 70 would be wide open. Robert casually told John: 'Oh, and she has predicted that you will be dead by the time you are 20'. John was a scientifically minded young man, so it was much to his own surprise that he could not shake a horrible and growing anxiety about the 'prediction'. Whether this foretelling came from Ivorine or Robert is unknown, but Robert explained that whether it would prove to be correct or not Johnny should live his life as if every day was the last.

> Which is all very well but was no comfort at the time, and many projects would never begin. I was 18, possibly with two years to live. Annie [Hill-Smith] thinks that Robert was a psychopath, but I think

that's an exaggeration. [...] Although, even if the message from Ivorine were true, why would [Robert] tell me? Either he was somewhere on the spectrum or he was experimenting. It is the kind of thing you'd keep your mouth shut about if you didn't want to terrify your younger brother. (Johnny Lenkiewicz, Interview, September 2017)

The full impact of Ivorine's prophecy struck Johnny the day before his twentieth birthday.

On the eve of my twentieth birthday (it was the custom to come down and see Robert) I hitched down to Cornwall. Hitching was very popular in those days. The first lift I picked up happened to be going right past Robert and Mouse's cottage. In those days, they had three-lane roads with a central overtaking lane. My driver would get into that shared lane and put his foot down at 70 miles an hour, somehow missing lumbering oncoming lorries. He would absolutely face these lorries down, never pulling away, and at the last minute the lorries would somehow miss us. Of course, I was by then convinced that this prediction was going to come true. I was literally shaking when I got out. (Johnny Lenkiewicz, Interview, September 2017)

In October 1960 Ivorine was pregnant. Whatever Robert might have felt about the news, there is no record of him making any adjustments to his behaviour which might suggest a long-term plan. A steady job did not seem necessary or desirable to him, and his classmates recall that the series of love affairs at St Martin's did not suffer. In terms of art Robert remained a model of creative industry and was held up as such by his tutors. Fellow pupil and lifelong friend Aury Shoa explains:

I knew of him and his ability because my introduction to St Martin's was being taken to the assembly hall when everybody had come back from summer holiday. [The point of this assembly was] to show us all what productivity really meant. St Martin's building was shared with another college known as The School of Distributive Trade. The institutions shared a huge assembly hall in a half-basement. We were called in there, and we saw one gigantic scroll, over three hundred feet long, maybe ten to twelve feet high, circling the entire assembly hall. The theme was horses, stables, local people, the trotters, iron workers: then there were three stacks of accompanying sketchbooks, very high-quality sketches. They said to us 'Next time you have a summer holiday, think of this as a model for productivity. Don't say you were too busy, or you had a headache, or a recurring cold: you have three months, and this is what is possible.' If Robert had been stupid, he would have been called an 'idiot savant', but he wasn't stupid. So, there was this aura; even before I met him I was very strongly affected. He had done all this at the age of eighteen over the summer holiday. (Aury Shoa, Interview, September 2017)

Here the influence of Alice von Schlossberg was likely an unacknowledged factor. Though far from perfect, she undoubtedly instilled in Robert the meaning of perseverance and the value of hard work. Isaac and Axel were not loafers, but as models of industry they paled when set next to Alice. Robert also had the manically productive Schweitzer, Rembrandt, and Nietzsche as role models, but they arose from books: powerful spirits, but spirits nonetheless. Everybody who knew her agrees that Alice was a living monument to hard graft and, in this respect, she was one of the best exemplars a young artist could have.

Robert could produce such large-scale paintings partly because of the liberation from the Shemtov: some of the semi-derelict properties he used as studios allowed much more workspace. They also allowed a very different kind of social space and his sexual, intellectual, and artistic relationships multiplied accordingly. His freedom was far from unlimited: social conventions and the ordinarily warped principles of 'herd morality' still applied. Alongside other early works the large scroll was destroyed by an irate landlady with a love of fire. One version of the tale says it was the result of a bitter dispute over unpaid rent, another that the landlady was Catholic, devout, and outraged by Robert's seduction of a young nun. It does not take a close reader of Nietzsche to note that the depressing common denominators between both versions are the interwoven desires for property relations, 'proper' sexuality, and the conflation of justice with revenge.

Robert's informal studies and conversations with Bertrand Russell, Alfred Reynolds, and Axel Ney-Hoch were bearing fruit, and he was putting forth strong and well-formed arguments about the deep history of art and culture. When Aury Shoa first met Robert in 1959, Robert was 18. What follows is a small fragment of Aury's recollections: what shone throughout the entire interview was the sense of how extraordinarily gifted Robert was as a thinker and an artist. One day, Aury sat in the canteen near a fascinating couple including 'a very attractive young lady called Susan Taylor, very blonde. I always noticed her in the common room and drawing rooms. My eyes were hungry for her. Robert was introduced to me by some friends in the canteen. Susan Taylor was at the table but even with her present, I was immediately drawn to such an erudite man' (Aury Shoa, Interview, December 2016).

We had glimpses of him and thought he was rather eccentric: he was one of the first men to have long hair; and remember this was before the hippies had gone to India [...] before all the rules broke down. He was incredibly exciting to listen to. He could think ahead and prepare at a distance something he would eventually approach in a serious manner: that was my first experience of communicating with him. I was desperately lonely for the first three months and was just starting to learn how to socialise thanks to my friends Jan and Erdogan, who were also foreigners in England. Robert was, unknown to me or anyone else at the time, having affairs left, right and centre. [...] He had a quality about him which was very attractive. Call it 'charismatic' for want of a better word. His sentences were measured and considered, he used language in a very evocative way, even though he was quiet, sometimes almost whispering, which is a great way of drawing people in. I was expecting something more profound but he asked me:
'What do you think about muscles?'
'What do you mean?'
'Just talk to me about muscles.'

Methodically as Socrates or Mr Plotnik, Robert repeated 'Anything else?' until Aury had nothing else to say on the subject. At which point Robert changed tack:

'Do you know anything about the ancient Greeks?'
'I've seen some films with Greeks and Romans in them, but nothing much more.'
'In theory the ancient Greeks were the entire foundation for European civilisation. Europeans have this conceit that they are followers of the Greeks, and for them the body beautiful, its function, its maintenance, and its ability to use it maximally, not just in war but in all kinds of skilful manoeuvring, was very important. But of course the Greeks also believed that in the same way you had to develop the mind, you had to

make sure that when you speak, you speak with accuracy, with measure, with prudence, proof, sequential thought, but that doesn't in the end make you right.'

Suddenly, in my first real conversation with him, this man was telling me about Greek civilisation, their philosophers, little anecdotes always interspersed with anecdotes about Alexander and Aristotle, especially Alexander's horse Bucephalus, or poetic references. This was the very beginning of Robert talking to me about the world of ideas. (Aury Shoa, Interview, December 2016)

Robert was delighted to discover that Aury's first language was Hebrew and the first stories he had learned were from the Book of Genesis and a vast range of Hasidic parables. Aury had become somewhat anglicised and was a proud atheist at that point, but 'Robert engaged me on this front also, and showed me a whole new way of dealing with material of this nature'. Robert was approaching 19, Aury approaching 18.

He told me tales of Jewish heroes. Robert would speak about how Rembrandt was a good friend of Menasseh ben Israel, an ambassador who argued the case for Oliver Cromwell to allow the Jews back into England. Robert was familiar with all the Hasids, with Martin Buber, Albert Schweitzer, and of course the Germans – Kant, Goethe, Schopenhauer, Nietzsche – all these threads he could weave together, effortlessly … he would talk of these ideas and I could never have enough.

It was unbelievable how much he was capable of linking together as such a young man. He opened up so many possibilities. We went from 'muscles' as a general introduction, to a whole world of ideas and art and stories and experiential intelligence. That was my introduction to Robert at St Martin's. (Aury Shoa, Interview, December 2017)

At his easel some days later Aury was surprised to find the strikingly beautiful student, Susan Taylor, was not in her usual place in the classroom but had moved closer to him. A lot closer. As they painted, her leg touched his. Thinking the contact accidental, he shifted away slightly and was pleasantly surprised when it happened again. As the lesson ended, she asked him if he wanted to go to the cinema with her. Aury accepted, and a wonderful relationship was born between experimenters and guinea-pig. For Robert had noticed that Aury was very interested in the muscles and related tissues of the delightful Susan Taylor, and had engineered the entire situation. Obviously leaving Aury out of the information loop, Robert had made a wager with Susan that she could not make Aury fall in love with her in the space of a week.

'She won that bet before I left the easel!' recalls Aury. The relationship with Susan Taylor lasted a matter of days, and when Aury found out the truth he nobly forgave Susan and Robert. The trespass was made purely in the name of knowledge, Robert claimed. They became lifelong friends. This casual cruelty, or at the very least the serious disregard towards other people's emotions, was in part balanced by an altogether more benevolent set of behaviours. Already Robert was dedicating much of his time to the support of what another friend, Tarun Bedi, described as 'the derelict people': a roving troupe of alcoholics, junkies, misfits, and outsiders who Robert liked to paint and help as best he could.

Initially these charitable tendencies might be credited to the influence of Schweitzer or the mawkish but moving scene in which Laughton's *Rembrandt* seemingly saves the soul of a broken beggar he has brought off the street to model for him. In later years Robert would laugh good-naturedly at what he called the 'messianic delusions' of his youth; but however his own evaluation of his motives might have changed, his commitment to painting and assisting the malfunctioning classes remained constant. Addicts, pariahs, those suffering from autism and schizophrenia, the entire rich and poor and sometimes dangerous spectrum of society, who Nietzsche called 'the botched and the bungled', were welcomed into Robert's studios from his teens onwards, decade after decade. The motto 'All Are Welcome' was not merely a slogan of youthful Messianism but a durable commitment to keeping his studios – and his mind – open to all possibilities. On several occasions this commitment nearly proved lethal, almost as if Robert had taken to heart Nietzsche's challenge in *Beyond Good and Evil*:

> If a man is praised today for living 'wisely' or 'as a philosopher' it hardly means more than 'prudently, and apart'. Wisdom seems to the rabble to be a kind of escape, a means and a trick for getting out of a dangerous game. But the genuine philosopher – as it seems to us, my friends? – lives 'un-philosophically' and 'unwisely', above all *imprudently* and feels the burden and the duty of a hundred experiments and temptations of life – he risks *himself* constantly, he plays *the* dangerous game. [14]

It is undoubtedly the case that throughout his life Robert risked other people's feelings and occasionally their bodily safety during his investigations. These risks were seldom finely calculated and often arose from experiments in which the person was not even aware they were a participant.

4.6 Robert on the banks of the Thames opposite Kew Gardens, *c.*1959.

5.1 Celia 'Mouse' Mills and Robert, London, 1961.
5.2 Robert with 'Mouse', London, 1962.

5

Food, Love, and Mouse

Robert's first child, Dorian, was born in St Mary's Hospital, Kensington, on 30 June 1961. The name likely reflects Robert's continued interest in Oscar Wilde. Robert was not present at the birth. Mother and baby returned to the McLaren family home at 75 Oaklands Road in Cricklewood. Dorian's birth certificate names the father as Michael McLaren.

> She hadn't told anyone that I was Robert's son. She hadn't told her father or her mother. Robert knew, but she never told me until I was seven or eight. Apparently, my grandfather [even when he] was about 75, still hadn't been told. (Dorian Lenkiewicz, Interview, November 2017)

If the responsibilities of fatherhood ever sat on Robert's shoulders, they did so very lightly before falling off altogether. It was not that he was insensitive to people's needs – far from it – but according to all those who knew him best, he was prone to prioritising the person standing next to him. On the rare occasions Robert had money in his pocket it would routinely and ungrudgingly be given to street beggars or visitors to his studios in need of food or the ever-popular 'cup of tea'. Robert was no fool when it came to the deciphering of codes; he knew he was feeding dangerous habits. Alex Donoghue recalls whenever he pointed out that the 'cup of tea' meant a fix of drugs or a bottle of wine, Robert would reply: 'They will spend it on whatever they need most.'

As Robert's involvement with Ivorine and the infant Dorian faded, his romantic involvements multiplied. His letters from 1961 name 'Elizabeth and Yvonne' as concurrent interests. 'Robert, possibly quite sincerely, claimed that children do not need fathers until they are in their teens. He used that to justify his absence quite a lot,' says Johnny.

In the summer of 1961 Robert lived and painted in a rented room in Fellows Road, Swiss Cottage. At almost the same time as the birth of Dorian, the woman who became Robert's first wife was moving to London from Cornwall: Celia Mills. Very wild, very innocent, very beautiful, she was nicknamed 'Mouse', despite her impressive stature, after a St Martin's student complimented Robert on being such 'a lucky cat to catch that mouse'. During her first year as a student she lived with her grandmother in New Oxford Street, Bloomsbury, amid a gorgeous clutter of antiques.

I was a wild girl, full of opinion and wanting adventure. My clothes were pretty crazy and I wore tons of black eye make-up. My grandfather was a deeply eccentric gent, a friend of Oscar Wilde, and my grandma, apart from her daily work, was a fortune teller. Grandma was wonderful, having lived a bizarre life of her own, and I came and went with no questions asked. Each evening I was invited into her sitting room and she would lay out the cards and tell my fortune by the gas fire. All she was interested in was money and all I wanted to hear about was love. She was divorced from my grandfather, but they shared the basement flat. He was a collector of weird and wonderful things: the place must have been stacked with diamonds and jewels worth a fortune, wrapped in tissue paper stuffed into the toes of shoes. There were suits of Japanese armour, swords, old Japanese paintings and first editions of the rarest books. When he died, Grandma sold everything for a pittance to dealers in Berwick Market. The remainder of her possessions she painted a vivid green, even the knives and forks. It was mind-blowing. Somewhere, I fitted into all of this, in love with London, in love with life. Everything is coloured by youth, and I felt long and slim and pretty, and tended to feel comfortable on the darker side of the moon. (Celia 'Mouse' Mills, Letter, August 2017)

She awoke one morning from uneasy slumbers to the memory of a vivid dream, the sensed significance of which seemed entirely out of scale to its mundane content. It was a job advertisement – not for lover, wife, and muse to a handsome young artist but merely a kitchen assistant. The very next day in St Martin's she noticed a canteen worker pinning a sign to the notice board: 'Washing up person wanted, apply within'. Unknown to Mouse, Robert worked in the kitchens. She was soon washing dishes as he dried and stacked them. The beautiful young people toiling at the industrial-sized sink could hardly suspect that their daughter would one day write:

Apparently Robert hung around with a girl called Sue Taylor at college. Robert had a strong aura about him and several of the girls – especially Monica Myers – flirted outrageously with him. Men would ask Mouse out during this time, but she was thinking of Robert mainly and she couldn't believe it one day when he walked over to her and said, 'Could I paint you tomorrow night?' Mouse of course said yes, and that night she told me she prayed to god that he would love her. She told me she was so scared and aware of Robert. She was doing her best to keep her expectations set in reality but it is difficult when you are crazy about someone. Robert then told Mouse that he had a child and she felt a huge stab of disappointment rush through her. He said he no longer lived with Faggot (Ivorine). Mouse arrived at Robert's studio at Fellows Road. She looked around curiously at the volume of paintings and murals. It was a dark room, faces gazed from paintings everywhere. He told Mouse to sit down and he painted her. They met the next time at Swiss Cottage and Mouse felt very daring as she saw him sitting on the steps, suddenly reaching out and touching him on the shoulder. They were very aware of one another, the beginning of falling in love. It was months before they kissed – they were so scared of each other – and finally in Soho Square he asked if he could kiss her. Then they just became a couple and were considered the 'odd couple' of St Martin's. Both incredibly good looking but definitely 'odd', eccentric and totally mad. (Alice Lenkiewicz, *When Robert Met Mouse*, 2019)

The alchemical principle of like attracting like may have been at play, but Mouse was soon to meet people far stranger. Of the following letters to Mouse Mills we have no certain dates but the first is from late 1961 or early 1962 – possibly even before they first kissed. They have certainly not yet moved in together and Robert is still calling her 'Celia'.

Undated letter to Mouse Mills, 1961/2.

Friday the 6th.
Dear Celia –
I enclose a self-portrait to ensure that your memory does not fail you with regard to my ['visage' deleted and replaced with] appearance. I humbly suspect the possibility, ridiculous of course. I trust you are well! I'm not; in fact, I'm perfectly miserable. You remember that professor chap we met in 'The Book'? [A café next to Foyles bookshop in Soho.] Well, he stayed the night at my place yesterday (Thursday night) and it was generally very interesting, he is convinced that in Einstein's formula the speed of light has been incorrectly ascertained [*sic*] and that it is – I quote 'infinite'. He has had corroboration of his theory

from people like Oppenheimer and Teller, the finest (reputedly) Physicist and Mathematician respectively alive; apparently Teller's reaction was a quiet 'My God' and Oppenheimer's reaction was to quote 'The Lord is My Shepherd': it may well pertain to mirth, but seemingly this misapprehension can have very meaningful if not dangerous effects with regard to scientific dogma, finance, and indeed politics. This Professor has been requested by the American Embassy to keep his theories 'quiet for the moment'. We also discussed Nietzsche, and the Talmud. Rainbow, the 200 lb lout I've discussed in previous correspondence, ate quite comfortably two razor blades, and lifted Faggot [Ivorine] off the ground with his teeth. He is very keen on developing me physically; he assures me that for my size he has never seen anyone so weak. My desire to wish you happy is a little ambiguous. I would like you to be merry, but [...]

And on that cliff-hanger, the letter ends. Whether Robert ran out of time, paper, or whether it was part of a carefully planned emotional fishing expedition is ambiguous. The identity of the razor-swallowing '200 lb lout' remains unknown. Another letter written on Shemtov paper lists his book buying interests:

I have now more or less got my passport, and guess what? I was crossing the road to have my photograph taken for my passport, when for no particular reason I glanced at a small bookshop and what should I find while perusing? I find a very interesting book by Nietzsche with some of his aphorisms, and ½ a dozen more on people like Shelley, Tolstoy, Wilde (with some interesting photographs), Homer, Mark Twain and others – all for a few coppers! I went into the photographers: he was a German, Ya! 'My young friend, *nnya nnya*, vood you lige some snuff?' No, thank you (laugh). 'You *shood*, you *shood*, you are carrying a book on Nietzsche, und he vas a great snuff taker! (Letter from Robert to Mouse, undated, probably 1961/62)

At this stage Robert's book collecting was modest but already finding its centre in philosophy and aesthetics. The habit would soon enough snowball into an outright vice. Ivorine was also developing a bad habit. Understandably depressed by her situation, still deeply in love with the father of her child, marriage crumbling, and with little or no support from anybody, she was initially prescribed amphetamines by her family doctor.

The doses rapidly became a routine rather than a remedy for her woes which were in any case emotional and social rather than a simple medical condition. Ivorine obtained larger doses and other drugs from illegal sources. Mouse and Robert were busy getting high on each other and the chaste pleasures of café dinners. Did Mouse know of Robert's continuing involvement with Ivorine?

> I knew that she existed, but he told me that they were separated, which was a lie. I remember being in a café with him in Primrose Hill and she was staring in through the window, and I thought ... there is more to this. But I was 17, I didn't care, all I cared about was love. I was selfish, but I was aware of it and it bothered me a bit. (Mouse Mills, Interview, July 2017)

Robert's mother was not overwhelmingly pleasant to anybody, but she was especially hostile to Ivorine. On one occasion Robert tried to introduce Alice to the mother of his son and her first grandchild. Ivorine was categorically refused entrance to the house and Alice would not speak to her. John recalls that the reason given was that Ivorine was not Jewish, but non-Jews had until then been made welcome at the Shemtov and many regularly dined there on Sundays. Alice was enraged that not only had her favourite child moved out but falsely presumed that Ivorine and Dorian gave him more reasons to stay away. Alice would hardly blame herself for this, and Ivorine became the helpless symbol of loss, ingratitude, and injustice. She was duly made the scapegoat for all the things that had gone wrong between Alice and her son. In the coming years, others among Robert's loves and children were made welcome and well-fed at the Shemtov: Mouse and the infant Alice were allowed to stay for several months. Robert was himself drifting away from Ivorine by this time and would regularly meet Mouse in the National Gallery or spend all day painting with her.

One obvious consequence of leaving the Shemtov was that three good meals per day failed to appear as if by magic and the combined intelligence and creativity of Robert and Mouse fell helpless before the mysteries of cooking. Their lifelines were the canteen at St Martin's and London's cheaper cafés like The Book in Soho and The Loft in Swiss Cottage. Robert was frequently penniless but his parting boast to Alice was not idle: he could and would work – in an emergency – often cutting out the use of money altogether. While still in his teens he developed a feeding strategy which lasted a lifetime. With nothing more than charm and a sketchbook he would approach a café proprietor with flexible terms of exchange: their food and tea bartered for his sign painting, menu designs, and, when hard pressed, 'sloshing and toshing' – Robert's phrase for the interior decorator's humble art. Many café owners must have thought twice before entering into what might be a devil's bargain with a hungry beast of such immense size, but Robert was no glutton and did not drink alcohol. His needs were modest. He was acutely sensitive to keeping the owners onside and he radiated an excitement which brought other people along: not all of them respectable paying customers, but always artists and intellectuals and beautiful young women. What little he cost the owners in meals Robert more than covered in 'buzz value' alone (Mouse Mills, Interview, May 2018).

Bernard and Mouse recall that in the cheaper cafés of early 1960s London, for the price of an espresso it was possible to sit and socialise for as long as one wished. As well as coffee, tea, and food, they served truly social and cultural functions, though the downside was that even the most basic health and safety regulations were as flexible as the opening times. Mouse conjures the atmosphere thus:

Off England's Lane [near Swiss Cottage] striking left was a small road then a mews which up a set of steps held The Loft. It was a second home to us and we went there most nights and played chess. A regular was Martin Carthy, the folk singer, and I remember him saying 'This new guy, Bob Dylan, won't amount to much ...' Winkle, a friend from St Martin's who became a table-tennis champion got up there, and Peter Sylvere, the son of a friend of mine. Peter had style. We were all at St Martin's together and he drew very well. He was one of the few people I remember Robert taking a real interest in. He respected Robert enormously [...]

To get back to The Loft, Kim Johnson ran it, a handsome bloke, with his assistant Eric with a massive beard. Eric was often seen doing a sly pee among the washing up in the sink. We were untroubled by this. [...] In our own way we were incredibly innocent. No drink, drugs, deviant sex – to an extent we were grown up children. (Mouse Mills, Letter, 14 March 2017)

Axel was a frequent visitor to The Loft and would often bring his daughters Maria and Stella. Not yet in her teens but already an accomplished chess player, Stella entered into a wager with Robert. He had no money but was in the habit of carrying books. We can be fairly sure Robert did not deliberately throw the game, because he forfeited his copy of Stubbs's *Anatomy of the Horse*. Letting go of books was painful for Robert and perhaps this was a memento of Isaac: decades later he tried to buy it back at a hugely inflated price. Stella returned it for free, no strings attached, and Robert reciprocated by painting a portrait of her son. The principles of barter and reciprocal gift-giving which Robert developed in the cafés were enduring.

Throughout 1961 and 1962 Robert's involvement with Mouse grew increasingly serious though exactly the opposite of solemn. Even before they were a couple and long before he proposed marriage to her in The Loft – where she declined this first offer – Robert was growing irrationally jealous and was doing all he could to provoke her jealousy. Yet she remembers their time together in these early days as full of silliness and laughter:

> What is never documented about him is his humour. We used to laugh till we were sick, literally. I remember sometimes collapsing on tube trains unable to move for laughing and missing our stop. I used to be convinced that I was the luckiest, most blessed woman alive and could feel that when we walked down the road, we shone. We used to sing nearly all the time – silly songs and opera. We warbled around the streets of London. How incredibly happy it must have sounded through people's windows. (Mouse Mills, Letter, November 2016)
>
> He disliked cigarettes, drink, and drugs. I imagine when we were together we were the cleanest couple in Britain. I don't know the source of this, as we mixed with smokers and drinkers. St Martin's was not rife with drugs to my knowledge. We were previous to the age of speed and LSD. There was the usual stuff, but we were not interested, saw it as a waste of time. What we were addicted to was food – huge transport cafés with steaming windows and treacle tart and custard. (Mouse Mills, Letter, October 2017)
>
> We had a vivid romantic, and jealousy-fuelled, relationship where we loved and hated in equal measure. We continually made the other one jealous. Sometimes I made up lovers and we wrote hundreds of letters. (Mouse Mills, Letter, November 2016)

We can gain some sense of the situation and its mutual provocations from a selection of Robert's letters, undated, but many from the early part of the relationship before he and Mouse lived together. Thanks to Mouse's generosity in sharing them we have a window into some of the processes which formed Robert – especially his experiences of jealousy, which eventually bloomed into an entire project on the topic. To grasp the cruelty and self-cruelty of Robert's machinations we should remember that Mouse was the great love of the artist's young life; she was his first human, female, and problematic grand passion.

To my Darling Mouse –

I am saying hello to my Cornish Mouse.
I am still sitting in The Loft – on the table before me is my brown box with paints and brushes – it is tied together with a piece of sheet that you never slept in.
    Last night I listened to Ethel Merman singing parts of 'Gypsy'.
I really can't tell you the things I've been doing with Elizabeth [a scribble, then an arrow pointing to the scribble] that says Ria [Ney-Hoch] and Yvonne – I don't know why I rubbed it out.
    I'd like to write how much I miss you – but that will doubtless make you hear at the moment extracts from various musicals or songs being played on the wireless – I wish you were here I could feel some contact then ...

Another letter, undated:

Elizabeth is a very intelligent cunning and amusing girl, why do I prefer you? Mai is tall and so slim with shortish blonde hair, she's so outstandingly beautiful, so striking everyone asks, 'who is she?' – She has the most wonderful liddy eyes, I'll try to send you photographs. Don't be jealous Mouse, not even in the slightest.

And another:

I've received a letter from Sue. I've received a letter from Elizabeth. I've received a letter from Ria. I'm still painting Elizabeth. What are you doing? I've been doing a marvellously cunning thing, you've no idea how cunning. What are you doing? I once knew a person – so hard up for money and things to do, that she used to write to her boyfriend (she was fed up with him) Fancy that! And ... what's more, when she wrote she used to write really cruel, unpleasant things, but at least she wrote!

And another:

I've just read your letter. You cow!

In gleeful retaliation Mouse had written to say she was involved with the singer Martin Carthy and various other likely and unlikely suitors. One fabulation interchangeably called 'Jon' or 'John' was spun out to the point of cruelty. Another source of pain was a wealthy farmer who Robert never met but loathed and nicknamed 'Fatty'. During a return visit to her native Cornwall, Mouse wrote with tales which drove Robert to high-pitched distress. His responses:

You haven't written yet and it's Wednesday – what happened, eh!? You'd better write or I'll phone. I'll give you till Saturday. [The former written in ink. Robert continues in pencil, obviously sometime later:] So Mouse you've written [...] How unfortunate that misery is your destiny. How UNFORTUNATE THAT YOU'VE APPLIED FOR TWO JOBS THAT 'REEK OF ATMOSPHERE' YOU CHEAT! I'll bet trying for jobs was in your mind when you were in London. 'Oh mother dear, I never want to go back to nasty old London'. I can just fucking well imagine it. You are a very sly Mouse, a very sly Mouse. Give my regards to Fatty.

The passion Robert had for Mouse bordered on the monstrous. One is reminded of several commentaries by Oscar Wilde and Nietzsche and Schopenhauer on the highly mixed and dangerous values crammed into 'love', and how much dark joy and torment are co-mingled in our most profound relationships with others. Though agonisingly raw and undeveloped in the above letter, many of the themes for Robert's later projects are here compressed: desire, devotion, compulsion, control, obsession, madness, sacrifice, and dismemberment. The overwhelming irony is that the sources of Robert's jealousy – John and 'Fatty' – were not even items on Mouse's to-do list:

We were tremendously jealous of each other, to a high degree ... he almost got a vicarious pleasure out of being unhappy. He imagined the Elysian fields with us walking hand in hand [...] we existed on just being young and happy, and jealous, which came a close third to the happiness. I was bitterly sad about Ria and others, and he ground himself into absolute despair over my often made-up boyfriends. John was a totally made up character, and he went through agonies over this John, who I built up into a bigger and bigger person. 'Fatty' was real ... he was a farmer and he was utterly boring, and I exaggerated him as well. (Mouse Mills, Interview, September 2017)

In spring 1962 Robert and Mouse's relationship developed into a more formal arrangement and they made the decision to live together. The first of their many shared addresses was 4 Eton Avenue, Swiss Cottage. Co-habitation did not diminish their mutual provocations to jealousy but it increased their happiness and Robert's productivity. He was in the grip of love and full-blown creative obsession, and when he was not making marks on any available surface, he was planning larger works and looking for larger spaces in which to complete them. That summer Robert discovered an empty property in Regent's Park Road: a rambling derelict mansion with its own ballroom. Avoiding the complications of informing the absentee owners, Robert and Mouse moved in and made it approximately habitable with the help of Des, a Jamaican poet friend. Robert used the space wisely. He began work on a series of full-scale copies of large works by Rembrandt, Goya, and Caravaggio – none of which survive due to the inevitable forced relocation which came within a matter of weeks.

They next rented a room in a house near Archway. This was supposedly once inhabited by the infamous Dr Crippen, for whom storage space had been a problem for much smaller items than Robert's works. But the ballroom had given Robert a taste of the studio space to which he would like to become accustomed and Mouse tells us it was around this time that Robert first began to formulate the concepts of his 'projects': discrete but overlapping series of large and small canvases, complete with research notes, historical and social observations, all united in the thorough exploration of a specific theme.

Alongside the canonically great painters Robert also admired and learned from the mass-produced images of posters, book covers, and comic books. He admired what he referred to as 'flash' art, the vivid if sometimes literally throwaway images which could present information or a specific emotion swiftly, decisively, and dramatically (Mouse Mills, Letter, September 2017). Visitors to his studio spaces could see Robert's close copies of Rembrandt stacked next to *The Beano* and *The Dandy* (Alex Donoghue, Interview, September 2017). Mouse recalls he was interested in the covers of pulp paperbacks and theatre and movie posters, often liberating the most impressive ones from their frames in the quieter stations of the Northern Line. What impressed him was the same compression of forces which he found in Caravaggio and the etchings of Dürer and Goya: achieving the maximum effect with the least gesture or simplest line (Mouse Mills, Interview, July 2018).

St Martin's continued to feed Robert's fascination with ideas – even the worst ideas – which worked in tandem with his artistic impulses. Copying the Old Masters was a key part of his apprenticeship, as was life drawing, but for Robert the processes of observation demanded by portraiture already went beyond what many of his contemporaries such as Marcel Duchamp would disparagingly refer to as 'merely retinal' art. Robert was acutely aware that the portraitist absorbs and transcribes much more than reflected light from the object of their interest:

> One incident that springs to mind was a guy who came along to model. He had about seven sittings. He was – the only word one can use is 'ugly', a young Fagin without his charm. He was a vicious guy with a deep hatred for Jews. After completing the painting, Robert thanked him very much and said 'I enjoyed this! Oh, and by the way I'm Jewish' whereupon young Fagin spat at him and roared with genuine pain 'You betrayed me!' I remember feeling shaken. (Mouse Mills, Letter, July 2017)

Listening to the Jew hater and attempting to understand the basis of his anger was more important to Robert than flatly contradicting him and thereby learning no more. This tactical stepping aside from the realm of 'personal feelings' – and moral judgement – may well have been inspired by Alfred Reynold's de-Nazification techniques and it certainly became a feature of Robert's later investigations into a wide range of social phenomena.

In early 1963 Robert and Mouse relocated again, first to 4 Steeles Road, Belsize Park then later in the year to 'a revolting room above Chalk Farm railway station – too awful to merit remembering the address'. The material hardships failed to dent their love: one evening in the crowded galley of The Loft café Robert took to his knees and formally proposed marriage to Mouse. She declined. 'I didn't see the need. We were happy as we were.' And they were. Robert was from a young age a deadly serious aesthete but that was only one aspect of his character. Against the mythology of the 'young struggling artist' we should set the image, full of love and good humour, of Robert on a leash, on all fours, with Mouse leading him down the steps of a tube station. This is possibly a reference to Dürer's etching of Aristotle and Phyllis, and possibly just young people having fun on the way to steal more movie posters from the Underground walls.

6.1 Celia 'Mouse' Mills with Robert at the engagement party of his twin
    Bernard, 1962. Seen left to right are: Mouse, Robert, Alice Lenkiewicz,
    Bernard and his fiancée Gillian, her brother Anthony, mother Bella and
    father Isidore. Robert's brother Johnny is on the right.
6.2 'Mouse' in the Eton Avenue studio where the couple lived, c.1964.

6.3 'Mouse' Mills and Tarun Bedi in the Eton Avenue studio, *c.*1964.
6.4 Robert with 'Mouse' in front of group painting, Eton Avenue, 1964.

6

Paris, Film Stars, and Crashing Back to Earth

Robert kept close company with many who used drugs in dangerous quantities – Axel was at this time regularly ramping up on amphetamines by day and later retiring with fistfuls of sleeping pills – but Robert had an iron-clad immunity to their lures. His interests were art galleries, ideas, bookshops, very attractive women, and café food. London has an abundance of all of these, but one can understand the obvious appeal of visiting Paris (which explains the necessity of the passport photograph mentioned in his letter about the snuff-pushing German barber). Robert travelled by coach to Lympne ex-military airbase in Kent, possibly then the worst airport in England. Once in Paris he stayed in a cheap hotel. How these modest expenses were met remains uncertain but the fact that all his letters from Paris to Mouse are written on Hotel Shemtov notepaper suggests that his mother was still a factor in his life.

The letters are all undated but the references to the 'two Russians in space' pins the Paris visit to the twin Vostok missions of June 1963, the first time two cosmonauts were simultaneously in orbit, one of them the first woman in space. Even with the distractions of Paris closely ahead of him, Robert could not shake off the thoughts of his unreal rivals or miss an opportunity to provoke a little suspicion:

Well! My beautiful Mouse, I am now on board my coach. I intend to bore you with fractional details, indeed so fractional that for them to register will necessitate enough concentration to take your mind off Jon or whoever it may be, for at least the time it takes to read this letter [...] There was a new maid at Mum's this morning [...] who worked previously at the Royal College of Music. I told her that instead of singing my customary three bar pop song while making breakfast I would sing Rachmaninoff's 18th variations of Paganini's theme. It took me till the end of breakfast to remember it but having done so she was well satisfied by it. [...] Pretty remarkable, eh! Those two Russians in space, imagine the affinity they must possess, no one to talk to except each other. If only such a feeling could exist between men on earth, eh!

I bet when they come down they get married. (Letter from Robert to Mouse, undated but likely June 1963)

It may merely have been the jiggling of the coach but the words 'they get married' are written in a thicker, heavier hand. Mouse's rejection of Robert's first offer of marriage had done nothing to cool his ambitions: more likely it amplified his desires. The letters from Paris illustrate a principle spelled out by a French researcher in human experience with whom Robert was not yet acquainted, the Marquis de Sade: that if our desires are denied to us for a little while, they multiply and intensify.

I am now about six miles from Paris, a few miles back I mistook an electricity pylon for the Eiffel Tower. I don't know why but I'm thinking about you all the time, and wondering what you're doing with Jon ...

I am sitting in an armchair in 'MY HOTEL ROOM!' It has a large bed with a red cover, a red carpet, two chairs, a sink and a wardrobe, and a telephone, in short it is bearable. Do you know the bed is an admirable size for two people, I would give all my francs and centimes to the OAS if you were sitting on the edge of it now, wouldn't it be marvellous? We could scour the Louvre, do everything – instead I'm sad and 99 thousand miles away, ever so sad in the most visually pleasing environment I've ever seen [...] My address is 16 Rue Lamartine, Paris 9, France. You may have time to write once (if you are so inspired) as I'm only here for 4 or 5 days. In fact I'll be back in London on Friday [...] Cheerio Mouse! Be good! Love Love Love Love Love Love ... Robert. (Letter from Robert to Mouse, undated but likely June 1963)

Each page of these letters was in high orbit around planet Mouse with no mention of the masterworks which Robert had crossed the Channel to experience.

Robert's return to London was joyous; Mouse was as chronically head-over-heels with him as he with her, his plans to move on to the Royal Academy of Art after graduating from St Martin's were gaining momentum, and his reputation as an artist was starting to show. Possibly via Mark and Emily, a young American couple who frequented The Loft, his work had come to the attention of Douglas Fairbanks Jr. Fairbanks was a great connection for any young artist. He was internationally famous as an actor, stupendously wealthy, a war hero, highly intelligent, with close friends in the British Royal Family and any number of movie studios. And he was keen for Robert to paint his portrait. Robert and Mouse were invited to dine with Douglas and his wife Mary in Hampstead to discuss the matter. Mouse remembers them as 'lovely people' with 'loads of dosh' and Fairbanks 'was *very* interested in buying paintings'. For reasons unknown, Robert was totally indifferent to the man, so Fairbanks's plans 'never materialised. It was weird. [Robert] was totally uninterested in money'. (Mouse Mills, Interview, October 2017)

The people who interested Robert were on the whole anything but 'good connections'. Mouse had already been alerted to the mixed company Robert attracted. In a letter prior to their cohabitation, possibly early 1962, he writes:

> Dear Mouseling
> How are you? I'm very well, I've been doing many interesting things Mouse, I've been having difficulties with a fellow called Lofty, out from the Moor [Dartmoor, a maximum security prison], no joke – he's hard, really nasty, and really nice, gives everything he's got away but nevertheless nasty and he's tough – dirty tough. (Robert, Letter to Mouse, 1962 or 1963)

Robert's ability to attract characters such as 'Rainbow', a razor-eating 200 lb lout, has been previously noted, but perhaps the decisive factor in his magnetism for such people was what he identified in Lofty: his seemingly natural communism in regard to money or resources. For as long as anybody can remember Robert gave paintings away where he could easily have sold them. Whenever he had money, he paid people like Lofty whatever small or large sums he had to sit for him and, when he had no money, he would stand them a meal at The Loft or The Moon and Sixpence and put it on his tab. Coupled with his erudition and charm, this made him a magnet for all manner of eccentric and often mentally ill characters. By no means all the crowd who came to visit, sit, or sleep over at his studios were damaged or deranged. Mouse provides an overview:

> The regular guests were 'Flowerpot', so called because of his seemingly permanent hat; he was permanently in trouble with money and petty crime. Lofty, an ex-Dartmoor convict with a facial scar and his French girlfriend Paulette, Peter Sylvere, beautiful gentle Peter, whose mother Irene modelled for Picasso. I loved her very much, and her me. One

truly remarkable guy called Michael de Costa who was very openly gay, very rare in those days, an actor; he made Robert and I laugh. He was very rotund and we used to wash cars together to get some cash. It was a carnival of friends, madmen and saints. Derek Winkleworth known as Winkle, the British table-tennis champion, Tarun Bedi, a shy and very sweet artist from India, friends from St Martin's like Milton Delaney, an Irish Jew brought up in London [...] Big Tony was another visitor, a very troubled soul, an actor who was on hard times; Ivan, a schizophrenic who consumed his own pee and worse, and was a pain, and frightened me a bit. (Mouse Mills, Letter, November 2016)

Robert's interest in the mentally ill had perhaps dawned early via the traumatised inhabitants of the Shemtov. He was unsentimental about the more disturbed and disturbing characters around him but consistently helpful.

Lofty wants to stay again – I've said no – he's disgustingly unscrupulous – I'm home and Big Tony (damn him!) hasn't got anywhere for the night [...] the only fucking compensation is that they will all be gone tomorrow! (Letter to Mouse, undated)

If they were gone tomorrow, they would soon enough return. Robert was by now developing quite an entourage of wild and eccentric characters. He was especially well disposed towards Pierre von Grunewald. By all accounts Pierre was a writer of considerable talent and a great storyteller, but terribly prone to self-destructive addictions: alcohol, amphetamines, opiates, raw ether, pretty much any intoxicant he could lay hands on (Tarun Bedi, Interview, June 2017). Whenever supplies ran out, Pierre had a habit of throwing himself like a drug-seeking missile though pharmacists' windows to grab whatever was available. Robert engineered an informal 'buddy system' among his friends, trying to pair those who could cope with everyday life with those who resoundingly could not. He painted everyone, listened to their stories, took their concerns seriously, and mulled over plans for future projects on vagrancy, obsessive behaviour, and mental illness.

His creative output was relentless during these moves between various addresses. Storing the growing collection of paintings was a problem. He often took works back to the Shemtov or gave them away at random because there was no space available in his lodgings. His creativity was not limited to art. He took his responsibilities for contraception as seriously as his fatherhood of Dorian: not at all. In the closing month of 1963 Celia Mouse Mills became pregnant with Robert's second child. For her the event happened as if by magic:

> I didn't know that I could *get* pregnant! I was that naïve. Terrible shock, and tremendous delight, but I was in terror of my parents. *My parents!* [...] Robert was delighted. (Mouse Mills, Interview, September, 2017)

The news did not change Robert's highly impractical attitude to work and money, though shortly afterwards he reproposed marriage and Mouse decided to take some time to consider it. They did not separate as a couple and were still giddily in love but 'took some time out' to formulate their plans with the clarity befitting grown-ups (Mouse Mills, Letter to the author, November 2017). Robert took paid work when the impatience of landlords demanded it: retreating to the Shemtov would be an admission of defeat in the face of the 'real world'. Yet he seemed oblivious to the fact that the opportunities offered to him by the Fairbanks class of patron would outweigh and out pay the 'emergency jobs' he took to make ends meet. For all his erudition, Robert was in this respect totally naïve.

For some months in 1963 Mouse was working in a bakery and Robert in a steelyard alongside somebody even more gigantic than himself, a Caribbean black man known only as 'Tiny'. On lunchbreaks they held competitions to see how many times they could lift various girders above their heads. Though their time together was brief, Tiny left a large impression, for two decades later Robert told stories of this silent Titan and their parting when they were laid off. They sat glumly on a wall. Robert pointed to his chest, then to the road leading to his studio. Tiny pointed to his chest and indicated the road to central London, and without a word the Leviathans parted, never to see each other again.

Still hero-worshipping Samson and Porthos, Robert respected physical strength and toughness. To Mouse's embarrassment he was constantly proving his mettle by hoisting people over his head or dead-lifting the ends of parked cars. On one occasion, when lifting the rear of a Volkswagen Beetle, the entire rear bumper came off in his hands: he placed the wreckage down gingerly and walked swiftly away (Mouse Mills, Interview, September 2017). Several photographs of Robert from this era show him triumphantly lifting nervous looking friends high above his head. More worryingly for Mouse, Robert's interest in tough guys took a bad turn:

Mouse, I have decided to give up painting and take up the fight game. I reckon I've got the strength, the speed, the stamina to be better than the greatest. I'm going to train and train and train – and in a few years I'll be so great I'll shake the world! (Letter to Mouse, undated, 1963 or 64)

This ambition was probably mere bluster and happily short-lived but one wonders why a man of high intelligence and handsome features would consider the fight game even for a second. Robert's close friend Alex Donoghue remarks that this was almost certainly 'part pose, part joke, part homage to Ali, then Cassius Clay. Robert was physically massive and strong but was incapable of hitting people'. Here lies part of the answer to the mystery: Robert had encountered a man of high intelligence and handsome features, and was profoundly and permanently impressed. That man was Cassius Clay, who changed his name to Muhammed Ali in 1964.

Well, heroes! When I was eighteen and Robert was twenty we were walking down Tottenham Court Road and there was this beautiful black guy – Cassius Clay – standing on a soap box. We stopped, amazed at his physicality. He was handing out autographs. There were only four or five of us there. He remained one of Robert's favourites. (Mouse Mills, Letter, November 2016)

Clay was in London that summer for a fight against Henry Cooper, but he was at that time almost unknown in Europe (he had yet to win the world title from 'unbeatable' Sonny Liston) and ticket sales were poor. Swallowing his considerable pride, Clay and his manager took to the streets to sell his talents, a tactic Robert would later emulate when times were tough. Robert was fascinated by Clay's beauty, self-promoting style, and exaggerated egotism, though the post-fight photographs in which Cooper resembles a car-crash victim leave no doubt about the brutality of 'the sweet science'. As Muhammed Ali, he was arguably the greatest boxer of all time, and perhaps more importantly a spokesman and activist whose efforts were no less sincere and effective than those of Albert Schweitzer. Schweitzer, of course, had received nothing but encomiums for his principled actions; Ali would receive a three-year boxing ban at the height of his powers for refusing the Vietnam War draft and campaigning against the war. Robert was fastidiously lucky in his choice of heroes. Boxing remained a fascination for him and his diaries of later decades record dreams in which boxers figure largely.

The year had been a happy, giddy rush but by Christmas of 1963 the demands of 'the real world' were pressuring Robert into swallowing some of his own pride. He was penniless. He had unwisely spurned a wealthy patron and had no others beyond café owners. He had little choice but to invoke the aid of his mother. Mouse was suffering from dreadful morning sickness and a curious sense of 'shrinking'. This is very likely Todd's Syndrome, a serious distortion of the sufferer's perception of physical scale and time. The cause is unknown but the stress of pregnancy, and keeping the secret from her parents, and her once happy but now chaotic and desperately poor life with Robert, are likely factors:

After my euphoric reaction at the doctor's surgery the sickness set in [smells became unbearable; she grew thinner and thinner]. Overriding all miseries was the guilt of not having told my mother. 'How are you? It's been ages since you phoned'. 'I'm fine, been doing a lot of painting'. I can't remember if I mentioned leaving art school. [...] Having been evicted once again for not paying rent, all that was available was this small room painted a washed-out white, the paper torn and mildewed [...] The door if left open let the putrid odour drift in from downstairs: an old lady we had been told was dying on the ground floor. The smell was almost visible, wafting through every crack [...] Facilities were in the shape of a leaking gas cooker, a thick, dull, yellow smell emitting from it which threatened annihilation.

We stared at each other in desperation. Where were the couple in London that made heads turn, the darlings of St Martin's? We had grown smaller. He said 'We won't be here long, try and bear it'. Nausea was in every part of my body. I dreamed of Cornwall and my mother's upside-down apricot pudding. The city became the enemy and I was indifferent to my man. I lingered outside fruit shops with no money, having heard that if you smashed a window the court would absolve you of responsibility if you were with child. I went as far as holding a rock in my hand but ducked out. I could have died for an orange. It was about this time that I started to become *little* [...] suddenly one shrinks to the size of a tiny creature and people appear like giants. The ability to speak disappears and the only sound one can manage is the tiniest of squeaks. I would wait in a terrified void for it to pass. [...] The accumulated smells of our room were too distressing to bear

95

and although it was late winter, I would have opted to sleep in the park. Robert's long-suffering mother paid a deposit on a reasonable place in Steeles Road, Belsize Park. It was much better, but as usual all the windows were blacked out, as he liked constant light for painting, preferring electricity to daylight. The smell of oil paint was making me even more ill, and I was desperately thin, and the shrinking episodes were becoming alarmingly regular. It was decided that I must return to the farm in Cornwall. (Mouse Mills, Letter, Summer 2017)

Robert moved back to the Shemtov. We have no record of how magnanimous his mother was in victory. Robert had certainly lasted more than Alice's predicted 'five minutes in the real world', but his return to dependent status could not have been easy for him. The greater part of his immense output of work had been given away, lost, confiscated, or destroyed by the vengeful commercial classes. At the Shemtov he had no money worries: Mrs Bobek served him wonderful Eastern European meals. Mrs Ryabushinsky and Mr Myers were helpful and kind. Many of the older residents had died off. Bernard, who had been a responsible adult since the age of 15 with his own successful business, was getting ready to marry. One of Robert's letters to Mouse mentions that Bernard bought Alice a new television for £100. Alice was getting no sweeter with age and tensions were rising. Though materially comfortable Robert was separated from his beloved Mouse and must have felt himself in a grim limbo when considering his own future. Bernard conjures the mood of the Shemtov in its later years thus: 'May I drop down dead before I finish this meal if these stories are not true. Robert left home very early because of my mother [...] She was a tyrant'. Bernard laughed as he described how his mother threw a bowl of soup over the head of elderly Mrs Lyons, who had dared to ask for it to be reheated: 'This is how she treated *paying guests*; nobody had immunity' (Bernard Leigh, Interview, March 2017).

And the residents were dying with grim regularity:

My fiancée of many years, Gill, soon to become my first wife ... her father said 'I think it's about time Gill met your family' and I thought – No! No! No! The wedding will never happen if she meets her future mother-in-law. We had one male tenant, Mr Goudella, a very old man, bachelor, been there for years, always sat at a little round table in the corner of the dining room. Dining room: two Corinthian columns in the middle where Robert used to play Samson destroying the temple of the heathen. I had decided the best time to take Gill to meet my mother was on a Sunday, because that's when Ma was busiest, and would have least chance to upset her. People came from outside the Hotel. Whatever else she was, my mother was a wonderful cook, so Sundays were very busy. When I [went into the kitchen and] said 'This is Gill' she said 'Ach, I haven't time for this now'. (Bernard Leigh, Interview, March 2017)

Happy to hear this, Bernard showed Gill the dining room and began making the rounds of introductions when,

Mr Goudella turns in his seat, acknowledges me, returns his attention to his soup, and collapses. His face *splatted* straight into the tomato soup and stayed there. No bubbles. Stone dead. I went into the kitchen and said, 'Ma I think something has happened to Mr Goudella: I think he's dead, and there is soup all over the wall.' Alice strode into the dining room with a towel over her shoulder, 'Oy veh! Ach! Oy vey!' *Straight past* Mr Goudella ... and started to clean the wallpaper before it stained. That was her priority; just natural. This was Gill's introduction to her future family. (Bernard Leigh, Interview, March 2017)

The brothers had to haul the corpse upstairs and lay it on a bed until the doctor came to certify the death. Bernard recalls Mr Goudella's heavy boots thumping against every step and banister along the way. Alice remained downstairs frantically attempting to restore the precious wallpaper, as Gill looked on helpless and horrified. 'That's how my wife was introduced to my mother, [who] came to the wedding. But for fifteen years of married life Gill didn't see her again' (Bernard Leigh, Interview, March 2017)

Robert wrote frequently and ardently to Mouse. Many of the letters reveal an understandable anxiety that he might be losing her, but the games of jealousy continue regardless.

Axel comes over quite often with someone for me to paint, he saw the photograph of me being led down the stairs, and you standing by the policeman, and the both of us by the Horse Guards with you on my back. He thinks you're wonderful! – but then he thinks that Elizabeth and Mai are wonderful too [...] He sends you his sincere love and 'congratulations' (I told him) and tells you not to be afraid, he thinks it's wonderful [...] I'm just starting to eat a succulent chocolate cake.

I suppose you told your mother how you had an affair with Martin Carthy and how he's pining for you: I don't know how you'll convince your ma about your dalliance with me, if you invent fictitious tales of blood and gore. Look after 'it' and yourself, and don't get stuck on other blokes – I wish I could go to bed with my pregnant Mouse. Love, Robert. (Letter to Mouse, January 1964)

Another letter from this period gives us an insight into the development of Robert's thoughts on the purposes of the painter's art.

Michael the painter with the wonderful studio is sitting right next to me [...] I think he's a lousy painter, he's all subject-matter – harmless enough of course, but he doesn't say anything with 'paint' (he's just looked at me, I feel embarrassed. I wonder if he suspects my utter and total disrespect for him as a painter, except for the fact that he paints at all, which I suppose must be significant) – he says it all with superficial images, and not the harmonies of essential paint alone! I know I don't either, but he doesn't seem aware of it. (Letter to Mouse, Jan/Feb 1964)

The letter was written in The Loft and it is reasonable to assume that Robert was spending as much time as possible away from the Shemtov. By February he had moved out again, probably with financial help from his mother: first to 99 Fellows Road and shortly afterwards to number 7 Belsize Park Road. Soon enough, money became a problem:

It's Friday afternoon. I'm still flat hunting but it will be alright. I've got money difficulties, the chap with the £2.10/– for my portrait can't come, I promised my landlady £2 on her phone bill to appease her but she took it seriously, she wants it tomorrow. I've got a job for one week at David's Hotel which will bring in £8.10/– hope I can get the flat for nought, the cat's hungry, moan, moan, moan ... Love, Robert. (Letter to Mouse, probably February 1964)

But news of his abilities was spreading. People came to The Loft specifically to incite Robert to paid work. This was not as simple as it should have been thanks to Robert's extraordinary ability to discourage any regular economic exchanges. His letters hint at a range of sitters and deals. He was approached for a portrait by an obviously wealthy Greek businessman, who Robert was delighted to learn was called 'Plato'. He talked enthusiastically about the importance of Classical proportion, took Robert by taxi to his family home halfway across London, offered him food and wine, and so forth (Letter to Mouse, undated). For reasons unfathomable, Robert abandoned this seemingly clinched deal.

Even at this early stage, Robert's marketability was hindered by his wilful disregard for the economic value of artworks. Buyers rankled when it was public knowledge that he often gave away large canvasses to people he hardly knew. Yet his letters record instances such as 'The doctor wants me to do another portrait – but only expenses paid this time (that's about 6 shillings) ... I've done a couple of portraits' (Letter to Mouse, undated).

It must have come as a huge joy to Robert when in springtime 1964 Mouse agreed to his marriage proposal. A date for the wedding was set – 21 March. She returned to London and lived with Robert at 24 Belsize Park Road. They both took up various menial and short-lived jobs. The wedding was extravagantly hurried and basic. At the appointed time and place – nine o'clock, Hampstead Registry Office – the officials were waiting. Mouse was running late: she had not even time to brush her teeth and the pink dress did not fit her pregnant body perfectly. She wore red shoes and clutched a bunch of yellow daffodils which had been hoisted along the way:

> There were seven or eight guests, one photograph, then we went back to our place in Belsize Park, near the tube station. We went into the Cauldron, which is a coffee bar near there. Then we went to work the next day, he was a porter and I was a chambermaid in the Cumberland Hotel [...] the only thing I got for a wedding present for myself was a packet of salt. I thought – you need that to cook [and I would have to cook once I was married. Up until then] we'd lived off restaurant menus. (Mouse Mills, Interview, September 2017)

Nevertheless, the newlyweds were deliriously happy and about to get happier with the arrival of the baby. And unknown to them, the strange and magical venue of Eton Avenue was just around the corner.

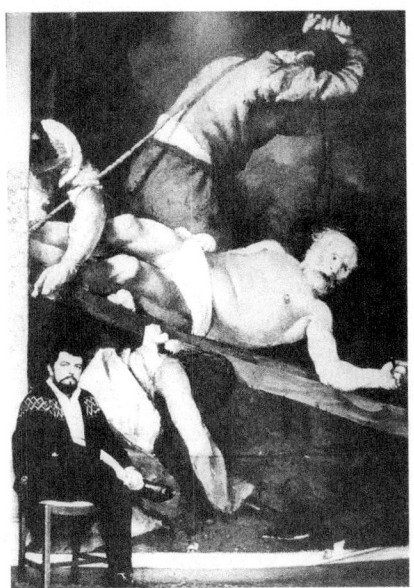

7.1 Alex Donoghue in front of Robert's copy of Caravaggio's *The Crucifixion of Saint Steven*, early 1960s, now lost.

7.2 Mouse with infant Alice, Eton Avenue, 1964.

7.3 Sitters and associates at Steeles Road studio, Hampstead, mid-1960s. Left to right: art students Derek Winkworth and Milton Delany. 'Lofty' (in profile), actor Michael de Costa (bottom right).

7

The Madness of Eton Avenue

The newlyweds rapidly moved to Belsize Park Road again. Then in a rare holiday into 'respectable' work Robert took a job teaching art in Drakewalls Junior School at Gunnislake, East Cornwall. Here he and Mouse rented a room in Drakewalls House. By all accounts Robert was very capable and well-liked as a teacher and some of the pupils stayed in contact with him for decades. But however much the pupils enjoyed the experience, it did not give Robert a taste for more of the same. As soon as the term was over he and Mouse headed back into London, first living in a small flat at 22 Oxford Avenue, Primrose Hill, then 'Fitzroy Avenue, an in-between place before Eton Avenue, and it was next to Primrose Hill. We had Pierre (von Grunewald) and Jo upstairs. Pierre was alcoholic but he was lovely; he wrote wonderful stories in tiny writing', Mouse recalls (Interview, September 2017).

Eton Avenue was about to be invaded by art and the growing tribe of outsiders attracted to Robert. He and Mouse moved first into number 4 then to a larger, more utilitarian but more chaotic studio set-up at number 53. Eton Avenue was a wide, beautiful Victorian road with tall plane trees which kept it shady by day and that 'shone luminous green at night-time. They were grand Victorian houses divided into flats. At the end [of Eton Avenue] one came to "The Washington" a large pink pub and "The Village" as we called it with its laundrette and various little shops: the proper name was England's Lane', Mouse Mills explains.

> The rooms inside were massive. We had the basement which had the advantage of large patio doors leading out to the garden. We had one enormous square room with a tiny kitchen and a decrepit bathroom with a gas heater which threatened extermination every time it was lit. A bath felt like a punishment. We had little by way of furniture, basically one large bed and a piano. (Mouse Mills, Letter, October 2016)

Mouse's health stabilised then improved as the pregnancy progressed. Robert painted at a frantic pace and the room was soon filled with canvases. It was also soon filled with mattresses and unusual people like Big

Tony, Ivan, and Lofty. Robert's interest in social outsiders extended to London's gangsters. The city hosted a fine collection of wide-boys, chancers, and rogues who saw Robin Hood as a role model to justify doling out menace and violence while robbing rich and poor alike. Robert did not completely swallow this bogus mythology but his fascination with outlaws was genuine enough.

One hundred yards from Eton Avenue in Fellows Road lived a prime candidate for Robert's curiosity: a plausibly Sicilian man with thick black curls, the massive chest and shoulders of a bull, neck wide as his head, immaculately dressed in tailored suits and Crombie overcoat. He came and went at irregular hours, followed no obvious trade and – perhaps the clinching evidence in an age when only the well-off could afford any car – he drove a top-of-the-range Jaguar. Fascinated by these symbols of successful villainy Robert craved an opportunity to paint the man but was utterly clueless about the etiquette of approaching what could be a Mafia soldier.

With touching and potentially lethal naivety, Robert did the worst possible thing: he made observations from what he thought was a safe distance, as discreetly as any long-haired poncho-clad paint-splattered giant could. As the object of Robert's curiosity left the house or arrived home, he often glimpsed Robert peeping around a distant corner. On several occasions he walked towards Robert to discover who was stalking him and why. But Robert fled when approached, thus digging the trench of suspicion deeper. This went on for two weeks until matters were forced to a head. The man was aware of Robert loitering as he approached his home but feigned indifference, put the key in the door, opened it, half-entered then pivoted and sprinted over to Robert, physically pinning him to the wall.

'What's your game? If you think you're going to put the hammer on me you're wrong. Every time I turn around you're lurking around and looking at me!'
'Oh no, Sir; I mean no harm. I'm a painter.'
'What, *houses*?'
'Sometimes, if I have to. But … I'd like to paint *you*.'
'Why didn't you ask?'
'I wasn't sure how you'd react. I don't mean any trouble.'
'Bugger off!'

'I live round the corner. If you change your mind I'd very much like to paint you.'

'I'll think about it,' said the man, releasing Robert who walked swiftly away.

'I'm not an alchie, I'm not a druggie,' said Robert, shakily, 'I just paint.'

Fifty years later the identity of this fearsome figure has been established. He even agreed to a series of interviews. As he recalls:

A couple of days later, at the house of [RC, a driver and bodyguard] I was at a dinner party. There were a few local artists there. [RC] was quite a competent artist. Several of his paintings were on show around the room. I hadn't met these other people before. In the course of the evening they talked about painting and [RC] brought up the name Lenkiewicz:

'He's only a young guy, but he's a *genius*. I'd love to be able to talk to him about what he's doing ...' The guests nodded and spoke of Robert with unalloyed admiration. I said 'Lenkiewicz? Young guy, tall, long hair, scruffy?'

'Yes, that's him.'

'Ah. He asked me if he could paint me.'

'He asked you? When are you going to sit for him?'

I thought, I can't say what happened, so I said: 'I told him I'd let him know when I had a bit of time.'

'I'd get round there sharpish in case he changes his mind.'

I had to laugh, because I knew nothing about art. But suddenly in their eyes, they thought I was his friend and knew everything about his paintings and ... well, I bluffed it for the rest of the evening. Next day, on England's Road, a shopping area near where we lived, I saw him and waved him over. I said 'When do you want to paint me?'

He said 'Well, if you're able to, now. All I need is one hour. One hour will be fine.'

'Let's do it now then.'

I had a brown overcoat on. I still have the painting. I went to Eton Avenue with him [...] A young woman I was later introduced to as Mouse was there. But what I recall most of all – I was totally gobsmacked. I walked into this large ground floor room and to my left was an immense mural, right along the wall, a fantastic, biblical thing. I had never seen anything like it. Then I noticed paintings all over the place, everywhere. The only things not covered by paintings were a bed and a fireplace. I said 'Who painted these?'

Robert said 'I did.' And while we were talking he set up an easel and brought turps and paints and I was walking round mesmerised, I didn't know what to think. I sat down.

In most of his studios Robert would black out the windows to totally control the lighting, but Alex Donoghue recalls the shifting sunlight through the large patio windows making large and dramatic changes to the room as he sat.

He had the canvas in front of him, blank, and he had this ritual I came to know well. He would sit, slap his thighs, sigh, squint at me through a hand mirror, and then begin. Swoosh, swoosh, swoosh, all over, he started to attack the canvas with a wide brush. I think I sat for him three times for that picture and on the final sitting, just like when he slapped his thighs and sighed to start the painting, he did exactly the same when he'd finished. He said 'Would you like a cup of tea?'

I said 'No thanks. Can I look at it now?'

'Oh yes. Do you want a cup of tea?' and Robert disappeared into the kitchen, which led out to the garden. I sat there for a minute then thought 'Go on then, I will have a cup of tea.' There was no reply from the kitchen. I got up and walked round to the canvas and I remember shouting: 'Who the hell is *that*?'

No reply from the kitchen, nothing. I said 'Is that *thing* supposed to be me?' I went to the kitchen, he wasn't there. I went into the garden, he wasn't there. He'd done a runner. Gone.

I walked back, sat in front of it ... and thought 'Is that what I look like to other people?' I looked like everything [Robert] thought I was, horrific, thuggish, a proper villain, blood-shot eyes, nose all over my face, it was brutal. I was not happy at all.

I looked around the area but couldn't find him anywhere, so I went home and Betty, my partner. She could see I was angry. [Then] a guy, who eventually became extremely bad news, had a love–hate relationship with Robert. I'd spoken to him once before; he knocked on my door. I asked what I could do for him and he said that Robert had asked him to pop round and see how things were: 'He's asked me if he can come round and do some drawings of you.'

I said, 'Do me a favour, fuck off.' I looked out of the door and Robert was standing at a distance, on the corner. I said 'Why didn't he come himself?' and the guy said 'He is a bit worried because you were upset about the painting he's done. He wanted to explain to you.'

I said: 'Fuck off' and shut the door. Soon afterwards the doorbell went and Betty went to the door. It was Robert. He said 'I'd like to do some drawings of your husband and if there is anything he'd like to ask me about the portrait I'd be happy to explain.' (Alex Donoghue, Interview, June 2017)

It was fortunate that Betty got to the door first. Her 'All Are Welcome' temperament outstripped even Robert's and she was an expert in smoothing troubled waters. With Betty present Alex's gentlemanly streak got the better of him:

He came in and I said, 'What was all that about? It wasn't exactly flattering, was it?'

He said, 'I don't do flattering,' and I learned later that he certainly didn't. While I was sat there, he was already casually sketching in his sketchbook and Betty was looking over his shoulder and nodding approvingly. Robert said, 'I'd like to do another one of you,' and I said, 'No way. That painting might one day or another end up in a gallery, and people will say "Who's that bastard?" No way!'

Robert said, 'I don't think galleries will be interested in my work and besides I want to give the painting to you. Then you can make sure whatever happens to it is your choice entirely.' So I agreed to a rematch. And that was the beginning of ... well, I don't know how many hundreds or thousands of hours I sat for him over the years.

Alex Donoghue was no gangster, but his skills as a wrestler, strongman, stuntman, driver, horseman, and actor made him as much of a social amphibian as Robert. As a genuine tough guy geared towards physical theatre, Alex could thrive alongside the highest and lowest elements of culture. His contacts included bouncers, underworld enforcers and bodyguards, movie directors, some of London's finest Shakespearean actors, playwrights, and producers. And for the next 40 years he was Robert's dearest, most consistent, and trusted friend.

Betty was keen to help the poverty-stricken newlyweds. She often brought food across from Fellows Road to Eton Avenue. She and Alex sourced several jobs for Mouse and Robert, and time and time again Robert proved his resilience when threatened with regular employment. Alex was busy with film work and saw a good opportunity to ease his new friend into a creatively meaningful job:

> I was constantly thinking how [Robert] could make money to support himself and Mouse. I suggested he approach the film studio and I said, 'Show them some of your work, they'll love it and you'll be happy as Larry if they take you on. They've got *vast* studios, you could paint murals from morning till night. When you see movies like *Rembrandt* they need artists to replicate the artworks – Charles Laughton didn't do that! And they always need huge backgrounds and titles, like the opening of *The Vikings* – they'll *jump* at you Robert.' And he really liked the idea. We talked about it over a period of weeks, and I offered to go along with him to introduce him to people, but he just didn't do it. I said, 'You'd make a good few pounds and it won't restrict you that much at all, you'll enjoy it – *big* works!' I told him how the studio walls go on forever, and he liked that idea ... but he never went. Mouse sometimes had a go at him, she was quite rightly getting tired of him dodging paid work. So he made the concession of going into Camden Town to apply for a job as a dustman. (Interview, September 2017)

Alex drove Robert to an interview for the humble though regularly paid and socially vital job. All that was required was physical strength and the willingness to work five mornings a week: apparently one requisite too far for Robert. The interview should have been a mere formality but Robert threw it by speaking in an exaggeratedly plummy accent reminiscent of Noel Coward, thus making it excruciatingly clear that if in the unlikely event that he did fit in, he would not stick at it. The interviewing official 'bundled Robert out of that office' and the exasperated Alex drove Robert back to Eton Avenue. Robert was far from disappointed.

In all but an economic sense Robert's work continued apace. 'He was totally uninterested in money' and fortunately, says Mouse, 'so was I.' 'His painting was a discipline, but it came to him so easily: if he had time on his hands he rarely took to a book or anything – it was always a pencil or paintbrush and paper in cafés, in the street, on the loo, anywhere: he was a compulsive visual artist, and when he wasn't painting he was planning a painting.'

Mouse was introduced to Axel, whose drug-fuelled violence was seemingly invisible outside of his long-suffering family. She found him charming, 'a real character, he spoke well at Speakers' Corner, I used to enjoy listening to him [...] he was great fun.' She was also introduced to Robert's mother, who despite not being invited to the wedding, treated Mouse well, though not at first meeting particularly warmly. Alice's usual standards of rudeness had been raised for Ivorine but inexplicably lowered for Mouse. Mouse in her turn raised her already high levels of generosity of spirit. She became genuinely fond of Alice and respected her enormously. Though Robert had seemingly spurned the official refuse collector's trade he took it up as a freelancer and made money at a better rate than if he had worked for Camden Council. Scavenging through the ruins of North London, he generated a haphazard but occasionally lucrative income:

> At the top end of Fellows Road, the Council placed compulsory purchase orders on a long row of houses and were in the process of demolishing them. The stuff that people left, like on a bombsite, was incredible! A wild-west style pianola was just left there, with all the cylinders, and it worked perfectly! Robert was incredibly strong; he somehow hoisted and pushed and took it home and later sold it. We used to scavenge wood to make frames and stretchers for his canvasses. One day he found a large black statue of an Adonis, slightly damaged, but still worth £120, just lying in the rubble. Robert had a radar for that kind of thing, he could have made a fortune finding and buying and selling. That was at least a month's wages in one go, for no work, but I wouldn't have been surprised if he gave it all away in the same day. He headed for The Loft; he bought food for everyone, handed out five-pound notes to anyone who asked. (Alex Donoghue, Interview, June 2017)

However much good luck Robert had foraging, the money left as swiftly as it arrived. His reputation for generosity was becoming something of a handicap and often led to dangerous situations far beyond the inconvenience of Pierre von Grunewald and other desperados interrupting the flow of his work. On one occasion a visitor to Eton Avenue was in the throes of such violent heroin withdrawal he soiled himself then lapsed into fits, then total blackout. Robert thought the man was going to die. Purchasing heroin to supply to others still carries a potential life sentence under English law, and administering a drug without consent is another serious offence: thus the following account was given under promise of anonymity:

We scraped enough cash to go to Paddington where [a friend] knew somebody who could sort out a bag [of heroin]. It was a freezing night, very windy, and rain, rain, rain, and waiting with [the friend] for this dodgy geezer. Well we did it ... but by the time we got back to Eton Avenue, we were shaking like junkies ourselves. We were *wretched*. Street heroin is a moody drug, it varies so much even seasoned addicts can get caught out.

Overdose is likely from a rare unadulterated batch. And conversely, what a family doctor might consider a lethal dose might not even take the edge off the withdrawal symptoms for a long-term user. The drug was mixed on a spoon and filtered through a cigarette-end then injected in small increments until the addict regained a semblance of humanity. This was probably not Robert's first criminal act of charity and it would certainly not be the last.

It must be reiterated that only a fraction of the visitors to Eton Avenue were addicts or lunatics. Writer Colin Wilson was a regular visitor. His book *The Outsider* was almost a field-guide to the sensibilities of Robert's higher-functioning friends. Alfred Reynolds, Alex Donoghue, Heathcote Williams, Axel Ney-Hoch, and Aury Shoa were not only 'theatrical characters' in their vibrant and flamboyant personalities, they were also, via their own experiences of hardship and creativity, acutely aware of the 'theatre of the world'. What united the attitudes of most of the group centred on Robert was not exactly contempt for the 'ordinary life of ordinary people' but an awareness of the dangerous absurdity of passively following the rules of the 'real world'. Some expressed this intellectually, some via artistic struggle, while others had no more resources than gut feeling and a desperate urge to alter 'reality' via drugs. Intellectuals, creative types, addicts, and madmen: each category of person brought their own joys and problems, and Robert and Mouse welcomed them all.

Not everybody who is awake to the theatricality of the world is necessarily a 'theatrical' character. In the painting *Group Portrait, Eton Avenue* (1964) behind the figure of Alex Donoghue we see a young Indian man. This is Tarun Bedi, whose wealth of high and low experience was at that time wrapped in painful shyness. Tarun first met Robert in the spring of 1964. The story of Tarun's presence in England was magical and Robert was always keen to know more about his travels, about Indian art and philosophy, and the Himalayan paradise he grew up in.

He was born in the extreme north of India to an ancient and noble family of warrior-scholars, direct descendants of Guru Nanak. The family had dealt in horses, supplying the British Army and thus substantially increasing their wealth and status. They lived in a mansion high in the mountains close to the Tibetan border, with servants and cultural riches to rival any European prince. Tarun's father was a significant artist and poet. Tarun was from an early age a serious and skilled artist, painting from the heart and body rather than the head: he was fascinated by the Surrealists. His father was abroad, busy about cultural and political work for the Sikh community in London, where he was tragically and swiftly killed by a brain haemorrhage. Tarun's mother was swindled by relatives: possession of the enormous house, its art treasures, and a considerable fortune in money and vast areas of land passed to a villainous side of the family. Tarun, his brother, sisters, and mother were utterly destitute.

Tarun himself was penniless but by no means helpless. By first selling clothes in the street, then working in menial jobs, he managed to hold the family together and still make time for painting and music and art. One of the many great hardships the Bedi family endured in their descent from their Himalayan paradise to the grim city was the constant threat of violence. Sikhs were targets for Hindi and Muslim bigots, and Tarun was often beaten or robbed on his way to school. In the spirit of his warrior forebears he refused to be passive in the face of wrongdoing and founded a street gang called 'The Tempest'.

Tarun travelled to Delhi, alone. He tried to maximise whatever small sums of money he could send back to his family. He tried to cut out paying rent and buying food entirely. He watched what the goats and birds ate and followed their example, trusting the wisdom and kindness of Mother Nature. This made him terribly ill. He was living in the ruins of a Moghul palace alongside beggars and wild animals. By utter chance in the city one day he met an old friend of his father, a man who ran a major gallery in the city. Taking pity on Tarun he told him that the back window of the gallery would always be left open for him, though he would have to make sure he was not seen as he made his way to bed each night by climbing a drainpipe. Thus, Tarun became the sole resident of this vast unofficial hotel, sleeping and waking among one of the finest collections of paintings in India.

One morning as Tarun sat sketching on the gallery steps, he was approached by an English backpacker of the sort who visit India in the hope of cultural and spiritual enrichment. This was Ken Hinkin. He asked

Tarun if he knew anywhere he could sleep and get food. Tarun instantly offered to let Ken stay with him. Three months they camped in the art gallery, with Ken living a strange double life. Though destitute by day Ken was often invited to parties and art evenings by wealthy English ex-patriots. He always took Tarun along:

> He used to dress me up properly, I didn't know how to make a bow for a necktie, I had only one shirt, one pair of pants, I used to take a bath every day and wash my shirt and pants at the same time as my body. (Tarun Bedi, Interview, June 2017)

Soon after Ken Hinkin returned to London, Tarun decided that it was time to seek his fortune in new lands and, when he followed on, it was Ken's pleasure to return the help and hospitality. 'This was the very cold time of 1964. Mouse was pregnant, Alice was not yet born,' Tarun explained.

> Ken lived in Hampstead and when I was there one day he said, 'I would like to present you to my painter friend, Robert.' He took me to Eton Avenue. I liked Robert immediately. I talked to him about Michelangelo and other artists, we had a long talk and when Ken was ready to leave I said, 'Robert can I come and see you again sometime?' I was a very lonely person, I had no friends apart from Ken at the time in London so I always went to Robert to converse. I brought small gifts with whatever money I had left over after I had sent money back to India for my mother. Pierre [von Grunewald] I met a little later. He came to Eton Avenue in the evenings, regularly: then he had a big crisis with his wife, and Robert was worried about the violence. He was a strongly alcoholic person, very wild. He was interesting, I liked him ... but crazy. I met all sorts of crazy people coming and going through Eton Avenue. A lot of them were writers. Robert had only one small bookshelf at Eton Avenue, not many books at all [...] He may have had books elsewhere: I think [Robert] had another place in Swiss Cottage. Anyway, Pierre stayed with me. He did many horrible things. I didn't drink but I took him to a pub once a week, I could not afford any more than that, but he would go and break glasses and sometimes he would raid liquor shops. Many times he would come home with his knuckles open, blood pouring out, with deep wounds. Sometimes the shop owners would put coloured liquid in the bottles to look like whiskey or

rum, precisely to stop people like Pierre – so he took [those] then when he got to my flat and realised it was coloured water he would fly into a rage. And then he used to take ether. He would soak a handkerchief and hold it on his face, sometimes he would go to sleep like that and fall into a coma. (Tarun Bedi, Interview, June 2017)

Robert and Tarun's parallels and affinities are many – noble families forced into decline, horse-dealing fathers, a profound interest in religion without the fanaticism of belief, the ogre of exile and shadow of violence, a cultural richness woven close with material poverty. Most of all they shared the drive to create art under any conditions whatsoever. They became great friends and Tarun spent time with Robert and Mouse almost every day in Eton Avenue. They discussed philosophy and art while the various loafers and madmen and friends drifted in to take turns to sit or beg a little money. Alex Donoghue recalls that many of them slept there in a chaotic rotation scheme on mattresses which Mouse had provided for them. They were given shelter, food, and human kindness when there was none to be had anywhere else. When people on occasion became aggressive and demanding Alex would step in and ask if they needed seeing on their way: 'Some of them I could *smell*, I didn't have to turn around to see who it was. I knew before the wheedling started: "Have you got fifty pence or a pound I could have?"' (Alex Donoghue, Interview, September 2017)

Robert was aware of the consequences of his generosity, which often came via money from Alex's pocket. Alex says that Robert's stock response when questioned about the wisdom of his charity was: 'Once I've given them that pound, it's entirely up to them how they spend it'. Robert knew his generosity was making a lot of the visitors worse and that he was fuelling their addictions: 'If he'd asked me for a quid [for Mouse], I'd have given him a fiver. I actually told him off a bit about that: *she* should be your first priority, those addicts have got no chance' (Alex Donoghue, Interview, September 2017). But Robert was staunchly literal about the 'All Are Welcome' motto. 'All' meant even the intolerable, the disturbed and disturbing, the stinky, the bearers of lice and scabies, and those who brought bad news and police attention with them every time.

Tarun talked of Robert having another studio in the Swiss Cottage area, and some, including Robert himself, suggest there were many studios, lock-ups, and hostels for vagrants throughout North London. This may be true but is slightly misleading. According to Alex and Mouse, almost any enclosed space in which Robert painted was referred to as 'a studio'.

We should understand the term to mean something like a magnetic field centred on Robert's eyes, hand, and brain. Wherever he came to rest for a while became a studio: he was at that time constantly making images: 'It was pure compulsion,' says Mouse. She recalls him sitting on a toilet, door open, frantically sketching the hallway.

It was mentioned earlier that Robert had applied to the Royal Academy. In this he had been successful, but the great institution seems to have had no discernible effect on his painting or life in general. Mouse recalls his attendance was poor, and that he 'somehow just did not jell with the place' (Interview, September 2017). All the people who recall this period – John, Bernard, Aury Shoa, Tarun Bedi, and Alex Donoghue – have little or no information on Robert's time there. Various reasons have been suggested for his departure, none of them any more or less plausible than the others. A selection of anecdotes and speculations include: he thought he had nothing to learn at the place so simply stopped attending; or there was an awkward affair with one senior member of staff; or one of the director's daughters became pregnant thanks to Robert and he was unofficially bounced out. When asked about his departure in later years Robert most often claimed that he could not remember. This may be true. He had a lot of affairs and was bounced out of many places: it would be unfair to expect him to remember all the reasons and details. As Mouse pointed out 'there are only so many hours in a day' and perhaps Robert 'felt that intellectually there was more to be learned from other people' at Eton Avenue and The Loft, and artistically 'there was more to be learned from the National Gallery, where he spent days and weeks making more full-scale copies of the Old Masters' (Mouse Mills, Interview, July 2018).

Eton Avenue was a hothouse for ideas and art but was becoming a circus besides which the Shemtov was a model of reason. The many mattresses were filled with irregular guests, Big Tony vexed the ears of all and sundry with his violent piano playing, and the police often visited to look for persons of interest. Mouse occasionally attempted to restore order: 'Sometimes I would lose my temper and tell them all to get lost, and they melted away only to return again a few days later' (Mouse Mills, Letter, August 2017). While she was away visiting her parents that summer Robert's spelling deteriorated sharply under the stress and he wrote:

Tony's going THANK GOD! He's unbearable on the piano. Ivan the tramp's gone but he's a periodical nuisance. He came running up to me a couple of nights ago saying he only had half an hour to live unless he drank a man's pee, so I said I'd give him some in a bottle. 'No, that's not the way he wanted it!' 'Fuck off' I said. Strange thing is I haven't seen him for 3 days. It's a funny life. Your cousin Jane called – I wasn't here but she knows you're in Cornwall. One bastard smashed open the meter – I was dead worried but the caretaker said he'd fix it up on the quiet. Whoever did it (I think it was Flowerpot) wrote 'Robert it wasn't me'. (Letter to Mouse, Summer 1964)

As frustrating as some guests might have been, it was overall an idyllic time. When there was electricity, Robert played music by Mozart and Paul Robeson on an antique record player and despite almost all space being used for art 'we all sort of melded. People slept on the floor chrysalis-like, and generally there was a good vibe. There were complaints from neighbours but on the whole being self-contained in the basement it was okay' (Mouse Mills, Letter, August 2017). In summer, the newlyweds sat out in the garden listening to the West Indian boys in the flat above singing Spencer Davis songs. Mouse remembers Robert and Alex's regular contests of strength. How many press-ups can you do in one minute? How many one-armed press-ups? A regular entertainment was a competition to see how far they could throw a 14 lb sledgehammer. This would be swung from the shoulder in larger and ever-faster arcs until let fly at as close as possible to a 45-degree angle. The neighbours must have been nervous wrecks.

Mouse's third trimester was happier and healthier than her first, but she thought it wisest that the birth take place far from Eton Avenue. As the due date approached, she planned for another visit to Cornwall. Perhaps less wisely she tried to press Robert in the direction of regular work, with predictable levels of success:

He pretended to work in a garage, I think he lasted one day. Then he used to scurry off with Alex, pretending to work. I have to say I was a bitch at the time, I used to say – let me see your nails – and I knew he hadn't worked. [I think he temporarily worked as] a hospital orderly in Hampstead Hospital. Some of these jobs lasted days, I don't remember a regular job. (Mouse Mills, Interview, September 2017)

Robert continued to bring paintings back to the Shemtov to show Alice. Her approval was in some way sought, if not wholeheartedly courted. She was also a source of emergency rations. Alex tells us, Robert asked if I would drive him over to his Mum's place. I said, 'Yes but let's have no arguments today please Robert.' She had a mountain of Green Shield Stamps, and Robert had asked her for some money, and she gave him a knock-back on that but she had *millions* of these stamps from all the food she was buying for the Shemtov. So Robert took these Green Shield Stamps to a shop on Finchley Road and picked out things which people might want to buy. (Alex Donoghue, Interview, September 2017)

Alex advised him to get practical items like pots and pans and kettles and so forth, durable items which could be sold door to door. This Robert did, but money generated soon evaporated. Betty intervened and cajoled her boss at the supermarket to give the heavily pregnant Mouse a job as a cashier. On her first day Mouse was checking things through and adding things up when a customer slammed a gigantic, whole, and still bloody ox tongue on the conveyor before her. Mouse very nearly fainted. She quit the job the same day.

Alex and Betty were key contributors to the upkeep of Eton Avenue and Tarun Bedi helped in every way he could, especially in the problem case of Pierre von Grunewald. Mouse recovered from her nasty shock and found work at another local supermarket on a wage so meagre she sometimes had to steal to feed the growing tribe at Eton Avenue – she recalls regularly smuggling packets of soup home in her bra.

Robert could have used his knowledge of books and art to make money, but rarely did. In 1964, around the time that he worked as a porter at The Cumberland Hotel, there is a confirmed sighting of Robert selling a book. Alex Donoghue recalls:

Walking back from Camden through Chalk Farm, we passed a second-hand shop. Robert pointed at the window, stopped dead in his tracks and said, 'That book, there!'

I said, 'What is it?' It was open and there was a picture of a horse in black and white.

'That,' said Robert, 'is a Stubbs.'

We went into the shop and chatted to the guy. He got it out of the window and said, 'A fiver.'

Robert turned to me and said, 'How much do you have?'

'Thirty bob' [£1.50] and I whispered, 'Don't look so damned enthusiastic. Haggle.'

For some reason Robert *never* haggled, at least not over books. Robert relieved me of my coins and treated the shopkeeper to his most charming performance, sincerely promising to return within the hour to pay in full, and even pay more on top for the trouble of waiting. With some cajoling the shopkeeper agreed, and I was resigned to never seeing my 30 bob ever again. I walked home to refuel my empty wallet, returned by tube, paid the difference, and sighed: 'Robert, I can't believe you just paid five pounds – my five pounds – for a book.'

'Alex, it's a first edition Stubbs. It's worth a lot of money. Unfortunately, it's the black and white version. Colour, it would be worth thousands.'

'So how much is this worth?'

'Oh, hundreds,' said Robert, casually and confidently.

We went directly to Foyles bookshop in Tottenham Court Road. Robert must have regularly traded books here because the assessor greeted Robert warmly by name as he entered his office via the back staircase. The assessor passes his critical squint over the tome and announced: 'Eighty quid.'

'Thank you,' said Robert and the deal was over. With no haggling.

(Alex Donoghue, Interview, October 2017)

Alex was not surprised but once again exasperated that in Robert's mathematics 'hundreds' meant eighty. When it can be found for sale in the early 21st century, the book changes hands for anything between £30,000 and £50,000 depending on condition. Back in 1964 the difference between £80 and £100 was more than good week's wages, but to Alex's despair Robert could not be bothered to talk money. Worse, he was characteristically oblivious to the norms of responsible generosity, causing a rare moment of friction with Alex, who came close to shouting at him:

Mouse, waiting, hungry ... and Robert wanted to go to The Loft to get risotto for everyone [so I said] 'Give me some money and I'll give it to Mouse, I can't eat with you if she's at home hungry.' [Needless to say] 'the money went quicker than it came.' (Alex Donoghue, Interview, October 2017)

Mouse's due date approached and she retreated to the comfort and nutritional safety of her parents in the West Country. Robert wrote almost every day. In Tavistock maternity hospital on 13 September 1964 Robert's first daughter was born. Mouse recalls it was an easy birth and she and the child were 'rampantly healthy'. Robert was in London at the time of the birth but came to Cornwall as soon as he got the call. The new arrival was named Alice, partly in homage to Robert's mother and partly as a memento of Mouse's mysterious shrinking sensations during the first trimester. The couple-turned-trio returned to London just a few days later. Whether it was quoted by either adult on the train journey or not, Robert and Mouse knew the following passage well enough:

> 'But I don't want to go among mad people,' Alice remarked.
> 'Oh, you can't help that,' said the cat, 'we're all mad here.'
> (Lewis Carroll, *Alice in Wonderland*)

In London, Mouse and baby Alice were welcomed unreservedly by Alice senior at the Shemtov and she insisted they live there for some weeks. Perhaps Alice senior interpreted the naming of the baby and Robert's slightly improved attitude to fatherhood as peace offerings, or at least as a small move in her version of the right direction. But living alongside his mother was never easy for Robert. He, Mouse, and little Alice soon returned to 53 Eton Avenue. From a very early age little Alice loved the piano, which she 'banged on lustily. She was the easiest of babies and accompanied us everywhere, at 2 am to all night cafés, usually The Moon and Sixpence, or laughing in her pram. She was a joy' (Mouse, Letter, March 2017). While Alice senior mellowed somewhat, Robert was not inclined to meet her halfway on matters of art.

Both Johnny and Bernard say they never knew Robert to shout in his many disagreements with his mother. He could be contrary, even deliberately hurtful, but never violent. Alex Donoghue recalls only one incident of shouting in all his years of friendship with the artist. When he accompanied Robert on a return to the Shemtov, Robert had as usual brought fresh work with him to show his mother, who rapidly formulated suggestions for improvement. The discussion snow-balled into an argument, not of the philosophical sort, and Alice stormed out of the room and returned with her beloved father's self-portrait. Holding this idol aloft with one hand and beating time with the index finger of the other she screamed at Robert: 'Vy Kann You Not Paint Like This?' After a moment of silence, Robert replied at similar volume and rhythm: 'Be Cos It Is Crap!' then wisely but less than nobly ran for the exit, leaving Alex to deal with the aftermath (Alex Donoghue, Interview, June 2017).

Alex continued to seek out work for Robert, work which paid and allowed him maximum artistic expression. In autumn 1964 Alex struck up a conversation with the owner of a series of North London pubs and suggested on Robert's behalf that they employ the artist: not sign writing or 'sloshing and toshing' but for artistic and serious murals. Robert liked the idea and started to plan a double-mural interior for a Hampstead pub called The Cruel Sea. He would be paid a tidy three-figure sum on completion. If both artist and client were happy with the results there was an option to repeat the deal in numerous other pubs. Robert began the work with enthusiasm.

In return Robert arranged some work for Alex. It was of course charity work of a less than dignified nature. Robert had become aware of a very old lady who lived some way along Eton Avenue, without family and neglected by social services. She was virtually immobile, and the home-help meant to be supplied by the council had not seen her for many weeks. Robert arranged what may or may not have been a disinterested act of humanitarian assistance. Alex explains:

> Robert said, 'Would you give me a hand with this, Alex?'
> 'To do what?'
> 'To give her a bath. She hasn't had a bath for over a month.'
> 'So ... exactly *what* do you want me to do, Robert?'
> 'Well, could you help me lift her into the bath? We've talked it over. She's quite happy to be helped.'
> 'Well ... if that's all, yes, I'm happy to help with that, but you can't ask me to help after that. I don't want to wash her. I'm out after she's in the water.'
> 'Alex, that's fine, that's all you have to do.'
> When Alex arrived at the house the old woman was waiting in her wheelchair.
>
> We picked her up. Carried her to the bathroom. She was laughing as we picked her up and gently put her in the bath. She was very pleasant, it wasn't at all embarrassing. And I left the rest to Robert. After some time [Robert] called me back into the bathroom and we lifted her back into her wheelchair. She was really pleased about it. I saw her several times after that; she used to invite me in for tea. (Alex Donoghue, Interview, June 2017)

Temporary jobs continued to vex Robert until the end of 1964. Mouse and Alex recall one which was telescoped by Robert's memory into a series of employments. Mouse writes: I worked in a nightclub as a hostess in west Hampstead and made a packet, enough to pay the rent and keep

Alice fed. I read various things about Robert having various teaching jobs in London. I remember one, which lasted a very short time; I read loads of inaccuracies in articles and books. Robert was fanciful and a lot of information was stretched. (Mouse Mills, Letter, October 2017) Any London teaching job certainly did not interrupt his flow of painting and drawing:

> Robert worked at a school behind the Tate; he had a place there he used as a studio. When the job came to an end he was getting rid of absolute treasures, huge copies of classical paintings, dozens of portraits and studies, and two large very fine drawings of horses; he was throwing them out. I said, 'Don't throw them away, I'll have them!' And I framed them and put them up on the walls in Fellows Road with *The Creation* and the Caravaggio [*Crucifixion of St Steven*].
>
> He came to me one day and said, 'There is a couple moved in along the road, lovely people, but they've got problems, anyway, could I have those two drawings of the horses back? I promised to give them to this couple.' Robert had struck up a conversation with this couple, the woman had said how much she loved paintings and drawings of horses, 'and it sprang to mind that you had those two, so I just said I'm sure Alex would let you have them, he's a very kind man.'
>
> So I never saw them again. To be honest, I wasn't very possessive of things, but it seemed strange that he was so generous he'd give anything away ... even my stuff! He had a very loose sense of property and ownership. (Alex Donoghue, Interview, June 2017)

A decade previously he nearly lost the book to Mr Shapiro (head-teacher of the Menorah School), but Robert was still carrying the ideal of Robin Hood around with him. He was being naïvely – some might say dangerously – visible about his affiliations with outlaws at Eton Avenue. The local community and the police who serve the 'respectable' elements thereof were growing uneasy with his behaviour and reputation.

It was around this time that Robert painted a mural for his near neighbour Michael Mills – no relation to Mouse. Mills lived several houses along Eton Avenue. He was on some accounts a charming though shady character, very fond of drugs, and according to some he enjoyed gangland connections, although he may have exaggerated this aspect of his life for reasons of leverage. His basement was easily as large as that of number 53 but considerably less cluttered. Alex explains:

This was a huge basement flat with a wall, a plain white wall about two and a half yards tall and a good seven yards long. Everything that size was a blank canvas for Robert. He did a magnificent painting in blues and oranges, biblical theme, with such a sense of movement! It was very beautiful [Many years later when the house was refitted, the Irish builders were asked to remove the painting, but they refused: they 'revered' it. So they reached a compromise and put a plasterboard wall over it instead. If time and humidity have been kind] it is possible that the painting is still on the wall in Eton Avenue, hidden, four or five doors up from Robert's flat. (Alex Donoghue, Interview, November 2017)

Though 'flash' with money when he had it, Michael Mills was not a good patron: far from it. On one occasion he came to Alex's door asking him to 'look after some things' which he had no room for in his own house. Alex was wise to the danger and sent Mr Mills packing. But some time later Mills asked Robert to 'look after some things' and naïvely he agreed. Unsurprisingly these things turned out to be stolen goods including, it was alleged, a Stradivarius violin. Whispers spread that some wealthy grey-market people were very unhappy and about to commission some goons to recover their property. Robert wanted to give the boxes of goods straight back to Michael Mills, but they had mysteriously disappeared. Whether they had been stolen by one of Robert's criminally inclined visitors or by Mills himself is debatable. Alex is not the only person who suspects that Mills engineered the situation to compel the penniless Robert to pay off the 'legitimate owners' of the 'Stradivarius' in paintings. It is possible that the owners and their goons did not exist, and Robert had been hoodwinked into surrendering paintings due to a few boxes of junk and a good story from Mr Mills.

On the subject of good stories, Robert was at this time privy to some restricted ones. Ken Hinkin, who had introduced Robert to Tarun, was working as a reporter for *The Daily Sketch* and regularly visited Paris to investigate what he took to be an international political scandal. Tarun explains: 'It wasn't allowed to be printed in English newspapers, it concerned paedophilia and necrophilia, it was totally taboo in England at the time' (Interview, June 2017). Alex was close to the Hinkins. Sent home from the maternity hospital one snowy night, Mrs Hinkin spent the last hours of her labour in Alex's house, then his car, and very nearly gave birth with him and Betty as attendants on her own staircase. He too was told that the political scandal involved politicians at the highest level and nec-rophilia. Both Tarun and Aury recall that Robert was energetic in pressing Ken for details. Unlike the 'Ballets Roses' scandal of 1959, the Profumo Affair, or the well-publicised political murders of Mehdi Ben Barka and Stevan Marković in the mid-1960s, the story investigated by Ken never 'broke'.

Perhaps the reason for this is simply that it was rumour and hearsay rather than a successful cover-up. Nevertheless, we must remember that Robert was close friends with at least one member of Her Majesty's intel-ligence services and that his unconcealed interest in sordid sexual politics, plus his seemingly communistic lifestyle, plus his closeness to Axel Ney-Hoch and Bertrand Russell, may have made him 'a person of interest' to the authorities. This is speculative but not fanciful. Cold War paranoia was rampant under the Wilson Government. Russell and the CND were heavily monitored, as was the independent think-tank at Chatham House where Alfred Reynolds and Axel Ney-Hoch both had connections. It is overwhelmingly likely that Axel, a Russian-speaking stateless immigrant who roused the rabble at Speakers' Corner, was 'on the radar'. In such a climate it is plausible that a figure as visible as Robert would come to the attention of London's notorious Special Branch.

As far as can be established, Alex was talking to Robert, who was atop a ladder repainting a sign for the falafel shop on England's Lane. Two plain clothes detectives appeared and announced that they would like to talk, privately. Robert descended, looked at Alex, and nodded silently. The police told Alex to stay where he was and took Robert inside 'for a quiet word'. This word took quite some time: well over an hour, and Alex had to attend to other business. He strongly suspected that Robert had been ar-rested, so as soon as he had the chance visited Eton Avenue to tell Mouse. To his surprise Robert was already there. Alex asked what the detectives had wanted with him. Robert was taciturn:

'Oh, they just wanted a word ... about some bloke.'
'Anyone I know?'
'No, just some bloke.'
I said Robert, 'It's me you're talking to. Don't pull that one'.
'Honestly Alex, it was nothing.'

I think that was the only time he flatly lied to me. What it was really about, I don't know. I never found out [...] that was the only time I personally saw the police bother him. I'm sure there were other occasions, but that was all I saw myself. Obviously, if the police were looking for someone dodgy, they would pay a visit to Eton Avenue but it never happened while I was there. I'm sure they did, because for alchies and junkies, all roads led to Robert. But some of the stories I heard about him being run out of the neighbourhood because he was bringing the area down ... that's rubbish. Those people were there already. Junkies, alchies, drifters, loonies [and other people like that] are all still there today, I'm sure. It's just that Robert associated with them in a very public way, he didn't shun them. Maybe the locals around his particular apartment didn't like to see these people coming and going, but [a lot of the locals] didn't have anything to do with Robert. Maybe they disapproved of him anyway because of his long hair and how he dressed – still wearing the fireman's boots and army-blanket poncho he had made a decade earlier in the Shemtov. (Alex Donoghue, Interview, September 2017)

Robert and Mouse began to discuss leaving London altogether. Increasingly hostile pressure from the police was no doubt a factor. Mouse and Aury both recall Robert seeming uncharacteristically shaken one day and telling them that while he was high up a ladder painting a pub sign, two uniformed police gave him the 'we've got our eye on you' talk. When Robert refused to engage with them one of the officers – perhaps in light-hearted mischief, perhaps not – began to kick the bottom of the ladder. Malicious or not, it was a clear extra-judicial hint from Her Majesty's finest.

Other factors and gentler forces were pressing upon them. Mouse was understandably tiring of London with its precarious housing arrangements and the energetic day-to-day concerns of raising a baby in the 24-hour circus of Robert's studio. Robert himself was feeling cramped by the situation. Police visits became more regular and the flow of inspiring, supportive, magical, demanding, and mad companions was eroding his painting time (Mouse Mills, Letter, May 2018).

There is no single reason why Robert left London but there are many indications that he felt he was losing control. In London he had the safety net of his devoted mother and friends like Alex and Betty, Tarun and Aury, Alfred and Axel, Colin and Heathcote. He had creative and philosophical inspirations from The Bridge Circle, Speakers' Corner, the great public libraries and galleries. But his ambitions to stand in the centre of all this as the creative ringmaster were being hijacked by his ever-growing collection of crime-clowns and drug-monkeys. He was also becoming vexed by questions of his own purposes and values as a painter: discussions with Aury and Tarun about Surrealism, Abstraction, and Representation were weighing heavily upon him. He and Mouse considered their resources and options, made a decision, and acted swiftly. It was time to change the conditions of production.

8.1 Robert, 'Mouse', and baby Alice at Trevawden Cottage near
Lanreath, during a visit by Tarun Bedi in 1965.

8.2 Tarun Bedi with Robert and Alice, Lanreath, 1965.

8.3 'Mouse', Tarun Bedi, Robert, and Alice at Trevawden Cottage, 1965.

8

Lanreath to Plymouth

Mouse Mills's parents had roots in the Cornish farming community, and they arranged a place to stay deep in their homeland. Trevawden Cottage near Lanreath was owned by Michael and Elspeth Millburn; he was a military commander, she an artist. When Robert arrived in early autumn 1965, Trevawden was a no-nonsense two-storey, square building, eight miles from Liskeard: 'One of the remotest spots in Cornwall', according to the BBC reporter Alan Towers (BBC South West, 13 April 1966). It consisted of six rooms: three up, three down, most with broken windows. The sea wind whistled on its way through the derelict out-buildings. The young family settled in and rejoiced at their good fortune despite the Atlantic weather and isolation. Mouse recalls:

> Living in the cottage at Trevawden was for me like childhood, a continuous summer. We could live there rent free if we did the place up. Did we? Did we hell?! We started out with good intentions, scraping the wallpaper off panelled walls and then ... that was it. We were so ridiculously happy and naïve. My culinary skills were nil, but we kept healthy. Alice chugged along in her little red wellies mixing quite happily with the cows around. I made endless jellies with flowers under the surface, and grey mashed potatoes. Rats gnawed away at the vegetables in the kitchen and we lived totally happy beside them. (Undated letter, spring 2017)

The days were peaceful but far from idle. Through the autumn of 1965 and spring 1966 Robert painted, contemplating the problems of representation in art. He was considering the huge wager placed upon 'paintings which look like things', teasing apart the exclusions and overlaps between the concepts of 'artist' and 'painter'. He was also preparing his response to challenges raised by Cubism and Surrealism, as well as the emergence of Pop and Conceptual Art.

In the approach to Christmas 1965, Peter Sylvere's mother visited and talked about when she modelled for Picasso, but it was normal for an entire week to pass during which the family had no news of the outside world.

Robert sometimes painted all day and on into the night while Mouse read out loud from art historian Gombrich or novelist Dostoyevsky.

It is difficult now to imagine a life without clocks, phones, screens, or money but, apart from these, they were also entirely free of London's flow of wonderfully strange and often needy visitors. As a result, Robert had more time and energy to wrestle with some fundamental issues in his artistic practice. These concerns found their material expression in the painting *Mouse With Wool*, which was possibly in planning as early as 1963, but not completed until late 1966 or even early 1967. Between the starting and ending of this pivotal painting there was unfinished business with London, for Robert had begun a large double-mural titled *The Cruel Sea* and was still working on it from Cornwall.

The work was site-specific to a large Victorian pub at the top of Heath Street NW3, named after the book and later film *The Cruel Sea*. The commission was arranged in early 1964 by Alex Donoghue who by now resembled Robert's ever-busy and ever-unpaid agent. Plans to paint a series of works for the chain of pubs and eateries were scuppered by Robert's insistence that he work according to his own timescale. Work on the mural continued through the weeks and months at Trevawden, with Alex frequently visiting to model for him, then driving back to Hampstead to fix completed sections of the painting onto the pub walls.

What did the eminently peaceful Robert bring to this theme of war? In Jewish mythology the unbounded sea symbolises strife and chaos (Genesis 1:9, Psalms 74:13, 104:7–8, Job, 38:8–11). One of the most sacred and mysterious objects of Ancient Israel was the *Yam Mutzak* basin at the Temple in Jerusalem. The term translates as 'the molten sea' or 'bronze sea' and whatever its ritual function, it is likely that the vessel was a symbol for chaos subdued by Law. Kabbalists interpret its features in terms of the *sefirot* or divine emanations through which God continually makes and remakes the cosmos. Robert knew of the *Yam Mutzak* and its symbolism. He was also aware of the book and movie, but the finished mural was no simple recreation of Nicholas Montsarrat's World War II yarn about Royal Navy ships hunting U-boats in the Atlantic.

Alex Donoghue preserved several early studies for the mural depicting the brutal force of mechanised naval warfare and the sea itself. Ships-of-the-line, immense cannons blazing with welters of gold and orange flame, rock madly towards their objectives. Man is trying to eliminate his fellow man while the raging waves, painted with great energy in the coldest of blue-greens and greys, grind away at the impersonal and motiveless destruction of all and sundry. These studies prefigured the background of the mural which in the foreground of the battle depicts a haunted-looking Lord Nelson. He is flanked by groups of figures who variously attempt to assist each other, or at least to bury each other at sea with some dignity amid the chaos. The mural extended to some seventy feet in length and eight in height.

The work gained a measure of public attention before it was completed and installed in Hampstead. A television journalist was sent to discover what this unlikely visitor to Cornwall was about, and thanks to them we have some idea of how the finished mural might have appeared (BBC Television South West, 13 April 1966, interview conducted by Alan Towers). Robert seems wooden and unusually inarticulate in the interview: Mouse recalls that this was due to a large and painful mouth-ulcer. The BBC team hooked up several hundred watts worth of lighting and camera equipment to the cottage's perilous electrical supply. Fortunately, Alex was there. He suggested that the BBC should take responsibility for any fires or shocks and contribute to the electricity bill, which was sure to be hefty. 'Robert didn't think about the economic side of anything. He could have completed the mural before he left London. It was months after he finished it that he picked up the money' (Alex Donoghue, Interview, September 2017).

Cornwall was windy and cold but the winter of 1965–1966 was fortunately a dry one. Trevawden's roof was barely rain-proof. The poster-paint and lining-paper mural could easily have been dissolved by water and it was Robert's only source of cash income. He was reluctant to evolve his business model beyond the primitive barter of paintings for food with the local shopkeeper. Good luck and lots of good will prevailed. Alex and Betty were generous in shipping food and other supplies from London. Aury Shoa had recently acquired an Austin van and likewise made mercy visits. Axel Ney-Hoch was making himself increasingly mentally unwell with drugs *en route* to his total mental breakdown of 1966, so he was out of the loop, but many of Robert's London contacts remained helpful – especially his mother. With the help of Alex and Aury, Robert sent completed paintings to London for storage at the Shemtov. Ma handed over money for food and art materials and more or less helpful advice. Yet Robert's favourite and entirely untrue version of his leaving London in 1965 was as follows. Having been warned by the Police to leave London, his younger self approached the ticket booth at Euston Station and asked about the next departure. He was told a train was leaving in five minutes time, bound for Plymouth. Without hesitation he replied: 'Give me a one-way ticket' and off he bravely strode into his future.

The story echoes Robert's fabulated account of leaving the Shemtov: a personal myth of self-reliance and an individual act of will. Precedents are plentiful. Robert was immersed in tales such as Empedocles striding into a volcano to achieve divinity, Thoreau quitting human society to glorify nature at Walden Pond, Saint Anthony seeking God in the desert, and Pinocchio embarking on his adventures of self-creation. Robert likewise championed the value of living decisively and of acting alone, even though he did not actually do so. His personal mythology erased all mention of the wife and child he undoubtedly loved and made no mention of the extensive help from family and friends because he preferred people to believe that he marched without so much as an easel or brush into the wide-open future.

Such glorious isolation was at least in one sense true. In the wilds of rural Cornwall, the 24-year-old Robert acknowledged few teachers but the dead. He certainly thought that nobody in London was willing or able to teach him anything about painting. In Trevawden he was communing with the spirits of Caravaggio and Rembrandt via his books, via the material activity and energy of his own painting. Alongside such artistic semi-shamanism and ancestor worship we might also weigh an entirely contemporary mode of individualism. Robert had been schooled in 'the value of the individual' by Bertrand Russell, Colin Wilson, and Axel Ney-Hoch. From the writings of Nietzsche and Sartre he had absorbed the modern myth of 'the sovereign creative individual' acting in anguish and splendid amoral isolation. Against his fabulation of his departure from London we should weigh a piece of self-criticism which is remarkable for a young and ambitious artist:

> He knew he was very good as a painter and that wasn't vanity. Everyone else, his teachers, other artists, everyone said it. But he knew he wasn't great; he knew he wasn't up there with the people who mattered to him ... Rembrandt, Michelangelo, Goya' (Tarun Bedi, Interview, June 2017)

These ancestral spirits rose in Lanreath: Mouse tells us that 'the only concession' Robert had made to luxury in the cottage was his library of around a hundred books mainly dedicated to the Old Masters, with a smaller percentage on modern painters and philosophy. Robert was not atavistic. It was not nostalgia which fuelled his admiration for the Old Masters but 'a living relationship with the materiality of paint', as Tarun Bedi would say (Interview, June 2017). Robert respected and admired several of his contemporaries such as Francis Bacon, Frank Auerbach, and Mark Rothko. He was 'fascinated by Surrealism', although this may have had more to do with 'the force of the ideas driving the movement' than a love for any particular artist (Tarun Bedi, Interview, June 2017). Robert's isolation from contemporary problems in art and aesthetics was far from total: the anti-painterly forces of Marcel Duchamp and Conceptualism troubled him.

Tarun came to Lanreath from London in January 1966. Robert and Tarun's friendship was a pure and simple one: they gave and took from each other nothing but ideas and art, they shared whatever small amounts of money and food they possessed. In Robert's numerous sketches and paintings of Tarun he is most often depicted as a family member, quietly reading on the sofa with Mouse, or with baby Alice on his knee. Tarun recalls that Robert was uncharacteristically 'snagged on a series of problems' in painting *Mouse With Wool* which he recalls as having been started in London: 'It was a struggle, an inner struggle' (Tarun Bedi, Interview, June 2017).

Despite Mouse's recollection of Trevawden as idyllic, Tarun experienced the house without the glow of marriage or summer: 'You have no idea what it was like living in that run-down cottage. No doors or windows closed properly [...] at night time I could hardly sleep as strong cold winds would rattle the windows and doors and sneak into my room to make me shiver [...] It was like living under a constant 6 Richter-scale earthquake or in a boat lost in the high seas rocked by huge waves' (Email, 21 January 2018) Fine-tuned in abandoned temples and some of Delhi's harsher streets, Tarun's survival skills played a part in making Trevawden more habitable. There was no heating and no tools, so Tarun and Robert resorted to gathering and smashing firewood with large rocks until a sizeable store was laid up. Shortly after Tarun's departure in spring 1966, Robert and Mouse were befriended by Alan Bryant, who had seen Robert on television and was interested in his work. He invited the young Lenkiewicz family to Sunday lunch in Stoke, Plymouth. This became a weekly event which allowed the family to top-up on much needed nutrition.

The cottage electricity supply became increasingly erratic and at times dangerous. Cooking required wooden implements: metal ones delivered nasty shocks from the mis-wired live hob. The bare lightbulbs regularly blew out. The nearest shop for replacements was several miles away and Robert trudged over the ploughed fields with paintings to barter for essentials. Mouse and Tarun recall that staples such as bread, potatoes, and peas formed the larger part of their diet. Robert's abilities as a cook were not entirely lacking but where they did exist, they were woeful. On one occasion he was left unsupervised in the kitchen after a gigantic pot of bartered and scavenged vegetable stew had been prepared in the hope that it would provide several days of reheatable meals. Robert thought it could be improved by cracking several eggs into the mix. This created a ghastly omelette soup which in the absence of refrigeration would rapidly become a holiday camp for malevolent bacteria. Mouse disposed of the toxic mess before anyone was injured and Robert was happy to comply with suggestions that he should never again attempt cooking.

By February Mouse was again pregnant. Robert was overjoyed at the news, although the early pregnancy was marked by severe morning sickness. Tarun returned to London and as spring progressed the last section of *The Cruel Sea* was finally shipped to Hampstead and the idyllic pace resumed: 'Alice was an easy and happy baby, really lovely. [She] wandered in the fields amongst the cows ... we were idiots, but we got away with it. We were healthy and young, and we had a glowingly healthy child' (Mouse Mills, Letter, September 2017). On sunny days they cycled to the coast together with Alice balanced in a baby seat. The cottage was as ramshackle as the day they moved in but, with summer approaching, they did not care one jot.

Robert's thoughts on the future of his artistic practice were chronic and intense but not solemn. Mouse recalls that they still spent much of their time laughing, and Robert made several cartoons in the style of *The Beano* for Alex, such as the portrait of the artist being chased across a field by an irate bull. Throughout the summer of 1966 Robert worked hard to bring *Mouse With Wool* to completion but could not do so despite several rethinks and many repaints. As far as we can discover no other painting had provided him with such a chokepoint on his practice. There were others he later found frustrating, but none took up so much of his time and effort. *Mouse With Wool* remained incomplete in August when with the help of the Bryant family the Lenkiewiczs moved to Plymouth.

Robert first saw Plymouth's Barbican in the summer of 1966 when it was picturesque but still very much a working port, resembling Korda's dockside scenery from the movie *Rembrandt*. Fishermen dried their nets on the cobbled quays; pedestrians had to negotiate cables stretched between stone bollards and the timberheads of the trawlers which moored directly aside the fish market. In summer months, the working boats could increase by as many as 200 extra vessels from other West Country ports. There are many reasons why Robert was drawn to the area, not least of these the historical links to the Elizabethan era – the Barbican being the point of embarkation for *The Mayflower* in 1620, which he was by then studying extensively. He was particularly fascinated by the tradition of English Alchemy and hence the pivotal Elizabethan Doctor John Dee (1527–1608), spanning the medieval writings of Francis Bacon (1561–1626) and Isaac Newton (1642–1726) in the 17th century.

Robert was less influenced by practical considerations: on leaving the cottage at Trevawden he would have to find money for rent. Plymouth offered him more opportunities for work and barter but at this time he was seldom minded to take them (Mouse Mills, Letter, August 2017). Much as he would have loved to set up studio in the Barbican, it was beyond his means. Thus, his first lodgings in the city were terribly basic and cramped after the wide-open spaces of Trevawden. Arthur Bryant helped to arrange the rent of a small flat in the North Hill area. By small we mean tiny. Number 24 Clifton Street was a mid-terraced house and the Lenkiewiczs did not have claims on all of it, merely the two rooms on the upper floor. These did not include a bathroom or toilet: those facilities were accessed via downstairs rooms belonging to a vexed and vexatious older couple, the Kings. Fortunately, the neighbourhood provided ample opportunities to meet younger and more interesting people than the guardians of the privy (Mouse Mills, Letter, August 2018).

Terry Goldstone lived opposite at 19 Clifton Street, also in poverty. Terry was rich in other ways, being a native Yorkshireman, cultural Jew, politicised atheist, and proud socialist of the practical type. As well as quoting Marxist principles, Terry acted on them, and took the trouble to feed the hungry and house the homeless. Robert and Mouse met him in the street where he was selling Communist newspapers. Mouse recalls that Robert 'revered Schweitzer but said nothing in terms of overt social consciences and political persuasions. Perhaps he was different with men friends like Axel Ney-Hoch and Alfred Reynolds, but I really don't remember one time that we even touched upon politics, strange as that might sound. [...] He preferred actions to words when it came to it. He couldn't stand hypocrites' (Mouse Mills, Letter, September 2017).

This goes some way to explaining his choice of friends and his utter disdain for professional politicians. Terry introduced Robert to other bright and creative characters such as Phil Sheardown, Jim Pascoe, Lynn Brogan, and Monica Quirk [née Shannon]. Lynn met Robert and Mouse in November 1966 and went on to study Sufism with them. Unlike many of the people around Robert and Mouse, Lynn Brogan was not a social outsider. Sober, intelligent, and hard-working, she became homeless with a shocking jolt thanks to the racism of her landlord.

Persons from Terry's house soon spilled over into Robert and Mouse's rooms, where the motto 'All Are Welcome' prevailed even under the most claustrophobic conditions. Here we should spell out how much Robert and Mouse's and Terry's generosity could arouse hostility from the 'decent folks' of 1960s Plymouth. Lynn Brogan explains: When I moved in with Robert and Mouse, I didn't tell any of my family where I was living. [I had a cousin who was a policeman] and he came up the stairs at Clifton Street to try and rescue me from this terrible place. I was forced to have a polite family feed a week later at Eton Park with him and his wife, my uncle and my mother, while they tried to explain that it was not a good idea for me to live there. (Lynn Brogan, Interview, April 2018)

Phil Sheardown recalls how he was invited there from the bus station by Jesus. Phil and 'Jesus' were technically vagrants, but of a practical and canny bent. Phil worked as a sailing instructor in the summer months then went nomadic for the rest of the year, hitch-hiking, sofa-surfing, and finding temporary jobs: 'I wasn't on the street, I was on the road [...] and worked with Jesus and Kit Gribble in the "dark satanic mills" of Marple' (Phil Sheardown, Interview, March 2018). Jesus was also a seasonal worker. He 'had to get somewhere, he wasn't crushed by being on the road'. When Phil returned from working 'up north', the first person he met at Bretonside bus station was Jesus, in his usual sandals, with long hair, and a split lip, and he said:

'Come and meet Robert! Come, he'll give you a cup of tea!' I thought he was going to take me to meet a vicar or something. But he took me for a walk [up to Clifton Street] and there was Robert Lenkiewicz, in his studio, above the maddened middle-aged people downstairs. He was cutting out of paper a *gigantic* stork, with a model baby in it. I said what are you doing that for? He said, 'I'm going to give it to the nurses who brought my child into the world.' [...] By that time of my life I was mad for education. And here was this bloke who was full of observations, stories, and histories of great philosophers. (Phil Sheardown, Interview, March 2018)

Phil and Jesus and their friend Ricky Penner were soon resident in the upper rooms. 'There were always visitors,' says Phil, 'the people downstairs were not happy.' Notice how effortlessly Phil describes a tiny upper room of a terraced house as a 'studio' – a testament to how easily Robert transformed space.

Mouse's pregnancy came to full term and on 28 October 1966 she gave birth to their son Wolfe. In a rare nod to custom Robert took up a tiny celebratory glass of whisky. He attempted several sips but did not finish it (Mouse, Letter, August 2017). Wolfe was a healthy, quiet, and undemanding baby but the Lenkiewiczs were running out of space. Their two rooms served as home, nursery, cooking area, studio, and micro-gallery.

The book collection had grown to several hundred volumes, still fairly evenly divided between art and philosophy (Phil Sheardown, Interview, March 2018). Robert gave occasional philosophy lessons but it is not clear if this generated any income. He was still working on *Mouse With Wool* and had plans for larger canvasses. He had not abandoned his interest in anatomy and on occasion he dissected the unluckier creatures of the woodland and roadside, further infuriating the couple downstairs. Complaints had already been made to the landlord. The final straw was a misdemeanour which led to Robert's first of many appearances in the Plymouth newspapers. The Lenkiewiczs were soon sent on their way again.

9.1 Monica Quirk holding Mouse's daughter Alice, Rectory Road, Plymouth, 1967.

9.2 Monica Quirk with Robert at Rectory Road, Plymouth, 1967.

9.3 Monica with Robert's son Aaron Reuben, who was born in April 1968.

9

Rectory Road, Monica, and the Cowboys

Robert and Mouse did not fret about being 'bounced out' of the rooms in North Hill, just as they had not agonised about leaving the cottage:

> We didn't agonise about anything. We were both absolutely blasé. [But after the peace and quiet of Lanreath ...] it was agony, because everyone came to visit us, and downstairs were the Kings, very old and conservative, and we would go down with bottles of pee and things like that [and eventually] they took us to court because we put a nude painting in the window. [...] we *were* a pain, with our music and stuff. I went down to the Western Morning News and said 'Please, please don't put this in the paper, because my mother is ill ...'. She wasn't, but of course it came out on the front page with a picture of him [The newspaper] gave him no leeway at all. (Mouse, Interview, September 2017)

And so in August 1967 under clouds of moral disapproval and unpaid rent the family was evicted. Jesus and Lynn went to live with Terry Goldstone. With help from friends and relatives the Lenkiewiczs gathered enough rent money to relocate to a larger house west of the city centre, close by the Dockyard. The move was not easy. It involved dozens of back-and-forth visits carrying cases, easels, canvasses, books, and boxes on a three-mile round trip with some challenging hills. But it was well worth the effort.

Number 7 Rectory Road was far superior to the house they had been forced out of. It had more and brighter rooms, three of them bedrooms, a living room to the front, a dining room to the rear, all with high ceilings. It had a working kitchen with safe electrics, plus a useable attic and a bathroom and toilet they could call their own. But not only their own: they immediately resumed their efforts to bring comfort and decency to society's outcasts.

Not far from Rectory Road was an area known as the Brickfields. It was not quite the municipal dumping ground Robert later described it as, but from 1915 onwards the zone had limited success as public playing grounds. There were goalposts and a swampy rugby pitch fringed with scrubland, sometimes used for fly-tipping waste. The official municipal dump was the then 'new' landfill facility to the east of the Barbican called Chelson Meadow, which was the home of the most famous of Robert's 'dosser' companions, Mr Edwin 'Diogenes' MacKenzie.

In 1967 the Brickfields and several nasty public parks were favoured by the homeless, the drug dependent, and the mentally ill. They were less likely to be harassed there by the police than in the 'respectable' parts of the city. Also, they were close to the Salvation Army Hostel in Devonport which was a life-support system for many of them. Mouse recalls the neighbourhood as 'decent, working class, poor. We didn't have any curtains and some local people rushed over to us and said, "Have some curtains!" but then ... lots of complaints about all the tramps coming down to see us' (Mouse, Interview, September 2017). They were legion: Jesus and Ricky dropped in and stayed for days. Sid Smith took up permanent residency in the dining room. Sid was old and mentally ill and wrote reams of sad but truly awful poems. Albert 'The Bishop' Fisher arrived along with the first wave of dossers who would populate Robert's 'Vagrancy' exhibition: Paddy, Corky, Harmonica Jim, Taff, Black Sam, and a rare female vagrant called Winnie who was sober but in constant dialogue with several inner selves (Mouse, Interview, September 2017). Many brought trouble with them: ranting fits in the street, seizures, lice, fleas, and police attention. In a few months Robert had managed to re-create the stresses of Eton Avenue, plus several entirely new levels of nuisance. As Mouse observed, 'Energy – we were young and Robert enjoyed talking and painting people and their stories fascinated him. Food – they fed themselves in London but not in Plymouth' (Mouse, Letter, October 2017). Help was needed and it arrived in the form of Monica.

Monica arrived in Plymouth with her children in 1967, travelling by rail from northern England. In the days leading up to her journey she had contacted Terry Goldstone by writing speculatively to his local pub and Plymouth Arts Centre. Terry met her at the station and unhesitatingly offered her sanctuary in Clifton Street:

> He gave me a little flat in the house and said he had met a very interesting man called Robert Lenkiewicz: 'He doesn't smoke, he doesn't drink, and he's married, but he's an artist!' [...] At the time Robert was just hoping and praying to find a little gallery. He had been in Plymouth for some time since the last half of 1966 or early 1967. Terry told me he [Robert] was doing a lot for vagrancy. What were they doing?

They were making food and taking it over to the guys who were sleeping rough on the Brickfields at the bottom of Rectory Road. (Monica Shannon, Interview, November 2017)

Monica, Mouse, and Robert became emergency hygienists. Mouse recalls her horror when for the first time she saw lice teeming beneath Winnie's headscarf: 'and there was sick, and scabies, flea bites, [we were all] painted with purple dye, and Monica and I were a team – we had to be. And we dealt with it' (Mouse, Interview, October 2018).

The situation worsened when in late 1967 the police began to 'tidy-up' the Devonport and Stoke suburbs. Monica recalls:

When the police moved [the dossers] off the Brickfields Robert wanted to take quite a lot of them in. [...] although the Sally Army had a big place [...] it was one strike and you were out ... three days if you wet the bed, or if you were found to be taking alcohol. Looking at it from the Salvation Army's point of view [...] they weren't professional social workers or nurses. They weren't being paid [...] and a lot of them were older, in their sixties, so they couldn't cope with the ruined beds: it wasn't just ordinary bed-wetting. (Monica, Interview, November 2017)

Mouse had Wolfe and Alice, Monica herself had Jimmy and Emily. It was going to be a crowded house.

It was decided that four was the maximum, and there was one old lady out there, Winnie. She didn't drink, she just talked to herself. [There was] Paddy, and Corky, he was one of the original ones but he's not on any of the paintings that I know of, he died fairly early. [...] Sid was one of the original ones: he was simple minded, and totally devoted to Robert. He was very childlike and could get cross, he only had eyes for Robert. He didn't understand Robert at all ... but he loved him. (Monica, Interview, November 2017)

What was most remarkable about Robert, Mouse, and Monica housing, feeding, and delousing these unfortunates was the fact that they themselves were close to destitution. Lynn Brogan recalls visiting and finding that basic supplies such as milk, tea, sugar, and bread were utterly lacking, though when she offered to buy some Mouse and Monica would always refuse (Lynn, Interview, April 2018). And Mouse remembers in the winter of 1967/68 'Monica putting the sweeping brush on the fire because there was nothing else to burn. We were freezing!' (Mouse, Interview, May 2018). Robert painted daily: dozens of portraits of the dossers in oil on canvas when he could afford it, and many more in watercolour or pencil.

Throughout 1967 Robert and Mouse's marriage absorbed the pressures of art, children, dossers, and poverty, and by early 1968 there was a parting of ways. A relationship between Mouse Mills and Jim Pascoe soon developed:

> Then it was my birthday. I felt very loved, it was very touching, and they put on a party for me with food and balloons and everything. Jim came along and we went on the Brickfields near Rectory Road and we kissed and that was it.
>
> Jim lived with me and more tramps came along, and it was quite hard ... There was a sad young boy called Jesus who was in love with me. He had a cleft palate. He followed us and spied on us, and it broke his heart. He went back to Manchester. And Quiet John who had this weird growth on his nose, he was always around, lots of characters. And The Bishop, that's when he came along, and Corky, and all of them.
>
> I got this gas cooker on credit; it was the only new thing I'd ever had, and I guarded it with my life. Gradually it got blackened, and filth encrusted, but the delightful part was dancing! We used to dance every night, The Beatles, Vivaldi, The Rolling Stones, we used to dance and dance. (Mouse, undated Letter, Summer 2017)

This sweet-natured beggar's banquet was only one facet of life among the dossers. In subsequent years as the crowd grew so did the possibility of violence: 'Brother Blair, he was from Birmingham I think, he was terrifying [but that was later, with the arrival of] some of the younger ones, quite dangerous some of them, very different from the original crowd' (Monica, Interview, November 2017).

Despite the evictions and moves, lack of studio space, the emotional crises, new children, and ever more dossers arriving, Robert continued to produce art vigorously. A small indoor mural was completed at The Purple Onion Boutique in Tavistock. This is possibly where he first met his later lovers the Pecorini sisters, Belle and Janine. We can discover no subject matter or mention of wages for this mural. He was also making portraits of the dossers, the children, friends, and local characters – the list of models is conspicuously clear of paying customers. Somehow Robert found time and space to make large papier-mâché models. With transport laid on by Alex or Aury, collections of paintings were ferried back to London where Robert would minimise his time with Ma and maximize his visits to libraries and galleries.

Monica was pregnant, Robert was still searching for studio and exhibition space. In harmony with his art and his practical help for the dossers, Robert read the works of Danilo Dolci, a northern Italian working mainly in southern Italy. Dolci's book *To Feed the Hungry* (1955, translated 1959) and his numerous campaigns to meet the basic needs of Italy's poorest people created enemies on several fronts. Dolci was accused of Marxism and often actively opposed by the lawful authorities as well as the Mafia. Dolci was a creative troublemaker on the side of the poor, a chronic nuisance to the hypocrites and profit-skimmers of church and government. The affinities are obvious, and Dolci's non-violent interventions inspired Robert to plan a similar campaign of squatting empty premises to house the dossers, who often referred to themselves as 'Cowboys'. At the same time Robert was increasingly worried that his canvases were also homeless and vulnerable. He began to make large plans which would bear fruit several years later in the Vagrancy Project, but he needed large, inexpensive spaces and in the closing years of the 1960s these remained unavailable to him.

'All Are Welcome' was a fiercely contested proposition in British politics in 1968. Enoch Powell made his infamous 'Rivers of Blood' speech opposing immigration. Powell was pushed out of the Shadow Cabinet for his efforts, but populist racism remained a live force. The Irish were not behaving as London thought they ought to, and their civil rights marchers were regularly battered by Her Majesty's Royal Ulster Constabulary, while throughout the United Kingdom people with darker skins or too much pride in their gayness were treated no better. The passing of the Race Relations Act in November 1968 meant an end to hotel signs saying 'No Blacks No Irish' but the sentiment remained. Jews were regularly targeted by the pamphlets and boot-boys of the National Front. Terry Goldstone again provided a safety net when Lynn Brogan was evicted because a landlady discovered her boyfriend was Indian. Though odd, Robert's appearance was not conspicuously Jewish or 'foreign'. On his return trips to increasingly multi-cultural London he experienced no bigotry, and even in the overwhelmingly white, Christian, and nationalistic port of Plymouth he was safe until the 1970s.

On 26 April 1968, Monica went into labour and was taken to Freedom Fields Hospital. At ten to midnight, ten minutes before her birthday, she gave birth to Aaron Reuben Lenkiewicz. In those times it was customary for the father to be far from the event, either pacing and smoking outside the hospital or in his local pub. Robert was at the scene making drawings of the birth. The obstetrician was so impressed he asked if he could have copies made.

Aaron Reuben was almost always known by his second name, a bright and healthy child who settled easily into the organised chaos of Lenkiewicz family life. Robert was delighted with the new baby and increased his work rate to cover the costs of an expanding family.

> When we were at Rectory Road, I used to go door to door with little paintings, some of them in the style of [Jacques-Louis] David, copies of famous paintings, so many of them I can't tell you. He had to do that, and local watercolours [as a concession to making money]. He used to imitate a Cornish accent and call them the 'shippy-whippy' paintings. He tried to take some better stuff around the Barbican, but the gallery owners wanted pictures that the tourists liked, views of the Hoe, the cannons. [...] Also at Rectory Road there was a grocery shop, and if we had no food, so he'd take [a painting down] and come back with a big box of groceries. Some paintings went to the landlords of the places we lived in. (Monica, Interview, January 2018)

Terry Goldstone continued to help in any way he could. He inherited a lump sum with which he bought his previously rented house at 19 Clifton Street. Soon afterwards his home consisted largely of holes. For very obscure reasons he carved hatches into the loft space, interior portholes between rooms, short-cuts from the kitchen up to the bedroom, and so forth, often with rope-ladders connecting the various zones. Several interviewees used the phrase 'like a Swiss cheese'. Mouse and Alice and Wolfe and Jim Pascoe moved here in 1968, before moving to Turnchapel on edge of Plymouth Sound. Robert and Monica stayed a few months longer in Rectory Road but once again Robert was feeling the pressure of disapproving neighbours and the rising tide of unpaid rent. It was only a matter of time before he would be asked to move on again.

That time came in May 1968. Robert was following two long-running news stories with great interest – the arrest of the Kray Twins for their murderous gangsterism in London, and the student uprisings in Paris which increasingly resembled a new French Revolution. Both sagas possessed drama and scope for philosophical reflections on justice, injustice, and force, and they appealed to his interest in outlaws. Robert himself was soon forced into close personal acquaintance with questions of *what is legal?* versus *what is ethical?* His neighbours at Rectory Road had complained and pressured the landlord into moving swiftly on the matter of late rent. Robert was forced out. He swiftly arranged to rent a flat in the North Hill area.

An advance was paid to the new landlord. The property was empty, and Robert had already been given the keys, so he could move beds and other furniture in. This was done on the Friday, but the contract stated that the period of residence began on the Monday. Exhausted from moving and with no beds remaining at the hastily vacated Rectory Road, the family decided to stay the night. Somehow the new landlord found out. He demanded that they move out immediately. Robert and Monica offered to pay the minuscule difference in rent. The landlord was not swayed and promptly called the police, who sided with the landlord. Thus, the family was evicted before their residency started, long after midnight, with three children, one just months old, out into the dark streets and Atlantic weather, all under the eyes of the law. They were told they could collect their belongings at a later date and swiftly moved along. Terry Goldstone's place was once again the safety net.

The moves were frequent and complex. Mouse, Monica, and Lynn lost track of the precise number of Robert's evictions and flits. Fortunately, all involved were young and robust enough to cope: 'I didn't drive, he didn't drive, and we were poverty stricken. We couldn't afford a bike, let alone a car. The only thing we had with wheels was a pram. He walked everywhere, and he carried huge loads, huge canvasses. In moving flats we used to go back and forth like an army ants' (Monica, Interview, November 2017). He lived for a time at Radnor Street, but was back in Clifton Street when, in autumn 1968, Alex Donoghue and his mother paid a visit: 'He wanted us to stay overnight. He showed my mother a room for her to sleep, and there was a dead fox in the corner of the room. He was dissecting it. It stunk to high heaven and so we didn't stay the night' (Alex Donoghue, Email, 9 February 2018).

Robert most likely found these remains like many others via Dr Philip Stokes, an academic, a photographer, and bone collector ('I always carried a large paper sack while on Dartmoor'; Stokes, p. x) He became a close friend and an invaluable documentarian of Robert, his working practices, and his companions. A decade older than Robert, Stokes was aware of this newcomer to the city as 'an artist with an enormous output of paintings, dealing largely with mystical subjects, based upon arcane learning in the areas of alchemy, Jewish lore and magic'.[15]

Robert's interest in rare and unusual books grew stronger as he matured. By 1968 English alchemy, Jewish mysticism, and art remained the main zones of interest, but latter-day occultists were also claiming his attention, most notably Ouspensky, Gurdjieff, the Hermetic Order of the Golden Dawn, and the Crowleyites. The English witchcraft revival movement under Gerald Gardiner and Alex Sanders also interested him. He met Myriam Rivera, a Columbian woman with practical experience of witchcraft and shamanism who became a companion for several decades. He possessed many of the texts which were the DIY manuals for a reconstruction of 'Wicca', such as Robert Graves's *The White Goddess* and Margaret Murry's *The Witch-Cult in Western Europe*. But Robert lacked the money to expand his research collection at the speed he would prefer. Once again we must draw a veil over one of our informants:

> Robert was in Plymouth but occasionally he would come to London and I would have to be his chauffeur, even, at one point, while he was stealing books from libraries. I was literally the getaway driver [...] He used to do a lot of London libraries. He would get to know a library really well, and if he found out that nobody, absolutely nobody paid any attention to some books no matter how interesting and valuable they were [...] it was his way of awarding himself a research grant. Semantics became part of the process ... euphemisms and so on, but there came a point when it was discovered, in Plymouth, and he decided it was a game that would not be profitable for him anymore. His bibliomania was always there. He was not in denial, he often said that if there was a fire he would save his books first. He was inordinately fond of his books. Sometimes with a really old book, he would just open it and sniff it. It was really visceral. He had no doubt that books were an important aspect of his life and ... he developed techniques to include them.

In later life Robert said that the written content of the book was not the primary concern: this was available in any number of new editions. The materiality of the book, the reality of its history, was far more important:

What appealed was that I didn't just have Renaissance literature on the shelf in the form of paperbacks but that I had the actual artefact, the first edition as it would have been hot off the press.[16]

As Plymouth's heavy industry withered in the late 1960s one of the side-effects was a slight rise in Robert's material comfort. The Dockyard stopped shipbuilding in 1968 and workers migrated away: thus housing availability increased. Robert and Monica moved to 1 Keppel Terrace (now Keppel Street), the first in a row of large and handsome regency houses. For a nearly manageable rent they enjoyed the entire lower floor with its high ceilings and large south-facing bay windows, which unfortunately made it costly to heat properly in the winter months. They were not joined by the entire crew of dossers. Robert perhaps realised that the people around him needed some breathing space. He was also starting to create unofficial 'Hotels' for the vagrants. These were usually vacant factory units or storage spaces left by the shrinkage of local industry, nowhere-places with few neighbours to complain to the police. Keppel Terrace was thus a quieter zone than previous houses, although there were still visits from schizophrenic Winnie and her lice, Snowy, or The Bishop. The upper rooms were by autumn of 1968 occupied by Jim Pascoe and Mouse, who was heavily pregnant.

One of Robert's sketches from the late 1960s shows a typical household scene. In the living room, which is also Robert's studio space, Monica sits reading in an armchair, seemingly unaware of the monstrous beast whose hooves seem ready to crush her, held back only by the chain around its neck. The creature was a gigantic papier-mâché unicorn made to advertise some local business. It was so large that when it was dry and painted Robert had trouble removing it from the room in one piece. Monica remembers it as almost ceiling height, so it was possibly eight feet tall. For all his ambitions Robert did not see artisanal work as beneath him, and he made many such works for boutiques, pet shops, pubs, and restaurants, the latter being literally 'bread and butter' income for much of his early career. He also took pride in being able to make items such as a pelican rocking-chair for the infant Reuben. Philip Stokes visited around this time and recalls: 'a big piece of work in progress, destined for The Purple Onion boutique [...] partly a Tarot-based design incorporating a certain amount of 'pop' imagery [...] the farther right-hand side was violently three-dimensional, in the shape of a life-size horse's head [...] Strangest of all, on the floor below the painting lay stretched out a sleeping tramp with a brimming pot of piss at his feet'.[17]

In December of 1968 Mouse gave birth to a daughter, Rebecca Dorothy Lenkiewicz. 'I didn't see much of [my mother and father] during my pregnancy but they understood it was Jim's baby'. Mouse's father wrote to Jim's father expressing 'shock and concern over the whole affair [...] At Becky's birth Monica and Jim and the midwife were there in the early morning at Keppel Terrace – I heard the milkman. Robert was definitely not there' (Mouse, Letter, April 2018). It was a fine home birth with mother and baby in excellent health.

Robert's friendship with Jim Pascoe was a deep though often unstable one, possibly fuelled by the fact that both possessed powerful though incompatible creative energies. They had a great deal of respect for each other, alloyed with a variety of adversarial emotions:

> A man such as Robert attracted both hero-worship and envy. With Jim and Robert the strength lay in them both having complete confidence in their own field [Jim with words, Robert with paint]. They had no rivalry as to who was better [...] just a joy in finding a soulmate. The imbalance came from the huge charisma that Robert had and his attention from women. They were both stunningly clever. I only saw the relationship disintegrating towards the end of Robert's life. I never discussed how sad Jim was with his death [...] but I imagine it was a huge loss. (Mouse, Letter, April 2018)

Robert's interest in communication with the 'outside of the human' and the borderlands of experience expressed itself in many ways. The anti-social and often plain mad world of the dossers was one line of inquiry. Several other lines were in development. At the close of the 1960s he was actively researching links between Kabbalism, the Tarot, and Renaissance magic with its 'planetary daemons'. He was fascinated by card number zero in the Tarot, The Fool. 'There was a time when Robert talked about nothing but The Fool', says Aury Shoa (Interview, June 2018). The Fool is linked by association to the Kabbalistic sign of aleph, the silent letter of the Hebrew alphabet which precedes all other letters. Zero and silence are places from which to begin and Robert's new beginnings in Plymouth were growing towards some exotic lights. The most prominent of these was a brand of Islamic mysticism known as 'Sufism'.

10.1 The Parade in 1970 before Robert's arrival at No. 25, between the
     Nash fruit wholesale business (now The House That Jack Built) and
     the former gin bottling plant that would host the Barbican Mural.

10.2 The Barbican Mural underway in 1972.

10.3 Robert at Trevawden, painting the Mayflower Cinema mural, *c.*1970.

In 1970, Plymouth marked the 350th anniversary of the sailing of the Mayflower colonists to America. This canvas and the *Barbican Mural* were Robert's visual interpretation of history.

A Seeker Among Seekers: Sufist, Prisoner, and Pnoob [18]

On the cusp of 1968 and 1969 Robert visited London for his birthday and New Year celebrations. On such trips he brought work to be stored at the Shemtov and took the opportunity to socialise with Bernard, John, Alex, Betty, and Ria Ney-Hoch. Axel remained in a state of mental collapse, further confirming Robert's low opinion of drugs and alcohol. He kept sporadically in touch with Ivorine by letter and telephone but was not a dutiful visitor to her or Dorian. Ivorine had also 'pretty much screwed up her health with drugs' by that time (Dorian, Interview, November 2017). We cannot determine if it was on this visit to London that the following episode occurred, but it was some time close to the end of the 1960s, as Dorian recalls:

> When I was about seven or eight, a tall bloke turned up at the house where I was living with my mother [and we] were left alone together. We chatted and I remember thinking: 'Why is this bloke talking to me? Why is he not downstairs with the adults?' He seemed a nice enough guy, but I didn't feel that he really knew how to talk to children. We chatted about various things. After he left my mum said, 'Do you know who that man was?' And I said 'It's obvious. That's my real father.' [...] Nobody told me, but it was almost instinctual. I knew [the man] who I had been told was my father wasn't. I knew pretty much as soon as I saw Robert. Children want to believe what they're told [...] but I always assumed there must have been a good reason for my mother's behaviour which wasn't simple narcissism. (Dorian, Interview, November 2017)

Though Mouse and Monica worked hard to keep Robert's children in touch with each other and even visited 'Ma' at the Shemtov, he did not see Dorian again for many years. Robert returned to Plymouth where, by early 1969, a leaderless collective of seekers after the truth was forming. Lynn Brogan had regular work in nursing and was the most financially stable of the circle, thus her flat in North Hill became the base for what we might loosely call a 'mysticism research group'. Unusual religious encounters were certainly one aspect of these informal studies, but they examined all aspects of anomalous human experience and development. Alchemy, spiritualism and seances, UFOs, telepathy, and magic were on the menu for discussion. This topic list might suggest the group was a meeting of loose heads spouting freely about 'cosmic stuff' while passing spliffs around. Far from it: by all accounts, the atmosphere was more like a post-graduate seminar. Self-selecting and self-motivated they worked at their own pace, undertaking close readings of key texts. There were lectures, presentations, reasoned discussions, and evaluation of evidence.

Lynn and most other members of the group were interested in esoteric matters long before meeting Robert. He was not a 'leader' nor did he aspire to become so, although he was one of the more proactive participants and sufficiently well informed to present a series of lectures at Lynn's place at 2 North Road. Throughout late 1968 and 1969 he lectured on Blavatsky, Ouspensky, Gurdjieff, The Golden Dawn, English alchemy, and the wealth of information and suggestions harvested from Frances Yates's books *Giordano Bruno and the Hermetic Tradition* (1964) and *The Art of Memory* (1966). These two books Robert held in the highest esteem. Their bibliographies provided Robert with wish-lists for further book acquisitions.

> Robert was always looking for hidden meanings and secret societies ... it's strange, because you can be so intelligent and interesting on a certain level but also have naiveties, and that was his. The dossers knew that they only had to tell him a story about seeing a ghost and he'd want to know where it was and how it happened ... while silver changed hands. It was a sweet, naive side of him. It didn't totally overwhelm him, but it meant that he had to follow the lead wherever it might go. (Monica, Interview, March 2018)

Robert certainly maintained this child-like wonder in the face of all things anomalous and outlandish. He was genuinely open-minded. Without asserting their reality, he would eagerly discuss ghosts, telepathy, the transmigration of souls, UFOs, or sorcery. He was easily charmed by the possibility of the miraculous, and this aspect of him was charming. Less sweet or naive is an item found in his library after his death, possibly from his school days. It is a notebook of coarse paper with wide lines and a pastel card cover, containing charts of symbols, page after page. These codes, so easily mistaken for the alchemical sigils or symbols of sulphur, mercury, and lead, are Robert's catalogue of badges. The catalogue is extensive and maps out minute distinctions between German and non-German Jews, political prisoners, homosexuals, Jehovah's Witnesses, and anti-social or mixed elements: the entire social-Darwinist ranking system of the death camps is set out with a saddening and obsessive neatness. Language is a form of magical code which works: categories are to be imagined, crystallised, promoted, and made into a real social system to distribute power, slavery, pain, life, and death.

Theories concerning UFOs were rife in the 1960s and 1970s, most of them bordering on lunacy. The group of friends remained rational about possible explanations:

> We talked about versions of alien intervention. If there is some kind of conscious, super-intelligent group in space which wants to come to earth, it's not going to put itself into flying saucers [...] What about the immense time and distance involved? The saucers in the photos all look so small. Where do they keep their supplies? People talked of humanoid occupants but if the occupants were anything like humans they'd be splattered on the walls. How are you going to shield [a physical body] from the immense acceleration? I've been a hobby physicist ever since. (Phil Sheardown, Interview, March 2018)

Though open to the idea of physical aliens in nuts-and-bolts machines Robert was more interested in the possibilities of subtler beings. He made extensive studies of the Elizabethan mystic Doctor John Dee and his shady assistant Edward Kelley. Dee's mathematical abilities were such that he was offered a readership at Oxford University while in his 20s but declined. He travelled Europe and returned with new mathematical techniques and instruments for map-making. He exhausted the writings of the previous generation of Hermeticists: Ficino, Agrippa, and the master of codes, Trithemius. Dee planned the expansion of English sea-power and is credited with being the originator of the term 'The British Empire'. As an alchemist and astrologer, he sailed close to prosecution for treason and sorcery. He was a lover of books and had the largest library in England, trained a generation of navigators, and designed their instruments. As an invaluable political asset, he was appointed special advisor to Queen Elizabeth. He produced the highly esteemed Cabalistic *Monas Hieroglyphica*, and most remarkably of all he spoke with angels in the language known to God and Adam, Enochian. Little wonder that Robert's knowledge-affair with Dee was profound and lifelong.

> On a cold day in April [1582] at his house in Mortlake, Dee was in his study [when] there is some disturbance in the garden, and he goes outside, [...] his story, and we have only his story, is that an Angel descended in a ball of light and gave him an object, which is to this day on exhibit in the British Museum. [...] a piece of black polished obsidian which he called his 'shew stone'. You could look into the shew stone if you had the right talent and it was a magical theatre: there were gods and demons and spirits swirling around. For many years this stone was the guiding force on Dee's life [...] It is one of the most puzzling and undiscussed episodes in the evolution of Western thought. [19]

Dee had no ability as a 'scryer' or medium but employed several people who had. The most capable of these was Edward Kelley. Kelley was a rogue and Dee knew it: his untrustworthiness was as plain as the ears which were missing from both sides of his face in punishment for a fraud conviction.

> But if [Kelley] was a con-artist he must have been a con-artist of immense cleverness, because the Angels delivered very long messages in Latin, backwards, and Kelley would dictate this stuff at rapid speed and Dee would note it down. Then they would put away the shew-stone and laboriously re-write it from back to front, and it would be coherent harangues about what they should be doing, which figures they should support with money, who should be introduced to who, it was very political. [If he was just a fraud] what kind of a polymathic talent was Kelley? [...] Dee kept a diary over the years, one of the most astonishing books in English literature. [20]

The original 1658 edition of Dee's *A True and Faithful Relation of What Passed For Many Years Between Doctor John Dee and Some Spirits* was the only edition published until the late 20th century. As McKenna remarks, there is a huge gap in our history of ideas. Dee was a paragon of intelligence and honesty. The possibility that he was genuinely communicating with an 'outside' of human consciousness – if only with Kelley's unconscious mind – has been crudely swept aside by a dogmatic view of what science should be about (see McKenna's excellent YouTube presentations 'The Alchemical Dream – Rebirth of the Great Work' and 'Magic and the Hermetic Tradition', 38 minutes into the lecture). The adventure of consciousness research was thereby set back by centuries by a growing dogmatism – the allegedly scientific prejudice for reductive materialism.

What fascinated Robert about Dee and other alchemists was the fact that these were the most rational men of their era, giants of logic and learning. Often named as one of the fathers of 'true chemistry', Robert Boyle on three occasions saw what appeared to be alchemical transmutation. He tested the gold and found it exceptionally pure, and petitioned parliament to repeal the law that forbade the process. Scientists of Boyle's calibre are unlikely to have been three times duped by passing conjurors. What had Boyle witnessed? Who or what was speaking to Dee?

Such speculations led Robert into the deep roots of the Hermetic tradition, beyond Judaism and Christendom into the alchemical and mystical traditions of Persia and the Middle East. Much of the wisdom of the classical Greco-Roman and Egyptian world had been systematically eradicated in Europe by the Catholic Church between the 9th and 11th centuries, but texts survived in the Eastern monasteries. The knowledge of the ancient Mediterranean world was preserved and transmitted by the sages of what is now Syria, Iraq, and Iran. Under the banner of Islam this mystical and Hermetic tradition continued in various guises. Initiates were variously known as 'The People of the Pledge', 'The People of the Design', or *muridin*, 'Those Desirous of Knowledge'. Later, in Europe, they were called 'Sufis'. Like alchemy, Sufism proceeds largely under the veils of coded metaphors and allegories. Though steeped in poetry it claims to be a science directed to the activation of humanity's latent psychological and spiritual powers. Its goal is the purification of matter and spirit. Robert first discovered the writer Idries Shah via *The Secret Lore of Magic* (1957) but was by 1970 familiar with almost all of the works Shah penned as a mystical spokesman: *The Sufis* (1964), *Tales of the Dervishes* (1967), *Caravan of Dreams* (1968), and *The Way of the Sufi* (1968). Thanks to Lynn Brogan, Mouse Mills and Monica Shannon we have three interlocking accounts of Robert's earliest involvement with Sufism beyond the written page.

How it came about: there was an advert somewhere for a book group to do with mysticism and Robert contacted the two doctors who were running it. Robert told people who were interested, then the group was set up to talk about Sufism. Again, that took place at my flat in Lipson Terrace, so we had the neighbours intrigued as to why twelve people would be walking up to my flat once a month. I remember them standing outside their flats and watching people come down. I'm surprised they didn't report us to the police. (Lynn Brogan, Interview, March 2018)

And Lynn recalls:

Through those group meetings we eventually came to visit Langton House [Idries Shah's palatial base of operations]. Robert went a few times, but I only went once or twice when [Robert] was there. [This was] possibly 1969, but more likely 1970. [...] there were some wonderful people at Langton house. Robert Graves [...] and Ted Hughes, and Doris Lessing. We used to sit and have a meal and [Idries Shah] would sit and almost give a lecture, and I'd be terrified to say anything. We would all be doing jobs sticking envelopes down or weeding the garden, menial sorts of things. (Lynn, Interview, March 2018)

Monica recalls:

Robert and I went to stay at Langton [House]. We were digging or doing something domestically useful every day. Robert was much more wholly convinced by all that than I was. It got him! [...] Robert was always looking for the hidden meanings, secret societies, witches in Cornwall. It's an odd thing. It didn't ever totally overwhelm him, but there is one lady who went to that group who is still going after all these years. It starts off as a hope of enlightenment ... then somebody has to be the leader, don't they? [And they get] a little following, and then ... well, they never need to pay for domestic help again! Some of them gardening, some making wine. It was a lovely holiday, but we had to work! (Monica, Interview, March 2018)

In summer of 1970, the participants were:

> Doctor Musgrave and his wife, who travelled from Somerset to encourage and direct the group. Doctor Stanley and his wife from Taunton or perhaps Newton Abbot. The local regulars were Robert, Monica, Mouse, Jim Pascoe, Phil Sheardown, Cath Shannon, Jack Shannon, and Peter Quiggley. We would meet in my new flat at Freedom Fields park, or out-of-hours in the waiting room of Doctor Hamlin's surgery in Stoke. (Lynn, Interview, March 2018)

It seems that Terry Goldstone's Marxist materialism kept him out of the Sufic orbit. Towards the middle of 1970, Monica first, then Robert began to feel uneasy about the leadership of the Sufi movement. On first meeting with Shah, Monica was struck by his lack of control in the face of a basic addiction such as smoking. Shah would:

> have one cigarette in the ashtray and another lit in his mouth, and I thought: if I understood anything about mind and behaviour I'd stop myself doing that [...] But it was very interesting so I kept my mouth shut. It was exciting: the [Nasrudin] stories are great, there were some wonderful people, it was full of doctors and teachers and writers. I met Doris Lessing, and even more interesting, Robert Graves. He was a fascinating man. He sat next to me at meals and he talked, he brought me out [of my shyness] a bit.
>
> I wasn't really cynical, but I smelt a rat, a bit like the Emperor's New Clothes. I kept my mouth shut, but in the end I started to say there was something wrong with that kind of guru-ism. Some of the other people were feeling similar things, Robert too, though he never denounced it in any major way. We just stopped going, although we kept in touch with a lot of the people. (Monica, Interview, October 2017)

In later years Robert would recount the precise moment of his break with Sufism. Though it may be a dramatic device, it is a telling one. Robert's version has it that during a stay at Langton House he was mulling over some point raised by the previous night's lecture and was keen to quiz Shah about some nuance or implication. Robert was aware of the near-universal principle of servitude as a form of initiation from Zen monks to Hell's Angels to Masonic Lodges: submission

153

of the ego to the 'higher powers' is the necessary price of becoming a full member of the club. The day's rota of spiritual improvements involved Robert sweeping the long and broad staircases of Langton House. As he was so doing the Great Spiritual Master emerged from an upper room. Robert had all morning been crafting the question he wanted to ask Shah and took the opportunity for a conversation. He began 'I was wondering about what you said concerning ...' and continued only a little before Shah interrupted him with the wisdom: 'Robert ... *the stairs*' and walked away. Whatever talents Robert had for discipleship evaporated at that point, although it might be fair to say that a kind of enlightenment arrived: he was no more likely to be spiritually improved by Idries Shah than Alice von Schlossberg had been by scrubbing floors for Mrs Stiebel.

It is unfortunate that Robert kept no records of his meetings with Shah or perhaps more importantly with Robert Graves. Graves was a close friend of T. E. Lawrence (he 'of Arabia' fame), the Templar-inspired warrior-mystic who was not only a man of action but a theorist of possibilities for human development. In later years Robert quoted Lawrence with high approval: 'All men dream, but not equally. Those who dream by night in the dusty recesses of their minds wake in the day to find that it was vanity: but the dreamers of the day are dangerous men, for they may act their dreams with open eyes, to make it possible'.[21]

An early notebook of juvenile sketches given to Barbican craftsman Trevor Pate contain what appear to be desert warriors at full gallop, probably inspired by Lawrence's legend. Robert was also impressed by Graves's love poetry and could recite some by heart, most notably 'Counting the Beats'. It would be fascinating to know what if anything passed between the painter and the writer on the topic of 'The White Goddess'.

Robert's concern with religious mysticism and the mysteries of the cosmos did not stall his attempts to solve the mystery of how to feed and house the growing ranks of dossers. He was largely successful in diverting them from Keppel Street and into the human storage areas known as 'The Cowboys' Holiday Inns'. Robert's children had some well-deserved respite, though Mouse and Monica also assisted at the 'Inns'.

The Cowboys' Holiday Inns were highly precarious places to lodge. Firstly, Robert was once again engaged in criminal acts of charity.

A good lawyer – which Robert could not afford – might make the distinction between 'unlawful' and 'criminal' a moot point, but the property owners would have respectability and a large bill for damages on their side. Secondly, these 'Inns' were often without electricity or water supplies, making them less than sanitary. Even when flush toilets were available many of the guests were nonconformists: 'You had to be careful where you put your feet' (Monica, Interview, March 2018).

Thirdly, if the squatters were discovered then the lawful owners could call the City Council and the police to evict them. Shadier types would simply use freelance goons. Fourthly and most dangerous of all, the dossers were seldom responsible custodians of themselves. There are good reasons why the cockney rhyming slang for an alcoholic tramp is 'paraffin lamp'. Not all were sozzled on cider or methylated spirit or cleaning agents from which they could alchemically extract their highs: but many were. Some were seriously mentally ill. Most smoked, and wrapped themselves in non-fireproof coats and blankets. On cold nights they made indoor fires, which was not entirely insane as survival tactics go but the potential for tragic mistakes was high. Add to this the awful algebra of addiction and the regular vices of extreme poverty. Characters like Brother Blair admitted they could 'cut anybody's throat for a drink' and this is not a metaphor. In Robert's words:

> I'd break into warehouses, disused premises, put new padlocks on them and get neighbouring shops to put in an extension lead for a single light. There were nine of them. I had good relations with local hospitals, and we got 170 beds, mattresses, and cabinets. I had to block up all the lift shafts because when they were drunk, they would have just blundered into them, and remove all the broken glass from the windows. [22]

Such large-scale charity did not stunt Robert's seemingly less humane ability to see people as material in his ongoing studies, and he often cast a harsh light on his own motivations:

> There was a book at each one of the places if I wanted to record anything. It was marvellous chaos. [The dossers'] greatest strength was that they knew nobody gave a shit and neither did they. If anybody thought

they cared about them they'd take them to the cleaners. Brother Blair was the main one for that. He'd say, 'The ones I really want to get are the do-gooders: I don't believe a fucking word of it!'[23]

Robert never saw himself as a do-gooder, though he surpassed 99 per cent of allegedly concerned and decent citizens in that regard. His rewards were instant, not heavenly. He got studio spaces, admittedly precarious, and plenty of very raw human material. The dossers were readily available as subjects to paint or draw and they provided him with a goldmine – or rather a teeming Petri-dish – of information concerning solitude, mental illness, love, exile, and addiction. They combined childish foolishness with harsh wisdom, and sovereignty with self-destruction. Some resembled living fossils of a mystical tradition Robert was keen to explore. Several of the 'Holiday Inns' served as studios but in 1969 none were suitable as galleries. The numbers of bodies always grew to fit the spaces. Robert, Mouse, and Monica struggled to keep them all fed with no regular income except the women's family allowances. These were desperate times: Robert's bookcases were starving.

At some point during the late 1960s Robert began to familiarise himself slightly too well with the City of Plymouth's Cottonian Collection, started by Robert Townson, a 17th-century merchant with a great love of books. The collection was expanded by subsequent owners until it included tens of thousands of pieces. There were rare watercolours and drawings by English Old Masters, sculpture, and shelf after shelf of beautifully bound volumes. William Cotton the Third donated this treasure trove to the City of Plymouth in 1853 for the 'amusement and instruction' of its people. His Majesty the King's Parliament commuted ownership to Plymouth City Museum and Art Gallery in 1915.

To steal from this collection meant stealing goods associated with high political powers. These books were sanctified by history and public spiritedness: rich men's things which were in any case free for the public to view. Robert had an intelligent plan to minimise the chances of detection, but this was a truly reckless choice of target. To any sentencing judge the crime would look like a rare simultaneous attack on both the highest political powers and the public. Hardly the Great Train Robbery, but Robert of all people should have been aware of the symbolic nature of the theft.

There are various tales of these crimes, and several others concerning Robert's detection and arrest. They are difficult to disentangle. Most likely there were a series of thefts, some of which he was prosecuted for, others not. One example is enough to show the craft of his operations. Our source wishes to remain anonymous:

> [In] Plymouth library Robert had spotted a volume he coveted. [Robert] explained that he had seen this book, and he was preparing to fake a copy of it [...] Robert wanted me to be at the heist just in case security guards came by while he was taking measurements. Next time, we were going in to swap it over. Time went by; he passed it to a book collector in Tavistock. Over a year later [1968-ish], the book collector in Tavistock sold it on. Whoever he sold it to realised it was stolen property, and that was when Robert was arrested [...] It hadn't been reported missing: the dud was there [in Plymouth library] and they hadn't spotted it. But the next customer that came to own it recognised that is was stolen property – because what was it doing out in the world? That is my understanding of [the situation]. (Interview, 2017)

Robert's defence was desperate but not entirely sophistical. The exact details are lost but Monica, Mouse, and Aury recall the gist of the plea. Although technically guilty he was not so much a thief as a freelance social worker, unilaterally adjusting the affairs of the City to fund emergency housing for its most unfortunate sons, the dossers. He acknowledged his idealism had gone too far, was very sorry, would not do it again, posed no threat to the public, quite the contrary, and his actions were guided by a principle of generosity similar to that of William Cotton himself.

Despite this being a non-violent first offence he was given a custodial sentence in the winter of 1970. The judge was not the only one to doubt Robert's plea of misguided philanthropy. Another account – though possibly of other thefts entirely – comes from Monica:

> I can't remember if he was arrested as he was coming out [of the library and museum] with the book or if they came to the house. There was a part of the library ... there were two places. The reason he went to prison was the theft from the Gallery [next door to the library]. There were some beautiful old bookcases, but I was thinking of the others that he took from the other side ... it was in the reference library. The

one which worried me more was a small section of books, a collection in a Jewish woman's name, books entirely on Jewish matters, and he started taking them. What I was worrying about was that the woman who donated the books might think there was some anti-Semite taking her books and throwing them away. It never occurred to Robert to think of that. [Q: Did he sell them?] No no no! He wouldn't do that. He wanted them in his library! (Monica, Interview, March 2018)

Robert gave his own version of the events to a theatre audience in 1996:

I used to go into the City Museum in those days – I can't believe that I did it, now – and I used to steal some of the rare books. Truly, I've got a fine library, far finer than the City Museum one. Don't misunderstand me, none of the contents belong to the Museum. I didn't steal that many, but I stole them because I thought … [here he taps his head] … well, they're sitting there and haven't been looked at since 1904, they're covered in dust, for goodness sake, they didn't even notice for four and a half years. (Robert, speaking at the Theatre Royal, 1996)

It is extremely unlikely that Robert was stealing books in Plymouth since 1965 while he was still based in London though we must remember that he is speaking during a performance and memory bends easily to self-image. In the same monologue he admits that Exeter Prison was an unpleasant place but throws a sunny aspect on the experience which none of his contemporaries recognise:

Anyway, I ended up in prison. Only a fool goes to prison. It was not very nice. Could have been there for a while, but in fact I was only there for a few months. I did portraits of people, in fact I think it was A4 Block [...] one of the attendants, or screws, as they are called, would open it up for an hour while I did drawings for people and I was always paid. My cell never had less than twenty-three packets of sugar on the table, but it wasn't payment that interested me. When I came out a chappie on the Barbican, dear fellow, John Nash, offered me premises. (Robert Lenkiewicz, Theatre Royal, 1996)

Monica says:

> He was only in for six weeks but it was upsetting for him, away from his books and away from his paints, away from his world. [Exeter] is a serious prison with high walls [...] It was a harsh sentence, it shocked him. He was in sort of ... disguise. He didn't look like himself, his hair was short. [Paints were not allowed but she was permitted to bring him a book: Shah's *Tales of the Dervishes*]. He wasn't in stripey clothes, but he was in prison denims and very, very close shaven, no beard. He was suffering, shocked. (Interview, January 2018)

Aury Shoa, Phil Sheardown, and Mouse Mills likewise recall him being profoundly shaken by his jail time. 'He was more serious, less ready to laugh. I think even his paintings got a bit darker for a while. Not just his art. Psychologically, his palette changed' (Phil, Interview, March 2018).

11.1 Robert works on a portrait of Monica Quirk and their son Reuben in the studio at No. 25 The Parade, 1970.

11.2 Robert seated in front of his study of Terry Goldstone, *Gentleman in Pierrot Costume*, 1972.

11.3 Robert and Pat Parker in the studio at No. 25 The Parade, 1972.

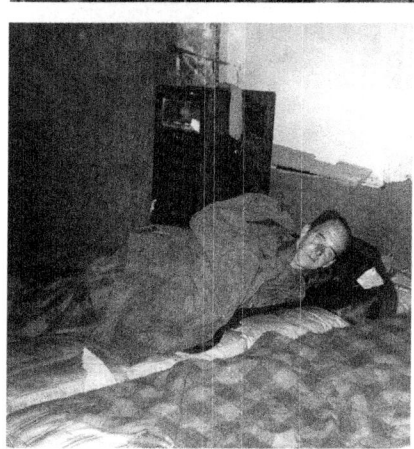

11.4 Robert started working in Jacob's Ladder studio, the venue for the Vagrancy exhibition, in 1970.

11.5 'The Fox' in Jacob's Ladder, one of the Cowboys' Holiday Inns, c.1970. Surplus NHS mattresses and cabinets were provided to vagrants.

11.6 Vagrant 'Black Sam' plays the piano in the studio, c.1970. He was born Samuel Eric Roberts in Plymouth in 1912.

11.7 Edwin Mackenzie, also called Blackie or Steptoe but named Diogenes by Robert, seated in front of his portrait with Harmonica Jim, 1973.

11.8 Albert Fisher, known as The Bishop, with the painting *Bishop with Cider Bottle* (1973) behind.

11

From Prison to The Parade

Robert's admission that 'Only a fool goes to prison' may have cemented his identification with the archetypal Fool of the Tarot card zero. We have noted that 'There was a time when Robert talked about *nothing but* The Fool' (Aury Shoa, Interview, September 2017). This time was the early 1970s when Robert began producing semi-philosophical, semi-autobiographical sketches of 'the Pnoob'. Pnoob's characteristic facial expression was one of wounded innocence, lower lip outthrust, astonished to find himself the target of moral judgement or criticism. These cartoons ran to dozens, perhaps hundreds, of pages of comic-strip wisdom and folly. The stories detailed the hapless Pnoob's encounters with jealous lovers, concerned friends, the authority figures of a wandering Orthodox Jew and a policeman, with many beautiful love interests both coming and going. Some episodes had the flavour of Sufi-teaching stories in which a nugget of fundamental psychology is revealed through 'the wisdom of the idiot'. Most of all they spell out the axiom that love is for fools and all fools are lovers, and that the terrible necessity of love – be it for books, women, or mystical beliefs – is a tragedy we must learn to live with, even though we learn almost nothing from our repeated patterns of foolishness.

Over the next two years Robert produced several exceptional paintings for the Vagrancy exhibition which foregrounded the figure of The Fool. Two of the very best are the *Bishop with Clown Doll* (1972) and *Terry Goldstone in Pierrot Costume* (1973). Robert considered this latter to be one of his finest works. He sold it, then years later repurchased it, and it retained a central place in his large library at St Saviour's Hall in Plymouth until his death. Death as a Jester inhabits dozens of Robert's canvases over the next three decades. Death in a Fool's cap appears in one of the largest paintings of the Vagrancy Project, *The Burial of John Kynance* (1970). A cloth clown-puppet features in several works: *The Bishop, Startled* (1972), the insuperably complex *The Judgement of Paris* (1974), and on through the decade and beyond via the mural in Joe Prete's café (1977), formerly situated on the Barbican's Southside Street.

Robert explored the deep connection between Death and Folly in several of his projects. Death is the greatest practitioner of the motto 'All Are

Welcome' and the Tarot Fool dances on the edge of a precipice, happy to accept Death as much as Life. Here we must introduce the figure of Diogenes, a taciturn vagrant whose journey with Robert extended beyond the phrase 'a lifelong companion'. His certified name was variously Edward or Edwin, McKenzie or MacKenzie. We do not know the date of their first meeting, but it was most likely in 1969 via Diogenes' loose connections with the other dossers. Diogenes did not drink and was not part of the usual dossers' weekly cycle of park squatting and Salvation Army stopovers. Robert explains:

> I called him Diogenes after the philosopher who lived in a barrel, because I found him living in a concrete barrel [...] at the foot of a tree looking down onto Chelson Meadow rubbish tip, a precipitous drop. I remember lifting up some of the coats that he slept on to find the whole thing teeming with maggots, so he was a pretty rough and ready character. He certainly looked like your archetypal medieval scholar, Trithemius von Spanheim, say [the founder of European cryptography], with a grey beard and so on. I became friendly with him and began to visit him up there and do watercolours of him on site. (*Robert Lenkiewicz: In His Own Words*, dir. Jeremy Elman 2011)

This reference to Trithemius provides us with another clue as to what Robert gained from the often unpleasant company of the dossers. They were both ciphers and rare substances: living, mumbling keys to the depths of the human condition. Like clowns whose anarchic behaviour and appearance suggest oblique access to truths beneath the veneer of domesticated humanity, the dossers were the basest sociological zero-point from which knowledge of the human might truly begin. In alchemical terms they were the filthy 'primal matter' which begins the Great Work: 'a mysterious chaotic source material called *materia prima*, containing opposites still incompatible and in the most violent conflict'.[24] Some seemed more promising material than others. Robert held an especially deep respect for Albert 'The Bishop' Fisher, a man isolated by profound psychosis but radiating an aura of mystical contact with realities far beyond the range of ordinary humanity. In moments of lucidity he spoke in aphorisms worthy of a philosopher:

> What you see is nothing, the head manufactures the world. It takes a lunatic to see what is really going on. You are now talking to a lu-

natic, Sir! A lunatic is someone who takes an interest in something no-one else takes an interest in. For the rest, there is no escape. (Albert 'The Bishop' Fisher, 1973) [25]

Characters such as Bishop and Diogenes were outsiders even to the outsiders. They were difficult and strange but only tangentially dangerous, though I found The Bishop terrifying on some unspeakable, metaphysical level. Other elements lodged in the Holiday Inns were potential killers. Robert was released from Her Majesty's Holiday Inn, Exeter in April 1970. We must give due credit to Mouse and Monica who along with Terry Goldstone and Barney (Barnaby Stephen Brown) kept the Holiday Inns functioning for the duration of Robert's incarceration.

The local community might not have been unanimously sympathetic to this flamboyant giant whose art and philanthropy had been highlighted in Plymouth's Courts and newspapers: but those who liked his style liked him very well indeed. Jack Nash's family ran a fruit wholesaling business in a building on the Barbican that later became 'The House That Jack Built', a charming three-floor warren of independent boutiques, jewellers, and record shops, later with its own tiny café. It is uncertain how Jack first met Robert, but he was impressed enough to persuade social landlords The Barbican Association to find Robert a workspace. The Barbican Association was a charity created after World War II to preserve the historic Barbican from obliteration by post-war planners, who often seemed eager to complete the task of demolition begun by the Luftwaffe. The City Council viewed many of the surviving properties, rightly, as little more than slums, but agreed to their preservation provided they were used as commercial properties rather than dwellings. And so a low rent cultural quarter was born. After some wrangling it was agreed that Robert should have a ground-floor room in the building next door to the former gin bottling plant whose 11.2 x 15 metre blank rear wall loomed over The Parade. After years of seeking a space for the public to view his work this straight-out-of-jail gift might have led Robert to think there was no such thing as bad publicity. Money remained a serious problem. Monica fed him, bought paints and brushes, and:

> As far as the canvasses were concerned, he painted on sailcloth, hardboard, anything. He used to go out and get sailcloth from the fishermen. We used to live on my family allowance ... poverty! He was bringing food in by swapping paintings with shop owners, and

Mr Downing bought some paintings. He mostly painted in oils on canvas, and gouache crayon or watercolours on paper. Ma [Alice] still sometimes gave him money for paints and things. He used to write notes about paintings all the time, and he was reading a lot at the time, philosophy [...] he was fascinated with the medieval world. Alchemy and Roger Bacon, he was greatly involved with the whole world view. His greatest love in art was obviously Rembrandt [...] He'd always had big ideas and liked big spaces, but the [Barbican Mural] grew out of all his reading and study at the time, the excitement of the alchemists and the natural science of the time. [He especially loved] the Aristotelian worldview, gathering in all the previous knowledge and organising it, seeing it as a whole, and scrutinising it more deeply. (Monica, Interview, March 2018)

The Barbican in the 1970s was:

... a bohemian world, yes, but still very much a fisherman's world. There were fisherman's cafés, bread shops and chemists. It was a working class world there, but there were also people who were renting studio rooms because rents were cheap enough back then ... drop-outs from Plymouth, right in the very beginning, no wine bars, just working-class pubs which had been there a very long time. There were people who wrote poetry. It had a wholly different atmosphere. But once Robert arrived things really began to take off culturally. Plymouth City Council had never met anything like him before, and they were worried. They didn't understand him ... and there were some things which would have worried some people. He had a very innocent streak in him, Robert really couldn't see the dangers when he was sailing close to the wind. [But] I was quite maternal towards him ... and I didn't want people to turn against him or break his windows or anything. I wasn't being moralistic, just nervous for him. And the journalists were dying to do it. He was the sort of man they would love to get because he was easy to get at. I worried. [Also,] he painted a lot of real nutcases [such as] anti-Semitic people of a nasty kind. (Monica, Interview, March 2018)

25 Parade – usually addressed as 'The Parade' – was at that time a very modest niche: approximately 12 feet of shop front with a central window and two doors, the room extended backwards no more than ten feet. An interior door led to a staircase and toilet. The shop seemed hemmed into

a grey corner of the Barbican called Basket Ope. Directly opposite were three decks of grey concrete council flats and the shop was dwarfed by the huge bare cement wall of the bottling plant. Number 25 might not have looked like a golden opportunity to any but the most imaginative occupant, but the expanse of blank cement was a joyous provocation to Robert. His ambitions and sense of scale soon turned this shop space into possibly the most productive private studio in the British Isles and the cement wall into the largest mural in the land, possibly the largest in Europe. From here on, 25 The Parade deserves a capital letter: the Studio.

There is an ancient and terrible tradition that wherever a new temple is founded a sacrifice must be made, and Robert's 'All Are Welcome' policy was about to draw some of its direst consequences. Robert was working in his Studio window space which in summer 1970 was the only space available at number 25. Throughout the early season he made pencil sketches of curious locals and tourists for a pound a time, sometimes two, but was working mainly on oil portraits of the dossers, or else Barbican residents, friends, and family. He sat brush in hand, surrounded by paints, paintings, easels, with a medium-sized canvas in front of him. Monica was modelling with the infant Reuben perched on her knee. The doorway darkened and there was a flash. The doorway darkened again and a splash of bright clear liquid arced upwards then down, landing partly on Robert, missing the child, but Monica was soaked. It was petrol, and plenty of it. The figure in the doorway held out a box of matches and scratched one into flame.

With no time to think and nowhere to run, Robert sprang from his seat and lifted Monica and Reuben from their chair. As he did so and by sheer luck the canvas and easel canted sideways, providing a moment's shelter from the advancing arsonist. Robert hurled Monica and Reuben through the tiny door leading to the toilet and stairs, slammed it, then turned to face his assailant. The man had fled. This was not the first time Robert had been faced with violence from one of the dossers, but it was the first full-on assassination attempt.

The incendiary was well known to Robert: a schizophrenic alcoholic freighted with fierce anti-Semitic impulses. By sheer chance a police constable was passing. The incendiary was taken to the police station but for reasons nobody can fathom Robert decided not to press charges. His judgement here was very poor. Even if the lunatic did not return to the Studio, Robert was by no means the only Jew in Plymouth. However sympathetic one might be to the problems of mental illness, however convinced of the principles of communitarian anarchism, Robert took a foolish risk in leaving such a hazard free to roam the city. Reuben was too young to remember the incident. Monica was obviously shocked and horrified by coming so close to an agonising death with her babe-in-arms for company. Somehow she held her nerve and goodwill and continued to assist the full range of 'troubled souls' in Robert's orbit.

Robert's interest in the Islamic mystical tradition remained steady despite being dented by the behaviour of its main UK salesman and he continued reading about Sufism even after Shah's rascality was fully exposed. But there were many more strings to the mystical bow. Alongside Sufism, Robert was interested in the emergence of the 'New Witchcraft' of the early 1970s, drawn in by the plethora of symbolic objects and actions. The ceremonial nudity by which the trend was sold to the public was less of a temptation – the painter already had access to plenty of undraped flesh. His interest was in the philosophical and sociological aspects of witchcraft. As Monica noted at the time, Robert was naïve about the dangers posed by the populist reception of such material. Taking a very public interest in 'the occult' exposed Robert and some of his children to more than a few risks.

The rise of the 1970s witchcraft counter-culture is well sketched in Anna Cafolla's article in *Dazed* magazine.[26] Via an examination of Gary Parson's work, Cafolla describes how 'witch-sploitation' soft-porn movies were a political buffer for much more serious explorations of psyche and sexuality:

> *Legend of the Witches* [1970, Border Films, was] one of the most complete, serious investigations into modern day witchcraft on film [...]
> Certainly horror films didn't help at the time, you had a film called *The Blood on Satan's Claw* that mashes together Wicca with what happened with the Manson family – you're getting a warped view of it' explains Parsons [...] Other films of the era like 1972's *Virgin Witch* or *Black Death* [...] and *Mark of the Devil* (1970) offer a debauched, hedonistic lens on the culture. And though this porno perspective on witchcraft is all sorts of awful, the genre is a product of its time, illustrating conservative factions of society's struggle with the spiritualist, sexually liberated rebels.[27]

Cafolla's comments frame the central problem of Robert's researches: he was unwittingly fanning flames for Plymouth's less nuanced thinkers. On one occasion he was shadowed by a group of drunks chanting the accusation 'Satanist!' as he walked on the Barbican. His considerable size and steady nerves prevented a physical assault. Conservative Christians of the political variety were unwilling to threaten physical violence, but many played longer and nastier games of slander against him. Robert would later characterise Plymouth as a city 'limping along between the twin crutches of the Dockyard and Methodism'.

We turn now to one of England's finest pieces of 20th-century public art, Robert's occult-themed Elizabethan Mural, which these godly factions welcomed into the world with a characteristic lack of grace or charity.

12.1 The Barbican Mural in progress in 1972. Robert's portrayal of Dr John Dee is on the left above the running figure of Simon Foreman.

12.2 The finished Dee figure clutches his most famous works. The sign leaning on the mural asks visitors not to touch the wall, 1973.

12

The Elizabethan Mural (1971–1972)

The wall of the McMullin brothers' warehouse was an immense and irresistible temptation to Robert. Philip Stokes recorded a conversation in which Robert talks of the genesis of the project.

> The inclination to work on a very large scale, which is a kind of psychological condition if you like, has always been there [...] it was a question of finding some sort of subject, some theme, which from a popular point of view would either be of some interest, or anyway, acceptable, as far as any committee or council which was going to permit the whole project in the first place was concerned. (Robert, in *A Portrait of Robert Lenkiewicz*, Stokes, p. xi)

Robert was on this occasion canny about local politics. Firstly, he made early consultations with the residents of the flats opposite. Their views – in both senses of that word – were paramount. A single objection might scupper his plan, but as council tenants their overwhelming support would grease the wheels of Town Hall approval. Robert was quick to seize upon a benevolent emotional lever. He went door-to-door with his preliminary drawings which emphatically included a large group of children in the foreground. If they so chose, the residents could have their children model for the mural, and perhaps themselves appear in some cameo role.

Secondly, he made use of his allies amongst the Barbican traders. The Barbican was far from derelict in the early 1970s, though parts of it were distinctly neglected. The fishing industry had been in decline for years. Tourism and leisure were a realistic hope for revitalising the area. A huge public artwork celebrating the Barbican's world-historic past would surely help the local economy, and the artist was prepared to work for free. John Nash, the local residents' group, and the Barbican Association spoke to the city councillors and aldermen in the language of culture, but with a strong accent suggestive of money, jobs, and votes. The bait was in the water but the political classes would not swallow it whole, for the potential for embarrassment was high. They wanted to know exactly what they were approving before they signed the paperwork.

And so began what Aury Shoa described as 'a game of cat-and-mouse with the City Council'. The plans Robert showed to the residents and shopkeepers 'were somewhat different to the plans he was hawking to the Town Hall, all very different from whatever he had in his head at the time' (Aury Shoa, Interview, June 2018). Funding such a large project was no easy feat and Aury suggested that part of the costs might be covered by sponsorship.

Robert turned to John Hall & Sons, a Bristol-based paint company. In exchange for paints and expertise they would get free publicity. Enthused, they sent a surveyor and paint specialist from their Bristol research centre to Plymouth. They saw the plans, climbed ladders, examined the wall, talked to Robert, and shook hands. Mr McMullin was doubly happy: he would get a mural on his building, in preparation for which John Hall paint laboratories would chemically seal and damp-proof his exterior wall too. Monica recalls how Robert spent the autumn and winter of 1970 re-doubling his researches into Elizabethan metaphysics and alchemy, building chaotic stacks of notes and sketches for the mural. Meanwhile, she and Mouse tried to keep the various spokes of the family together despite Robert's unwillingness to be the paternal hub. Mouse recalls:

> I would still see him once a month or so, but there was no interest in his art, no connection. The children took an interest in him, they loved him, but they had to make appointments. It wasn't 'Let's go down and see Dad': it was never 'Dad', it was 'Robert', but to them he was the most incredible father. He never remembered birthday presents. I bought a piano and pretended it was from him; I should never have done things like that but I did, to keep the children from hurt. I felt pity, real pity for Dorian, but he was closer to Monica than to me. (Mouse, Interview, June 2018)

Dorian was invited to Plymouth by Monica in the hope that some kind of relationship with Robert might be encouraged. Dorian recalls that Ivorine told him:

> very little about Robert, and her stories were inconsistent [...] She was not a massive drug addict, but she did a lot of amphetamine. [...] I went into his shop [25 The Parade] and I didn't tell him who I was,

and I sat and paid him a pound to have my drawing done. He did a drawing of me, which actually wasn't that great, [during which we didn't talk]. When it was finished, I got up to leave. He obviously did recognise me, because as I was leaving he said: 'I do know who you are, you know'. (Dorian, November 2017)

Dorian returned to London with no insights or Oedipal wranglings about his mysterious father. Robert was merciless in his unwillingness to fake concern where he felt none. This trait occasionally backed up into comedy. His eldest daughter Alice recalls 'I was actually in a very bad way at the time but I can't remember exactly what it was. It could have been a sprain as I was training a lot at the time [...] it was one thing after another. I phoned him at one point and said I am not well: this keeps happening to me. He replied 'Yes, unfortunately it's part of our genes. You come from a family of cripples'. (Alice, email, June 2020).

Relations between Robert and Monica were loosening throughout late 1970. She became aware that she did not have his undivided attention:

When I decided I would have to go, he came over and wanted to get back together, and he moved into my place on Priory Road. At that time [1970] Priory Road was two separate houses. (Monica, Interview, March 2018)

Lynn Brogan recalls:

Robert was at that time involved with a woman called Liz. I went for a meal with her at Priory Road in 1969, in the house which would later be owned by Robert and named 'Death House'. (Lynn, March 2018)

Robert also became increasingly involved with Pat Parker. Mouse says:

Pat Parker was the most beautiful woman I ever saw. The photographs and even the paintings don't show half of it. It was the way she moved, and talked, and smiled. (Mouse Mills, Interview, April 2018).

The complexities of Robert's emotional and sexual life in the early 1970s are impossible to disentangle, and not only for reasons of historical distance. Cross-referencing the memories of half a dozen interviewees, the only conclusion can be that things were chaotic and Robert frequently duplicitous. Mouse says:

> I got the innocent part, when he was just a boy, with love and enthusiasm. I think I got the best part really; it was from the heart, immediate. There was a lot of game playing with love, but it was real, young love. I don't have any angst, none at all. I just remember it all as joyful. [Robert definitely] played far more games when he was older, he was much more manipulative. (Mouse, Interview, November 2017)

In a whirl of relationships, uncertainties, metaphysical speculation, historical research, coded references, and wild promises to pay the scaffolders at a later date, the great work began. Throughout the autumn of 1971 the physical preparations were in full swing, with scaffolding in place and the surface of the wall being treated with chemical primer. One of the more capable dossers, Barney, was helping Robert with various tasks when he was approached by two strikingly beautiful young women. One of these was Jeny Lelya Bremer, a second-year art student from Holland who had come to England with her friends and hitch-hiked along the south coast. In Holland and London they had lived in communes of artists and theatre performers, and when they saw Robert's Studio:

> [We] sensed kindred spirits. Barney was sanding down wooden furniture outside, and we asked him if he knew of places to stay. This was September or October, a warm day. Barney took an instant like to my friend and said he would find us somewhere and he went inside to talk to Robert. He was painting. (Jeny Bremer, Interview, May 2018)

Jeny could see Robert 'making observations from his window' as Barney returned with an offer of a place to stay and a request from Robert that Jeny modelled for him. Jeny recalls Robert's ability to swiftly create a sense of profound intimacy:

> When I modelled for him that first time, he asked me all sorts of questions about love, about death. He told me Jewish stories, he recited Khalil Gibran. I was a bit shy, but so was he: though already at first meeting I found him very attractive, and him to me too, I think. I felt like I was his wife already. (Jeny, Interview, May 2018)

Their relationship became physically and emotionally intense almost instantly. Robert's previous relationships were obviously highly significant, but Jeny seems to be the first to enter Robert's life as a straightforward accelerant or muse:

> I was sitting for him almost every day when I was with him, more often for sketches and watercolours for the notebooks but lots of oil paintings too. That first portrait was in a round brown chair in the Studio [at 25 The Parade]. Many of the dates I have seen on the paintings [in books] are wrong. I am sure some were a lot earlier, some later. (Jeny, Interview, May 2018)

A joyful and ferocious libidinal economy was emerging. Robert's drive to produce images at speed and in high volume had been present from his youth. But something had changed. It may have been a sense of romantic or sexual mourning – a possibility hinted at in an interview where Robert discusses the beginning of his explorations of 'aesthetic fascism' – an expression coined by him and which refers in part to our innate tendency to be attracted to certain individuals to the ruthless exclusion of all others:

> I was looking at it empirically and the guinea pig I could use constructively was myself, which I proceeded to do. It really began when I was about thirty [1971] with the ending of a particular relationship, when I was carefully analysing my own withdrawal symptoms, which were intense. (Robert, in *Paintings and Projects*, p. 12)

The jolt of his prison sentence may also have played a part. Likewise the milestone of the 30th birthday. Alex Donoghue recalls that Robert 'was convinced he would not live long' (Alex, Interview, September 2017) and as Robert aged, he was increasingly aware of the race between creativity and death. By 1971 Robert's modus operandi was firmly established: a voracious feedback-loop between the intensities of artistic production, philosophical research, and sexual relationships.

The ideas informing the mural are complex. Robert devised a booklet listing dramatis personae, historical snippets, and philosophical notes to accompany the work, but all this was merely the tip of the iceberg. Here is the place to speak of the traditions which preoccupied his artistic practice at the time, and for many decades to come: Pythagoreanism, the Hermetic worldview, and the mysticism of the Kabbalah.

Even the most glancing acquaintance with Robert's murals, paintings, and daily notes reveals treasure troves of magical and mystical references. He continually searched for signs and patterns as if he wanted to discover evidence of God at the scene of some cosmic crime. He found inconclusive hints and partial fingerprints everywhere, but never enough to tip him over into belief. Here is a small sample from the 1970s, very likely written in response to Henry Lincoln's *Mysteries of the Templars* (1972):

April 1656 = Poussin had a secret. Sacred body of knowledge reserved only for the initiate.
'Base metal into pure Gold'. 'La Tour Magdala'.
Sounier Pentacle at Renee le Chateau Mary Magdalena Venus The Pattern that Venus draws every 10 years is the Pentacle.
The Hidden Pattern and Venus – the Magdalena. The link between Matter and Spirit.
The real treasure is not in Gold & Jewels. The real treasure is a Pentacle.
Certain shapes DO certain things. Can a Pentacle really do something?
As Above – So Below.

It is interesting how Robert capitalizes certain letters, as if in reverence. For example, the G in 'pure Gold', which is perhaps to distinguish alchemical Gold from sublunary variants. But also 'Pentacle', and 'Hidden Pattern'. Steeped as he was in philosophy, Robert knew that the pentacle and the pentagram were symbols of the Pythagoreans long before their association with the dark end of the metaphysical spectrum. And from his early interest in astronomy and astrology he was aware of the concept of the cosmic harmony known as 'the music of the spheres'. According to Marcus Tullius Cicero (about 60 BC) it was Scipio Africanus who said that the divine music of the heavenly bodies is produced by:

the onward rush and motion of the spheres themselves: the intervals between them, though unequal, being exactly arranged, in a fixed proportion, by an agreeable blending of high and low tones, various harmonies are produced. Therefore this uppermost sphere of heaven, which bears the stars, as it revolves more rapidly provides a higher, shrill tone, whereas the lowest revolving sphere, that of the moon, gives forth a lower tone. For the earthly sphere, the ninth, remains forever motionless and stationary in its position at the centre of the cosmos. (Cicero, *De Republica*, 6: 18–19)

This cosmology illustrates the first principle of the Hermetic world-view: 'That which is above is like that which is below, and that which is below is like that which is above' (Hermes Trismegistus, in *The Emerald Tablet*). The infinite inversions and recessions of the Pentacle symbolize this perfect transmission of geometric properties across all scales, from the infinitely small to the infinitely large. In the Hermetic tradition, the cosmos itself was 'tuned' by divine forces, and sympathetic energies and harmonious correspondences could help adepts to achieve their designs upon excellence or perfection. The above illustration shows a monochord with the corresponding planetary motions. Robert possessed copies of works by Robert Fludd, including a first edition of the major cosmographical work showing relationships between the microcosm and macrocosm. If his doctrine of resonances, correspondences, and invisible forces seems implausible to the modern mind, think of opera singers cracking glasses at a distance or the famous collapse of the Tacoma Narrows Bridge in a relatively light breeze. In Fludd's time, the actions of magnets and navigation compasses were seen as proof positive of the alignment of the macrocosm and microcosm.

Much of the English alchemy which fascinated Robert and featured in the Elizabethan Mural had its roots in the philosophies of Pythagoras, along with the Neo-Platonic and Alexandrian thinkers. By the late Middle Ages the mathematics of music was widely accepted as the most perfect model for all the arts including architecture: 'We shall therefore borrow all our Rules for the Finishing our Proportions, from the Musicians, who are the greatest Masters of this Sort of Numbers, and from those Things wherein Nature shows herself most excellent and compleat'.[28]

The composition of the Elizabethan Mural is based around three figures. Firstly, the octagon, a symbol of the cosmic harmony of the octave. Secondly, the pentagon, the perfect image of the Golden Ratio. Thirdly, the 'Aleph', the soundless first letter of the Hebrew alphabet, a symbol of the profound but largely silent influence of Jewish mysticism on the cultural climate of Elizabethan England.

The Aleph is the sound that is made before one speaks, a silent clearing of the way for meaning. It is written as a long diagonal stroke (a 'vav') descending from left to right. Hebrew is written right to left, so the line marks an ascent. Either side of the diagonal is a dynamically formed dot called a 'yud'. One strain of Hasidic mysticism suggests that absolutely everything is already contained in the Torah, and before that, secretly encoded in the ancient Hebrew language itself. The Aleph is a symbol expressing the original division of the upper and lower waters in Genesis, the path between exile and redemption, the division of man and God, and the unity-in-opposition of the microcosm and the macrocosm.

In contemplating the blank 3,000 square foot wall Robert noticed that for most parts of the day the shadow from 25 The Parade cut diagonally across the surface. Preliminary sketches place heavy stress on this line, as if acknowledging that the position of the sun and the earth must be taken into account for the mural to work successfully. 'That which is above is like that which is below, and that which is below is like that which is above.' The mural is in this sense a gigantic talisman, with the levitating rabbi at the top right acting as one 'yud' of the Aleph and the fleeing figure of the astrologer Simon Forman, about to fall, forming the lower 'yud'. Robert was open-minded about magic. Can a pentacle *do* something? Can an Aleph *do* something? He did not know, but the evidence suggests that he was developing strategies to find out.

Robert's addiction to the metaphysical and 'occult' ideas informing the mural should not be mistaken for anything 'heavy'. Despite the themes of fanaticism, secrecy, poisoning, and persecution, the overall development and execution of the work was not Saturnine. The overwhelming effect of the mural is a sense of energy, brilliance, and for all its hidden structure, a kind of giddy, chaotic levity. The production of the work was virtually a carnival. Among the first of the historical figures Robert painted was Sir Phillip Sydney, modelled by Philip Stokes, and the gorgeous, murderous Lady Frances Howard, arch-schemer and seductress at the Elizabethan Court. She was:

> [A] client of Simon Forman, whom she paid to supply her with love-potions, in the hope that the King's favourite, Sir Robert Carr would fix his attentions solely upon her. Part of the intrigue involved the elimination of Sir Thomas Overbury, whose part in the whole affair was one that jeopardised Lady Francis Howard's ambitions. Overbury was poisoned by her in the Tower [of London], with the help of Mrs Turner, a friend of Forman. (Robert, *Notes on The Barbican Mural*, 1972)

Equally shady but bloodless intrigues surrounded the portrait of the Lady. Monica and Pat Parker would remain friends for decades to come, but a decisive change had been wrought in Robert's attentions. Monica recalls:

I was the first [sitter for Lady Frances Howard], but we had our quarrel and then our departure from one another at that time, and Pat Parker was on the scene, so I didn't finish sitting for the painting. Anyway, he probably would have preferred to paint Pat Parker then, so it ended up as a hybrid. It's difficult to say who it predominantly looks like because it really is a mixture of us two [...] So much of it was funny in retrospect. (Monica, Interview, October 2018)

Wild-haired men like Terry Goldstone and Barney waltzed the square in Elizabethan costume, and Jack Nash cavorted as a jester. Reuben was a shield-bearer, Alice carried a knight's jousting lance. Brother Johnny, Alex Donoghue, Aury Shoa, and other visitors from London became alchemists and scientists, mixing with a cast of dossers and locals and admiring spectators, although Robert was careful to keep large sections of the mural under wraps to ensure the Council could not see and thus not object to any content before the grand unveiling. Alice recalls:

I particularly loved the mural [...] not just because of the painting but because of the memories I have of the time in which it was painted. Robert was so full of energy at this time and the atmosphere around the scaffolding and studio was equivalent to something like Rodin. It was magnetic. People were everywhere. Robert just knew so many people and many of the people painted in this mural were close friends of Robert and my mother. (Alice Lenkiewicz, blog)

She remembers that 'the street was packed, there were radios playing David Bowie and T-Rex, children dancing. It was magical' (Alice, Interview, March 2017).

[T]here were beautiful women and characters and intellectuals, young and old, academics, everyone combined in this one corner of the Barbican. [...] The whole atmosphere was rather like an Elizabethan play but instead it was the 1970s and something quite eerie about it too. [...] Most men did have long hair anyway; people did walk around barefoot. Women had long hair with flowers in it. It was Elizabethan and the Summer of Love combined, which was incredibly atmospheric and then on top of this you heard the hammering of the scaffolding and shouting and the press and people in and out and the general public becoming very excited as the image before them began to grow and develop. It was a kind of magical and alchemical chaos. (Alice Lenkiewicz, blog)

The Renaissance magic which so fascinated Robert involved 'tuning the invisible strings' of the microcosm and macrocosm. If the planets, and the people around you, your own intentions, and the objects you assemble around yourself are misaligned, then the result will be disharmony. But the magus is an artist working upon reality itself, with knowledge of the turning of the heavenly spheres, and correctly aligned energies: the magus can use hidden sympathies and resonances of objects and words, can 'tune the strings of the soul' and bring about complexity and order from chaos. Even the lowest elements of human life can be lifted towards perfection, and even the highest transfigured to greater heights.

Robert completed the transformation of McMullin's north wall from eyesore to splendour in July 1972.

> The mural was complete and the staging removed. It caused very much of a local celebration, especially among the people who lived most immediately around the site. I ascribe this in part to their appreciation of the huge, bright image and the work which had gone into it. But a major factor must have been in the way that Robert incorporated numbers of local and near-local adults and children as his models. Even I knew some of them by name and many more by sight, and for me, it underlined the still-surviving atmosphere of the Barbican community. To Plymouth as a whole, I sense that the mural gave a sense of haughty pride – and a relief that the painting did not disgorge its figures amongst the womenfolk for a wave of midnight ravishment. (Philip Stokes, *A Portrait of Robert Lenkiewicz*, Introduction, p. x)

There was extensive local news coverage, which was almost entirely positive, though some of it slightly mystified. Perhaps some journalists had not taken the trouble to read Robert's *Notes on The Barbican Mural* which were clear and concise, though broad in scope:

> The theme of the mural concerns itself with metaphysical ideas current in England during the period 1580–1620. These ideas cover the following activities: Philosophy, Alchemy, Cabala, Ceremonial Magic, the symbolic aspects of poetry, music and art, the cult of melancholy,

chivalry, and similar allegorical trends. It is to be understood that as
a survey of this aspect of Elizabethan culture, the mural is limited.
Although the presentation of the theme is subjective, the technique of
painting is academic and traditional. The painting does not pretend to
reflect any aspect of present-day art theory [...] It is intended that the
Barbican mural should convey some feeling of the demoniac brilliance
of the Elizabethan age, a time of tremendous skills, flights of imagina-
tions, and great brutalities, a time – very much like our own. (Lenkiewicz, *Notes on The Barbican Mural*, June 1972)

As Mouse and Monica recounted, the Barbican already had its share of artists, poets, and musicians because space was cheap. But the mural became
a beacon for more of the same. Its completion was something of a turning
point in the development of the Barbican from a fishing dock and tourist
attraction to a major cultural enclave. In less than a year a penniless companion of vagrants, surrounded by his coven of beautiful women and wild
men, did more to inspire and raise the spirits of the community than the
political and religious nabobs had managed in decades. Thus and therefore
the middle ground was washed away, and local opinion polarised. Robert's
name was a matter for admiration – or resentment. With a predictable
'moral squint' the 'Reverend L. of St Judes, Plymouth' pronounced:

> 'I was rather appalled when I saw it. It seems to be negative, macabre,
> and horrific, not the sort of thing one really wants the public to feast
> its eyes on. The Barbican is a big tourist area and lots of children visit
> it. I think they might find this kind of thing rather repulsive. There is
> no Christian message of Death in it. There is nothing of heaven, light,
> and purity. It is all destruction and hellish'. [29]

More mysterious than anything in the mural is why the Reverend L. expected an atheist Jew of German-Polish ancestry to promote the theology
of the Anglican Church. Robert was not painting for the clergy but for
the general public, and doing so without condescension. He knew droves
of 'men and women in the street' who, like Mouse, Jim, Terry, Monica,
Lynn, Alex, and Aury, gladly engaged in conversations about mysticism,
symbolism, art, and alchemy. Momentous, even 'heavenly' ideas are signalled in the work if one wishes to explore them, and if not, it is possible
to appreciate it at the level of sheer visual beauty. Permitting viewers to
participate at the level they most desire is a sign of greatness in art, and an

antidote to what Robert called 'aesthetic fascism'. Priests tell people how to interpret myth, scripture, and history. Artists deepen the mysteries and multiply the possibilities, reminding us that there is more than one way to decode the world. The great Elizabethan plays can be taken as simple revenge dramas or as contributions to existential philosophy, and many other things besides. Good art works on many levels, bad art insists upon staying on one level: 'Buy our product! Believe in god! Vote Communist! Vote Nationalist!'.

Robert frequently described his work as 'a provocation to thought'. But some people prefer belief to thought and may genuinely have found the mural 'horrific' and 'repulsive'. Most residents, shopkeepers, tourists, artists, children, and philosophers did not. The consensus was that it added both glamour and depth to the area. Before the paint of the mural was dry Robert was busy with more projects – soon to become 'Projects' – exploring the combination of seeming opposites: surface and depth, sensual intelligence, and intelligent sensuality.

13.1 The Vagrancy Project in Jacob's Ladder studio in 1973. *The Burial of John Kynance* (1970) hangs on the far wall.

13.2 Amongst the vagrancy canvasses Robert and Jeny Bremer are portrayed as Columbine and Pierrot, the Fool, *(right)*, characters from the *Commedia dell'arte.*

13.3 Smaller studies of the vagrants hang in Jacob's Ladder studio.

13.4 The large canvas of *The Apotheosis of Albert Fisher* (1973). Diogenes appears as Harlequin in traditional chequered garb, Belle Pecorini and Terry Goldstone to his right.

13.5 The small canvas on an easel to the left is *Mr Albert Ernest Fisher Shitting Himself Outside a St Andrew's Cross Building*. To its right is *Mr. Edwin Mackenzie Flying Past the Salvation Army Hostel in King Street Plymouth at 12 Noon*.

13.6 A visitor to the exhibition views *Mr. Fisher With Clown Doll*.

13.7 *Opposite:* Opening night of the Vagrancy exhibition, August 1973.

13.8 Alice Lenkiewicz, Johnny Lenkiewicz and Belle Pecorini.

13.9 Diogenes and other guests at the opening of the Vagrancy exhibition.

13.10 *This page:* Belle Pecorini invigilates in Jacob's Ladder studio during the Vagrancy exhibition. The self-portrait *Mr. R. Lenkiewicz* can be seen centre.

13.11 & 13.12 The Bishop makes his way to the Vagrancy exhibition.

13.13 Robert and Pat Parker in Jacob's Ladder in 1973.
13.14 Robert and Belle Pecorini in Jacob's Ladder in 1973.

13

The Vagrancy Project

During the years-long struggle painting *Mouse With Wool* Robert was pre-occupied with Nietzsche's questioning of the *value* of art. Not the economic price determined by the tastes and wallets of buyers, but the complex questions of why the artist should create anything at all, what the personal and social consequences might be, and what purposes or goals are thereby served. He was fond of the amoral aesthetics of Oscar Wilde but unconvinced by the maxim that art is and should be gratuitously beautiful and useless. He was even more sceptical of the 'improvers of mankind' who judged art by its moralising effects. Robert's notes from the late 1960s and 1970s contain no fully worked out rationale for his fixation upon the project form which gave shape to a lifetime of creativity. But as Mouse, Aury, and Alex have already testified, the concept was in place at an early stage of his development.

The ur-document of the Vagrancy Project are Robert's archived notes from 1967–1969. This bundle contains around one hundred sheets of sketches, letters, biographies of the vagrants, plus their writings and poems. These latter are mainly the limerick-like doggerel of the elderly Sid which despite – or perhaps because of – their comedic incompetence convey a moving sense of isolation. The documentation and presentation of the widest range of materials came to underpin all of Robert's artistic practice. By 1974 he sounded certain that the 'project form' was his optimum mode of expression. In his preface to the Death and the Maiden Project he wrote: 'It is hoped that those with a more specialised interest in the implications of this and further collection[s] in the series will read the notes *which will always accompany the exhibitions*' (my emphasis).

Taking the notion of conceptual art entirely seriously but convinced that the demise of 'merely' visual art was an ill-founded rumour, Robert determined to combine ideas, painted images, personal statements, scholarly and literary books from his library, and human lives into artworks of a scale hitherto unimagined. We cannot know whether memories of his semi-mythical maternal grandfather and early exposure to Wagner's idea of the Bayreuth experience as a 'total artwork' played some part. But even his Elizabethan Mural – at the time one of the largest outdoor murals in the world, certainly in England – was not large enough for his sense of scale. The project form provided Robert with three new frontiers for expansion: firstly, it was a solution to the separation of idea and image engineered by Duchamp and subsequent artists and theorists. Secondly, the form gave him a green light to indulge his bibliomania. Thirdly, the limitations of space and location were to a large extent overcome. A project could function like a gigantic mosaic-mural or a hologram containing many thousands of square feet of visual material, as well as written words and living witnesses to the phenomenon under investigation.

> I might do five hundred paintings on a theme [and] to me, the whole project, the whole collection, is the one painting [...] the atmosphere you get from the whole collection, *that* is the picture. (From 'Robert Lenkiewicz: In his Own Words', at 3 min 30 sec)
>
> I liked the idea that I could put together a body of work on a theme. But at the same time I could only do that innocently and energetically if I didn't worry about 'art'. I decided not to worry whether I was going to be a 'good' or 'bad' painter or a 'modern painter' or a 'man of my times'. I had to consciously shut these things out, and in the process I rather shut out my connections with other painters. I thought that the *humanitas* involved in putting this project together was of more importance and more depth than any art theory. (Robert, in *Paintings and Projects*, p. 11)

Some of Robert's sitters and witnesses for the Vagrancy Project require special attention. Without his intervention Albert 'The Bishop' Fisher and Edwin 'Diogenes' MacKenzie would have left little impress on the world besides mouldering police and medical records. In a sense Robert curated these characters, but even with his drive to experiment on people he could in no way control them. They were nobody's creatures: not society's, not Robert's, not even their own. But Robert provided settings in which their profound oddness could be exhibited to the public via arts which included but were not limited to painting. Inspired by the work of Danilo Dolci with the Italian peasantry, Robert made the invisible visible and created spaces in which the silenced could speak. His initial notes for The Bishop read:

> Forty-one years old? Born in South Africa? Father a rector, may support him financially (partially). Seen on the 24 of February 1969 [...] in

lively and healthy state. Still living at the Salvation Army, and fairly tolerant of his circumstances. Seen under the 'Gas' building on the 14 March 1969. He seemed well, discussed his relationship with Norman Shirley [a vagrant]. He felt like Norman that there was little to do, that he was too well known, that Plymouth was too small for him. That many more years of similar circumstances could create all kinds of difficulties, that Norman was certainly making a rod for his own back, if he intended to remain in Plymouth for the rest of his life, as his unpopularity both with the public and the authorities would put him in Moorhaven [a psychiatric hospital] on several more occasions yet, and that eventually, being emotionally unable to leave Plymouth, he would become a deranged tramp. (Lenkiewicz Foundation Archive, Vagrancy, Item 21b)

Despite The Bishop's considerable insight into Norman's condition nobody could mistake him for a voice of reason. He was eloquent and educated, he possessed a truly great voice and a wicked sense of humour. But at times he exuded a kind of metaphysical menace similar to Anthony Hopkins's Hannibal Lecter. As Reuben Lenkiewicz observed: 'You couldn't talk to The Bishop. He would kill you.' (Reuben, Interview, June 2018). This may be an exaggeration of The Bishop's capacity for violence but I can confirm from personal experience that Reuben's feelings were spot on. Mere proximity to The Bishop induced a creeping panic which was amplified by the sense that there was no identifiable reason for the fear. But it felt like sitting next to a badly wired-up landmine. Thirty years after The Bishop's death I mentioned his name to Eliza Gunning [Massey]. Her flowing conversation almost ground to halt:

Ah ... The Bishop. *Him* I was scared of ... him. Quite scared. The unpredictability. Whereas Diogenes, and Snowy, he was a complete poppet. If he hadn't been so stinky you could've given him a cuddle. But The Bishop ... The Bishop was ... *something else*. (Eliza, Interview, September 2019)

The Bishop talked to animals, street furniture, celestial bodies, and a world of spirits like a sozzled version of William Blake. Robert's document continues:

As for Albert himself: 'As long as I have my "sustenance" all's well, we must indulge mustn't we, oh yes we must indulge. What else is there? You indulge in your way and I'll indulge in my way and if we don't bump into anybody on a dark night, then we're all right, aren't we? Yes, oh yes. Yes, yes, we're alright.' He is still staying at the Salvation Army and looking forward to summer 'When I can lay down on that grass, with my good friend (pats his bag of "vintage" [cider], and talk to that Sun there, oh yes, that Jolly Old Sun, and what a stranger he's been.' (Lenkiewicz Foundation Archive, Vagrancy, Item 022)

As Robert noted in the cases of many of the vagrants, such 'indulgences' were attempts to self-medicate through some trauma or chronic mental illness. It is likely that The Bishop was some way along the psychotic/schizoid spectrum. In Robert's words:

He was an extraordinary man with large hands and a great red beard. He would sleep beneath a tree in Stoke Damerel graveyard and believed himself to have mystical experiences. He came rushing in one day and said that the sun had been shining through the tree, and every single leaf had turned into a man with a top hat, that each man with a top hat had a pint of beer in his hand and that each and every one of them had wished him 'Good morning!'. In the posh Oxford accent he had cultivated he said – 'I had a *vision* there. Not a dream, not a nightmare, but a *vision* there.' (Robert, in *Paintings and Projects*, 2006)

This articulate delirium explains Robert's fondness for the man and the extraordinarily high quality of his portraits of him. Robert was intellectually and aesthetically aroused by visionaries like the prophet Ezekiel, the schizophrenic Judge Daniel Paul Schreber, and Saint Antony the Great. These 'over-human' types, to borrow the Nietzschean term, not only survived their profound isolation and extraordinary perceptions, they also *grew creative* under these unlikely conditions. Their lives partly mirrored those of the modern outsiders near and dear to Robert, the Fools and pariahs which morally judgemental types class as 'sub-human'.

The Bishop, Startled (1972) suggests a man levitating through a diaphanous background into the stratosphere of a cosmic realisation. Awestruck, The Bishop grips his chair and raises his eyes to the far distance. His pose invokes an explosive energy: he might burst out of his layers of crumpled clothes like a mad butterfly. The stylised apple in the lower centre of the painting suggests the myth of the exile from Eden, the *felix culpa* which enabled the greater perfection of humanity's redemption. If The Bishop stands, the Fool on his lap will fall. *Mr Fisher with Bottle of Strongbow* (1973) presents him almost as a brother to Van Gogh, pensive eyes searching the heavens. In both paintings Robert includes zones of primary colour which sing out with the clarity and resonance of church bells.

In other portraits of The Bishop the mood is decisively sinister: *Mr Fisher in Pierrot Costume with Clown Doll* (1973) resembles a man facing a firing squad. Even the doll seems horrified by whatever it is looking at. Their shadow is granted an uncanny solidity by the lower blues echoing the doll's limb. A dark downward slash adds to the suggestion that the shadow is holding a knife. Robert's handling of the white-into-white areas shows how far he has technically advanced as a painter since he set himself a similar problem in his *Portrait of Ivorine* (1959–60). A later work *The Bishop Asleep on Red Chair* (1974) likewise conveys a sense of death being close, but in this case death is seeping out from inside The Bishop, his hand supporting a head which might be flayed back to the skull.

The theme of death emerging from within is present in many of the paintings of the dossers. In *The Burial of John Kynance* (1970) there is a double vision of Diogenes, as if his spirit and body do not coincide. The doubling is repeated more forcefully years later when Robert painted *The Putrefaction of Diogenes* (1974), a visceral horror show representing the sitter first as a live person, then as a split sack of surreal organelles with an obscenely bloated tongue and hands like rotting marine polyps. The exhibition price list offers a dare: 'The left hand academic portrait section, is to be given away free to the purchaser of the right-hand section'.

Unlike The Bishop, Diogenes was in no sense a bogeyman, nor was he obviously deranged. Monica remembers him as 'lovely, almost shy, but when he was on the door [at times of exhibitions] nobody got past him without giving up their five pence' (Monica, Interview, October 2108). Mouse remembers him with great affection, noting how he was 'devoted to Robert' (Mouse, Letter, September 2017). In life, death, and after-life Diogenes would become one of Robert's best supporting actors. He gave rise to profound meditations on mortality as well as frivolous journalism such as 'Embalmed Tramp Found Hidden in Artist's Drawer' (*Daily Telegraph*, 12 October 2002).

The nickname Robert chose bears some analysis. Diogenes of Sinope was born in 412 or 404 BC and first achieved fame by being exiled from his home city for deliberately mangling and thus devaluing its coins.

He wandered the Greek world until he settled in Athens. Here he refused allegiance to the city and declared himself to be a 'cosmopolitan' – the first recorded use of that word, meaning 'a citizen of the cosmos'. Diogenes considered himself subject to no human laws. He saw wealth and honour as traps and lived without job or money in a large ceramic vase or barrel in the marketplace. Thus, in a foreshadowing of Albert Schweitzer's dictum 'My life is my argument', Diogenes was a living example of 'performance philosophy', constantly enacting rather than merely talking about a critique of society.

His words are unrecorded except by myth, but his influence was profound. The philosophical schools of Cynicism and Stoicism are heavily indebted to him, though he would doubtless scorn the concept of indebtedness. One legend has it that Alexander the Great approached the philosopher's barrel to ask if he could do anything for him. Diogenes replied 'Yes, you can stand out of my light'. According to another version he made a harsh joke about the warlord's dead father. The scene has been painted many times. Cornelis De Vos's canvas (1651) shows Alexander's retinue, including a dismayed hunting hound, turning to Alexander awaiting his response to this Holy Fool. Fortunately for all involved, Alexander avoided the mistake which Pontius Pilate would make several centuries later. The historical Diogenes' vagrancy was not so much a geographical wandering but a self-imposed and solitary exile from any nation or society. He escaped what would later be called the 'social contract': the conventions of money, family, rank, and what our neighbours (however powerful) might think of us. His life was a concerted attempt to answer the question: How can I be free from slavery in all its forms?

> Diogenes, his real name was Edward MacKenzie, he lived on Chelson Meadow Rubbish Tip about a mile and a half down the road, in the cleft of a tree in an old, corrugated barrel. For obvious reasons he associated in my mind with Diogenes the Greek philosopher. He certainly looked the part. Although he was capable of arcane wisdom such as 'Live while you can and live in clover, when you'm dead your dead all over'. That was about the limit of it. (*Robert Lenkiewicz, In His Own Words*, dir. Jeremy Elman 2011)

Robert speaks too swiftly here, for that was by no means the limit of it. Similarities between Diogenes of Sinope and Diogenes of Plymouth went far beyond their housing arrangements or sayings. Both lived without work, family, and social rank. Interviewed on the opening night of the Vagrancy Exhibition in 1973 by Westward TV, Diogenes expressed the heretical position that work and money are not the solutions to his problems: he had no problems, and did not want them 'solving' by becoming a useful citizen:

> Interviewer: Why did you become a vagrant in the first place?
> Diogenes: Well, that's a question I've been asking ever since I was three and a half years old … and I've been one ever since. Interviewer: Would you describe it as a good, happy life? Are you happy with your lot?
> Diogenes: I am. Because I'm better off. 'Cause I could go and get a job tomorrow at forty-five pounds a week, but it ain't no good.
> Interviewer: Why?
> Diogenes: Because I'd be on the bottle.

Presenter Angela Rippon then visited Diogenes at his cylindrical country abode at Chelson Meadow tip and asked 'You seem pretty contented with your lot … would you say you're a happy man? The tramp replied, 'Well, I always been brought up with a contented mind and I stuck to that. … I'm far more 'appy I am now in this way, with little money coming in … there's an old sayin' "What you ain't got, you don't miss".'

Diogenes was one of the few vagrants who was not a drinker and he clear-headedly lived the philosophy of Apollo at Delphi – 'Know thyself!' He also knew that the solutions suggested by 'benefactors' like Social Services and the Sally Army were a Trojan Horse. Robert says: 'I was interested in [the vagrants'] amorality and their psychotic behaviour' (Robert, in *Paintings and Projects*, p. 11). Against this we must set Robert's conviction that one is never interested 'neutrally'. He disdained the notion that anyone could have 'concern about the welfare of another human being independently of one's own needs [...] Our attraction towards the person has nothing to do with their welfare' (Robert, *In His Own Words*, at 5 min 40 sec). An insight into Robert's own aesthetic agenda vis-à-vis Diogenes is found in the diary entry for 27 March 1976:

> Diogenes shaved off his beard and cut his hair. Purchased a suit and new shirt and shoes. He looks slightly ridiculous. I feel sure that no-one will want to know him now. Disconnected from romantic preconceptions of the 'tramp', he has become a tiresome, 'silly', lonely bore – domesticated out of life and into the English cess-pit.

What needs did the vagrants meet for Robert? His interest was fuelled as much by their abilities as their disabilities. They lived precariously but not without strategies and skills. William Burroughs once commented that if one wanted to become rich then watch what a junkie does to make money, but don't spend the money on junk. A similar principle applies to time. To be rich in time one could do worse than observe vagrants, but don't spend the time getting drunk or begging for money. Without jobs, family attachments, or any other responsibilities, the vagrants had more free 'life hours' per day than anybody else in the city. In this sense Les 'Cider' Ryder, Diogenes, and The Bishop could be counted as teachers of practical philosophy for Robert. They did not influence wider society as did Schweitzer, Nietzsche, or Russell, but whether Robert acknowledged them as such or not, they were amoral exemplars. They taught how *little* one could live with and how free one could be if only one was prepared to be ruthless – towards oneself as much as others.

The Bishop commented on the necessity of 'our indulgences', and Robert himself recognised the compulsive nature of his own behaviour:

> It seemed to me that these people [the vagrants] fulfilled the same function in our society as the fools and jokers who wandered through medieval Europe. They remind us too of the medieval dance of death [...] Generally speaking, I regard my interest in vagrancy as a romantic indulgence, which I am not likely to change. I don't think though there's any genuine altruism behind it. (Robert, in Stokes, p. xii)

The theme of the dance of death informed one of the larger and curiously more jolly canvases of the Vagrancy Exhibition. *The Bishop and the Painter Dancing to Mahler* (1973) is painted on sailcloth scavenged by the vagrants themselves. Cider Ryder, The Bishop, Robert, Corky, Snowy, and Cockney Jim are cavorting inside the 'Jacob's Ladder' Holiday Inn, depicted in blue-green, leaden grey, and gun-metal hues. The liveliness of their death dance is accentuated by the wave-like positioning of the foreground figures. The effect is more mischievous than sinister, as if the group are gleefully anticipating the trap which the Salvation Army and local politicians would soon walk into. It is a joyous painting. But there is a piece of information which Robert took the trouble to record in his notes and raise in at least one televised interview (*In His Own Words*, 7 min 45 sec). They were dancing to Gustav Mahler's *Kindertotenlieder* – Songs for the Death of Children.

The *Kindertotenlieder* song cycle was a lifelong favourite of Robert's and was played continuously during the painting and opening night of the Education Project. As Mahler's title suggests it is a profoundly anguished series of studies. Highlights from the libretto include 'Now I see well, why with such dark flames' and 'In this storm, I would never have sent the children out. I was anxious they might die the next day. Now anxiety is pointless'. Perhaps Robert wished to signal that there was something super- or sub- or extra-human about the vagrants' ability to dance to deep tragedy. The painting captures a moment of joy, but viewing it while listening to the music gives a sense of how seriously demented these characters were. A similarly daemonic but more subdued and Saturnine mood presides over the second largest painting (208 x 513 cm in its eventual cut-down form) in the Vagrancy Project, *The Burial of John Kynance* (1970), inspired by Gustave Courbet's *Burial at Ornans* (1849–50). The composition is staged from the point of view of the dead man in his grave. All of the figures, including Death in a jester's cap, seem to be folded in upon themselves, arms crossed, with hands clasped or wedged into pockets: all apart from the central figure of Barney Brown in his shaggy fur who is reminiscent of the Great He-Goat in Goya's *Witches Sabbath* (The Black Paintings, 1821–23). The vagrants' faces are exquisitely painted in expressions of stoical knowledge: this too will be their fate. The background is curiously indeterminate but powerfully evocative, suggesting the toxic London fog of Robert's youth. Several works in the project contextualise the scene – the haunting *Study of John Kynance One Week Before His Death* and the two pencil sketches *John Kynance – A Few Minutes Before Death by Cancer*. On the reverse of these Robert wrote: 'Vagrant character of rare qualities. Completely out of tune with his thuggish companions'. It is noteworthy that of the 78 works Robert included in the exhibition catalogue, the only ones marked 'not for sale' were the pictures of John Kynance. The smaller work survives but *The Burial of John Kynance* was destroyed by fire in 2012. After its appearance at the Royal West of England Academy in an exhibition entitled 'Robert Lenkiewicz: Still Lives' in 2011, it was destroyed along with several other large works in an arson attack at Chilford Hall in Cambridgeshire, home of patrons Sam and Fiona Alper.

In a fabulated movie scene which Robert found very moving, Charles Laughton's Rembrandt (in Korda's 1936 film of that name) comments to a vagrant that his trade seems slow. He quips 'No worse than yours [...] You're the man who paints beggars. Decent painters paint decent people. Gentleman of rank, fine ladies, kings'. Rembrandt replies: 'Then I will paint you as a king'. Many artists have depicted vagrancy and addiction. But few if any rival Robert in the extent to which art and life were interwoven. When painting *Andy Lynch with Oak Leaves* in 1981, Robert borrowed Lynch's coat to complete the portrait of the dosser-as-king with an oak branch sceptre. The never-washed garment was so befouled it almost sat upright in the chair all by itself; the stink, Lynch's trademark, nearly made the painter retch, but he endured several hours alone with it for the sake of authenticity.

With the help of Mouse, Monica, Terry, and other kindred spirits, he fed the dossers, housed them, mopped up vomit and excreta, carried them in from the streets where they had collapsed, took them to hospital, and on several occasions was present at the hour of their death. Whatever we make of Robert's many disavowals of altruism, he cared for these people. And willingly or not, consciously or not, they taught him about life, death, religion, addiction, mysticism.

> The Bishop, Brother Blair, Mouth McCarthy, Scarface Fitz, Brighton, Psycho Jock, Big Brummie, now dead [...] so many of these characters, some of whom believed that they communed with Jesus, like Harmonica Jim [who] would light fires in derelict buildings then urinate them out in some strange private language of communion with the infinite. (*Demon or Delight*, dir. Cathy Sayers, 1996, 11 min 30 sec)

Robert's early Vagrancy notes reveal similar suggestions that the vagrants were haphazardly involving themselves in some kind of archaic magic. *Mr Fisher Talking to the Sun*, *Mr Fisher Conversing with a Fox in Stoke Damerel Church-Yard*, *Mr Fisher Conversing with Death*, *Mr Fisher on What He Terms 'An Astral Plane'* – the very titles suggest that The Bishop wilfully rejected consensus reality in favour of something akin to shamanism.

I discussed this with Robert in the late 1980s when he was reading the anti-psychiatric authors Laing, Cooper, and Szasz. Robert speculated that at least some of the vagrants were self-medicating on alcohol and pills to fend off the intensities of 'madness', but this madness may well be an artefact of an overly restrictive society. He wondered what insights the vagrants might achieve if only they could loosen the brakes of addiction and instead *accelerate* their strange journeys. I recall him enthusing about how they might be lost forever, or might return like the Marco Polos of human experience with tales of New Lands. A similar thought appeared in the Exhibition Notes for the Vagrancy Project:

The relationship [between the vagrant and] Death and the Fool might in these terms become clear. The Fool survives where the wiser person might die: the survival of the Fool does not make sense, it is as if part of the Fool operates in another dimension [...] The Fool reminds us of the ancient and essential possibility that life is not what we think it is and that there may be another order of things operating under our noses. (Vagrancy Exhibition Notes, 1973)

Robert had cleaned up too much blood and vomit to romanticise the vagrants as noble psychonauts but he was determined to prove that they were not merely 'human waste' or souls to be saved from sin. In the first collection of its kind in the United Kingdom, perhaps the first anywhere, Robert recorded the views of over 60 people on the topic. A handful were probation officers or welfare workers, but the vast majority were the vagrants themselves. They were asked how they defined the term 'vagrant', whether they would self-define as a vagrant and why or not, whether they thought vagrancy was a problem in Plymouth, and if not, why not. The cumulative effect of their answers supports Robert's insistence that the project as a whole is the artwork. Here are a few of their self-definitions:

'A man without home or habitation – he has no future in life' – Thomas Dunstan.
'A wanderer' – David Louis Helingoe.
'A man who has outlived his usefulness to society and is a drop-out' – Victor Johnson.
'No visible means of support, just fiddling and scrounging' – Eugene McDonnell.
'A man that wants to go his own way through life' – Leonard Wotten Hill.
'A vagrant is someone who thinks he's escaping to something when in fact he's escaping from something' – Alan Paul-Wrece.
'A misfit – an escapist' – Samuel Eric Roberts.
'It's a fear. Not being able to communicate with people' – John Casey.

Escape, exile, displacement, inability to function, isolation from the organs of wider society – these concepts inform much of the visual content of the exhibition. In the decades to come Robert developed these themes in visceral images of incontinence and disintegration. This was not so much a personal or even social exploration as a philosophical problem for him, an existential sense of homelessness in a cosmos where God and heaven are nowhere to be found, despite the glimpses and mirages afforded by Shah's Sufism or Harmonica Jim's fire rituals. Alongside the considerable painterly and intellectual work for the Vagrancy Project, Robert managed to complete an indoor mural for the Hoe Theatre with the title *History of the Harlequinade*. It was accompanied by extensive historical research on costume, character, and symbolism.

The opening of the Vagrancy Exhibition was set for March 1973 at the former Olivetti building, 58 Southside Street, also known as 'Jacob's Ladder' or Holiday Inn Number Three. This likely began as a squat, for it was an industrial-sized space, and at the time Robert certainly had no means to pay rent. Sometime before the opening of the exhibition he must have negotiated with its owners, if only to head off the possibility of paintings being confiscated. He also negotiated with the venerable Alice von Schlossberg, who was brought from London for the premier by Johnny. It was a theatrical event. The book of observations and the exhibition notes had been printed up and the local political and artistic classes invited. Philip stokes recalls:

> The opening ceremony was performed by The Bishop, who explained 'While I had generally found myself to be here, it seemed most likely that what was over there would be more interesting, and so I always felt that one should move from here to there in order to discover what actually that interesting thing was that one had seen here, when over there, before moving from there to here ...' This monologue proceeded for some time and was liable to restart at any moment, irrespective of appropriateness, as some switch closed in The Bishop's mind. (Stokes, *A Portrait of Robert Lenkiewicz*, p. xiii)

Robert made sure that several local dignitaries had a chance to speak, some of whom talked their way straight into his trap: they denied that vagrancy was a problem for the city, and one claimed that there were only a handful of genuine cases. On hearing this Robert gave a pre-arranged signal and several dozen vagrants shuffled in to mingle with the finely dressed crowd of 'middle class people gently interested in the arts [...], members of The Salvation Army, Plymouth Guild of Social Services, and the official Welfare bodies' (Stokes, p. ixx)

Robert would be suspicious of the terms 'performance philosophy', 'political theatre', or 'art-activism', but the Vagrancy Project contained elements of all three as well as being a vast and original work of social documentary. Building on Schweitzer's axiom 'My argument is my life', Robert widened the limits of ethical and political philosophy beyond what is merely said or written. The 'artwork' was the overall event, the entire aesthetic impact of the project. This continued some way beyond the opening night. The exhibition was a carefully staged collision between the City authorities and the bodily existence of the vagrants. Some elements of the City authorities were thus provoked to treat Robert himself as a vagrant force, prejudicial to 'good order'.

In what might be seen as a peace offering or a further provocation, Robert gave a gift. On 26 October 1973 the artist, accompanied by Diogenes dressed as a Clown, attempted to present a canvas and a poem to the Lord Mayor. It was a piece of performance philosophy worthy of Diogenes of Sinope, and the authorities showed all the gratitude one would expect. 'This is not the right way to go about things. Proper arrangements should have been made through the Lord Mayor's Parlour,' said Alderman J. C. Porter (*Western Morning News*, 27 September 1974). The painting was titled *Mr Albert Ernest Fisher Shitting Himself Outside a St Andrew's Cross Building.* St Andrews Cross was a modern part of the city consisting of banks and local government agencies, all of which refused entry to The Bishop. The Alderman commented that the painting 'was in poor taste' (ibid.) but did not comment upon the point it made. A citizen of Plymouth was denied access to a public building to meet the most basic biological need. A painting of the consequences of the exclusion was also inadmissible.

The episode underlined more than the barring of the vagrants from civic buildings. Their exile from political discourse, from the bare awareness of 'decent people', was tantamount to a collective neurotic denial. The vagrant is intolerable, and even his painted image is unacceptable unless it is suitably sanitised. Hogarth's etchings of addiction and dissolution (*Gin Lane*, 1751) are not considered to be 'in poor taste' because the miscreants are long dead and their behaviour bleached by moral condemnation. Robert's non-moral observations on the base materiality of the vagrants spoke truth to power. It is worth recalling that the Vagrancy Act of 1824 included a provision for a person to be prosecuted for the crime of 'circulating obscene images'. The local authorities did not threaten Robert with obscenity charges for this exhibition: that came later.

Robert said of Diogenes that he 'had never met a man who was less harm to anyone' (ibid.) and may have said so without irony. Everybody interviewed for this book recalls Diogenes as a gentle soul. But the figure of the vagrant is a political agent of the most important kind. Like the very existence of the Jew in the Reich, the vagrant is *ontologically* harmful to any authoritarian model of the state.

The vagrant's essential feature is that of a deserter from normal social reality. Desertion is the most fundamental act of non-compliance with power. It is Satan's crime – 'I will not serve'. Great generals fear and detest deserters, for they may be the contagious example which undermines all their power. Robert could be humorous and even frivolous, but much of his joking was deadly serious. 'Not by wrath does one kill, but by laughter', wrote Nietzsche (*Zarathustra*, Part 1, Chapter 7). Diogenes of Plymouth had an axiom: '*Always* a true word spoken in a joke' (Vagrancy Project Notes, 1973). Many people in positions of authority intuitively understand Diogenes' point, which goes some way towards explaining why so much of Robert's work stuck like a fishbone in the City's throat. Robert chose the first line of the following quatrain as the title of a 1982 documentary about his work. Borrowing from the joyful wisdom of Nietzsche, it summarises the artistic and philosophical problem which united all the projects. It also summarises the local political reaction to 'Vagrancy'.

> *Go, said the bird, for the leaves were full of children*
> *Hidden excitedly, containing laughter.*
> *Go, go, go, said the bird: human kind*
> *Cannot bear very much reality.*
>
> (T.S. Eliot, 'Burnt Norton', 1935)

14.1 Poster for Death & The Maiden, 1974.

14.2 Robert's sketch of 7 Clifton Street. The gallery name was changed from 'Pnoob' to The Fool prior to opening in 1974.

14.3 Annie Hill-Smith in front of Robert's self-portrait in the Barbican Mural, *c.*1974.

14.4 Diogenes and Annie Hill-Smith at The Fool gallery, 4 June 1974.

14.5 The largest painting in the Death & The Maiden project was described as: 'A painter in a graveyard/(large study for mile long painting)'.

14.6 Death & The Maiden at The Fool in Clifton Street, 1974.

14.7 These works on paper were marked 'these studies are not for sale' in the catalogue. They were later bound into a large folio titled *Death and The Maiden, Paintings: R. O. Lenkiewicz.*

Death & The Maiden at The Fool in Clifton Street, 1974.

14.8 *The Judgement of Paris* (1974) above the diptych *The Putrefaction of Diogenes* (1974).

14.9 *Opposite, top:* Robert painting Diogenes on a small canvas that references the painting *Gentleman in Pierrot Costume* (1973).

14.10 Diogenes in front of the large canvas *The Judgement of Paris* (1974).

14.11 Model Francesca in Pierrot costume with Robert's friend and patron
Peregrine, Lord Eliot, in the Round Room at Port Eliot, 1974.

14.12 Robert with Francesca and Peregrine in the Round Room before it
was lined with canvas to hold the *Riddle Mural*, 1974.

14

Death and the Maiden

Robert began work on the Death and the Maiden theme long before the Vagrancy Project was exhibited. A note from 1972 depicts three blue-grey cadavers devotionally spilling their innards. Alongside it he wrote:

'And yet we would not know love were we to live indefinitely' – Anatole France. Three Magi Presenting their Entrails to the Virgin & Child. (The world) 'Perhaps sexual desire is only the frustrated desire to eat human flesh' – Novalis. The active, passive neutral principles present their own future to their own past.

Even at this stage of his development a casual glance through Robert's output reveals a chronic engagement with death and sexuality, but it would be crude to raise the wail of misunderstanding often directed at Sigmund Freud: 'It's all just sex and death'. Robert's ambitions for the projects were diverse – love, education, old age – he intended to explore the fundamentals of all human relationships.

In 1973 Robert first met Annie Hill-Smith, a social worker who had just relocated to the West Country from London. Annie would later help Robert develop a new gallery to focus on his Projects and they would have three children together in the 1970s:

At the end of 1972 I left London, started a course in Plymouth and moved into a derelict property on the Moor – there was a 'back to nature' movement going on at the time. I was dimly aware of the artist on the Barbican. But only very dimly aware.

I organized a conference on poverty in Plymouth in the summer of '73 and the artist was an obvious person to invite. Local and interested in the theme. After the conference the artist messaged me. I called down to the Barbican a month or so later to pick up feedback on the conference and that was how I met him. (Annie Hill-Smith, email, September 2020)

Most people achieve a stable 'character' by their third decade, and though much of Robert's work was tinged with darkness he was certainly not a gloomy Romantic sensualist. Apart from the period of shock during and after prison, everybody recalls him as light-hearted, even when discussing the most serious subjects – full of optimism, charm, and humour. He enjoyed the company of his many lovers and friends and, on occasions, his children, taking time to see movies such as *Fiddler on the Roof* (Alice Lenkiewicz, Interview April 2017). This he loved and in subsequent years visitors to his studios might hear him yodel-doodle-doing his way through its highlights. Despite severe financial strain throughout the 1970s, Robert was in Ivan Illich's sense 'philosophically convivial'.

The philosophy research group centred around Lynn Brogan's flat was showing signs of wear and tear. The Sufi trajectory proved divisive. Some people had 'found their higher purpose' at Langton House, and speaking in 2018 Lynn said 'at least one woman [from our original group] is still involved to this day'. Monica, Robert, Mouse, and Jim had been pleased to meet the creative intellectuals in the organisation but were unconvinced by the 'master' and his motives. Shah was not the only person suspected of psychological manipulation.

Phil Sheardown was interested in Robert's seemingly magical ability to attract women and asked how to improve his technique:

> He did two portraits of me in the early days: one of me is sitting in a chair. When he painted that first portrait [...] I said to him, 'Rob, do you ever write poems?' Just for a minute he was [...] not offended, but hurt. He was quiet for a long time. He carried on working, his lip didn't tremble [...] but it came near to it. Minutes later he said, 'My paintings are my poems'.
>
> It was through hanging out with Robert I met Lynn [Brogan ...] one woman that he didn't pull! I said to her, 'He could have pulled you if he wanted to, but he didn't want to.' She said 'No,' but I took up with her.

Interviewed jointly in 2008, Mouse and Monica hinted at the life-altering effects Robert's charismatic 'teachings' could have:

> [Monica]. There were men who hovered about Robert because they [...] wanted to be the guru and it got them more female companions. [Mouse]. That did a lot of harm. There were men who gave up their

vocations and started posing as little demi-Roberts and they are still doing it.

Phil's path to enlightenment led him to state:

> [Robert said] it was often a matter of 'making yourself useful. People like to be helped; you have to find ways to help people. [...] He said to me 'If you are going to find out these things, Phil, you are going to have to use your natural intelligence.' Nobody else said that to me, not before, or since. Robert said to me – 'One of the things she wants is to have babies.' After a while our first child was born [...] Robert Sheardown, he's called. We moved out of Terry [Goldstone]'s house [...] I went away that summer to Salcombe to teach sailing, and I knew it was my last holiday. [Our son] Ben came along, and then came Katie. I had to get a job, so I applied to be a long-distance driver. [...] Time went by, we moved to Somerset [...] I felt like I had been stuck with Robert Lenkiewicz for about three years [...] I thought: I've got to get out of this, I've got to stop thinking like him, I needed to build on what I already knew. I've got my own brain here.

Taken in isolation the deep ambivalences in Phil Sheardown's recollections and his sense that Robert was to blame for pushing him into some regretful decisions may seem peevish, but given Robert's track record with his brothers and friends it is not implausible. The effect of charismatic individuals – people who exercise 'a compelling charm which inspires devotion in others' – is to make separation psychically costly. For Phil, the pain and emotional price of splitting from Robert is palpable in these remarks nearly four decades after the event:

> Robert liked to have a little bit of power over people and get them to do things. There I was, surrounded by my children, driving trucks, and if I didn't stop driving trucks I would still be driving trucks today: and it twisted, and twisted, and twisted, [that] Rob had [...] kind of pushed me in that direction. [...] I've never told anyone – you're the first person I've talked to about it – but for that reason I did not go to his funeral. I think I had to abandon him. There were terrible consequences for the whole family. I was screaming inside and out – let me out! I stood underneath the viaduct, feeling very sorry for myself, right under the spot where my body would land if I did jump, and my ghost

would be there forever, moaning, and nobody would know. (Phil, Interview, July 2018)

Robert's *Portrait of Philip Sheardown* (possibly 1970 or 1971) is a fine single-statement piece in grey-greens and blues, suggestive of Captain Nemo brooding on the fate of the oceans. It is also one of the earliest examples of a compositional device Robert developed throughout the early and mid-1970s. The 'headroom' above the sitters came to increase so that large fields of tone and colour could be the object of the painting equal to any human representational content. Robert had a deep admiration for Turner and Rothko, and was pursuing research into the aesthetics of colour via the philosophies of Goethe and Wittgenstein. This expansion of 'the portrait' beyond merely representing the head allowed him to explore paint in ways which included psychology and the creation of 'mood' but also dovetailed with his growing interest in the physiology of visual perception. The projects might have distinct zones of interest, but Robert was resistant to the risk that his paintings became 'all subject-mattery', to recall his criticism of the American artist at The Loft. The paint itself was not to be hidden behind its representation of another object.

Three examples are especially worthy of note. The *Portrait of Jeny Bremer, An Allegory of Folly* (1972) contains a subtle geometry in the large background, inviting the eye to explore the beauty of the paint before returning to the beauty of the sitter and the detail of the little monster Fool in her lap. The Fool makes the traditional gesture for silence – finger pressed to lips – yet the cockerel atop his fool's cap will crow out anyway the secrets that should have been kept. *The Painter with Courbet's Self-Portrait* (1974) is perhaps 80 per cent uniformly lamp-black, adding a doubled sense of both closeness and isolation to the faces of the artists depicted. The *Self-Portrait with Monica* diptych (1975) presents the faces of the sitters almost as footnotes to the vast colour surfaces and volumes conjured above them. Had this trajectory continued the portraits would have become skyscapes.

The down-to-earth problems of rent and square metres of workspace continued to vex him. In 1973 Robert still mainly operated from the front window of 25 The Parade, but the economic ill-fortune of the entire city once again played to his advantage. Small businesses suffered, and when the Post Office at 7 Clifton Street was closed as unprofitable, it was suggested Robert might turn it into an exhibition space. The Elizabethan Mural had increased his public 'consumability' but he remained suspicious of the commercial gallery system. The mural caught the attention of Peregrine Eliot, Earl of St Germans, who approached Robert to paint a large indoor mural in the Round Room of his mansion. Thus began a friendship and patronage which endured for the remainder of both their lives. The relationship was cemented by the facts that Perry genuinely valued culture far beyond the index of money and possessed an interest in the arcane symbolism of heraldry. Perry was helpful with money when he saw it was needed but respectful in making claims upon the artist's time: so much so that the Round Room mural remained a work in progress for decades. And Robert was careful not to make many financial requests. Despite the possibilities implied by the term 'wealthy patron' there is ample evidence that Robert was unwilling to take advantage. Throughout the 1970s his diaries contain dozens, perhaps hundreds of demands from printers, utility companies, and bailiffs. These he met at his own pace or failed to meet and risked having paintings confiscated.

The idea of losing paintings hardly bothered him: his books and the housing of them were more important. To further his vision of a private library at the Priory Road cottage he resorted to trying to borrow large sums from the bank (Diary, 25 June 1974). The manager was understandably unwilling to act without any guarantees. Robert's outgoings were many and random. Thousands of pounds were needed to upgrade and damp-proof the semi-derelict 'Death House' at Priory Road. Any loan would have rapidly evaporated. On 22 May 1974 Robert wrote: 'Sent £100 to Belle [Pecorini] in India, phone call from Mr Butt, feels like I might be conning him. Gave him £100'. 11 April, 'Gave Maria £10, gave Scotty £5'. The diaries record Robert paying bail-money and fines to keep various dossers out of jail, in addition to regularly feeding them.

His concept of paternal responsibility remained woefully under-developed. He was happy to make creative gestures like designing and building a dragon see-saw for the children (this was by all accounts a thing of wonder), but he had no sense of priority and was wilfully bad at turning paintings into money. The people who were raising his children and helping with the dossers were not at the back of the queue. There simply *was* no queue.

> There were times he would get someone to take us up [to London] in their car, and he'd put some beautiful big paintings on the roof of the car. There was a triptych, and only one panel survived. The rest ended up splattered on the motorway. He never burned his bridges with Ma

[but] he always used to dread Ma ringing. I used to feel sorry for her. When your *raison d'être* is doing the best you can for your boys [...] and he was her pet [... Mouse and I] had been penniless for a long time, and it was the starting of school; again, Wolfie had no shoes, it really was difficult times [...] In the end, Mouse and I decided that we had to hoist some books from Priory Road. We thought [...] we would take half a dozen of the books, take them back to our flat, then send a note saying we had them, but we must have £20 each for the books. [Robert] had a new girlfriend and was throwing [money] about a bit and we [Monica laughs ...] we were just the old discarded ones! And so we kidnapped his books, and it was only a small ransom demand, just enough for shoes and a few bits, but [when he came around with the money] he was white as a sheet and shaking, he was so worried about his books. You could have pinched one of the paintings and set fire to it for all he cared, but not the books. (Monica, Interview, June 2018)

John Nash continued to be helpful with gifts of food and money, as did Alex and Betty. Ma could be relied upon in emergencies. Perry Eliot and several lovers ensured Robert did not want for paints and brushes. Arrangements with café owners like the jocular and fiscally patient Joe Prete meant he was not at risk of starvation. Robert would have scorned the idea of a 'business model' but the complex and overlapping forces of the Holiday Inns, fragmented families, multiple relationships, and artistic production became increasingly chaotic throughout 1973. Some concessions to organisation were required if he was to fulfil his ambition to 'paint more paintings than anyone else, ever'.

Whether Robert was incapable of resisting disorder or merely unwilling to do so is a moot point, but it was a piece of good fortune that in the summer of 1973 he began his relationship with Annie Hill-Smith.

When I met Robert [September 1973] he was living a precarious life but had begun to think he needed to create a space that would enable him to show his projects. In the spring of 1974, I bought a run-down house in North Hill area and we passed the derelict building that would become The Fool on Clifton Street every day. The idea of acquiring that building began to take shape and we approached the Council, who owned it, and they accepted my offer, surprisingly. This was the spring of 1974. We did as much work as we could, as quickly as we could, with help from anyone who was willing to climb a ladder.

214

We had less than no money ... it was hard to find materials, but we opened it as The Fool on 20th July 1974 with Death and The Maiden. There followed three years of running Project exhibitions there. The last Project there was Jealousy in 1977. It was a busy, creative, productive and stimulating time for us and we earned almost no money from our enterprise. (Annie Hill-Smith, email, September 2020)

For some years Robert had been documenting his raw materials for the projects by biographising the dossers, taking philosophical notes, delving into the history of art and ideas: but prior to 1974 the biographical paper trail is haphazard. From 1 January 1974 we have resources to trace the trajectories of his development thanks to Annie's intervention: she encouraged him to keep detailed accounts of his paintings, reading, and relationships.

Thanks to Annie's prompting we have a trove of day-by-day, year-by-year records for Robert's life with the exception of one diary, for 1975, presumed by Robert to have been taken away by a woman of unclear conscience. In later years Robert told me he did not involve himself with married women as there was 'enough free-range stock around not to be a poacher'. This was a lie. He poached mercilessly and on occasions people were endangered by it. The habit was inexcusable considering how many single women were advertising their availability. Pat Parker had moved away from Plymouth but wrote regularly and with open longing:

Hello Robert. I do wish I'd seen more of you in Plymouth. There were so many things I wanted to chat with you about for a long time, but I guess you were busy, and so was I, sort of. The visit was strange, very good in some ways, not so good when we parted. I feel like I would like to see everyone again, but alone. Do you go to London much? Because you know you could stay here with me for a couple of days. I know you are busy and the emotional pull is not strong enough for you to spare the time, I understand all that, but I sure would like to see you. [...] I'm interested in your work progress, and I was disappointed that I hardly got a chance to hear about it. Also, naturally, your affairs of the heart [...] Love. P.P. (Pat Parker, Letter in the 1974 Diary, Lenkiewicz Foundation Archive)

His affairs of the heart were insuperably complex. He was concurrently involved with at least 20 women at greater or lesser distances. Some like

Jeny Bremer were close in his affections but living abroad. Others like Belle Pecorini lived locally but were sometimes made unviable by other relationships, unilateral choices, and international travel. Others again were reserved for Robert's London visits: many of the women mentioned in the jealousy-inducing letters of his art school days were now actively involved with him, such as was Axel Ney-Hoch's daughter Maria, with whom he remained especially close. Then there were the local muses, models, and maenads who formed the largest cohort. Add to this the 'exes' who were in many cases merely semi-detached, and we still do not have the full picture. Code names in the diaries suggest he tried to keep some affairs secret.

At the close of 1973 Jeny Bremer returned from Holland to stay at Priory Road and subsequently visited Robert during the summer, Easter, and Christmas holidays: a migratory muse. She recalls a gathering of the dossers for a Christmas meal at 'Death House' with several of Robert's present and former paramours busy cooking: 'Nobody was jealous or difficult, we were all good friends. Belle and I spent most of our time laughing like naughty schoolgirls' (Jeny, Interview, April 2018). With each passing year the numbers of vagrants grew until Priory Road could host no more. By the middle of the 1970s the concrete overhang of Bretonside Bus Station was the regular venue for the 'Cowboy's Christmas Feast'. The organisation of such large events, the day-to-day complications of the Holiday Inns, and the balancing act of multiple relationships did not deplete Robert's energies.

It seems likely he was energised by this level of complexity and experimentation, painting under conditions ruinous for most 'sensitive artistic' temperaments. Once again we should pause to recognise the efforts of those around him in preventing the complexity breaking down into utter chaos. The mothers of his children bore the full brunt of parenting, and Mouse and Monica were still supporting vagrants with any time and energy they had left over. Johnny had matured from his role as little brother to an erudite friend. Robert was immensely proud of Johnny's academic achievements in anthropology, sexology, and gerontology, which fed into much of his own researches: Johnny often located and photocopied rare books and journals for him. Terry Goldstone and Jim Pascoe were helpful in providing surrogate fathering as well as intellectual friendship and labouring skills. Builders such as Dave Johnson, who were owed large sums for work and materials at Priory Road, shared the kindly forbearance of the Nash and Prete families. It was known that Robert would not actually 'rip anybody off', but it was not in his nature to have the right sum of money at the right time unless books were involved.

Robert's affairs – artistic, business, erotic – were a mad jungle, and Annie toiled to turn as much as she could into workable lands. Her first triumph was the insistence upon daily record keeping; second was the creation of The Fool Gallery in Clifton Street, a task she began in late 1973. Opened in 1974, The Fool was more than an outlet for art and craft: it was a centre for aesthetic education. We have already noted the archetype of the Fool was an obsession for Robert. Throughout the late 1960s and early 1970s he scripted and drew many tales of a clownish figure of his own creation, the Pnoob. Aury Shoa explains:

> We set up our own Fool [in London] and Robert liked it. [...] We were very popular, we were selling clothes internationally, a real cottage industry. This was the heyday of the *crafty* world of the hippie, not the deluded. None of us had any interest in drugs or sentimentalised, ethical religion. We loved the emancipation of craft and the breakdown of barriers in fashion [...] We made clothes for Annie on sale-or-return, Robert got Clifton Street, which was a semi-corner shop. Annie immediately took to me and Myrna. From very early on I was a regular guest at Annie's house and became an honorary member of the family. Annie did all the work, and Robert gave advice, and helped her with the signs for The Fool.
>
> Robert's conversation about The Fool was philosophical, whether it was the court jester, or Herschel Austropolia, the Yiddish *meshugganer*, or Nasrudin the Trans-Caucasian Fool. There were schools of metaphysical education which were based strictly on telling the jokes of Nasrudin! They are brilliant! Brilliant at describing the arc of a certain psychological nature, describing accurately the characteristics of man. So many of them are word-for-word taken from Eastern Europe, from the Land of Fools, the land of Chelem. As a teaching figure, as a symbol, [Robert was] utterly fascinated by The Fool [...] and it engaged us all, philosophically. A lot of our designs were medieval, all our clothes had historical names: tabards, firkins. [Later] Robert came with us to Europe, to France and the Low Lands. (Aury, Interview, October 2018)

It is entirely appropriate to the theme of ironic wisdom that neither Annie nor Robert suspected how The Fool might cause as many complications as it solved. Different complications were already being prepared by Robert. He began exchanging letters with 'Warren – prisoner number 5A6366' in Dartmoor – one of the toughest jails in England – with a view to arranging art lessons for the inmates (Diary, 11 January 1974). He made visits to Freedom Fields Hospital to support The Bishop, who was in precarious health (Diary, 27 January 1974). Alongside these avowedly amoral acts of kindness he expanded his portfolio of lovers. On 17 January 1974 he notes in his diary: 'Lord Eliot visited with a strange girl (who is the next "book")'. The 'next book' is a reference to an emerging method of investigation. In the 1970s Robert asked lovers to keep 'relationship notebooks'. He too would document the tides and seasons of each relationship, a practice that would reach its zenith in the beautiful and disturbing 'Mary Notebook', begun in 1977.

The winter of 1973–1974 was unkind to Plymouth, with heavy rain driven by unlucky winds and tides which caused the Barbican to flood. Fortunately, 25 The Parade and its canvasses were spared. The roof of the Hoe Theatre was damaged and letting in enough water to make the electricity supply a hazard to audiences (*Western Evening Herald*, 17 January 1974). Thus began the slow destruction of Robert's *History of the Harlequinade* mural in the theatre foyer. Robert was unconcerned. The important thing for him was the preservation of the accompanying research. He had already edited his copious notes and watercolour studies into a small book which he collected from the printers on 19 January 1974, with a promise to pay later. The diary shows that by Friday he was enjoying a performance of Hedda Gabler at the Swarthmore and a night out with Mouse and Jim who were at that time 'totally skint'. Robert settled the printer's account eventually, but he often steered by Oscar Wilde's maxim 'The only way to live on in the memory of the commercial classes is by not paying your bills'.

Robert and Annie visited Lord Eliot's estate in early February accompanied by a young model referred to as 'Thrush' in the diaries, an early nickname for Eliza Massey. Robert made paintings of her in a Pierrot costume and began to develop ideas for the Round Room mural. They were at this stage very broad and dark: 'War/aggression/false altruism/unrequited love/suicide/murder/etc.' (Diary, 13 February 1974).

Though far from finished Robert regularly referred to his book collection as 'the library' and Death House in Priory Road as 'home'. He had no interest in returning to base himself in London. The myth that one must be part of the London Scene to count for anything in British art was and still is a powerful one, but nothing suggests that Robert believed a word of it. There are no reflections on the enormous potential of the Shemtov as a studio space he might inherit. He was happy to visit London to see friends and view exhibitions of interest, but his artistic roots favoured the edge-lands of England over the putative centre, much as his intellect favoured the wilder regions of thought. He was enjoying the role of The Outsider and cultivating his reputation for being 'eccentric' in all respects.

The strange richness and precariousness of Robert's daily life in 1974 is best conveyed by a compressed sample from the diaries. On 1 February he visited Dartmoor Prison to teach Warren and associates, then visited Barney in Exeter Prison, who was doing 18 months for possession of cannabis and LSD (*Western Evening Herald*, 15 September 1973). On the second day he was teaching Lelya's partner Henk to paint and 'worked hard isolating his problems and demonstrating weaknesses of a basic academic nature', then watched Bronowski's *The Ascent of Man*. Later that evening he travelled to Lord Eliot's estate to continue the mural. He spent the third day talking with Lord Eliot and a visiting American painter called 'Willy, a student of [Pietro] Annigoni', one of the few truly talented 20th century painters still working in the Renaissance tradition. Still keeping up with his esoteric interests, Robert found time to read work by Ouspensky. On returning to Plymouth he continued his preparatory research for the Death and the Maiden Project. On the seventh day he rested not, but found time in the evening to visit the Guildhall where he viewed a propaganda film for the Marhaj Ji, a guru claiming to transmit direct knowledge of God. On the eighth day the metaphysics ran out – 'Debt collectors came, asked for £15 [...] arranged to pay in a fortnight'.

Although he had been exploring the topic for many months previously, Robert emphatically announced in his diary on 28 January: 'STARTED WORK ON DEATH AND THE MAIDEN THEME'. He began a process of immersion which he called the 'deep-sea-diving' of his art, though he seldom referred to himself as an 'artist' and much preferred the term 'painter'. It is worth noting his methods here, which he applied to all subsequent projects. Scornful of the Romantic model of the Great Artist languidly awaiting inspiration, Robert favoured the Alice von Schlossberg model of long and serious graft.

He intensified his reading, made extensive historical and aesthetic notes, searched out the very best images of the topic from the late Middle Ages onwards, sketched and painted while his portable record player repeatedly trilled out Saint-Saën's *Danse Macabre* and Schubert's *Der Tod und Das*

Mädchen. This latter piece Robert came to evaluate as altogether too light for the subject matter: 'Schubert's Death is merely a kindly but implacable "doing his job" policeman chasing the Maiden. Perhaps he was unaware of the sado-masochistic undertones generally conceded in the theme'. There is little evidence that Robert was drawing on the works of Georges Bataille, whose incisive *Erotism* reached similar conclusions to Robert's research, though an English translation had been available since 1962. But the tenor of Robert's notes, images, and reflections are at times so close to Bataille's one could easily mistake one for the other: 'Licentiousness alone is capable of contact with "the old gentleman" [Death]. Through wanton and sacrificial behaviour, the very edge of Life is sensed. Oblivion is replaced by the orgasm' writes Robert, closely echoing Bataille's analysis of the violence of 'sacred' pleasures beyond anything the ego could desire. In this project Robert commuted the central Jewish theological problem – that of the impossibility of adequately representing God – to the problem of representing the relationship between the brief beauty of Life and the immensity of Death.

Robert's work rate and the intense darkness of his theme took a toll on some of the sitters. Monica was under considerable stress due to family and financial worries, but she regularly modelled for four or five hours at a stretch. She suffered from worsening episodes of depression, and while it would be far too speculative to claim that hours of immobility listening to Schubert's music worsened her condition, it is fair to assume this cannot have helped. There are several watercolours depicting Monica as the Maiden cradling a child while Death looms behind her unsuspecting back. Any young mother with an atom of religiosity or superstition in her body might feel anxious about tempting Fate in such a manner. Monica suffered for Robert's art, and to his discredit he made several ungrateful and graceless diary entries about demands she made upon his time. Although he had rejected the Romantic idea of the artist passively awaiting the Muse, he keenly embraced the idea of the artist as tyrant. Monica still adored him and behaved decently towards his many lovers, but she could not tolerate being one of many. Schubert himself perfectly describes the melancholy of Monica's situation: 'Some people come into our lives, leave footprints on our hearts, and we are never the same'.

The Death and the Maiden notes explore the profundity of this feeling of loss, which is itself a foretaste of death. And the paintings dramatise it – sometimes tenderly, sometimes with utter revulsion. Robert's point is that in losing our love, we also lose our life, either in small part or in its entirety. This is not a Romanticisation of the situation, as he went on to demonstrate in the Suicide Project. Some of the most powerful images from the Death and the Maiden series are the gentle and brooding paintings of Death presenting a peace-offering to the Maiden, often in the form of a dove. While the subject matter is firmly based in the 15th and 16th-century traditions which cast Death as a suitor, several of these gentler pieces are stylistically reminiscent of Edvard Munch's works from the late 1890s, for example *The Dance of Life* and *Jealousy*. In *Death Presenting Peace to the Maiden* (1974) Robert uses large areas of indistinct darkness to support a bold composition of tonal peaks, which like the crimson of Death's entrails are vivid but not violent. The morbidity seems moonlit.

In contrast to these dream-like and nocturnal pieces Robert produced several large paintings which were almost floodlit in their horror. Following a trajectory begun with his 1972 watercolour of the three disembowelled Magi, these paintings explore Death as a self-giving gift. The concept finds maximally gruesome expression in *Study For The Magi Presenting His Entrails to The Maiden* (1974). Death's flowing organs resemble a swooning lover, his hands buried in her red hair. What is most disturbing is Robert's choice of a fabulated anatomy over a biologically accurate one. This foray into surrealism was no accident. He knew human physiology from the outside-in from decades of painting nudes and he knew it inside-out from his books, which ranged from Andreas Vesalius to vivid photo collections of forensic pathology. His stylistic choice of surrealism took the word at its deepest meaning: 'sur'-real, over-real, more real than ordinary perception. He paints the howling cadaver with the leg bones of a bird or reptile. Pustules and prolapsed organs billow from the ribs, tendons and tubules conveying a vigour which should *absolutely not* be present in a corpse. Thus the painting achieves a monstrous sensuality; just as the aesthetic weight of our nightmares frequently possess more reality than the feelings of our waking hours. Death spills into life, night into daylight. This is not the horror of what might lie in the dark, but the horror of *night itself* spilling from the inside of daylight.

The diptych *The Putrefaction of Diogenes* (1974) is executed in similar style, with over-real grotesqueries sprouting from the dead Diogenes. The swollen, almost placental, tongue was modelled by a lobe of ox liver. The Maiden appears as a pregnant ghost connecting the two panels, linking the living Diogenes to the dead one. Of all Robert's paintings this perhaps best exemplifies his oft-repeated maxim: 'To paint oneself is to paint a portrait of someone who is going to die, and the same applies if one paints anybody else'. It is almost impossible to look at the image of the living Diogenes for more than a few seconds. The bold horizontal stripe of the background and the colours of his ghastly double drag us away, with hardly time to notice the Maiden. Robert was exceptionally sharp in the use of such visual and psychological devices to make a philosophical point. In this case, the suggestion is that we move so swiftly and inexorably towards Death that we fail to notice that the passage involves life and fecundity. Our condition, described by existentialist philosophers as 'death-bound subjectivity', carries the risk that a thoroughly *morbid* fascination for Death makes a ghost of Life itself. Yet there is more than a little ironic humour in the work. A shadow in the left-hand panel strongly suggests the reversed form of the Maiden pressing her pregnant belly against Diogenes' face as if to listen to the new heartbeat, though he is unaware of her. And while all living matter is sloughing downwards to oblivion in the second panel, Diogenes has if anything perked up, a curious reminder that the objects which outlast us might say *memento vitae* while our skulls howl *memento mori*.

As well as such studio works Robert was immersing himself in the landscape of death by painting in cemeteries. He may also have been reflecting on his personal experience of the relationship between lost love and death. Several diary entries from this period repeat the phrase 'Nostalgic, etc.' in relation to Mouse, and their meetings are often followed by powerful and poignant episodes: 'Friday March 1: Saw Mouse and Jim in his rooms. Nostalgic, etc. Saw Alice and Wolfe shortly before they left for Cornwall. [...] I was visited by "Christmas to Come" and decided to carve and cut my own gravestone, to be laid in the lawn outside my home, as a constant reminder'. The next day, as he made watercolours of tombs in the sprawling necropolis close to Central Park, he heard thousands of human voices 'suggestive of hordes attempting to escape from Hell, or [confined] under the ground'. The mundane explanation for this was Plymouth Argyll supporters suffering another defeat in their nearby stadium; but it was a powerful inspiration, nonetheless.

As Robert laboured on the project, Annie, Terry, Lemon and a host of helpers laboured on The Fool gallery. Much was needed to renovate the building. On top of the physical work and expense there were problems with various City officials who had to be kept on-side. Residents of Clifton Street remembered Robert well, but not all of them fondly. The process would have been far easier had he kept away. In mid-February he went to inspect 'new shop/studio to view, etc. Shop very interesting. Police came, suspecting break-in. All explained [...] Await permission to go ahead from authorities with anticipation' (Diary, 15 February 1974). It did not occur to him that some neighbour – untroubled by the prior activities of Annie or her helpers – had phoned the police due to Robert's involvement. Later that month worries were conveyed to the Council that the ex-Post Office would soon be a hippie commune or shelter for drunks. Robert wrote letters to the relevant offices to clarify his intentions. In a belated moment of clarity he writes in his diary: 'First row with A[nnie]. Must leave shop set-up to her' (Diary, 17 February 1974).

The Vagrancy Exhibition continued to resonate. In March 1974 Robert was visited by the TV presenter Bernard Falk who was keen to interview him and some of the sitters. Robert chose The Bishop and Diogenes as his ambassadors. The situation gave him pause for thought on the relationship he wanted to cultivate with the media. The diary entry is not quite contemptuous:

[Falk of the BBC] wants to make a film about me as painter/social Pnoob, etc. 11 million viewers to his programme. Will film Diogenes and Albert, etc., and me painting/mural/Lord Eliot's, blah blah blah. Emphasised my desire to create a balance between inevitable social preconceptions about my work – and my 'actual' position. Had poo. Considered problems.

Falk and the TV crew arrived on 6 March. The electrical circuits of 25 The Parade were as treacherous as those at Lanreath and Jack Nash had to rig up several extension leads from The House That Jack Built to save the shoot. Robert's poverty must have been apparent, as was that of Diogenes. Albert did not make an appearance. After filming, Falk took Robert for 'an extremely posh dinner at Bella Napoli' – it is not recorded if Diogenes was invited, nor if Falk was embarrassed by spending so much on luxuries while discussing vagrancy. Robert wrote 'Extraordinary waste. But nice. [...] BBC men came to [Priory Road], saw library, children's books/get a better idea of what I'm doing. Listened to Hasidic songs/ Mahler/ Cabaret to consider background music for film, but decided on nothing' (Diary, 6 March 1974).

Robert virtually co-directed Falk's documentary, suggesting locations, selecting characters, highlighting or de-emphasising elements of Plymothian street life and art. One immediate consequence was a small but much-needed financial boost. The documentary was not to air for several weeks but word must have circulated that Robert's works were worth buying before prices rose: 'Mr Roberts came to shop, wanted to buy paintings. Mr Sherrington came to shop, wanted to buy watercolour of Diogenes, £25' (Diary, 8 March 1974). On the 15th Annie drove almost 250 miles to London delivering drawings and watercolours, presumably to buyers offering more than the petrol money. He received a commission from the landlord of The Shakespeare pub for another large indoor mural. This mural is lost but Robert kept notes on the theme which centred around the mysterious and possibly non-existent 'School of Night' which fed into his extensive English alchemy notes.

Robert's already chaotic sexual adventures flourished as the Death and the Maiden Project gathered pace and intensity. We recall how the young Aury Shoa was impressed with Robert's ability to stage complex situations at a distance and observe the behaviour of the witting or unwitting participants. Mid-March 1974 was especially busy in this regard as Robert engineered situations with the models Victoria, Francesca, Viv, Elizabeth, and Miranda:

16 – Lord Eliot picks me/Francesca/Miranda up to go to estate, start mural etc. Francesca made up as Pierrot, Miranda as Jester, both very striking. [Returned to Plymouth] gave Monica £10, put off arrangement for tonight. Miranda came back with me. Pleasant evening, etc.

17 – Miranda/Brekky. Francesca came back from Eliot. Amusing developments. Everything according to plan.
Interesting 'open' talk with Miranda and Francesca – curious joy over set-up. Annie back from London.

18 – Annie/Brekky, Viv drove me back from house. Amusing and decadent talk about 'honesty' and 'sex'. Amusing but potentially very dangerous.

Ruti, Myrna Shoa, and her son Nahem came from London to help with the gallery and pose for paintings. Aury had to take care of business at the London Fool but was in frequent contact by telephone. He had done well in business since his St Martin's days and was generous with both money and advice to make sure The Fool in Plymouth would be ready for the exhibition opening. Robert's band of helpers began moving paintings from the Jacob's Ladder site on the Barbican to the new Clifton Street Fool at the end of March 1974. Many of these were the smaller canvases from the Vagrancy Project.

Clifton Street residents were not unanimously delighted by the impending outbreak of culture. One of the first paintings to appear at The Fool confirmed their suspicions: *Portrait of The Bishop and Diogenes Naked* (1973). There were thousands of Robert's works which might have found their way to The Fool. Perhaps the choice was motivated by the oft-misjudged maxim that there is no such thing as bad publicity, or an equally misjudged notion that compulsive moralising about nudity was a thing of the past. The style of painting and the poses are low temperature, far from erotic, presenting the evidence of ageing bodies with honesty and *humanitas*. In terms of what the newspapers describe as 'graphic content' the prudes didn't know how lucky they were. Robert could have taken inspiration from Giacomo Balla's *Dynamism of a Dog on a Leash* (1912) and its multi-legged dachshund to capture his subjects' full range of movement. During the painting process Diogenes and The Bishop had two uncontrollable problems. They couldn't stand still for laughing, and they were laughing because, unused to the sensuality of being observed naked, their penises were running though rapid cycles of inflation and deflation. Considering what Robert could have painted, the work is a paradigm of dignity. After some press attention and haggling with the authorities the canvas was moved to the hind parts of the gallery.

The Fool was imperfectly finished but in good shape by March 1974. Robert aimed to complete the project by June but it was already sprawling. New themes, new ideas, sub-themes, and philosophical tangents multiplied as he worked. New and old lovers complicated the schedule for sitters, and when Maria Ney-Hoch came to visit, Robert was unusually constant, though not of course exclusive, in his attentions, waking up next to her almost consecutively from 28 March until 10 April when she returned to London. In early April he began work on the large and insuperably complex painting *The Judgement of Paris: Death and the Three Graces* (1974). This is a visual maze of false reflections and double echoes dealing with the problems of time and representation that we noted in works as early as *Self-Portrait in Room Number Three* (*c*.1955).

Despite the joyful colours and bright tones of *The Judgement of Paris* it is a disturbing painting. It re-visits the most famous beauty contest in Greek myth, with the winner receiving a Golden Apple from Paris, the nemesis of Troy. Robert is again applying more than paint and uses his knowledge of visual perception, mythology, and psychology to provoke the viewer to thought. Initially it seems The Bishop is looking in through the Studio window, until we realise that the mythical Golden Apple he is offering is some way forwards of the glass. Looking to the main group we see that The Bishop is doubled, and the gold of the apple has been rhymed with Pat Parker's vest. Which of the Graces she or Monica represents is a mystery, and it is uncertain if there are three Graces or two, with the doubled Grace on the extreme right apparently wearing Diogenes' coat. The doubling of Terry Goldstone is especially threatening: he floats like a vengeful ghost who has emerged from a mirror. But our assumptions about what is a mirror, what is a painting, and what is a painting inside a painting are continually confounded. When we return to the left-hand side of the canvas to consider The Bishop offering the apple, the available interpretations collapse. Like Paris himself the viewer is presented with an impossible decision.

Why *this* painting as the centrepiece of the exhibition? The classical theme had inspired countless interpretations in the Western Art canon from the late Middle Ages onwards – painted by Lucas Cranach (The Elder) alone over twenty times. Another version by Peter Paul Reubens in the National Gallery collection would have been well-known to Robert. But, just as significantly, the theme had proved a perfect illustration for radical critic John Berger's re-interpretation of the nude in art and the 'male gaze' in his 1972 TV series *Ways of Seeing*. The TV program and the accompanying book feature both Cranach's and Reubens's versions. 'Behind every glance is a judgement', states Berger. 'Aesthetics when applied to women is not as disinterested as the word Beauty might suggest'.

However we try to establish a visual frame of reference for Robert's painting, whether we choose to think of the apple being offered via a mirror, painting, or window, the image must break. For all its stylistic differences, the philosophical impetus of *The Judgement of Paris* has strong affinities with *Mouse With Wool*. The doubled paintings 'in' the painting must already have been completed, and this visual insistence prompts thoughts of Necessity and Fate. As with the apple of Eden, both the possibility and impossibility of a 'free choice' carries Death with it. Aphrodite accepted the apple from Paris on the promise of the gift of one woman's beauty: unknown to Paris this was also the gift of destruction and death for all of his home city of Troy. The Jewish and Greek mythologies resonate richly with Robert's 1972 notes quoted at the opening of this chapter: 'We would not know love were we to live indefinitely', and 'The active, passive, neutral principles present their own future to their own past'. In years to come

Robert explored these ideas in relation to Jung's archetypes, mythological time, and Nietzsche's doctrine of 'The Eternal Return'.

Self-exiled from London's cultural life, the new televised arts programmes provoked responses from Robert as much as his regular trips to London galleries. Berger stated that he wrote *Ways of Seeing* as a response to Kenneth Clark's monumental BBC2 series *Civilisation*, broadcast in May 1969. Robert's diaries, starting in 1974, contain many clippings from the Radio Times programme listings, often accompanied by reminders to get himself to a companion's home in time to watch a show. Most of these prestigious TV series were accompanied by well-illustrated publications. In the case of the *Civilisation* book, there is a compelling piece of evidence that Robert relied upon it for *The Burial of John Kynance* (1970) – note the completion date. The painting is an homage to Gustave Courbet's *Burial at Ornans*. But that painting has more than forty figures in it; *'Kynance'* just eleven, not counting Death. It can hardly be argued that Robert wasn't up to the task of painting a multitude – he did that with the two dozen or so sitters for *The Apotheosis of Albert Fisher* (1973). It seems that the answer is in the way the illustration of *Burial at Ornans* is cropped to fit the page in the Clark book, with just the central portion of the canvas being shown and the few figures at the graveside book-ending the cropped composition. The resemblance to the *'Kynance'* canvas is striking.

Berger's Marxist critique of the mystification of the work of art as a market commodity are closely paralleled in Robert's 1976 project 'Paintings Designed To Make Money: The Diogenes Con Show and The Masterpiece Museum', his humorous and ironic investigation of the relationship between art and commerce. Berger's influence persists through other paintings featured in his book, in particular, Frans Hals' group portraits of *The Regents and Regentesses of the Old Men's Almshouses*, which later inspired two key works in Robert's 1979 Project on Old Age.

Exploring the heights of myth and philosophy did nothing to cancel out Robert's fascination with the gangland scene. Plymouth had few underworld 'firms' to match those of London but several Dartmoor inmates known to Robert had served time with Frank 'The Mad Axeman' Mitchell and other criminals of the most serious and organised type. Robert was visited by two brothers, local men of renown keen to commission a painting. This they explained would be a touching scene of a panther being mauled by to death by an English bull terrier. They returned later in the day to show Robert various weapons (Diary, 14 May 1974). It was a day of menace. There is no reason to suppose it was anything but coincidence, but underneath he writes: 'Visited by Black Sam. BIG TROUBLE. Burnt his mother's house down. She is in Paternoster House, Efford Lane [a terminal care unit]'.

Two days later the police called into the Studio. Whatever friction Robert had with the authorities, they recognised and sometimes respected the fact that he took a genuine interest in the city's 'invisible people'. One of the vagrants had been killed. 'I thought it was Vernon. Showed me photographs of badly mutilated man [...] seems to be some confusion about identity' (Diary, 16 May 1974). The police speculated the victim might have been dragged underneath a car for some distance, making it impossible to determine whether he was dead or injured before the impact. No driver stopped or reported the incident, thus it was anybody's guess as to how accidental or otherwise the killing might be – or if indeed a car was involved, though the body was so mangled it was unlikely to have deposited itself in the alley-way behind Bath Street Mission. In the following days Robert was visited by another of the dossers, Thin John, who referred to 'a curious paranoid vendetta' between Vernon and some local taxi drivers. Robert redoubled his efforts to establish 'Holiday Inns'. He commandeered an empty City Council building and 'arranged a large van to collect (in instalments) 14 mattresses from Mount Gould Hospital and 40 bedside lockers' (Diary, 20 May 1974). The hope was that anywhere would be safer than the streets, although Harmonica Jim would soon prove this wrong.

And so throughout 1974 Robert's reputation as Plymouth's go-to 'social Pnoob' grew, for better and for worse: 'Visited by John Arnott [a Probation Officer] re: Rob L., 15-year-old animal mutilator and thug. Could I put him to work?' (Diary, 21 May 1974). It is unlikely Robert could offer anything appropriate to this youth's skill set, and hopefully didn't suggest people who could. 'One of the ... brothers came by to see about the panther/terrier rubbish. Now wants baboon vs. terrier. Better have it done in a week or so' (Diary, 30 May 1974). The phrase suggests that this painting actually exists.

The new Holiday Inn stung the City Council's pride. A senior social worker telephoned Robert to discuss it. Robert wrote:

> Looks like more response has been effected through this venture than anything before – including [the Vagrancy] exhibition. Imperative the Derry [slang for a sleeping-place, also called a 'skipper'] is looked after.

228

Discussed 'death' of Vernon Stevens/ Steptoe/ Fagin/ G.F. Parks. Both of us are unconvinced by the police 'identification'. VERNON is still missing. Police seem to be taking an unusual interest in this case. All rather odd. (Diary, 22 May 1974)

The huge and sustained pressures of raising children without help from their fathers, looking after the dossers, and the intensely dark modelling sessions exhausted Monica's health. She was hospitalised for several days in May and Robert took Reuben to live at Priory Road for a while. Reuben was not unwelcome, but the diaries give no indication Robert did much to alter his schedule to make time for the boy. It seems Annie was largely left in charge of such matters as getting children to school while Robert wrote and read and painted, often until four in the morning. On 28 May Robert records that Annie made breakfast – as usual – and as he left the house he encountered:

A curious grave/shrine on the lawn. Something wrong. Went to [25 The Parade]. Harmonica [Jim] very aggressive. Knew trouble was on the way the moment I clapped eyes on him this morning. Followed him to CH-1 [Jacob's Ladder]. Observed him collecting paper and lighting fire. Am sure it was psychologically necessary for him to avenge 'the flies' and 'the shit' through a form of sympathetic magic. Extremely interesting proof of intense emotional religious response to fire. Had to 'shop' him. Expecting police visit.

Harmonica was causing exactly the kind of problems Robert needed to find answers to in his dialogue with the City authorities, who now engaged with him on a semi-formal level. They sometimes invited him to their offices for advisory meetings (Diary, Friday 31 May). The mental strain must have been enormous for Robert as he pushed the Death and the Maiden Exhibition towards completion while placating the representatives of law and order:

Police came to tell me that Harmonica Jim has been attracting young children to the skipper (8-year-old girl, etc.). An official complaint has been lodged with the police. Warned me that if Harmonica Jim remains at the skipper they will close the building down immediately. Monica in hospital again (kidneys), Reuben with Maria. (Diary, 9 June 1974)

Robert does not record how or if he squared the circle of the Harmonica Jim problem, which is as close as one would like to image as a limit-case for his 'All are Welcome' axiom. Harmonica Jim was possibly a sexual hazard to children, a known pyromaniac, and likely to force the closure of at least one Holiday Inn. The common objection that 'such people should be allowed to live somewhere, but not next door to me' is far from vacuous: it is likely that in this instance Robert would concede that society must be defended, especially the part of society with a temptingly combustible private library.

Far from leaving things to Annie at The Fool, Robert was busy making sure things were 'organised so that a more authoritative and personal arrangement can be designed' (Diary, 5 June 1974). He finalised the exhibition poster, an ingenious German Renaissance design of a handsome gentleman, which when rotated became a winged skull with flames billowing from the mouth. With the help of Jim Pascoe his huge volume of research was edited down to form an exhibition booklet of almost 40 pages which remains a first-rate contribution to the philosophy and iconography of death. The quality of this work is consistently as worthy as any doctoral thesis.

Robert also found time to visit London for his mother's birthday and took some suitable paintings as gifts. Alice was mentally strong as ever but her bodily health was declining. Bernard, Johnny, and Robert took her for a meal and then, duty visit done, Robert attended to the business of relieving Johnny of a copy of Robert Fludd's metaphysical work *Utriusque Cosmi*. The following day he spent with Pat Parker: 'Saw Mahler, National Gallery, Duccio, Cézanne, Foyles, Royal Academy summer exhibition, Book café, stayed at Zvia's place – with Parky' (Diary, 14 June 1974).

Returning to Plymouth on the 15th he began several new and fairly large paintings in an attempt to meet the hard target he had set himself: *The Times* of 27 June ran an article in which Robert boasted there would be 200 paintings in the exhibition. In early July he arranged his notes for the appendix to the Death and the Maiden booklet. It is impossible to estimate how much labour was involved in sourcing this obscure alchemical material prior to the existence of the internet. He selected and edited the historical images for the booklet and made final changes before delivering it to the now-paid printers. From the middle of July onwards he was too busy painting to make anything but the briefest diary entries. On 19 July he framed and hung paintings at The Fool with Annie and Terry. They 'worked all through the night until 11am' (Diary, 14/15 July 1974).

The 200 paintings Robert aimed to exhibit were not in place but it is astounding to consider what he had created in under half a year. The exhibition itself contained 30 major pieces and 50 smaller studies. There were many more pieces which did not fit the overall design of the exhibition in the available space. Then there were the extensive research notes which surpassed what many PhD students might achieve in a year. The exhibition opened on 25 July 1974.

Critical reception was good as far as it went, but the exhibition received far less press attention than its labour deserved. In fairness to the 'art and entertainment' journalists, even with the best will in the world they would struggle to convince a lazy editor that humane intellectualism was better than a story about Britain's largest marrow. Robert's concerns about the 'inevitable social preconceptions' and 'misunderstandings' in the media were justified: the intense compression of information required by newspapers risked pushing readers towards a total non-understanding of Robert's intentions.

'A Shocker from the Mural Man' – was the headline penned by an unnamed reporter for the *Sunday Independent*. The writer had the benefit of a preview some weeks earlier and needed to tell the public how they would feel about the works, should they see them. 'A disturbing exhibition [...] it will shock some people. Others will say the paintings are obscene and pornographic. Many will enjoy them. A few will understand them.' The paintings themselves are described as 'vivid, sensual, amusing, sad, and brutal'. The quote from Robert seemingly accepts the compromise between shock-horror publicity and the seriousness of his intentions:

> People down here might be shocked by this first one. I expect it. It will be considered objectionable by some, but for those who consider it obscene I would ask first of all if the philosophic issue has been clearly understood and if it has, can they think of a more successful image with which to convey it. If they can, I will be in their debt. (*Sunday Independent*, 7 July 1974)

Robert went on to make the Socratic point that if people 'inevitably' find his material irritating, such irritation is a well-intentioned provocation to enriching their lives. Whether Robert needed this kind of short-form publicity or not, he mainly desired it. He detested the mauling of his ideas, the salacious reduction of his work and behaviour and his person to crude cartoons. But for the rest of his life he walked a tightrope between using journalists and being used by them. The article in the *Sunday Independent* was not a terrible result given the obvious constraints: if the tone of reportage was set before the exhibition opening, at least Robert had some active part in setting it.

What was highly significant about the Death and the Maiden Project was something no journalist could be expected to see, which was how far Robert had travelled as an artist and thinker since the Vagrancy Project. 'Vagrancy' was an almost entirely empirical documentation of a social situation in a particular city, at a certain time. Death and the Maiden marked a huge expansion of attention, an expansion of consciousness itself towards the edge, towards Death. Peculiarly for Robert, the canvasses became smaller. This cannot credibly be explained by the constraints of the proposed venue. Robert seldom worried about where a huge canvas might be hung or even if it was possible to get it through a doorway without butchering it. More likely was the consideration that he was playing a numbers game, aiming for 200 works, accompanied by the thought that 'The Old Gentleman' is never far behind us. And perhaps the meticulous record keeping of pictures sold hint at a new pragmatism regarding income.

There is a unity of style to the Vagrancy paintings. In Death and the Maiden this unity is decisively abandoned in favour of a variety of approaches. We noted the visceral surrealism of *Study for Wise Man (Magi) Presenting his Entrails* and *The Putrefaction of Diogenes* in contrast to the softer more lyrical images of works such as *Death Presenting Peace*. The vast array of watercolours, pen-and-ink studies, and smaller oil canvasses for this project are so varied it is not obvious that they are the work of one artist. Expressionist and post-Impressionist gestures reminiscent of Matisse, Munch, and Nolde appear alongside delicately cross-hatched line drawings and watercolours redolent of the imagery of Hans Baldung Grien (1480–1545), the Northern Renaissance master of macabre *memento mori*. Robert was not 'playing with styles' in an attempt to find a single 'mature' set of techniques which would be adequate to his artistic vision. On the contrary, the variation in genres and visual grammar is a kind of meta-palette in the service of the project as a whole. It was now over a decade since his virtuoso copies of Caravaggio and Rembrandt. He was no longer 'painting from' the history of art. But he was painting *with* the history of art, and all the ideas implied by such an endeavour. It takes an immense and difficult dilation of the mind's eye, but we should take him at his word that each 'individual' work achieves its full value and meaning only in relation to the entire project.

The project was also shown for ten days from 25 November 1974 at the Wilmas Galleries in Coventry. In between the shows, the most enduringly popular painting 'in' Project 2 was painted – *Diogenes and Belle at Prayer with Chairs* (1974) – when Belle Pecorini made an unannounced visit to Plymouth. 'Also known as *The Red Chair*, it was submitted to the Royal Academy Summer Exhibition as *Diogenes and Belle Kneeling Behind Two Chairs* on 17 Feb 1975 and then figured in *The Daily Telegraph Magazine* Number 548 May 30 1975'. [30]

Around two metres square, *Diogenes and Belle at Prayer With Chairs* evokes a dreamlike, paradoxical space. It is highly intimate yet so spacious it might be a landscape. It is in several senses 'an interior' though obviously not Robert's studio or anywhere else he spends time, for it is bare and tidy. Belle Pecorini and Diogenes kneel behind two chairs. One is blood red, almost glowing from within. The second is of unpainted wood and supports a human skull. The skull in turn supports the humblest of vessels, a disposable plastic cup; the standard tea conveyance from Joe Prete's café. With these simple elements Robert stages a complex dance of ideas and perspectives.

The spatial geometry is fractured in a very wily manner. As in *Mouse With Wool* the multiple perspectives are partly modelled on Duchamp's *Chocolate Grinder*, and in this painting Robert uses the tilting planes of reference to create a sense of the viewer moving closer to the praying figures. His line and tone work is outstanding here, for although the figures are hidden by the chairs and their thick, heavy clothing, the image captures their hidden body language. Diogenes seems stoical as ever, eyes hooded by his hat, arms hanging loosely in an attitude of relaxed rather than rapt contemplation. Very little of Belle is seen, but the gesture of clasped hands is conjured entirely successfully by the outline of her coat. This is clearly a silent moment where calm bodies and quiet minds turn their attentions inward: an inwardness echoed by the foreground skull. Here the tilt of the perspective draws the eye downwards into the plastic cup, suggestive of a funnel or a trepanation: perhaps there is a way of peering into the thoughts of death.

The rim of the cup is the highest tonal point of the painting and seems linked to an analogous zone on Belle's living skull, an area which is tonally close to the darkest point of the painting. It seems likely that *Diogenes and Belle at Prayer with Chairs* is linked to a watercolour study for another canvas work in this project, *The Burial of Monica Quirk and Belle Pecorini*. The watercolour depicts three sinister figures, shadows made substantial, lowering the lifeless bodies of the women into a circular hole atop a giant skull. The idea of the skull as a container for experience, the terminus of all our sensations and memories, haunts much of Robert's work.

The saturated colours and high tones are only part of the painting's liveliness, a liveliness infused with fecundity and calm like a harvest scene or the golden hour of a mild autumn day. Large areas of the canvas are given entirely to colour fields: the carpet on which they kneel is deliberately inchoate, but if one were to think in representational terms, it closely resembles a cloudscape against which the chairs and figures float. There is also a wild vigour to Diogenes' beard and locks, and Belle's hair of glorious gold sings out against the deeper ones of the under-painting: the blood red gloss of the chair reflects its own structure in a way which suggests one can see through its solidity.

The concept 'seeing through' is a way of exploring the entire painting, a way of seeing things related to the seeing of *nothing*. The painting of an *absence*, using the metaphor of an empty chair, is a recurring leitmotif in Robert's work dating back at least as far as the London studio years. Robert is as ever concerned with 'seeing through things', decoding the surfaces of signs to look further into the world as in Nietzsche's 'Where does man not stand on an abyss? And is not all seeing – a seeing of abysses?'.[31] One wonders whether Robert considered his compulsion to paint as a mode of prayer, a devotional act. If prayer is the near-universal call to connect with 'the other side', or the 'outside', or the innermost reality, then Robert's inquiries and methods are candidates for the title. And he had a deep acquaintance with the process of 'seeing through' what is apparent to what is not present, but entirely real. The empty chairs which feature in so many of his images are related to his experiences at the Hotel Shemtov, where an empty chair in the dining room almost always announced that one more life had ended.

We see through the ribs of the chair which holds the skull. In the gaps between those ribs the brain – not the eye – conjures the body and clasped hands of Belle. And if we continue on our journey of 'seeing through' just a little way further, it is almost as if we are looking through the body of Belle at some internal, distant, and nocturnal landscape, set within her outline. Robert later uses the technique more overtly in several paintings, most notably *Man Watching Woman Walk Away* (1977, Jealousy Project). Again, Duchamp is a point of reference here. Beyond the suggestion of the dark interior landscape, I must resort to poetry. For reasons which may be entirely subjective I cannot help but link the painting to Rilke's words: 'Only, at certain times, the veil of the pupils slides up soundlessly – an image enters in, rushes down through the stillness of the limbs, plunges into the heart – and is gone'.[32]

Robert took the trouble to include 'a small display from a variety of the painter's sketch-books dealing with the Death and the Maiden theme. They are exhibited in order to clarify or emphasize certain aspects of the present collection and to indicate the various associations'. After the exhibition these works on paper were mounted into a linen and leather-bound folio on heavy cartridge paper: the large 16 x 24 inch folio *Death and the Maiden, Paintings: R.O. Lenkiewicz*. The exhibition price list states in capital letters 'THESE STUDIES ARE NOT FOR SALE'. They included *Death Lies With The Maiden as a Child* – still discretely omitted from posthumous exhibitions of facsimiles of the folio – or the study of The Bishop grappling with a 3-foot phallus, or Jeny Bremer, skirt lifted on the streets of Amsterdam as 'Death inserts his tongue into Love's anus'. Fortunately, an iconic watercolour of the study of Diogenes in his corrugated pipe/barrel dwelling was also not for sale. The image is captioned: 'But there is no "Woman" in the picture. (It depends upon the sex of nature – and upon the sex of man)'. This is the scene which Robert is seen painting on the cover of *The Daily Telegraph Magazine* (Number 454, 13 July 1973), which bears the caption: 'THE ARTIST AS ENTERTAINER ... PHILOSOPHER ... AND SOCIAL CONSCIENCE. Plymouth's portrait painter.'

Two appearances on *The Daily Telegraph Magazine* cover in as many years. Could national fame be far behind?

15.1 & 15.2 The poster and gallery handout used at The Fool in 1975 for Project 6.

15.3 In May 1975, paintings from The Masterpiece Museum were shown at the Blenheim Gallery in London, including the trio of self-portraits with Courbet, Van Gogh, and Rembrandt respectively.

236

15.4 Diogenes stands in front of *Diogenes and Belle at Prayer with Chairs* (1974) with two studies from The Diogenes Con Show, 1974.

15.5 Diogenes serving tea at The Fool, 1974. A portrait of Ruti Cohen and Robert's daughter Laila, born in September 1973, hangs on the wall.

Love and Romance exhibition at the Reynolds Gallery in 1975.

15.6 The poster for Project 4, based on the work *Lovers in Joe's Café*, 1975.

15.7 'Barbican Boys' in the gallery entrance with Andy at the rear, who modelled for *Orpheus & Eurydice (below, top right)* in Project 4.

15.8 Project 4 at the Reynolds Gallery, 1975. The diptych *(lower left)* has Robert and Monica as *Two Humans or John Donne and Anne More*.

15.9 Upper row: *And She Dreams of Faraway Lovers, Lelya on the Cross with Peselino's Saints, Francesca with Grunewald's Christ in Cranach's Landscape, Belle with Mantegna's Dead Christ in Bellini's Landscape, Human Heart.*

15.10 A few works from Death & The Maiden were also shown, including *'The decay of love/the putrefaction of Diogenes'* (top right).

239

15.11 Paintings in the Barbican studio, 1976.

Left to right:
Portrait of Jeny Bremer, An Allegory of Folly (1972), *Mr. Fisher With Clown Doll* (1972), *Study of Pat Parker* (1972).

15

Masterpieces, Money, and Mental Handicap

'At forty-five, I want to paint a masterpiece and save Modern Art from Chaos [...] Cézanne is very popular at the moment, but in time to come Meissonier will sell for much, much, more [...] Well, there you are,' he would say after an outburst of this kind, 'You've got your money's worth. Time's up now.' (Salvador Dali quoted in *The New York Times* by John Russell, 24 January 1989)

During the mid-1970s Robert investigated the relationship between art, time, and money, but this research did not help him organise his life in a more economically rational way. As some locals had feared The Fool become a magnet for wanderers. 'Once he had the downstairs shop in Clifton Street [the] tramps came from far and wide. They knew he was a soft touch – no sooner had Robert made a tenner than they'd be lining up for a handout' (Monica, in *Robert Lenkiewicz: Self-Portraits*, p. 24). Visiting during the summer of 1974 Aury compared The Fool to the mythical town of Chelm where Pnoobs and *schlemiels* play out their roles in life's tragi-comedy.

And as other locals had hoped, it became a centre for aesthetic education. In addition to his visits to prison Robert regularly taught at the Charles Street School. Paid teachers such as Mr Chapman and Mr Ward were 'sympathetic, if not enthusiastic' about Robert's ambitions (Diary, 6 May 1974). Their ambivalence is understandable. Robert was a great resource and worked for free but it was obvious that his skills and erudition were far in advance of any school-teacher and the last thing the staff needed was further erosion of their authority. Robert noted problems with vandalism and 'inadequate class structure' (Diary, 6 June 1974). For one whose life was in such disorder, the latter phrase is an interesting hint at how systematic his approach to teaching was, at least in regard to painting. Public opinion concerning Robert and his benevolent or baneful influence intensified. Aury recalls Robert's studios in the London days were populated with 'a huge diversity of human life, from junkies, prostitutes, homosexuals, bisexuals, extra-sexuals' (Aury, in *Demon or Delight*, 1996).

241

The visitors he encouraged at 25 The Parade and The Fool were similarly diverse. His encouragement mainly came via genuinely non-judgemental interest, such that a large and very masculine cross-dresser popping in for a chat did not faze him in the least. Few topics signal a fundamental difference in character types than that of sexuality. Robert's amoralism was risky, and the aesthetic education taking place at The Fool gallery was sometimes at the edge of acceptability.

In the 1980s Robert told me that when a group of teenage boys inquired what a clitoris was, he asked a nude model who was present to show them. This she did and the mystery was solved without embarrassment or confusion. Word reached the boys' parents who were 'fortunately all earthy working-class types' with no axes to grind, but Robert added 'there would have been hell to pay' if anybody had been morally outraged. A moment of well-intentioned instruction might have landed Robert and the model on the sex offenders' register, and newspapers would take the most damaging and salacious view. They were already recycling and embroidering old 'news' in a manner which utterly degraded Robert's labours. An article with the title 'Down and Out' from August 1974 can be quoted in its entirety:

> An artist stuck a fig leaf on his latest picture yesterday to save the blushes of Plymouth's elderly. The portrait of a naked tramp was the centrepiece of Bob Lenkiewicz's exhibition – but so many elderly people complained to the police that he stuck a fig leaf over the offending parts, and left a note on the leaf saying: 'Lift this if you dare.'

Next to the clipping Robert wrote 'Fictional rubbish in the Mirror/Guardian today' (Clipping dated 1 August, Diary entry 4 August 1974). This compression of serious inquiry into titillation became the news industry benchmark for much 'Lenkiewicz appreciation' in the decades to come. Robert was not deterred by such trivialisation and throughout 1974 worked on a project which contained a sustained joke about his fall into provincial obscurity: 'Paintings Designed to Make Money – The Masterpiece Museum and the Diogenes Con Show'. Recall that Robert's earliest inspirations contained 'provocations to thought' on the economy of truth and art, most notably Charles Laughton as Rembrandt.

However right or wrong it might be, the beggar's idea seems simple enough. But that movie scene and its subsequent redemptive schmaltz raises profound questions about the social, personal, spiritual, and economic value of art. Mercantile Amsterdam was a hot-house of early capitalism and a perfect historical backdrop to such questions, but the Anglo-American art world of the 1960s and 1970s had the same operating principles. 'Paintings Designed to Make Money' was in some ways a comedy after the darkness of Death and the Maiden. But it was a serious comedy exploring the themes of time, death, and money. Aside from a means of getting more books Robert was interested in money mainly because of its symbolic functions. According to Johnny, Robert condoned Sigmund Freud's analysis that 'money matters are treated by civilised people in the same way as sexual matters – with the same inconsistency, prudishness, and hypocrisy'[33], shrouded in shame and taboo. Robert was in even greater agreement with Ferenczi, who interpreted money as abstract, desiccated, deodorised faeces. The punk rocker shitting coins in the *Last Judgement* mural of 1983 (formerly on The House That Jack Built) confirms this as a long-held view.

Robert did not dislike filthy lucre or the people who, like Perry Eliot, just happened to have plenty of it. But he abhorred the adoration of money, and detested people who tried to use it as a lever to manipulate him. Diary entries from the 1970s describe egotistical businessmen and collectors as 'psychotic fascists' and 'vulgar idiots'. The upper-middle classes seemed to be his main target. Here is a typical encounter:

> Couple from Bristol came to shop: inquiries re. Portrait of Company Director. How much, how long, etc. 'Oh well you see if it takes so little time they may not feel they're getting their money's-worth. We've already considered one or two [Royal Academy painters] but their prices bear no comparison to yours' – blah-blah – puke.

Robert's response:

> £40 for one hour, none of the ritual portrait painting shit, £40 for one hour for you ... £40 for one hour for the Queen.

Reflections on the relationship between time and artistic value featured largely in the Paintings Designed to Make Money Project. In what was confusingly known as 'The Free World' during the Soviet era, the dominant evaluation of human worth was the hourly wage. Persons 'free' from wage relationships, such as vagrants, the mentally ill, and the very old, become socially and politically invisible. Along with very beautiful women,

243

these were precisely the kind of people in whom Robert took an interest. We will gain a better insight into what Robert was aiming at in this phase of his development if we spend a little time exploring the nature of his foe, the 'art market'.

For most Western economists of the time, the overwhelming 'proof' of capitalism's superiority – even in the vilest dictatorships of South America – was that it converted human life-time into consumable products more efficiently than the Soviet and Chinese models. Without banging a Marxist drum, Robert used the project to foreground the irrational brutality of this evaluation of human creative labour. 'The Diogenes Con Show' element contained over 30 paintings, all but one of which had titles linking time and money: *This Study Took 8 Minutes £40*, *This Study Took 30 Minutes £90*, *This Study Took 1 Hour 18 Minutes £100*.

Contra one narrow view of the 1960s and 1970s as a playground for beatniks and freedom-loving hippies, many artists were happy to sell the putative 'edge' to the centre. The revolution of Surrealism had been tamed to mere commerce thanks largely to Salvador Dali, whose name was contemptuously anagrammed to 'Avida Dollars' by Andre Breton as early as 1939. Warhol began as a commercial artist, and by the 1970s openly stated that 'business art' was the highest form of art. This is a safe cultural bet in any land where the measure of artistic success is the work's financial value. Historians such as Frances Stonor Saunders have established beyond doubt that the CIA funded foundations and galleries to control the 'revolutionary' leading edge of the art markets. Head of the CIA International Organizations Division, Tom Braden, sums up the Devil's Bargain of the 'Free World':

> We wanted to unite all the people who were writers, who were musicians, who were artists, to demonstrate that the West and the United States was devoted to freedom of expression and intellectual achievement. [...] I think [the I.O.D.] played an enormous part in the Cold War [...] In order to encourage openness we had to be secret [...] It takes a pope or somebody with a lot of money to recognise art and to support it [...] After many centuries people say, 'Oh look, the Sistine Chapel, the most beautiful creation on Earth!' It's a problem that civilisation has faced since the first artist and the first millionaire or pope who supported him. And yet if it hadn't been for the multi-millionaires and popes, we wouldn't have had the art. [34]

This plea for cultural unity under the micro-management of the rich and powerful would have been welcome in the 'fascism' section of Robert's library of irrational beliefs. We include it for two reasons: firstly because Robert himself took an interest in the CIA's 'culture wars' (Diary, 21 March 1976) and secondly, because it encapsulates so much of what Robert's art and life was dedicated to resisting. The idea that popes and millionaires are not only the *best* arbiters of artistic value, but also the *real* source of human creativity, is pure delusion. But the dogma did not fall from the skies. It is a collective delusion imposed by people upon themselves, with a social function that is not very different from archaic human sacrifice to make the crops grow, or the witch-hunting crazes of Europe. One of the strongest implications of Robert's lifelong resistance to top-down authority is that we should not value art because it serves God, the State, the Market: nor even the abstract ideals of 'freedom of expression' and 'intellectual achievement'. Those too are idols. Robert's position was far closer to that of Nietzsche: art is valuable only in as much it is necessary for living a fuller, stranger, and more beautiful life.

Thus throughout the autumn of 1974 Robert planned Paintings Designed to Make Money as a critique of the socially accepted benchmarks of artistic worth. The idea of a painting as a trading token or investment was his most obvious object of derision, but the entire pantheon of 'guarantees of value' comes under sustained and humorous attack. He derided the 'high ideals' of the artist as moral exemplar, the drive to be 'understood' by critics and one's peers, the hope of being remembered either as an individual genius or as part of a celebrated artistic movement. The negative part of the critique is scathing. His positive thoughts on the topic are wide-ranging but not in the least nebulous. He describes the political economy of art as an extension of the drive to own another person's productive power. In this respect today's 'art market' combines elements of archaic magic with the technologies of advertising, with the aim of extracting the life force or 'soul' from an artist:

> The innuendo of the 'masterpiece' is that its creator has transcended both himself and Society, that it is in some sense, prophecy. If the item has been purchased, then we are reminded of a slave-trader who has been wily enough to buy 'good stock'. Such images develop like institutions or minor religions imbued with qualities that we conspire with. The 'masterpiece' can be seen as an abstracted extension of the 'hero',

and its function in Society operates as an amulet or talisman. (Robert, in the exhibition notes for Paintings Designed to Make Money, 1974)

His thoughts on the relationship between magical beliefs and contemporary society had been focussed throughout 1974, when the nation suffered a general reaction to William Friedkin's movie *The Exorcist*. This Robert viewed on a visit to Aury in London on the 23 April, almost immediately upon its UK release. He was less interested in the movie than the moral and religious panic it created. The diaries contain dozens of news clippings which chart and to some extent fuel the hysteria. Robert's views on the metaphysics of magic will be explored in a later chapter. For now we note that despite his constant refrain that he was responsible for nobody and that 'altruism' was a pathology, he was concerned enough about the likely impact of the movie upon Monica to be insistent that she not see it.

The centrepiece of Robert's exhibition concerned the relationship between making money and possession by spirits of a very material sort. *Plymouth Mourning Over Its Unfortunates* (1975) is a sombre and terrifying allegory of the triumph of commerce over consciousness. To the left of the canvas lie the prone bodies of three sleeping alcoholics, expressions empty as the bottles in the foreground. In the far room a fourth body lies dead-still beneath more empties. Centre, foreground, in the glorious finery of his official uniform is the City Town Crier, who may indeed be weeping. He is deep in thought or silent prayer. The rich colours of his costume, the high polish of his buckles, buttons, and bell amplify the surrounding squalor.

To the right and behind the Town Crier there rises up a figure resembling a damned soul. The flesh tones are rotten, but this head carries the only lively emotions on any face in the painting. Robert has captured such stress in the muscles of the forehead and neck that it seems as if the eyes and mouth are being stretched further open in the dawning realisation of guilt or horror. With a gruesome visual pun the raised right arm of one sleeper melds into the left arm of this anguished ghost, suggesting a collector of severed heads who possesses and is possessed by the spirits of his victims. The effect is heightened by the disembodied face floating over his heart and the bearded head hovering in his bowels.

The figure of the Town Crier serves a double role in history and the painting. During the centuries in which rumour and hearsay could cause murderous disorder, the Town Crier was the sovereign authority shouting official truths about local witches, Jews, Flemish weavers, or the foreign powers whose galleons were only 45 minutes away. He was also a fore-runner of the food standards inspector with the task of announcing what was fit to eat and drink, a pillar of the market economy with the right to demand free samples. Alcohol addiction was unlikely to be an issue for the town halls and their representatives so long as the freebies and tax revenues kept rolling in. Their job was to ensure that goods circulating within the system were of *saleable quality*, not to wake people up with a critique of a system determined to make money whatever the human cost. Robert's diaries often record the normalisation of alcoholism in the city, as when walking on the Barbican he saw seven '12-year-old boys drinking large bottles of cider. So sad. So nothing' (Diary, 20 February 1976).

Plymouth Mourning Over Its Unfortunates foregrounds a theme which unites many of Robert's later projects: the ruthlessness and amorality of 'normal' social functioning. This he views as the promotion of one kind of addiction over another, while noting the same evaluation applies to his own elevation of social critique and art over money:

> *The Masterpiece*, or, *Plymouth Mourning Over Its Unfortunates*. Value? Priceless. This complex work conceals a large amount of allegorical symbol, suffice it to say that what is known of its underlying meaning covers the following associations: *The Seven Sleepers of Ephesus*, *The Studio* by Gustav Courbet, social art at its worst, the mythology of sleep, etc. (Exhibition notes, Paintings Designed to Make Money, 1974)

The exhibition opened on 20 January 1975 at The Fool Gallery then moved to the Blenheim Gallery in London in May. In what was by now becoming a pattern, the critical reception was good though muted in the few serious articles, but with merely a trivial mention in most newspapers. Robert never talked down to people, he trusted the public to be intelligent, and the press too, he expected them to be interested and make an effort. And that's great, but sometimes it can be a mistake. When you're putting all that work into an exhibition it's easy to misjudge how quickly people consume things. You put on a banquet but there are a lot of people who still want the McDonald's [version of art and knowledge], so that's their basis of understanding. (Aury, Interview, May 2018)

The ironies of Robert's position were complex. Despite the long shadows of Duchamp and Dada the art market had not yet stabilised its responses to anti-institutional artists. It would be almost another half a century before people were prepared to pay thousands of dollars for works like Carpenter's daubed slogans *Kunst* = *Kapital* and *Die, Collector Scum* (2009). Robert's critique was more nuanced and good humoured, even when conducted quite literally at his own expense: his exhibition notes probably deterred more buyers than they seduced via an amusing but acute 'business diagnosis'.

> This gallery has chosen to acknowledge an aspect of the now forgotten painter Robert O. Lenkiewicz. Though dead only a few years, we have thought it proper to present this small selection in the recognition of the fact that he might as well have been dead for a hundred. [...] In drawing the public's attention to the work of Lenkiewicz, it is not to be assumed that we have formulated any opinions about his products. [...] We know through unpaid bills in the Court Archives that he purchased paints and canvases on a very large scale, and assume therefore, that he was a prolific worker.
>
> There are many similar personalities in the colourful pageant of 'art heroes'. Few share the distinction of achieving so complete an obscurity in so short a space of time. This obscurity must be attributed to some degree to the nature of the work itself. And we can only conclude therefore that his undeniable skill was technically and philosophically obsolete. Today we recognise that those who purchased from him made a mistake. Vainly hoping that they had selected an interesting investment, they were soon to be let down and disappointed by History's indifference to their fantasy.
>
> For this reason we have selected a painter of no consequence today (notwithstanding the alleged stories of his fame and success in his own times), as an indication of the treachery of taste and the futility of treating 'art' as anything other than 'good' or 'bad' business. ('The Painter R.O. Lenkiewicz', Mayfair Gallery notes, 1975)

Once again Robert was busy with other projects before 'The Masterpiece Museum' was hung. Several pieces for the planned 'Love and Romance' and 'Love and Mediocrity' Projects were complete or under way. These projects were themselves cogs in a larger machine, for his ambition was to provide a comprehensive survey of human attractions, interactions, and breakdowns. This would be referred to as the 'Relationship Series' within the projects. By now it appears that the alchemical maxim 'as above, so below' applies to Robert's projects: they were a macrocosm to the microcosm of his sexual and emotional relationships. Mouse Mills observed that 'Robert only really fell in love with what he couldn't have. As soon as he got that full measure of devotion, he wasn't interested' (Mouse, *Robert Lenkiewicz: Self-Portraits*, p. 36). The exhibitions were not entirely formalities, but as soon as Robert felt close to grasping 'the full measure' of the human material in any given Project his attention refocussed on another topic. This sometimes happened long before completion, and as we shall see in the case of 'Observations on Local Education' Robert's relationships with his projects were not always harmonious.

Belle Pecorini returned to Plymouth in the summer of 1974. Robert insists that he was 'calm, friendly, and gently pleased to see her. No traumas. No intense eroticisms' (Diary, 14 August). He records this fact beneath a block-capital headline in thick marker-pen: 'BELLE WALKED THROUGH THE ARCH 12 NOON'. Later in the day he writes 'I am still intensely attracted. But it is easily coped with, thank Christ'. The last note of the day is a rare and poignant thing for Robert: 'Slept on my own. At Barbican'. The obvious implication is that he was hook, line, and sinker in love with Belle and not yet absorbing the shock. When Belle resumed her travels he accompanied her to the airport. When she returned he noted 'God knows what will happen' (Diary, 11 September 1974). The relationship intensified and the diaries frequently record staying up with Belle until the early hours and getting out of bed late, with the occasional reminder 'MUST WORK HARDER' (Diary, 19 September 1974). Robert viewed monogamy as akin to painting with only one colour. He was not about to close off any possibilities with other lovers, but Belle was clearly a strong favourite, as hinted at in an 'aesthetic note' of the period which refers to Belle's creativity in establishing compelling erotic subtleties. Robert would not acknowledge anybody as irreplaceable, but the rare event of him sleeping alone was more than once occasioned by some upset in the Belle situation (Diary, 12 October 1974). The yearning disturbed his nights for years to come: 'Difficult night. Dream re: Belle again' (Diary, 19 February 1976).

As 1974 drew to a close the pregnant but tireless Annie was running The Fool, keeping close accounts, and regularly selling paintings in the manner Robert would not. She arranged for the exhibition to be restaged at the Wilmas Galleries in Coventry on 25 November 1974. Despite her valiant attempts to wean Robert onto a diet of good economic sense, the numbers meant little or nothing to him. Even when presented with written figures showing an income of £70, Robert persists in random acts of charity such as 'Went to Courts, got Tony Prior bailed for £200' (Diary, 2 December 1974).

In mid-December another of the dossers was hit by a car and killed. This time the driver came forwards to explain, but once again the police could not identify the body. They issued a description in the local paper and the suggestion that 'his Christian name was believed to be Wally'. Robert pasted the item in his diary and wrote simply: 'Walter Quiggley' (Diary, 18 December 1974, news clipping unsourced). Another socially invisible candle snuffed out. The next day Robert records carrying bodies of Plymouth's unfortunates off the streets – living ones, but dead drunk – into the relative safety of a Holiday Inn. He began preparations for the 'Cowboys' Christmas Dinner' at Priory Road. There are several blank Diary pages up to and including Tuesday the 31st, where we find two very lonely-looking words: 'My Birthday'.

In early 1975 Dorian was six months into his teens. This according to Robert was the only time that children needed a father. Dorian was unconvinced and came to Plymouth only to see Monica, Mouse, Kath Shannon, and his half-siblings:

He arranged to meet up with me and I remember some other kid being around, not one of his but some street kid. And one of the tramps. The only thing [this tramp] had of value was a ring, I think it was his wedding ring. He'd cut all the skin around it, you could just see bits of the gold showing through this mass of scars. So nobody could steal it. We went to the café, Joe Prete's. It was mainly Robert talking. I think he was trying to impress me, I don't think I meant anything to him, it was just what he did with people, and I remember being quite bored by it. I was a bit of a misanthrope when I was a kid, I wasn't the loveliest character, and I told him how it's not possible to move one hand without moving the other, and he said it's nonsense, but I said I'll prove it to you. I got a box of matches [...] what you've got to do is hold two matches [against the box], balance a match across it, which he did because he has a very steady hand, then break the top match. He balanced it across, hit the top match, and both [the matches he was holding] lit. He just sat there with his fingers welded to the matchbox, looked at me and said 'Ah. I see'. I was impressed. He took it very well. I expected him to scream and throw [the matchbox aside] or something. I don't think you could make a deliberate choice in that situation, when your fingers are on fire, but he just held it and didn't move. After that we got on much better.

Next time I saw him I was about 17, I went down and stayed with Monica, he heard that I was coming down, and I remember getting a message that he had a spot available for me to see him at such and such a time. I thought – why does he think I'm going to go down and see him? If he wants to see me, he can come to me. So there was a bit of a stand-off, but the day before I was due to go back [to London] he did come to see me but ... being an obnoxious little git I saw him for about five minutes then went out to play rugby with [Monica's son] Jimmy. We were dealing with two quite large egos at the time. (Dorian, Interview, June 2017)

Throughout the mid-1970s Robert became stricter about his division of time, often dispensing it in homeopathic doses to people who needed significantly more care and attention. In his defence he was a workaholic, and when a project was in the 'hot phase' he would 'sometimes paint for eight or ten hours at a stretch, one sitter after another. He was relentless, ruthless with himself, really' (Monica, Interview, May 2018). But without wishing to sound prosecutorial, Robert's work rate was one factor in the emergence of what the diaries began to refer to as 'the Reuben situation'. Robert's notes on this are skeletal, but it was obvious to everyone except Robert that the child needed his father's attention: 'Walked to Barbican. Reuben chased after me for a bit. Strange boy' (Diary, 15 February 1976). Reuben provides a vivid picture of the effects of Robert's fragmented life upon those close to him:

Wolfe was very different then; he's very confident and capable now but as a teenager he had a very vulnerable side to him, he felt very clumsy and just not up to it. I find that quite funny because he was very like Robert [...] the two of them saw the silliness of each other, which is probably why they found each other difficult at times.

Monica was in love with Robert all her life, he was the centre of her world in so many ways, and they had a good friendship. Mouse [was in love with Jim Pascoe], a wonderful character, extraordinary man, and I was so fond of him. He was another father figure to me. Jim could be incredibly warm and giving, and sentimental, and kind, and erudite, and just ... a cool dude. Robert was much more a father figure, a strong All-Father like Zeus, who was also difficult to get close to.

[Monica] was very vulnerable, unwell, and had a difficult time in her life ... I was brought up into this culture which was very artistic, all these wonderful personalities. Then she met Peter Finch, who was a stabilising factor, and we moved to Durnford Street. Then we moved to North Hill, Clifton Street, then to Nelson Street. Wolfie was living with Mouse at Lower Compton near the Council offices. It was lovely there, very posh for a council flat. Alice, Becky, Wolfie lived there, and I used to stay there all the time. The Fool had opened by that time. Annie and Peter Finch and Terry Goldstone and John Mayhew's father worked really hard on that. That whole community was a very working-class community.

I started to have problems when I was about 12 or earlier. I felt something was missing, something wrong, and what that was was that I didn't have a father in the house. I'd go and see him, my mum particularly wanted that. He was such a huge personality and so colourful and interesting, he opened the world up to adventure, the wildness of life, a life full of characters and meanings and stories and culture and art [...] but then I was living at home, there were six of us, very chaotic, the stresses of everyday life. And I expected some kind of answer or meaning that would make me understand ... but it wasn't there. The truth is what we really needed was attention, validation, and that's not what Robert was about. He was about himself. He was very much a taker more than a giver in that way. An emotional black hole in that sense. You put yourself into him and had great expectations, but for him to be the way he was he had to be detached, to be an independent artist with no responsibilities. Above all, he had to have no responsibilities, he needed to be free.

I developed an attitude, and that anxiety started to come out in all sorts of ways. I started to steal, to look for validation elsewhere, anywhere, which is quite dangerous. Nothing crazy, but I wasn't getting the care I needed emotionally. I was taking time off school, still had a good relationship with mum and Robert ... but I was starting to behave in ways which confused and disappointed them, and that created stresses in my relationship with Robert. He couldn't or wouldn't help resolve that. Probably couldn't. Over a number of years, certain things happened that put fractures through it all that you never recover from. You deal with it, you come to terms with it. Robert was not good at dealing with it. (Reuben, Interview, May 2018)

The situation could not have been simplified by the arrival of another Lenkiewicz boy-child in the summer of 1975. Many paintings from the 'Love and Romance' Project incorporate the infant Sholem and his mother Annie, but Robert avoids the over-determined Mother and Child references in favour of a hard but (at least occasionally) tender materialism. 'Objects of our affections' are treated as precisely that: objects, no metaphor: 'The aesthetic reaction to, shall we say, the woman, is not necessarily as dissimilar as our aesthetic reaction towards wallpaper, and clothing, and ideologies'. Robert is obviously drawing on themes from Nietzsche's philosophy with its joyful anti-humanism and the titles of several paintings suggest he is not currently a member of the species: *Three Humans in front of the Jewish Bride, Human that Might Be in Love Looking in the Mirror at Night-Time', Human Heart*.

The year 1975 was busy even by Robert's standards. There were visits to London where the National Gallery had loans of work by Rembrandt in January, and a major Renaissance exhibition in August. There was a trip to the Netherlands to see Jeny Bremer and other items of interest and beauty, mostly in the Rijksmuseum and Rembrandthuis. There was the opening of two new relationships which were among his most profound and enduring – Gillian 'Mary' Pearce and Yana Trevail. And another new relationship, which was shorter-lived and vexed by distance but no less intense, with Amelie Cachia from Tunisia. There was the Love and Romance Exhibition accompanied by extensive research notes. Enough fame was accruing that Robert was sought out by the media. Joan Bakewell interviewed him, The Bishop, and Diogenes for the BBC *Summer of '75* programme (*Western Evening Herald*, 18 August 1975; Westward Television, 20 August 1975). And there was in September Robert's marriage to Keiko Nakamura in Hackney, London. This was reported in some quarters as a 'marriage of convenience' and there is something of that; but it was more.

Aury says:

> She had met Robert several times before and she knew of his charisma and eloquence and so forth, she was already curious about him. She had an affection for older men, and Robert was still young but he had this aura of a sage, an intellectual, a man older than his years. Keiko had worked in the studio with Ian [Godfrey, the celebrated ceramicist]. She got his recommendation, got the Arts Council recommendation, but the authorities refused to let her work in England. So we had to do the

usual thing: to find a husband for her. A very sweet, very good-looking boy called Paul said he would do it. But at the last moment he got cold feet – and she was desperate. When I mentioned this to Robert he said – 'I'll do it, as long as she promises that after three years she chases the divorce and I don't have anything to do with the paperwork'.

When I told her, she was delighted. But Robert was a naughty man, he was a tease. She had a relationship with a Jewish New Theatre director, a mama's boy from Somerset, but he wasn't available for marriage [...] so [...] he was at the wedding. I was one of the witnesses, and when the Town Hall official says 'You may kiss the bride' Robert gave her a really deep and passionate kiss, because he knew Brian was there. In no way did it disturb her, she just smiled afterwards. I said to that man Brian: 'You're a schmuck, you have such an interesting woman, you should have married her.' But Keiko was so relieved, so happy, and she kept her word.

I think they were both very touched when she discovered that she did not feel it was just an artefact or artifice that they got married. She felt a connection to him. Partly through my friendship with Robert, and her friendship with me, and partly through experiencing him in different situations. And he unconditionally helped her. Totally unconditionally! It was really very sweet, I felt so pleased it worked out for them both so well. I didn't dream of asking him if he would do it, he volunteered as soon as he heard that Keiko had been let down by this other fellow, and Robert had, I think, recently divorced from Mouse [...] so it was as if he just happened to have a space in his diary. (Aury, Interview, May 2019)

The wedding came shortly before the peak of Robert's preparations for the Love and Romance exhibition, but left no discernible traces in the work. If we had to find one word alone to characterise the paintings of this project, it might be 'earthy' or perhaps 'earthly'. Despite the inclusion of archetypal images which imply transcendence – the crucifixion, the rose in full bloom, references to androgyne myths, and the cult of chivalry – the uniting sensation is that of a thoroughly worldly, truly carnal mystery. According to Robert the veneer of moralising culture demands that all

sex desires should be thoroughly controlled by and under the influence of 'love' feelings [...] There is not a great deal of popular culture mate-

rial dealing with the idea of men and women enjoying sex consciously
without suffering some sort of unspeakable aftermath. The key word is
'consciously'. Unconsciously, the situation seems to be very different.
(Robert Lenkiewicz, *Love and Romance, A Note*, 1975 p. 7)

Under cultural conditions which Nietzsche described as 'the disaster of
monotheism', the old material deities of the Earth, Water, and Winds
largely became the 'repressed' or the 'unconscious' of Western theology.
Sky-gods and planetary spirits had a chance of assimilation as Christian
archangels and saints. Not so the divine forces of fertility in and under the
land, in and under the sea. The very term 'worldly' or 'earthly' became a
token of evil, especially if linked to joys or delights. The vast spectrum of
celestial and marine and chthonic (underworld) divinities was shrunk to
a black-and-white moral cartoon: the Good God versus the Devil. The
Love and Romance Project does not side with metaphysical evil against
the transcendent God but is rather a non-moral, non-metaphysical exploration of the nuanced darkness of our 'earthly delights'.

But it is not just that the earth colours dominate the series of paintings:
there is also a geological element to many of the compositions. Human
forms are pressed under planar surfaces like fossils in shale – whether under blankets (*And She Dreams of Faraway Lovers*) or blank ceilings (*Two
Humans*, left panel) or beneath rustic masonry (*Annie with Rembrandt
...*). In one of the few outdoor scenes (*Francesca with Grunewald's Christ*)
the mass of the earth rises like a wave to embrace the figures. And in *Orpheus and Eurydice* the earth has become the sky, with tombstones stack-
ing against each other over the heads of the lovers. The whole series of
images announces that despite our dreams of transcendent love the earth
has claims upon us and will settle those claims with amoral innocence and
tragic inevitability. The symbolism of the crucified body is used repeatedly; for instance *Lelya On The Cross With Peselino's Saints* and *Belle With
Mantegna's Dead Christ in Bellini's Landscape*.

In Robert's analysis the sexual fork of biology – then later, Death – must
divide the lovers despite their energetic rush towards unity. The image he
chooses for this division is stark. In plans for an exhibition almost mega-
lomaniac in its scale Robert envisages a towering skeleton presiding over
lines of visitors, men to one side, women to the other. He does not seem
aware of what to my mind are obvious resonances with the 'processing and
selection' on the ramps of Auschwitz:

At the end of the year 1977 I intend to present a collection of paintings numbering some two thousand five hundred. [...] The collection will be subdivided as follows: Love and Tragedy, Love and Humour, Love and Romance, Love and Mediocrity. Each of these four will be further divided into four and designed to emphasise a specialised area of academic interest [...]

The layout of the exhibition will be structured as a giant labyrinth, with two entrances, one male, the other female, and a 40ft skeleton pivoting at the sacrum scything over the visitors' heads. The visitors will divide into the appropriate sex and enter the maze.

As they emerge from the exit they will be confronted by a large mirror in which they will see themselves; the mirror will be set at the right height in order that they may then perceive their opposite sex emerge from the other exit. As the couples pass each other to enter their opposite sections and so conclude the circle, they will pass a giant canvas called I LOVE YOU: this canvas will consist of seven hundred life-sized self-portraits. (Love and Romance Exhibition Notes, October 1975)

Public sensitivities have changed since 1975 and Robert's staging might now trigger a social media crusade on behalf of the non-gendered midget community. Setting aside the blunt instruments of the right height and opposite sex and the presumption of couples, the point underlying his planned performance-philosophy event is worth considering. For whether the counterpart in a 'love relationship' is of the 'opposite sex' or not, whether the relationship is exclusive and binary or not, we enter it as we might a maze. The mirror is a hard symbol for two worlds of knowledge which are obviously similar and obviously opposed. Perhaps we should say 'blindingly obviously similar'. For we habitually forget or repress the fact that those two worlds can never touch: the mirror is a plane of tension between not knowing in advance where our passions might lead and a deeper level of knowing precisely that all passion is ultimately doomed. However 'perfect' a reflection may be it has neither temperature nor blood pressure nor any thoughts or feelings about us. It is not 'ours' any more than the other person in the relationship is 'ours'. Like Kafka's mighty guardian at the gates of the law, the reflection does not care whether we stay or go. And it is precisely this mighty phantom of 'love' which we willingly mistake for 'the truth' or an 'opening up of possibilities'. In Robert's analysis it is the most powerful self-deception and severest restriction in regard to both knowledge and 'earthly delights'. This, he reasons, is because our engagement with the 'falling in love experience':

> seems structured in such a way that once it has 'committed' itself to one other person it simply refuses to see the rest. If we find reasonably attractive one in every hundred persons we meet, let us even say one in every thousand, then we are aware that in relation to the present population we are finding strongly attractive and to our personal taste approximately 13 million men and women. By meeting just one of this army of possibilities we can, in many cases, find ourselves satisfied. This may be plain lifelessness or stupidity, but it does seem that many couples find genuine reward in exclusive relationships. A healthy suspicion may be levelled at such behaviour, for its very exclusiveness can so easily exclude the whole of the world. (Love and Romance Exhibition Booklet, 1975)

This thought soon becomes a cornerstone of Robert's thinking on 'aesthetic fascism' – how our strong preference for certain individuals amounts to mass dehumanisation of the excluded – and the social role of addiction. Echoing Nietzsche's dictum that 'the love of any one thing is barbaric: this includes the love of God', Robert draws our attention to the inconvenient fact that rather than being cosmically diffuse, or consciousness expanding, or overflowing with goodwill, the psychology and physiology of 'romantic love' tends towards calcification, jealousy, and enclosure. The idea echoes throughout the paintings in the theme of faces under strata of stone.

The exhibition catalogue lists only 48 works, though this was perhaps due to the limited space at the Barbican's Reynolds Gallery (16–31 October 1975). In November almost double that number found their way to The Fool in Clifton Place, though we do not know how many were watercolours or sketches from the project notes. We have no press reviews for the event but can read backwards from Annie Hill-Smith's comments on the following year's Love and Mediocrity Exhibition: 'It was a very good exhibition, as usual, and received no critical attention, as usual' (Facebook, 9 September 2020). Yana Trevail, an artist who studied with Lenkiewicz and later worked as his gallery assistant, recalls:

> I met him in 1975. I used to go up to The Fool in Clifton Street when I was a teenager, and I met him then but I was very scared of him; well, not scared, but he was very ... imposing. Then my mum asked

for my portrait to be painted for my birthday, so we went down to The Parade. I had various sittings and he told me the story that [his doctor friend and keen photographer] Hans de Rijke took an interest in who I was, and then Robert suddenly noticed me, and that's when I really met him.

So although 1975 closed with some promising new relationships and Robert's fame now extended to television appearances, there were few signs of the breakthrough he hoped for in terms of artistic recognition. He seemed blind to the implications of the ambition expressed to Jeny Bremer in 1971: 'I want to paint more paintings than anyone else has ever painted, ever' (Jeny Bremer, Interview, April 2018). The gatekeepers of the art market are wary of any painter intending 'to present a collection of paintings numbering some two thousand five hundred' in less than two years (Love and Romance Exhibition Notes, October 1975). As with diamond traders and high-end performances, scarcity is an intrinsic part of their value system. This is not necessarily cynical. If every provincial town had street violinists knocking out Paganini-level improvisations while singing like Enrico Caruso, it becomes normal. By that very fact 'the goods' become economically devalued: a diamond on a beach full of diamonds. One could (and should) entertain the suggestions of artists as various as Duchamp and Wilde and Blake: wit and wisdom may be found in a ceramic urinal, beauty in the leaden lump that was a statue's heart, and eternity in a grain of sand. But try selling the grain of sand or asking critics to engage with it, and you will have opportunity for a different kind of enlightenment.

The year drew to a close with a return to the Reynolds Gallery for a Christmas Show with '50 new paintings by Fred Yates, Michael Moss, Charles White, Robert Lenkiewicz'. The gallery notes stated:

Robert Lenkiewicz's first exhibition at Reynolds was visited by over a thousand people in two weeks. We have had many demands for some more intimate paintings by him and he has executed specifically for us a set of paintings on the theme of 'the Barbican area, Plymouth' – sometimes topographical, sometimes of people well-known in these parts. He has just finished two major portrait commissions in London, one of Sir Billy Butlin, the other of the Hon. Vere Harmsworth, owner of the Daily Mail, and has been studying Rembrandt and Van Eyck in Flanders and Holland. Next year he will have a major show on the theme of the mentally handicapped.

Robert's contribution embraced the seasonal spirit with three conceptual works on the theme 'A Christmas Breakfast', which included *Eclipse Over Lower Compton With Annie And Pnoobie: painted on a cornflakes packet (packet contains two brief pencil sketches of eclipse at night), Father Christmas Screaming At The Moon: painted on a breakfast plate, Father Christmas Pouring Out The Milk Of Human Kindness: painted on a milk bottle*. Annie Hill-Smith featured also in *Annie With Rembrandt Draped As Father Christmas Peering Through The Window*. A few pieces from Love and Romance appear, together with studies of Barbican familiars such as Diogenes, Dave Helingoe, 'Big Bill' and Andy Lynch. Two further night studies of vagrants were titled *Barbican With Human Interpolations*. The major study of *Diogenes at Night in the Studio Window* was also shown, together with early fisherman studies. Clearly, in this delightful hodgepodge of works, the Barbican was seeing a preview of what would later become the Gossip on The Barbican theme.

December 1975 was a traumatic time for Mouse and her daughter Rebecca (Lenkiewicz, though Jim Pascoe's child), now well known as one of Britain's leading playwrights, who had been severely burned. There followed several weeks in hospital undergoing plastic surgery:

> They were electrical burns and she was the only little girl in the Royal Naval hospital on Christmas Day. We sat surrounded by nurses singing Silent Night. I think Becky was four, which would have made me twenty-eight. We got through Christmas and my mother kept Alice and Wolfe at the farm. Bex was still in on New Year's Eve, and I went to see her and went back home [to Havelock Terrace] very depressed. (Mouse, Letter, April 2019)

The New Year brought ever more strange drifters. Robert records a couple of encounters with a character called 'Squire' who latched onto Mouse during a bus journey. She offered him a roof and a sofa until he could find somewhere to live:

> He had just come out of prison and showed me many drawings of his ideal underground city. He was unusual. Sadly, he fell totally in love with me and I found the situation impossible and asked him to move

on. I thought I had seen the last of him when I was again sitting on the back of the bus [and he climbed aboard with] a huge bunch of red roses in his arms. I slithered down in my seat hoping he wouldn't see me, knowing that the roses were for me. He looked incredibly happy. We met as he got off the bus and he came for a cuppa and I explained yet again that he couldn't stay. He was a sweet man, but to my horror when I woke up the next morning he had set up camp in my front garden. I got irritated after a few days of this and told him to hop it. (Mouse, Letter, April 2019)

The opening moves of Robert's year were complex. He and Annie had spent the holiday season in London with Aury, returning to Plymouth on 1 January. Page 1 of his 1976 diary notes: 'Belle "grumped" past. My first sighting this year. Just walked past'. It seems Mouse's analysis was spot on: Belle became more attractive in proportion to her ability to walk on by. Peregrine's spouse Jacquetta (née Lampson) visited, 'droning on about gossip'. Francesca and Nimadi, along with several other models and companions, were keen to see him and pose for paintings. Robert's reading on the theme of mental handicap intensified. Despite increasing domestic work due to young Pnoobie's (Sholem's) teething, illness, and bouts of vomiting, Annie organised an exhibition of paintings at Highbury School where Robert talked with the children and parents. The Deputy Mayor handed out presents. Meanwhile, the police were dealing with a spike in the murder rate.

Scottie and Maurice were friends of Mouse and Robert:

We all hung around together and Robert painted Scottie on the huge mural. Scottie's real name was Lancelot. He had curly hair and enormous blue sparkling eyes, a sort of baby face. He joined the army [straight out of school], went to Northern Ireland and eventually came back after seeing some horrendous stuff. He settled back into Plymouth life and I was friendly with him. And Maurice, everybody knew Maurice. He was gay when it was less common to come out, but he didn't give a shit. He was flamboyant and enormous fun to be with, tall and dark, with a mass of black hair, and good looking. I remember the date because it was New Year's Eve. [After spending all day and evening with Becky in the hospital I was] depressed and thought I may as well go out for a drink, and set out for the Breakwater at Cattedown. I remember little of the evening, I simply wasn't in the mood.

As we all linked arms for Auld Lang Syne, Scottie said 'Give me a kiss Mouse' which I did. It was quite a passionate kiss and I was surprised. Unknown to me, he had killed Maurice two or three hours before. (Mouse, Letter, April 2019)

On New Year's Day itself the corpse of 51-year-old Esther Soper was found in her home at Mutley Plain. She had been heavily bludgeoned with a cider bottle and choked to death. A grandmother and a member of the ultra-righteous Plymouth Brethren, Mrs Soper was the kind of victim the police liked to prioritise over the dead vagrants they asked Robert to identify. They made several calls to 25 The Parade in the hope of information about the cider-drinking strangler. But the righteous themselves were violent that New Year and one of the younger alcoholics, Dingo, was 'very badly knocked about' by the Reverend John Gardner at the Bethel Mission House. Robert records that the Reverend, 'in a very sacrificial mood' spoke to Dingo's mother, possibly with the aim of preventing criminal charges, bleating: 'I have hit your son and lost my career' (Diary, 5 January 1976). On 7 January amid many notes on money worries Robert writes: 'Police came/discussed the present spate of murders'. They revisited zealously in the following months, as did a private detective.

Word on the street had it that Maurice's murder was due to a simple and ugly outburst of homophobia. On 3 January Robert records a visit to Monica's where: 'Pete told me that Scottie has been arrested for the murder of Maurice. It seems to have attracted a great deal of unpleasant talk, etc. Several people have been down to the mural to view the face of Scottie' (Diary, 3 January 1976). News of another death came the same day along with other stresses: 'Jacquetta at shop/impertinent liar. Poor "Stick" is dead. [...] Impossible, irritating situation. Either she is too nervous to know what she's doing or she's a psychotic cheat. I'm finished with it. Belle came and cackled through the window. J freaked out'. The vagrant 'Smokey Joe' died later that month.

That winter's death rate among vagrants was high enough to warrant press attention. An application to open a 'supportive care hostel for single homeless people' had been knocked back by the City Council. The story ran as 'Homeless Dying in Plymouth Streets'. Robert's friend Gordon Wright is quoted: 'Four men have died in my arms [...] There are men dying in the streets, and I would be happy to take [the Council] around to see them'. They didn't accept the offer. As the Conservative politician Mrs Helen Fox was honest enough to admit, the crux of the problem and 'the trouble with every single one of us is that not one of us would have them [the vagrants] next door to us' (News clipping, Diary, 13 January 1976).

Robert inherited a problem. Working on a triptych at Priory Road he was 'disturbed by a knock on door. Troubled by an associate of Mouse's called Squire. Had to stay the night. Turned up very late, nowhere to go, sent by Mouse. Tiresome schizophrenic. Will find him somewhere in the morning' (Diary, 12 January 1976). He did, but the stay was short. On what evidence we cannot know, but Squire was hoisted by the police and questioned about the recent murders. Possibly it was nothing more than the fact that he was recently out of jail and the mayhem coincided with his arrival in Plymouth, but Squire was in anguish and the police were working overtime. Robert records: 'Inspector came to see me about Hugh Parry, 7.30 p.m. Go to see Squire in the cells. Poor Squire crying, very upset, terrified of being remanded. The usual horrific wire gate. Went to Victoria and got a few cigarettes etc. Dropped them in on the way home' (Diary, 15 January 1976). The Esther Soper murder was unsolved, and Squire could not have known that Scottie had already confessed to the murder of Maurice. But Squire's clothes had been confiscated for forensic analysis and it was likely he was 'a person of interest' in some serious matters. He feared he might be 'fitted up' for one or both murders.

> I had no idea that [Squire] was suspected of Maurice's murder. He went to prison for fraud. What came out [at Scottie's trial] was that Maurice had come on to him, and Scottie was suffering from his experiences in Ireland, and apparently inflicted a massive amount of stab wounds. He went to prison for, I think, eight years; I wrote to him for a while. It was tragic on two counts, mostly because Maurice was incredible, and hugely liked, but also because Scottie was deeply intelligent and so young. It was dreadful, and we were all in shock. (Mouse, Letter, April 2019)

Despite such tumult Robert was once again ratchetting up the pressure on himself, hot-housing his reading and the numbers of paintings for the Mental Handicap Project. He began work on what would be the centrepiece of the exhibition, a revisioning of Rembrandt's *The Night Watch*. This is possibly one of the most famous and exquisite paintings in Western art history so the stresses he placed himself under were maximal. Success or failure in this piece would be an act of ruthless self-diagnosis. Not that Robert was concerned with contemporary art critics, rather that he was consciously testing his skills against the highest available measure. The diaries record his preparations of the canvas and ideas several weeks before announcing its beginning on 22 February. Patterns are emerging: sexual activity is increasing, his consciousness agitated – 'Curious dream about Belle. Not very pleasant ironies' – and once again he is clocking his progress in numbers: '48 oils, 9 tempera, 10 drawings so far for the M.H. Project' (Diary, 18 February 1976).

By now the working methods for the projects were firmly in place. The 'artwork' is not the paintings, it is the trinity of paintings, plus 'fieldwork', plus reflections on theory. The fieldwork in this case involved close contact with the day-to-day realities of the mentally handicapped and the people caring for them. Robert made lengthy visits to various 'special schools' two or three times every week. He spoke to the 'younger parents of mentally handicapped children at Highbury, went very well. Managed to get a few more of the more harrowing cases booked [in for portraits]' (Diary, 2 January 1976). The spectre of Albert Schweitzer looms large in many of the notes and once more Robert's mistrust of his own empathetic feelings seems misplaced: 'Mrs Rogers came with Sharon (Mongol) – parents don't seem to accept that [diagnosis]. I had a very strong awareness of my desire to be a doctor' (Diary, 14 January 1976).

16.1 Robert with the canvas *The Night Watch*, in progress in 1976.

16.2 Robert in front of the canvas *Barbara Bridgeman and Caroline Young*, in 1976. To the right, Annie Hill-Smith holds their son, Sholem.

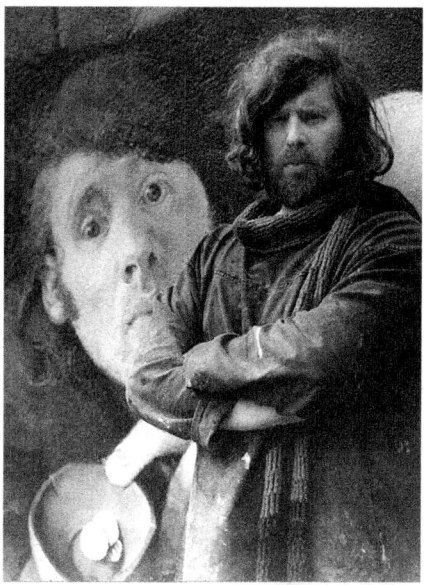

16.3 Robert working on a self-portrait with a *memento mori*, 1976.
16.4 Robert standing beside his self-portrait in the Barbican Mural, 1976.
16.5 Robert seated before the canvas *Study of Belle Pecorini in the Kitchen* (1973) and the Mental Handicap study *Couple Dancing* (1976).

16.6 One panel of the Wild West mural seen at the Yankee Burger café, formerly in Frankfort Gate, Plymouth.

The work filled the two longest walls, being 1.4m in height and 5.2m and 5.8m in length respectively. The mural was commissioned by the American café owner, John Desiderio, in 1976 and took roughly one year to complete. The well-preserved canvases are now in the United States.

16

Compassion, Tuberculosis, and Yet More Violence

On 15 January Robert visited Millford School to see the class 'for more severely handicapped and autistic children'. In the same month he tried helping a crippled boy to walk and noted with sadness the limitations of his 'amateur physiotherapy', though he suspected that with adequate professional resources the boy could be walking 'within two years' (Diary, 22 January 1976). Conversations on this and similar cases with Dr Hans de Rijke suggested that the 'problems of mental handicap' were often social and economic as much as physiological. Robert had boundless admiration for Hans and their friendship was permanently cemented by their sensitive but detached benevolence and stoical recognition of life's tragedies.

The theoretical elements of the Mental Handicap Project received a dramatic boost on 13 February with the arrival at 25 The Parade of Michel Foucault's monumental book *Madness and Civilisation*. The introduction to the translation of Foucault's book had been written by radical psychiatrist David Cooper, who in 1965 established The Philadelphia Association working with fellow psychiatrists R. D. Laing and Aaron Esterson. They attempted to redefine the understanding and treatment of psychosis and mental disorders, which they saw as the response of a sane individual to intolerable social pressures and an insane society. Laing's books in particular soon became counterculture classics and reinforced Robert's own observations: *The Divided Self: An Existential Study in Sanity and Madness* (1960), *Sanity, Madness and The Family* (1964) (with Esterson), and *The Politics of Experience and the Bird of Paradise* (1967), where Laing stated bluntly that 'normal men have killed perhaps 100,000,000 of their fellow normal men in the last fifty years'.

It is likely Robert was impressed by the French philosopher's style of living as much as the acuity of his thought, for Foucault's work ethic and experimental sexuality were truly first rate. Philosophy for Foucault was not a matter of lofty abstraction but a means of living a significant life. *Madness and Civilisation* cuts through the hallowed notion of moral or scientific 'progress' in the field of mental handicap. The range of the book is huge even in the cut-down English version Robert was working with, and we must do considerable violence to summarise its main argument.

Throughout the Renaissance madness was not merely evaluated in a different way, it was an entirely different object of inquiry. The 'unreason' of the Shakespearean Fool or rustic idiot was a valuable counterpoint to the working of reason, which was itself acknowledged as a limited tool. Although Foucault does not himself stress the point, the 'mentally handicapped' of the Renaissance had a social role not unlike the tribal shaman, with access to a different but important kind of wisdom. The 'Enlightenment' of the 18th century framed a drastic change in the relationship between 'folly' and 'good sense'. The terms were slowly but surely loaded with moral evaluations. 'Reason' was increasingly characterised as a military encampment defending society against 'unreason'. A *hostility* emerges, with 'mental handicap' or 'madness' refigured as a threat to be contained or an enemy to be fought. The offending fools were taken away from their families, villages, or city streets to be 'cured' in workhouses or exhibited in asylums. Foucault calls this 'The Great Confinement', in which the distinction between the mad and the sane was made by physical separation and 'professional helpers' who profited from the system. The modern treatment of the mentally ill and 'retarded' in special institutions is different from former centuries but can hardly be attributed to a triumph of lofty morals. The mentally handicapped have been made invisible and uncommunicative, whereas 500 years ago no European Royal Court would be without its well-integrated collection of loons, fools, and crazies.

Robert's choice of his ironic version of *The Night Watch* as a centrepiece for 'Mental Handicap' makes more sense considering Foucault's analysis. For Rembrandt's *The Night Watch* was not originally a 'night painting' at all. It acquired the title and reputation due to some well-intentioned lathering with dark varnish in the early 1600s. This drastic change in tone sanctioned a general forgetting of the painting's original title, which emphasised the work as first and foremost a military painting: *Officers and Men of the Amsterdam Kloveniers Militia, the Company of Captain Frans Banning Cocq*. The gentlemen portrayed were in effect very wealthy vigilantes, a self-selecting band of well-heeled and well-meaning citizens armed against the enemies of the civic order, real or imaginary, internal or external.

As with the Town Crier in *Plymouth Mourning Over its Unfortunates*, the characters in Robert's version of *The Night Watch* are not at all villainous. They are merely constrained by their roles in an economic and political order which diverts their good will and best efforts into a collusion with silence. So when Robert invited the Lord Mayor of Plymouth to unveil

The Night Watch in the Jacob's Ladder studio in August 1976, the gesture was more nuanced and generous than the dramatic scene where Korda's Rembrandt rages against the 'vanity and stupidity' of the disgruntled officials (Korda, *Rembrandt*, at 17 min). Mr Moore, the headmaster of Millford School, and Hans de Rijke were held in high regard by Robert, and it is interesting that Hans is painted in the costume of a more humane age. Mr Moore's attire is more ambiguous, but his expression and pose suggest strength and possibility: he appears to be presenting options. Even the political classes are not entirely mocked in Robert's depiction. The Devonport MP, Dr David Owen, then Minister of State for Health, looks determined, if somewhat melancholy and clueless. He holds a T-square used in technical drawing and building, also in Masonic and vernacular use as a symbol of fair dealings. But his thick white sash seems more custodial than ceremonial. He is a man with plans, but ironically confined by his official powers.

One more irony must be noted. Robert's image of armed men or builders planning the exclusion of unreason is doubly poignant, for no matter how wise or well-intentioned the players, all attempts to out-build or out-fight 'the darkness' are a 'folly of wisdom'. This theme Robert developed in later paintings such as the Project 18 'Aristotle and Phyllis' series. And for reasons or unreasons beyond the scope of this book, *The Shooting Company/The Night Watch* has been a magnet for persons of defective judgement armed with more than dark varnish. Rembrandt's canvas was stabbed in 1911, severely slashed 'in accordance with orders from The Lord' by an attacker in 1975, and sprayed with acid by another escaped psychiatric patient in 1990. Robert saw the original still under repair during his trip to the Netherlands that same year. His version, along with the entirety of Chilford Hall in Cambridgeshire, was incinerated in 2012 by a malicious addict and his autistic accomplice.

The project was in Robert's own words 'a complaint' against the double-bind of ignoring and/or sentimentalising the victims of 'mental handicap'. By 'victims' he included the entire web of people who were made socially and economically responsible for dealing with the accidents of biology, most of all the parents. What Robert communicates in these paintings is a sense of the mentally handicapped being *sacred* in the strict sense of 'set apart'. The 'Special School' was a place of exile for those deemed bio-socially accursed, and the parents and professionals were expected to function as insulation. The terrible mixtures of duty, shame, and pride which accompany this function are conveyed in canvases such as *Mr and*

Mrs Greep with Francis, Tracey, and Darren (1976) and *Wally Carter with His Son Martin John* (1976). Other canvases speak less of a social situation and more of the abyss at the edge of reason, which is very close indeed. *Boy with Cerebral Palsy* (1976) has an archetypal resonance with the Hanged Man Tarot card, his head lolling as if the device meant to hold him upright had broken his neck. For Robert, the image was also associated with the story of his childhood hero Pinocchio – but in this case, there is no magic, and the puppet will never become a real boy (Diary, 15 May 1976).

The bright, almost harshly lit, double portrait of *Barbara Bridgeman and Caroline Young* is particularly uncompromising in its forensic obser-vation. It is not grim but could easily be described as *stark*. Referencing Velázquez's portrait of King Philip's dwarf attendant Sebastian de Mor-ra, Robert paints Barbara and Caroline with the same recognition of hu-manity as he did the vagrants and other previously 'invisible people'. It is interesting to note that King Philip surrounded himself with his 'little people' – well over a hundred of them – because he trusted them more than the courtiers and political schemers who tried weaselling their way into favour. Sympathetic but unsentimental, Robert depicts the sitters for this project with the full range of feelings that they are perfectly entitled to – sadness, anger, defiance, frenzy – or the ambivalent joy and melancholy of a *Couple Dancing* (1976). Perhaps Robert trusted the feelings of out-siders more than those of the people who suffer under that tyrant called 'normalcy'.

Several of the paintings were visible to the public before the exhibition opening due to Robert's working conditions at 25 The Parade. The judge-ments of the man in the street were not always humane: "'He's supposed to paint lots of mad people. All he does is paint nutters and drunks. Look at that disgusting creature there" – Comments overheard regarding one of the MH paintings/someone looking through window' (Diary, 7 March 1976).

Sometimes a hostility to society's outsiders is well warranted. Barbican traders could hardly be called 'vagro-phobic' about dossers relieving them-selves in their doorways. Residents of the flats opposite the Studio were rightly concerned about large groups hanging around to beg from people, harass youngsters for money, and in general make a menace of themselves.

People in the block of flats where I reside are loath to let their small ones out to play because of them. They sit on the nearby wall with bottles of hooch at all times of the day drinking themselves into a state of stupidity. They then urinate in the lane opposite my lounge window [...] These people have rejected society; they contribute nothing to it other than to draw money from the DHSS for their "plonk" ('Hooligans and Vagrants on the Barbican', unreferenced news clipping in diary, 2 June 1976)

Hostility to such vagrants is not irrational. Several were becoming so intolerable that even Robert was forced to compromise his open-door policy. The main offenders were a group including 'Brighton' and 'Brummy' who were often loaded on random mixtures of drugs:

Dealt with 'troublesome Brighton'. Took pills off him (Librium/Valium?) Bombed out of their skulls already with the drink. They have been on pills all day. Identified one as Dalmane, 30mg. Apparently this drug with alcohol can have dangerous psychotic effects. 7pm. Painted Hans de Rijke [...] until disturbed by Cowboys. 'Brummy' tried to steal Annie's fur coat. Worthless anyway. Bad trouble with Brummy: tried to get heavy at the main studio. 'Brighton' showed him the way. Threw them out. Very difficult with 'Brummy'. Strong man. Had to lock the main door on them. (Diary, 1 June 1976)

They called back next day. Robert bought them milk and food 'They intend going "dry" again! We'll see'. The day after that, the inevitable: 'Brummy and Brighton seen getting bottles from the Octagon. They both turned up half-steaming, accusing me of putting them on a "bum steer". Cretins. Brummy stomped off' (Diary, 3 June 1976). And it got worse:

Brummy and Brighton got very bad. The combination of the Jake [a mixture of methylated spirit and cheap red wine]/pills and alcohol turned them mad. Brummy lifted a ladder and smashed it against Annie's van with the baby inside it. Brighton got up, and came into the shop full of people, understandably terrified. I threw him out and had to knock him down. His drink plus bottle of Jake smashed in his pocket. He went for me with a section of broken glass. I disarmed him. Annie dragged him to the police station. Brummy found half-conscious, spread-eagled on the ground down the road. Got him an ambulance. But the police took him anyway. He stared like a baneful chained Minotaur. Loathsome sight trapped in a police car. They will probably be released in the morning. And the trouble will begin anew. (Diary, 4 June 1976)

There is no real victory or defeat in such grim matters, but Robert was magnanimous. Later that evening he 'went to the police station, handed 40 cigarettes and a box of matches over to the constable at the desk' for the villains (Diary, 4 June 1976). News travels fast on the Barbican. Several of Robert's friends who were skilled in the science of communitarian justice offered to 'sort out' the Brummy and Brighton situation. Setting up an educational beating from 'Gypsy Joe' or 'Slugger Ray' was not at all Robert's style but he was at the end of his tether. After a poor night's sleep, he arrived at a partial but elegant solution. He put aside the 'All Are Welcome' policy and made it somebody else's problem:

> Pulled a pretty amusing stroke on Brighton and Brummy. Both had been fined £2.50 + costs and were feeling pretty rough, etc. I told them a story. That Gypsy Joe was angered at what they did and was gunning for them: that he was going to 'kill' Brighton, etc. They freaked and wanted to leave town. Put them on a bus to Bournemouth. (Diary, 5 June 1976)

With some measure of tranquillity in place Robert refocussed on the project and some necessary restoration of the Elizabethan Mural. It was barely half a decade since the undercoat had been applied by assistants of imperfect diligence. The weatherproof, acid, alkali, and frost-resistant paint was bubbling away from the wall. Harry Cooper led the Barbican Association in a spirited campaign to cover the necessary costs. Robert climbed the scaffold in the mornings and spent hours repainting the damaged sections, then lunched at Joe Prete's café before the relentless round of sittings began: '2.30. Mrs James and Mrs Martin, Down's syndrome children. 4pm Mr and Mrs Downing, continue double oil. 5.15, continue 'Night Watch' etc. 6.15 Mr Lowe, continue Andrew's portrait. 7pm, Ron Moore, complete figure of Captain Banning' (Diary, 22 June 1976). Late that evening he writes:

> sitting in the dark of my shop I saw a figure silhouetted outside. She seemed familiar. It was Gail [Steadman], student doctor/now a doctor at Freedom Fields. So sad somehow to see her again. [...] She looked very attractive and miserable [...] showed her 'The Night Watch' [...]

saw her back to the hospital. She suddenly turned around and said that she had come down to make love. Unexpected and moving development. Slept alone at the main studio. (Diary, 22 June 1976)

On 15 March he writes: 'Started "THE DEAD LOVER WITH MEMORIES" painting [Love & Mediocrity]. Enjoying this more than anything I have done in a year.' This upsurge of joy arrived on the eve of misery.

Until this point in his life Robert had dodged the effects of poor nutrition, rats in the kitchen, and the impressive range of diseases carried by the dossers: his only health problems were minor colds and the inevitable bouts of head lice. But March 1976 brought the first signs that his circulation might not be working properly. His feet began to swell painfully. He was 35 years old, a non-smoker and non-drinker, was not fat but weighed around 120 kg and spent many hours immobile in front of his canvasses. Hans de Rijke suggested he should spend less time standing. Robert 'went to Victoria's. Feeling very uncomfortable. Had a bath. Feet hurt. Read various possibilities and explanations (including death). Decided to go somewhere more suitable and terminate work (of a kind) for a day or two' (Diary, 16 March 1976).

As far as the records show this is Robert's first self-imposed slow-down or rest period (of a kind). The pain worsened and help was sought from a Dr Everett who took blood samples, made X-rays, prescribed antibiotics, and urged Robert to stay in bed for a week. The situation worsened. Robert's resolve to slow down his work rate was as futile as Brummy's intention to 'go dry'. Although he cancelled all his sittings at 25 The Parade for somewhat less than a week, he continued making notes and watercolour studies even when he was hospitalised on 18 March. Annie Hill-Smith was only days away from birthing her second child but:

Annie drove me to the Orthopaedic department. I was immediately X-rayed and blood-tested etc. Too tall for the machine – taken to another X-ray room. Asked to go in to see Dr Salz. To my surprise Hans de Rijke was there as well as Dr Montgomery. Such odd circumstances for a painter and his models. After examination they left me with the impression that I had some kind of tuberculosis. They also mentioned 'sarcoid'. Further diagnoses to follow. I observed curious infected area of lung on X ray. (Diary, 18 March 1976, marked up as 'Tuberculosis Day')

He returned to Priory Road that evening where he was visited by Hans and the vagrant Corky who brought food, though he was 'slightly drunk, but sweet, he yakked on about the Cowboys and other trivia'. Next morning Harry Cooper, Belle Pecorini, and Terry Goldstone visited, the latter with news that Monica had given birth to a girl. Annie immediately went out to buy silver spoons as natal gifts. Dr Dowson, a specialist in chest medicine, visited with mixed but worrisome news.

> Spoke to me about sarcoidosis. Explained that in 90% of the cases it could clear up of its own accord. But there were 10% where the effects were chronic with unpleasant complications: e.g. inflammation of the iris leading to loss of sight, and considerable pain, and severe inflammation of the lungs: a kind of tuberculosis. I explained about my work etc. and he suggested that a good compromise was for me to come into hospital for tests tomorrow. Come out tomorrow, work (sitting down) during the weekend. Go back into hospital and rest till Tuesday. Come out on Tuesday and work, etc. Worked a bit more on 'Sarcoidic tubercular self-portrait'. Poor piece. (Diary, 19 March 1976, marked up as 'Sarcoid Day')

Over the next week Robert was in and out of hospital. Much blood was extracted, reagents injected, a minor operation performed. He was also working at his usual giddy pace on two projects, and returning to 25 The Parade to make sketches of passers-by: 'managed to earn some money. Dr Hans de Rijke turned up/amused to see me working there [...] I worked on "Lover with Memories" for most of the afternoon. Completed drawing of dwarf with dog. Prepared and completed drawing for Daily Express man' (Diary, 20 March 1976). 'Completed Aragonese Dwarf. Completed a few Auto-sex studies. Terry turned up. No news' (Diary, 21 March 1976). The next day he admitted himself to hospital, met 'the inmates of Ward 15', made more notes, went to sleep, arose at '5:45 am, had liver biopsy operation at 9.35 am. Read and worked all day in hospital' (Diary, 22 March 1976). Early the next morning he was back at 25 The Parade: 'Worked at shop all day. Started new painting of Jacquetta's bedroom for Love and Mediocrity'.

Robert's excruciations revisited him in June 1978, this time in the left leg only; and his sensations were recorded in a pair of illustrations that combined his near-paralysed leg with detailed anatomical drawings, as if he intended to assist a doctor in the diagnosis.

On March 17 [1976] Annie called Dr Everett for diagnosis of similar discomfort. The condition lasted for some 10 days – but I did not seem unable to walk for more than a day or two. This time [11 June, 1978] the inability to walk is much more marked; have been unable to use the left leg for one week. Pain also more severe. Last time both legs; this time only the one.

The pain and swelling in his feet subsided, but he was not taking advice from doctors, friends, or indeed himself on the topic of rest. His schedule had changed but not slowed. He worried about few things but it was as if he feared he might miss the arrival of some vital clue which an unannounced stranger could bring into the Studio. And much valuable 'raw material' did present itself this way: 'Very unhappy woman came into my shop to discuss her suicidal inclinations after her recent breakup of a "romance" between herself and man 18 years her junior. She was 41. All very interesting in relation to my Love and Mediocrity notes' (Diary, 26 March 1976).

Robert must have been aware that tubercular sarcoidosis was a multi-system disease which could travel in all sorts of nasty directions, especially if there was a pre-existing genetic weakness such as that suggested by his father's early heart attacks. In an ideal world he and Annie would have been attending relaxation clinics prior to the arrival of the baby. In reality, he was facing court summonses 'for the Rogers' Debt. I have fourteen days'. The Department of Social Security were pursuing him 'Re: maintenance, Mouse and children' and 'Man from Courts came re. Taxi Driver £280 warrant, etc.'. 'Belle turned up. No comment. Annie took her away. Police came to ask me about Jock and Irish John' (Diary, 6 April 1976). All this in one day, on top of his painting and study schedule.

The atmosphere of violence thickened around 25 The Parade. Brummy and Brighton had returned from their short exile. One of the few rules Robert had for the dossers was that they must not vex any sitters or paying customers. On Saturday 10 April, Robert was feeling ill, 'T.B. ill'. A couple of American tourists were purchasing a portrait of a girl for £50. Big Jock, Corky, and Brighton were visiting, and Brighton's drunken antics nearly scuppered the sale. Later that day Brighton 'tried to beg a customer'. Seeking to avoid embarrassment Robert left the customer in the studio and took Brighton aside into the adjacent alley for a word about his behaviour. It was nearly his undoing.

Big Jock misinterpreted [the situation] and nearly jumped me with a knife. Dealt with both of them. 'Deafy Kelley' collapsed prone in the square. All the people in the flats [opposite the Studio] have had just about enough of them all. Woman started shouting at me about – 'Is this right, Robert? Is it right for my little Sandra to see this sort of thing? Is it right?!!?' I was too much pre-occupied with Kelley on my back to reply – fortunately. People even complained to Joe [Prete, who later that day] said to me 'Get Rid of those Cowboys, before the Cowboys get rid of you'. The police came three times. (Diary, 10 April 1976)

Joe Prete was a wise man and worth listening to. Running one of the busiest cafés on the Barbican gave him ample opportunities to notice who was talking to whom and saying what. Robert had strong support from people like Harry Cooper, the Nash family, George Wright, and Hans de Rijke. But Peter Wanstall and the landlord of 25 The Parade and a cabal of nay-sayers were plotting to close the Studio by any means possible. They would gladly amplify legitimate complaints from residents and the police reports of violent drunkies and junkies.

Another of the dossers died, this time by the causes natural enough to heavy drinkers. 'The Singer' was buried at Weston Mill in a pauper's grave. George Wright read extracts from Robert's Vagrancy book (Diary, 12 April 1976). And there was another Lenkiewicz birth: Annie had made arrangements with the Calders to look after young 'Pnoobie' while she was in labour, which began on the 26 April. Robert notes:

Belle and Annie went to Dudley's, I worked on self-portrait etc. Went to Dudley's, phoned Nina (Calder) to collect Pnoobie. Belle went to my house. I went to Annie's. Met Nina there who collected Pnoobie and drove off into the dark. Painted study of Annie having contractions for about ¾ hour. Walked over to Freedom Fields [hospital]. Annie produced a boy at 12.40 am. I saw its extraordinary little face come out into the hands of lovely nurses. Very long cord wrapped around its throat twice and once under left arm. Refined looking child.

Robert spent the night and next morning with Belle, then visited the hospital to see Annie and 'Pnoobie No. 2' (Jascha), then spent some time with Nina and Pnoobie No. 1 (Sholem). 'Everything was very pleasant' until Brighton visited the Studio with one of the few other dossers Robert genuinely feared. This was Brother Blair, whose presence was often noted with comments such as 'something unhealthy and dangerous about him' (Diary, 27 April 1976). Brother Blair would in due course hold a knife to the throat of one of Robert's children. The quality of Robert's visitors was always up and down: one day a street psychotic drops in for menaces, then the next day 'the Polish Ambassador to London visited. Did a bad drawing of his charming wife. Would I please visit them in London?' (Diary, 28 April 1976).

Nina Calder, daughter of Barbican antiques dealer Leonard Corkette, had been tireless in driving back and forth with Pnoobie and ferrying Robert to and from the maternity ward. During those five days she fell a little bit in love with the child:

> He was in a carry-cot he was too big for, squeezed up and fast asleep. In the morning when he started waking up I put him over my shoulder before he could see who it was, and it was quite heart-breaking for him when he leaned back and saw it was me. But then we really bonded. For those three days he was coming to me and [...] I can't remember how long he stayed, maybe a week. It was quite hard giving him back. (Nina Calder, Interview, February 2019)

Robert's relationship with Belle became hotter and less stable. Between 7 and 12 May he made three large paintings of her. He notes their pleasant conversations about Delmore Schwarz and Marcel Duchamp, then how she 'droned on and on and on' about nothing but 'food and sex and food and sex and food and sex'. He writes that she was 'very pleasant' and looking 'edible' but prone to 'tantrums'. There was a 'speedy incident in the back of the studio'. He records a 'sweet night. She actually made me breakfast'. The next night he completed a 'painting of Belle which she in her infinite wisdom censored in the usual manner. Scream, stamp, rage, throw, hurl, thump, kick, stomp, march, slam. Came back in ½ hour. Sweet night. Very pleasant incident' (Diary, 6 May 1976). And on the 10th: '10pm. "Les(ley) Miller", continued triptych of vagina study. Have watercolours for her vagina! Strange sad evening. Did nude masturbation study and worked on oil. Belle came with baby. Les Miller left. Did nude study of Belle.'

Once again this intensification of his sexual activity co-developed with his work rate on the project. Despite his recent hospitalisation, he was utterly restless. He worked all day and hardly slept at all. On 15 May he 'woke up early, walked to shop' and after 'working hard on [the painting of the] suspended child' and other artworks through the day and long into the night, he 'walked around until 4 am. Feet feeling a lot better, Found "Skipper" on his back in the gutter. Picked him up. Terrible state. Took him back to his doss. Went to main studio, worked on "Night Watch"' (Diary, 15 May 1976). The next day he rose early after 'bad sleep', spent most of the morning on the new Wild West Mural in Frankfort Gate (the Yankee Burger café), back to the Barbican for lunch, 'completed "puppet" spastic child', dealt with 'a large number of irritating customers', 'started another MH [Mental Handicap] painting of huddled up boy on floor', started to move 'all paintings on MH theme up to the main Studio', 'Finished "Blackbird's" portrait at 11pm precisely – went to Khan's, lost my patience with her. Thanked her for her trouble – said goodbye and put her in a taxi. Such a pointless waste. Went back to shop. Fucking rats running all over the Studio' (Diary, 16 May 1976).

During the mid-1970s Robert became more selective about the help he gave to the dossers. Aware that many chose drink or drugs over food, he sometimes made an offer to 'see me once a day at 5pm for food' instead of handing out cash. With one semi-competent addict, help was given on condition that the man 'leave his tools [presumably so he could not sell them, and that he should expect to] receive no money – only milk and cigarettes' (Diary, 11 July 1976). Robert was as last combining generosity with responsibility.

Robert's sympathies for the outsiders, addicts, and outlaws found another route for expression in an indoor mural he completed in summer 1976. This was a Wild West themed extravaganza in the large Yankee Burger restaurant, owned by American John Desiderio (who appears in one of the large canvas panels in modern sunglasses). Many of the gunmen were modelled by the 'Cowboys' from the Holiday Inns who, with names like 'The Janner', 'Big Jock', and 'Scarface Fitz', were the interchangeable ruffians of all centuries. Robert remained so poor he occasionally had to borrow money from the dossers and a restaurant mural was always good social insurance. His motivations were not entirely nutritional: his brothers, Mouse, and Alex Donoghue recall his prolonged interest in gunslingers. The mural gave him licence to research their histories, costumes, and characters. Almost inevitably Billy the Kid was Robert's favourite. The Kid's mythology resonated with his own. Orphaned at age 14, brought up in a crazy boarding house, imprisoned for theft, the Kid's early life diverged from Robert's only in his propensity for murder. His highly publicised death and folk tales of his 'resurrection' might also be noted as an inspiration. Several diary entries from March and April 1976 note how Robert's 'research' extended to borrowing an air pistol and holster to practice quick-draw shooting in the Studio. With no talent for bloodshed Robert chose old paint cans for targets rather than the plentiful rodents. John Desiderio, spoke to the *Plymouth Herald* in 2016:

'I commissioned Robert to paint the murals in 1976, he was given a key and allowed to work when he could. The project took a little over a year – it was worth the wait.' Mr Desiderio clarified one of the murals is 1.4m tall by 5.8m long and the other 1.4m by 5.2m long and was painted on canvas. But sadly for Lenkiewicz fans the murals were removed in 1985 by Robert Lenkiewicz and are currently in Mr Desiderio's possession in America. ... 'It's hard to find a 17- and a 19-foot continuous wall to hang them on and cutting them up was never an option. I contacted a few museums in the 1990s to see if they wanted to exhibit the murals, but none were interested'. (L Daniel, posted to This Is Plymouth, 19 May 2016)

In March 1976 Robert visited Aury Shoa in London, visiting galleries and talking philosophy. He also spent time with Jacquetta Eliot who was at that time involved with the painter Lucian Freud. Robert's old friend Tarun Bedi knew many London artists with underworld or gambling connections, such as Francis Bacon, who was perfectly gentlemanly about Tarun's heterosexuality and allowed Tarun to watch him paint on several occasions. But Tarun's exotic good looks were a red flag to Freud. He wrongly suspected Tarun was having an affair with one of his favourite models, or else used this as a pretext for some good old-fashioned colonial violence in the Colony Club one night: 'He grabbed my throat and said "If you lay one finger on her I will cut your fucking head off, you black bastard!"' (Tarun, Interview, June 2017). Neither Tarun nor Robert discovered whether the model in question was Jacquetta. Robert notes that things are 'very strange in J's world. Went to café – accompanied by Lucian's little son' (Diary, 9 March 1976). Robert's own children did not escape his notice. Speaking of his and Ruti Cohen's child, born in 1973: 'Laila charming. How strange to have such a pretty daughter' (Diary, 10 March 1976).

In what was becoming standard operating procedure Robert began his next project six months before this one was ready for exhibition. In a note from late January 1976 concerning a portrait of Judy Simpson he runs three lines through the word 'complete' and replaces it with 'start'. Beneath this, in letters more clearly formed and strident than usual, is an acerbic note-to-self: 'When I write "complete" I mean complete, pin-brain. This one you started months ago' (Diary, 22 January 1976).

On Saturday 10 April Robert was watching British sculptor and broadcaster Michael Ayrton's BBC TV programme *A Question of Mirrors* and saw a convergence of ideas with his multi-mirror self-portraiture for Love and Mediocrity.

> Watched study of 'Mirrors' by M Ayrton – shortly before he died. Philosophically very interesting. Though not connected in any way with the kind of interpretation I have been making. So curious. I had no idea of Ayrton's 'Mirror Theme'. Yet I have been working on exactly the same structural principles for the 'relationship theme'.

Ayrton's work focusing on the idea of the maze and the myth of the Minotaur was shown in Exeter Museum in 1975, though in the absence of the 1975 diary there is no evidence that Robert saw it there. Ayrton's catalogue notes for the show state:

> The maze has come to serve for me as an image of my own life and indeed of any individual's life. [...] The belly contains its entrail maze and the skull encloses the brain's baffling convolutions [...] That is why in certain bronzes I have strung the labyrinth like a lyre and the strings wind out from the maker's guts and nerves to supplant the navel cord. (Ayrton, *Maze and Minotaur*, Catalogue notes 1975)

But Robert's attention is already moving on, and the next day he is making studies for Love and Mediocrity. As soon as this project is rolling he begins planning a third project, on prostitution. This is one of several which never materialized but he got as far as enquires with local pimps and madams to see how the 'girls' would feel about posing. Most were hostile to the idea, for Plymouth was a swamp of hypocritical morality and recognition was not without its dangers. Later in the year Baroness Joan Vickers, former Conservative MP for Plymouth Devonport, wrote to Robert on House of Lords notepaper 'Be kind to the prostitutes' (Letter in diary at 27 August 1976).

17.1 & 17.2 Robert photographed Magdalena Rivera at his cottage garden
and in Compton village on 4 July 1976.

17.3 Diogenes at The Fool next to *Myriam in da Vinci's Grotto*, 1976.

17.4 George Fallick, a sitter for Project 3, with Robert and Magdalena at the studio, July 1976.

17.5 Robert photographs himself and Magdalena Rivera in a mirror at the Compton cottage, July 1976. No pictures of Magdalena's sister Myriam appear in the artist's diary until three years later.

17

The Remarkable Rivera Sisters

The Mental Handicap Project was not yet complete, and the Love and Mediocrity Project was developing alongside it throughout the early summer of 1976. But Robert was planning much further ahead:

> Exciting developments for next summer's project. The surgeon Dr Sutherland-Jones visited me saying that it would be possible for me to attend the anatomy course at Freedom Fields for doctors. I could also attend dissections and post-mortems. (Diary, 4 May 1976)

Already he had the framework for a lifetime's achievement: a series of 16 projects under the banner of 'Relationships: Attitudes Towards Love'. The projects would include key areas of human experience and the limits of that experience, such as Education, Gossip, Jealousy, Orgasm, Suicide, Old Age, and Death. His ambitions soon spread beyond these 16 projects first announced in the notebook for the Mental Handicap Exhibition. The writing and arrangements for printing were well underway when in early June he made another visit to London:

> Went straight to Ma's. She seems very skeletal: quite a bit changed from the last time I saw her. Johnny/Tova and Bernard/Gillian were there. Tova made a pleasant meal. Took Johnny and Bernard out to discuss matters. Must try and paint Ma soon. (Diary, 12 June 1976)

The alluring and exotic figure of Myriam Rivera re-entered Robert's life. He notes: 'Extraordinary letter from Myriam, born in Columbia. Came into shop a day or two ago. I remember her well. Curiously attractive. Sweet letter – I should not jump to conclusions' (Diary, 12 June 1976).

It appears that Myriam and her sister Magdalena were versed in some indigenous Columbian religion, somewhat at odds with the repressive Catholicism which had arrived with the Spanish:

> Annie drove me to Kingsbridge. Dropped me in the town. And commenced yet another of 'those' so strange explorations. Myriam Rivera

was waiting for me. I was taken to her by Magdalena, her sister, who was extraordinarily beautiful. Myriam made corn on the cob and some curious drink and took me up to her room. Candles, books, and silence. She sat in meditation for ½ hour. Did not want to talk about the reasons for this and that. Myriam behaved in the manner of the 'woman' in Siddhartha. Unnervingly open: giving and trustful. No demands, perhaps as natural as it is possible to be for someone without a teacher. Had many years of experience with the 'Magic Mushrooms' in Mexico. [...] Has been with no-one for seven months. Said that she just 'knew'. I must not worry about anything – just accept if I wished.

Got up early for breakfast in a small café. Walked around the town. Went into the museum. [...] went back to her room. [She] told me that I found her sister Magdalena very beautiful: that if I wished I should go into the next room and be with her also. It would be alright, she said, a good thing. Magdalena is one of the most beautiful women I have ever seen in my life. That is certain. I did not go. I stayed with Myriam until 4pm then taxi'd back to Plymouth. 'Go in Peace' Myriam said. It is difficult for me to take her seriously, but just as difficult not to. Whether I see her again or not – a remarkable person. (Diary, 20/21 June 1976)

The comedown from the heights of sexual mysticism can be cruel. Robert returned to the Studio to find his electricity cut off for non-payment. He took a taxi to Annie's house where there was some kind of dispute: 'Her behaviour was depressing. If only – but that is impossible in every scummish English possible way'. Later in the day he notes: 'She chucked me out'. Above this, in confident script almost certainly penned by Annie: 'You chucked yourself out' (Diary, 21 June 1976). Robert had a small salad at Dudley's café and slept alone in the Studio.

He continued to neglect his health. He had an appointment at the chest clinic to follow up on his X-rays, arrived early, waited a while, then noted: 'Too busy. I couldn't wait./Left' (Diary, 17 June 1976). And unless Annie, Eliza, or some other kindly woman cooked for him out of café hours he was helpless. His own dietary choices were cumulatively suicidal. The above-mentioned salad jumps out of the diary as a rare exception. None of the eateries which subsidised him were unsanitary but they served high-fat and almost exclusively fried foods. One of the greatest physiological mysteries about Robert is how he ran a muscular body on utter junk. He once boasted to me that he ate nine Mars Bars in one day. This adds up to 2,000 calories of sugar and fat. The mural Robert painted inside Prete's café in the mid-1970s gives a fair indication of his lunches. From basic nutrition to physical and intellectual companionship to erotic fuel for the projects, the women helped him live. He was fortunate that so many wanted to look after him, for without their concerted efforts he would surely have been obese and diabetic by early middle age.

And look after him they did. In an episode which was even by Robert's standards remarkable for its mysticism as much as its sexuality, the Rivera sisters created a *memoria* or *memento vivere* for him. We quote Robert's account at length for it contradicts a large prejudice that his exuberant sexuality was merely that of a greedy sensualist sleeping around with his models. Yes, he was a sensualist and he loved sex. His investigations shared features with the filthy materialism of Bataille and de Sade. But he drew at least as much impetus from the Christian mystics Catherine of Sienna, Julian of Norwich, and Hildegaard of Bingen with their projects of higher union, divine love, and *deliria synaesthesia*. Robert was of course capable of the most casual of sex and sometimes joked about the practicalities of his 'penetrating research' while Johnny pursued the scientific path of sexology. But for Robert the worldly pleasures could function as a gateway to a stranger, mythical zone. Explorations of the flesh pointed towards a metaphysics and poetics of 'the soul':

I sit in Joe's surrounded by people sitting in Joe's. All their backs are facing me. The café room seems like an aircraft or mobile taking us to meet Father Time or Peter Pan.

12:30 pm. Myriam and Magdalena meet at shop to go to the house. Get large canvases etc. They came looking extraordinary. Taxi'd to my house. Took off their clothes and made themselves at ease. Brought many fruits and goat's milk. Peaceful and very unusual time with two beautiful ladies. Strange tales are made of this but rarely written. Something learned and not to be forgotten.

Stories. Talked. Painted. Fucked. Stories. Music. A little food. Painted. Stories. Tales. Talked. Fucked.

Myriam. Very sweet evening. Many, many layers of human activity in this strange world. Unusual wise silent night. Something about her is very old.

Went upstairs, lay down with Magdalena and woke her up with a story.
Went for a walk with Magdalena. Took several photographs.
Painted her (very poor work, illustrational and hopeless).

Talked with Magdalena. Sudden change of situation with moving incident in the library. One of those images – *memoria*.

Taxi came to collect me from my house, and Miriam, and Magdalena. So strange to say goodbye. Like a sphynx and a black horse. I just
stepped out of the car. Looked and went. What strange times. (Diary,
4 July 1976)

The sisters wrote to him several days later and Robert records: 'They both
seem to wish to live at the house. Dangerous situation (for me). Irresistible undertones. The stresses would be so interesting. Very amusing letter'
(Diary, 9 July 1976).

On 15 July, Magdalena and Myriam came to live in my house. Arrived
[...] with food. So nice to see them there. 'Death and The Maiden have
come to visit you' was the first thing Myriam said. I typed my first page
for the History of Mental Handicap. Did a painting of Magdalena.
Went to bed: Magdalena to my left, Myriam to my right. So curious –
the old fool with two sisters. Very beautiful developments. (Diary, 15
July 1976)

The next morning, he notes: 'Perhaps one of the most unusual nights of
my life. So, so, strange. So, so, strange. Sweet, sad letter from Myriam'
(Diary, 16 July 1976).

The next day Myriam sat in 25 The Parade:

Myriam like a sphynx, saying nothing. No reaction whatsoever to
any of the dossers/Cowboys etc., even when Welsh Ray John came in
drunk and aggressive, she sat there reading as if the room was empty.
She thought there was no harm in the situation if I felt I wished to take
the stress. Father Confessors are usually anonymous and behind bars'
(Diary, 9 June 1976)

Robert himself was fairly unflappable in such situations, as when 'a large
group of Hells Angels crashed into the shop. All sorts of Manson-ish undertones: but quite sweet really'. But Myriam's non-reactions to the breaks

in normalcy are interesting. Most people have no choice – they are compelled to react. Those who can choose their reactions or non-reactions are a rare breed, and have usually cultivated themselves in some 'spiritual' way. Over the next week Robert slept most nights with the sisters. There are hints of something akin to shamanistic or at least 'occult' voyages. He writes: 'Myriam cleaned everything. Magdalena danced for an hour. Myriam so strange – so humanly explorative in areas better left alone' (Diary, 19 June 1976).

Robert's favourite word for the situation with the Rivera sisters was 'strange', but it is hard to make sense of why he went to a fortune-teller with Magdalena. He describes the visit with the oxymoron 'predictable/amazing'. Next day he mentions an unspecified event 'which could make the fortune-teller more prophet than fool. Reuben came. So good to see him get on so well with Myriam. Went to the police station. Myriam playing the game very well. How I hate to see it. Magdalena released'. Without charge, it seems, though why she was detained we are not told. 'How I hate to see it. The police feel so filthy. My years with them have taught me only how to loathe them more. The only group worth scapegoating. Beauty and the Beast. Only this beast grows uglier every century' (Diary, 25 July 1976). Stranger becomes stranger still: 'Strange night. Myriam made the tea. Magdalena: curious empty foreboding. They will both go and see my mother in London'. He gives no explanation of why they should do such a thing. But the next day he again feels the 'curious, empty foreboding'. Later he describes the situation as 'calm and agreeable. Trying to look at Reuben in a different way. Reuben waited for Myriam. An example of Faith I suppose [...] Magdalena bought everyone a meal. Drove to station to get times etc., for tomorrow's train for the two ladies. Magdalena and Myriam. The last night for the Trinity' (Diary, 25 July 1976). When they left the next morning: 'Myriam left me a letter. Very true. Wrote a note to my mother for Myriam and Magdalena to take to her. Last time at my house. Stood at the bottom of the path and registered their dark images against my old silent home.'

As if by magic the Rivera sisters' departure coincided with the arrival of Jeny Lelya Bremer, 'looking very good'. The accompaniment of her young son made liaisons a little difficult but she posed for many paintings. We mentioned earlier the capacity to react or not react that we saw in Myriam as an index of how 'normally socialised' – which is to say, how 'mass-produced' – a person might be. It was a hot day at 25 The Parade and The Bishop was sitting on the low wall outside the council flats. Jeny and Robert were in the window area of the Studio. To investigate their capabilities Robert asked Jeny to approach The Bishop, strike up a conversation, then while talking start to take her clothes off. This she did, slowly stripping to the waist before an old lady from the flats shrieked down as if a murder were in progress. Jeny put her clothes back on. She recalls how The Bishop had continued their conversation looking straight at her face, with neither her very good-looking breasts nor the screaming woman exerting the least gravity upon his eyes (Jeny, Interview, May 2018). This bears serious philosophical consideration. Unless totally hammered on cider The Bishop was far from 'insensible' – quite the opposite. He struck me as one who could hear clouds passing overhead on a dark night. I do not know how much of his altered perception was his choice, but this was clearly a man tuned to very different channels than the standard human being.

At the end of July Robert notes some 'sickening news about Belle. I wish her the best. No better way to cut connections than the 'aesthetic way'. No better than the way she chose. Strangely – a relief. Unpleasant, but a relief' (Diary, 30 July 1976). He had of course been dumped as unceremoniously as he had dumped Mouse eight years earlier. Ruti Cohen visited from London and spent several nights with Robert. This was 'very sweet [but] I keep thinking of M and M' (Diary, 2 August 1976). This despite his wholly positive feelings for the woman and their child: 'Ruti so sweet: far too good for me. Laila is a very pretty child [...] took her to a taxi, watched them drive off' (Diary, 3 August 1976). Jacquetta returned to Port Eliot and was keen to see Robert. His feelings for her were ambivalent: 'Jacquetta standing in the doorway like an emaciated demon. The clavicle opens [...] meet her at 5pm Wednesday' (Diary, 2 August 1976). The pace of Robert's relationships both sexual and non-sexual again increased, perhaps catalysed by the interventions of Myriam and Magdalena. And he became somewhat more fatherly to Reuben: 'Reuben came down today – bit of a nuisance [but] in a curious way he was very sweet and philosophically amusing today' (Diary, 4 August 1976). His diaries buzz with social interactions, and as he approaches the manic phase of the project's development he notes in block capitals: 'THE LORD AND LADY MAYOR WILL OPEN MY EXHIBITION ON TUESDAY THE 24TH AUGUST AT 7.30PM. I STILL DO NOT HAVE A RELIABLE VENUE'.

The Jacquetta situation tormented Robert but he seemed oddly or wilfully inept at controlling its pace. Engaging a troublesome love object in intimate discussions and unresolved erotics is sure to fuel the fire. It seems that this is exactly what he did:

> Went to Dudley's. Long talk, she became very depressed and aggressive. Always the same frightened, withdrawn attitude. Went up to main studio. I tried another approach. And another. Ridiculous situation developed. Absurdly unsatisfactory ... And could do a lot of harm to a foolish man. What does Lucian Freud do I wonder, about that one? There are some things she simply 'Does not know'. J. Drove off to her stupid bed. Taxi'd to the house. Myriam has cleaned the place. Everything so calm. (Diary, 4 August 1976)

In the calm of 'Death House' Robert assembled the hundred or so questionnaires from the Mental Handicap Project. Myriam typed these up into publishable form and translated more research materials. Robert chose quotes from Nietzsche's critique of the morality of pity, perhaps the most depressing and fateful form of what Nietzsche called 'slave morality' and 'herd values'. While keeping The Fool open for business and tending to the children, Annie found time to ferry paintings back and forth in her van as well as acting as Robert's chauffeuse. Funds were found to relight 25 The Parade with the help of an electrician. He 'even cashed a cheque of mine personally in order to get the electricity back on. I bought spotlights and the shop is ablaze again' (Diary, 12 August 1976). Robert could once again work through the night.

Sensing the growing momentum, many of the dossers helped as best they could. They brought scavenged furniture and timber to make stretchers, signs, and frames. Andy, Michael, and the rest of 'the Barbican lads' made the old Jacob's Ladder studio on Southside Street presentable with wooden panelling to cover all the obvious holes. But Jacob's Ladder was still unlit. 'Everything seems to be going fine. Next problem: electricity'. With no time or money for a professional fix Robert conscripted 'Hans de Rijke. He is the "electricity man" I need. Gave him £30 for materials etc. Will start tomorrow' (Diary, 16 August 1976). Advance publicity appeared in the local newspapers. Not all of it was good, and some of it so ugly that one wonders if Robert had entirely misjudged the interview or had been misquoted.

> Robert Lenkiewicz the Barbican artist has a shock in store for visitors to his new exhibition this week. For many of the 200 pictures of men-

tally handicapped children could be disturbing [...] one of the paintings shows a girl screaming while the girl next to her stares blankly into space. And there is one of a child who has only one year to live. This exhibition, however, is nothing compared to the shocks he has in store for Plymouth next year. He has just started work on his new exhibition. Its theme – prostitution. That collection will be shown next year. Also next year Lenkiewicz is going to show his 'most offensive picture in the world'. Only those over 18 will be allowed to see it. 'That one will really shock a few people' he said. (News clipping, Diary, 22 August 1976)

The writer may as well have used the word 'freak show'. Robert commented: 'Perhaps one of the most insensitive and stupid articles ever written regarding one of my projects. This must take the prize for sheer crassness. What does he expect the parents to think?'. Undaunted by the irony that so much study, goodwill, creativity, and *humanitas* could be swept aside in so few words, the next two days were an insane rush to the finish line. 'Painted all night. Still very much behind schedule. Slept for one hour' (Diary, 22 August 1976). 'Myriam came with food. Worked hard and late in preparation' (Diary, 23 August 1976). On Tuesday the 24th: 'Mad panic to erect "The Night Watch" [...] extraordinary amount of labour involved in getting everything ready. Still left with work to do after the people came. Incredible influx of people. Over 300 turned up.' And that was *before* the Lord Mayor officially opened the exhibition at 7.30 p.m.

The Night Watch was unveiled and the crowd was well pleased with it. Robert was roundly congratulated. And for once, without the slightest delay, money started to roll in. Sales of paintings and donations from the local bourgeoisie were brisk. Not a penny was for Robert. As the exhibition pamphlet had it:

> It is to be clearly understood that no altruistic intentions motivated this project [...]. All the proceeds from this exhibition viz: entrance money, paintings that are sold, will be for the use of the Plymouth Society for Mental Handicap. Although all the paintings were produced by the painter, they are technically the property of the Plymouth Society for Mental Handicap. Those paintings that remain unsold after the completion of this exhibition's tour around the cities of England become the property (free) of the parents concerned.

17.6 Robert with *Self-Portrait (after Franz Xaver Messerschmidt)* (1976), shown in the Mental Handicap Project.

17.7 Robert with Project 3 sitter Barbara Bridgeman. The canvas of the Greep family can be seen left, with the Bridgeman family to the right.

17.8 Paintings from the Mental Handicap Project crowd the Barbican studio, March 1976.

17.9   Poster for Project 3, 1976.

17.10   The entrance to Jacob's Ladder studio where Project 3 was shown.

17.11   Interior of the Mental Handicap exhibition.

17.12 Interior of the Mental Handicap exhibition.

17.13 The 4.2m tall canvas *The Night Watch*, unfinished, filled one wall
in the studio.

17.14 Belle Pecorini and her daughter Hayyam visited Robert in May 1976.

17.15 The artist's son, Reuben, with vagrant The Skipper, 16 October 1976.

17.16 Annie Hill-Smith with Robert at the studio, with their sons Sholem and Jascha, who was born in April 1976.

17.17 Robert at Port Eliot with small study attributed to Rembrandt on 30 December 1976.

Next morning the exhibition opened to the general public. The newspapers contained 'Nothing special [but] people started to come right away'. The painting of the Greep family sold almost immediately for £250. He gave an interview for local radio. Television crews from Westward TV and the BBC arrived. Throngs of interested locals mixed with the sitters and their families and talked about the issues raised by the paintings. All talked with the politicians, including David Owen, the Minister for Health, and Victoria Stennan, the head of the National Society for Mental Handicap. Robert records: 'People still going into the MH exhibition at 9 o'clock in the evening'. The same night he notes how he 'Began to re-organize [...] Make ready for the next project on Love and Mediocrity [...] Feeling really quite ill. Over 300 people went to the exhibition today' (Diary, 25 August 1976). Fifty or eighty pounds was a good week's wage at that time: in 24 hours over £1,000 had been raised for the charity. Bailiffs were circling, the roof was leaking onto *The Night Watch*, Robert's children were struggling for school shoes, but the art was flourishing. Reception in the local newspapers was not always thoughtful but it was mainly 'sweet' to use Robert's favoured term. An unsourced article in the diary at 26 August 1976 reads:

> Are these pictures too strong for Plymouth? Since he came to Plymouth the Barbican artist has been called disgraceful, shocking, and obscene. Some [including members of the City Council] have suggested that his works should be whitewashed over or scribbled on by vandals to hide it. But his new exhibition of 200 paintings on Mental Handicap which opened this week [...] seems certain to be accepted even by stiff-moraled Plymouth [...] Lenkiewicz is the master painter of relationships and this new collection takes the viewer farther behind the face of mental handicap than a pile of books on the subject could hope to. From the beginning of the exhibition the viewer is confronted with a mirror and told 'This Person Is Normal'. From then on he is on his own. Already the paintings have been acclaimed by Baroness Vickers and Lord Mayor Arthur Floyd. Now will the people of Plymouth recognise and support their local genius?

Sadly the closing line falls under that journalistic formula for writing headlines: Questions to which the answer is – 'No'. Or at least 'Not yet', except for the people of the Barbican who were perhaps 70% convinced. Sales were swift, footfall brisk, and media coverage good in terms of volume, if not always quality. But Robert's optimism was dented by a sense that 'people [are] lazy and aggressive towards the exhibition. BBC [coverage] very good, sensitive, gentle and dramatic. Westward [TV] very poor, cheap. Converted the whole Project into a horror show' (Diary, 25 and 27 August 1976). It was predictable enough that Robert's unsentimental handling of the material troubled some people. What was surprising was that some of the parents of the sitters were disturbed by the paintings.

This ambivalence was evident even before the exhibition: 'Mr and Mrs Ruse freaked in. They were in a very difficult mood. Would I please destroy the portrait of John, their Down's Syndrome child?' (Diary, 3 June 1976). This ambivalence extended to many of the public. Robert noted how some people who paid to enter the exhibition 'couldn't be bothered walking fifty feet' to see it in its entirety – 'simply can't be bothered' (Diary, 28 August 1976). Curiously, he does not consider the possibility that something other than laziness might prevent them from confronting the images. Robert's calibrations for 'normal' were odd but he was highly sensitive to people's thoughts and feelings. Perhaps he did not realise how much his works could unnerve the public. With paintings of such intimacy as *Mr & Mrs Greep with Francis, Tracey & Darren*, sensitive people might feel they were prying into a private tragedy. There are also people who through no fault of their own genuinely fear abnormality in any shape or form. But many do not, and for several consecutive days Robert's mood swung according to the motions of the crowd: 'Amazing to see hundreds of people at the exhibition. So strange to actually see a queue. People coming into my shop and congratulating etc., etc. (Diary, 30 August 1976).

Robert was starting to enjoy fame.

18.1 Poster for Project 5, exhibited in December 1976.

18.2 Annie Hill-Smith with Robert and their sons Sholem and Jascha, and Suli the dog, who appears in *The Night Watch* canvas, November 1976.

18.3 Robert unloading paintings at The Fool in Clifton Street, 1976.

18.4 Robert smiling up at Annie in The Fool, setting up the Love &
Mediocrity exhibition, 1976.

18.5 David Rogers and a Television South West film crew interview
Robert at The Fool on 1 December 1976.

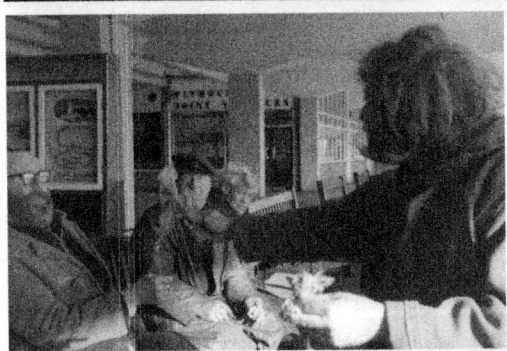

18.7 David Rogers interviews Robert for Television South West at The Fool.
18.8 & 18.9 'Cowboys Banquet – 12 noon at the bus station. Myriam helped
– semi/mystically'. (Diary, Christmas Day, 1976).
Attending were: Reg Hawke, Dave Helingoe, Big John Wayne, 'Sally Army
chap', Cockney Jim, The Bishop, Snowy, Irish (Barbican) John.

18

Mediocrity, Death, and the Mother

The Mayor of Bath visited Robert with offers to host the Mental Handicap exhibition in her home city. She left her business card and personal contact details. Beside her card Robert notes: 'Must contact Baroness Vickers, this could be very interesting' (Diary, 5 September 1976). The directors of an academic publishing company requested 'the pleasure of the company of Robert Lenkiewicz' for a champagne buffet with the Lord Mayor of Plymouth (Diary, 7 September 1976). Lord Eliot grew increasingly hospitable and was keen to introduce Robert to the Poet Laureate, Sir John Betjeman, and his daughter Candida, herself a formidable literary force. At Port Eliot Robert held the snuffbox which belonged to the artist Sir Joshua Reynolds and a small original painting by Rembrandt. He dined with Perry, Jacquetta, Lucinda [Andrew Beaumont's spouse], and 'some Home Office and Foreign Affairs chap' who 'wouldn't leave me alone'. He was shown 'the silver room – below stairs. I held £6,000 worth of African coins in my hands. Studied a strange "Death Defeating Life" seal (Italian?). Felt a bit like the Count of Monte Christo and his treasure hoard' (Diary, 8 September 1976).

Robert's hobnobbing with the Upper Crust had something of a comic flavour. He did not 'belong' among them anymore than with the lower and very much crustier characters who lurked just around the corner:

> The Taxi drove us back [from Port Eliot] to Plymouth. First thing I was greeted by was two rough looking cowboys sitting on the ground opposite the gates to the exhibition. One of them – grinning psychopathically – was Brummy, just out from Exeter prison – and down on his vendetta bit to 'do me in'. He became very aggressive – lumbered over, grabbed hold of me and started threatening, spitting at me, etc. in the middle of the road. 'Brother Blair' had said to him that I had 'paid someone £40 to deal with him' or some such gibberish. It was very difficult for me to avoid his aggression. Very dangerous and unpleasant situation. Felt quite nauseous for the remainder of the day. He is strong as a bull, and plainly unafraid of pain. Must be very careful indeed. (Diary, 12 September 1976)

Brother Blair was intent on harming Robert but without risking imprisonment. He resembled a vagrant prototype for Will Self's twisted psychiatrist Dr Mutki, who referred his most dangerous patients to a rival practitioner like 'dumb bombs in a deadly duel'. Robert was right to be worried. He knew there was no point appealing to reality when dealing with a psychotic. Brummy would not respond well to the fact that Robert saw him as mentally ill, or that £40 to have him bashed was a ridiculous sum because there was a queue of people happy to bash him for free, and Robert had declined their offers. Or the most obvious fact of all: paying to have a vagrant bashed was simply not Robert's style, and Robert's style meant more to him than morality, legality, or safety.

The following day was Alice's twelfth birthday. Robert met Mouse and the children for a cinema visit. Once again Robert reports a rare sadness, possibly a nostalgia for Mouse. In the evening, after watching the movie he notes: 'Strange melancholy business. Alice cried. We went to the Yankee Burger. Chris let me have credit – had a marvellous meal. Alice/Wolfe/Becky/Romilly/and two of Alice's friends + Mouse' (Diary, 13 September 1976). Two months earlier he wrote of Mouse: 'Wish I didn't feel sorry for her' – which easily translates to 'Wish I didn't still have feelings for her'. The theme of past lovers haunted him as he pushed further ahead with the Love and Mediocrity Project. Some were sweet ghosts, others were vengeful.

Predictably the next day saw 'trouble brewing in Brummy's sad wet brain'. He 'sat like a brooding behemoth on the wall opposite my shop. Grinning inanely/swaggering past/drinking, drinking, drinking'. Robert had no telephone at 25 The Parade so the complaints must have come from the flats opposite. 'The police came down at least three times. Slightly amusing chase – following Brummy – but they did not pick him up. Could now develop very badly' (Diary, 14 September1976). Brummy orbited Robert with closer and further menaces in the following weeks. How much he was directed by Brother Blair is uncertain. Though the air of madness thickened around Robert he was not going to close the Studio door to lock out any possibilities, however bizarre:

The extraordinary half-caste turned up again. She insisted on having me do a quick pencil self-portrait. There was no way in which I could dissuade her save the use of physical force which would probably have resulted in some unimaginable consequence. She lives in Texas, was never born, (just came) is 2,000 years old and her name is 'Baa'. She has 'always' been married; he is a Eunuch kept in a glass case on a shelf. He paints, writes, and plays music. Her 'skill' is to do the best for him. She describes herself as 'a nutcase' and tells me that 'If I was not already married, I would run away with you: you would not be given the chance to say yea or nay. I would just run away with you. You do not do yourself justice. I think you look like me. I think-in-you is a comrade'. Then she left, gaunt and intense with the drawing under her arm. (Diary, 26 September 1976)

Brute violence, symbolic violence, and psychic violence figure largely in the works Robert assembled for Love and Mediocrity. The project is all about human relationships and the paintings mainly show human bodies, though these are interwoven with solar imagery: wounded suns, setting suns, stars bleeding out into the street or desert sky. Double suns, one for the world of the living, one for the world of the dead. Black suns, resonant with the alchemical symbols of spiritual and cosmic decay. Several of the paintings contain dark figures with hoods, which could mark them as condemned prisoners, executioners, or both. Others depict the lifeless bodies of Belle and Monica being lowered into unmarked graves. This dying of the light, the fading of consciousness, the closing of life is encoded in the beginning of a relationship as much as the end. The executioners and/or victims in *Lovers Getting to Know Each Other* (1976) are presented in a pose of tragic innocence based on the archetype of Adam and Eve. The warmth of their naked bodies is as sure to fade as the pale sun setting behind them. It is bisected by a cloud resembling fresh viscera. Robert is again exploring the fundamental human relationship with the passage of time towards death. In *Lovers with Child* (1976) the eroticised nihilism is painful to contemplate. The lovers seem unaware that they are holding a child's severed head. Entirely beyond sensation, or blissfully unaware, all three heads are closed to the awareness that the biological future is already over. Nor is Robert's point an abstract one about archetypes: the dead child is clearly Jascha. The face is almost identical to the image in an aesthetic note titled 'Jascha, 3.5.77'.

It is not all bare bones and heartbreak. There is some humour, of the graveyard variety. *Lovers Dancing on the Graves of Previous Lovers* (1976) has the wicked energy of Grieg's 'Hall of the Mountain King', with its troll-like lovers stomping in an ecstasy of remembrance. The colours are rich and sonorous: the double flowers resemble bloody polyps singing, or Miro's 'animacules'. The deepest blue of the graves pulses with energy as

303

if death itself were the source of the living lover's 'orgone'. Despite such instances of painful humour, the overall mood of the Love and Mediocrity canvases is one of deep isolation with the similar cumulative effect of the Vagrancy Exhibition. It is almost overwhelming. In *Woman Watching Man Look at Himself in a Mirror* the woman is barely discernible as a shadow among shadows. The man, whose relation to himself is surely auto-erotic, resembles partly formed conjoined twins, fused at face and groin, sealed in a glass laboratory cloche. Robert's point is that even when we are 'doubled' with ourselves, we are *always alone*. The inevitable and equally tragic flip-side of this libidinal coin is that we are also *always with too many people*. Or rather, with too many of our own representations of people. This is evident in the studies of lovers with multiple heads looking through ghost crowds of remembered lovers, and the lovers hemmed in by memories of previous lovers. Robert conjures a world characterised by the consistent failure of anybody to encounter anybody else with their eyes open.

The paintings and the project notes foreground a decisive philosophical element in Robert's aesthetic and erotic practice – his insistence upon a fundamental isolation. This sense of isolation had been sharpened by his idiosyncratic readings of Kant, Schopenhauer, and Nietzsche. His position varies somewhat throughout his life, but the basic contention informing all the 'Relationship' projects is as follows. If we cannot know the world 'as it really is' but only as it appears to our senses, then 'true' knowledge of other people is an illusion. What we 'know' of the other person is merely our habitual response to the scintillations of our own senses:

> The mirror that you hold up in front of me whenever I am in your company reflects on my own mediocrity. As I move to another person, then again another mirror rises between me and you, and the relation-ship echoes the same mediocrity as before. 'You' are not to blame, 'You' do not exist, 'You' can never exist, not for a single moment can 'You' ever exist for me.
>
> 'I' am not to blame. 'I' do not exist. 'I' can never exist, not for a single moment can 'I' ever exist for you. (Love and Mediocrity Note-book, p. 5)

Robert's thought takes strange directions in the Love and Mediocrity Notebook, possibly because he hoists philosophical arguments out of their historical positions, ignoring the conditions of their development. This does not necessarily make them less effective, but it does change their functions and values. For example, he follows Kant's transcendental critique of knowledge through Schopenhauer to Nietzsche, culminating in the evaluation that 'the real world' is a myth. But curiously, Robert's notes often read as if Nietzsche had not developed transcendental philosophy into a critique of *values*, such that truth, beauty, and goodness are themselves under question. Because of this oversight, Robert's arguments concerning the untrustworthiness of the senses often sail close to the pre-critical, moral condemnations of Plato and Descartes:

> By assuming that one is able to identify the experiences which represent significant milestones in our lives we give birth to a melancholy vacuum of unsatisfying experiences. Nowhere is this clearer than in relationships. Romantic conditioned reflexes discourage subtler layers of perception, producing the inevitable sense of failure in 'achievements', which by their very nature were chimerical. Unprepared selectivity (emotive memories) have nothing whatsoever to do with the real nature of the experience of a relationship. By and large the major art of a relationship's 'meaning' or 'value' passes entirely un-noticed by both partners. (Love and Mediocrity Project Notebook, p. 23)

Robert's thinking often reintroduces the notion that there is a 'real nature' of things, and that it is rationally discernible, and must differ from the phenomena of emotion and memory. We will see more of it in the 'Mary Notebook' and the Self-Portrait Project notes. Robert's search for 'the truth' ranges very widely. At times he argues like a Platonist or Pythagorean, and at other times like the Blake of *The Marriage of Heaven and Hell*:

> Love is kindled through the senses. Nothing cures the soul as much as the senses. Nothing cures the senses as much as the soul. The 'finer feelings' are raised through the senses. And the 'finer feelings' are crushed by them as well. (Love and Mediocrity Project Notebook, p. 49)

The body and soul are divided from each other, the 'individual' is divided from themselves just as much as they are divided from society. One of the conclusions Robert was driving towards in the Love and Mediocrity Project was that relationships do not 'unite people' but ironically and tragically isolate them. This is doubly odd considering Robert was a twin and remained emotionally close to Bernard all his life. This thought that we cannot 'really know' others – or indeed ourselves – led Robert into a series of reflections of a semi-geometric nature. If knowledge was not to be found via the senses, then perhaps the axioms and deductions of rational thought might be more helpful. Thus, in the style of Euclid and Spinoza, Robert began to map out what he took to be the basic structures of desire. This may in part be a return to the Pythagoreanism he first announced in his 'Essay on Velázquez', but in 1976 the methods of Spinoza are also on Robert's mind. These he modifies in his own unique way:

> An old Pnoob legend tells us that the origin of the Milky Way and indeed that of the whole of the Heavens begins with the act of self-love. God so loved himself that he ejaculated. When Spinoza says that God Loves himself infinitely, he hints at his own secret acts. We do not know if Spinoza masturbated with a view of Amsterdam before him, lenses on the table, Descartes' *Meditations* on the shelf.

Indeed, we do not know, but Robert painted a lively watercolour of how he imagined the happy scene described above (Love and Mediocrity Notebook, p. 31, 'Spinoza Masturbates over His Lenses'). In the following pages we find dozens of geometric figures. These are Robert's maps of the structural features and load-bearing capacities of 'the necessary psychic pillars of human relationships' (Love and Mediocrity Project Notebook, p. 51). These surreal engineering diagrams are accompanied by musings on 'areas of primary vulnerability' and 'need for support'. He is at times aware that the structural analogy is considerably over-extended: 'A few graphic studies of applying pressure on or between points of a triangle demonstrate unreliable geometric results (Love and Mediocrity Project Notebook, p. 52). He continues page after page, and the resulting diagrams have some relationship to beauty, if not truth. The notes are couched in scientific terms, although how we might estimate 'aesthetic energy' or the 'potentials' and 'quota' for addictions remains obscure. The doubled intervals Robert develops in the charts resemble updated versions of Fludd's 'universal monochord' diagram from the Elizabethan Mural. There are tantalising hints that a mathematical function might be isolated from all this: 'The blue line is the time taken. It is independent of events within it. The time period remains constant but the addiction content is halved sequentially' (Love and Mediocrity Project Notebook, p. 58). But the formula does not appear, and Robert rebounds from attempted mathematics to a conclusion linked to dreams and memories:

The great Dream of the lover is auto-sexual. You cannot seriously believe that what you strongly desire ever happens in the way envisaged. The act may last for a day or two provided there is no work to do and there is food. But then it becomes memory, and that is falsified. So, what is there to do, but repeat it? You can only ever live now, they say. And when 'now' has passed, then you live in the next one. And if in that 'now' she has gone, then where do you live? Auto-sex and memory, that is 'love' for us, isn't it? (Love and Mediocrity Project Notebook, p. 65)

The bleakness of this sentiment is cushioned – perhaps with ironic humour, perhaps unconsciously – by the personal pronoun 'us'. By Robert's reasoning, this 'us' can only be a community of people with nothing in common except their isolation. We are exiled from one other, we are exiled from our 'selves'.

Brother Blair had been conniving all summer to get Robert threatened or actually 'done in' by other dossers. He started to write suicide notes. Whether this was an attempt to emotionally blackmail Robert, a genuine cry for help, or some other strategy we cannot know. Robert notes: 'Another "con" letter from Brother Blair' and 'Letter from Brother Blair – the suicide crap' (Diary, 8 October 1976).

On 12 October Robert draws two lines under the words '"Brother Blair" is dead'. Next to this:

List of Cowboys who have died this last year. Eddy Faden, committed suicide. 'Big John' Barr. 'Griffiths' (Bristol). 'Furgy' (Bournemouth). 'Whispering Jock'. 'Duke' McCloud. 'Kerbs' Ward. 'Punch Tyrone'. 'Basil'. 'Smokey Joe'. 'The Singer'. 'Jack Willet'.

News of Brother Blair's death came with reports that Brummy had been jailed for destroying a Social Security office he had found unhelpful. Robert felt a distinct sense of relief, but nothing in the diaries suggests he had any ill-will to his persecutors. Even so, the future must have looked brighter without Brother Blair in it. The problem was that Robert's initial instincts about 'the suicide crap' were sound. Brother Blair was not dead and would haunt Robert for some time to come.

Throughout the autumn of 1976 Robert received news about his mother's declining health via Johnny, Tova, and Jennie Celner – the daughter of the exploding Mrs Plotnik. They encouraged him to write and visit while there was still time (Diary, 25 September 1976). Ma was suffering from colon cancer. Johnny recalls that the treatment involving invasive tissue-freezing techniques was almost as awful as the disease. When she was not in the Royal Free Hospital, Johnny and Tova bore the brunt of her care. She was not a pleasant patient. They saw her every day, though when on one occasion they took a short break:

> Just for a weekend. She was not happy that we had been away. [On our return] as soon as I turned the key in the door my mother was swigging [...] she must have been waiting for me [...] she started swigging back this bottle of Brompton cocktail. (Johnny, Interview, May 2018)

Seldom used now, the Brompton cocktail was a staple of terminal care nursing in the 20th century. Morphine or heroin was dissolved in high-purity ethyl alcohol, mixed with cocaine or amphetamine to combat the drowsiness, then shook up in a bottle with chlorpromazine and cherry syrup. Self-administered dosages meant that patients had the option of a relatively dignified and painless overdose from this tasty 'elixir of death'.

> I asked her how much she had taken, and she was being very ambiguous about it. Deliberately, obviously, but she led me to believe it was about a third or a half of a bottle. A lot. I said – are you sure you took that much? – I rang the doctor and he was a bit critical about it; he said something like *too bad but not good enough at all*, so I didn't know what to do. In the end I called the ambulance, and they took her away while she was complaining about not having her glasses with her. We ended up at the Royal Free A & E department. The young doctor there said to me 'What should we do about this?' and I didn't at first understand what he meant. Later, it occurred to me that he was asking if we should just let her kill herself, a kind of 'do not resuscitate' situation. But I was quite angry with him and said, 'Do your job.' He went off, they took her in, and they kept her in for about a week. I imagine she was just a bit depressed and wanted a bit of attention. And she wanted to punish us for having a holiday. (Johnny, Interview, May 2018)

Robert wrote to her and made a swift visit in December, but left her care entirely to others. Ma was understandably unhappy about this. Robert asked if he could paint her portrait, again. She refused, again. In February 1977 Robert allows her voice to enter the Diaries.

'You vunder at vot I say? You should hear vat I think! Dat vood be something to paint!'

'I know you are mit no money and many proplems, but I don't gif a damn!'

'De only think a mother does wronk is to leave you alone in dis dirty vorlt.'

'No death with dignity, without a life with dignity.'

'What the hell do you think love is, an Irish maid?'

Alongside her words Robert notes: 'You are a malicious, vicious cow under that suffering exterior' (Diary, 26 February 1977). He is working on the Last Supper Mural in Prete's café, he is adding finishing touches to the Wild West Mural in Frankfort Gate, he is working hard on the Jealousy theme, he is arranging funerals for dead Cowboys, he is fretting about his less than successful relationship with Belle, he is starting long relationships with the art students Yana Trevail and Gillian (soon to be known as Mary) Pearce. Brother Blair emerged from false death and self-imposed exile to make some kind of peace and even buy tea for Robert (Diary, 14 February 1977). Yes, he is busy, but no, there is no time or attention given to his dying mother.

Menaces from Brummy continued. Robert was offered protection by the tiny but fearsome dosser bearing weapons and the name 'Psycho-Knife Jock'. He had recently finished a prison sentence: 'Nine months for GBH – stabbing a large Scot in the stomach. He seemed very affectionate, taking into account his Cowboy crack. Said that he was going to bodyguard for me during the summer. Amusing to think that a dwarf might defend me against the likes of "Big Brummie" – but he is such a little thug it could just work' (Diary, 12 February 1977). Indeed, it could. Knife defence is tricky at the best of times, let alone keeping one's nerve and balance against a man whose natural stab-level is your genitals.

When Robert eventually visits London on 24 February he spends most of his time with Aury, first in the National Gallery admiring Ingres, then in Portobello admiring the buskers, 'particularly a tap-dancer who I spoke with'. He paid a short visit to his mother on Saturday 26 February. This is the last time he will see her alive. He sketches her while she is semi-conscious. Granted Ma was terminally ill, but Robert makes her look like Max Shrek in *Nosferatu*. He leaves her to spend time with Johnny and Tova. The next day he is back in the National Gallery, then Hyde Park with Annie, Pnoobie, Aury, and Myrna, generally lollygagging around the city, feeding ducks in the Serpentine and so forth. If he has anything to say to his mother it has already been said, but Ma was not letting him get away so easily.

> Back to Aury's. Talked and joked much. Watched television. Johnny phoned. Ma had attempted another suicide. Brompton Cocktail etc. Difficult to know what has happened (I suspect nothing or very little). Dramatically timed for my expected visit? I phoned Tova a couple of times, she was fatigued and ironic about it all. (Diary, 27 February 1977)

Robert spent the next day with Annie, Aury, and others, preferring to see Kubrick's *Barry Lyndon* than visit his mother again. He returned to Plymouth on 1 March and dealt with some Studio business before spending a pleasant night with Myriam, then slipped out early for Port Eliot with Belle. He was pleased to see Perry and even more pleased to hear that the estate manager Andrew Beaumont had brought the tangled affair of the lease for 25 The Parade to a happy conclusion. Robert worked on the 'Death and Apocalypse' section of the Round Room Mural.

He was in telephone contact with Myriam in Plymouth and Annie in London, juggling priorities and painting schedules. On returning to Plymouth his main concern was the damp in his library at Priory Road which threatened his 16th and 17th-century books. The weather was so bad he often stayed at Priory Road to paint rather than getting soaked on the walk to the Barbican, but the time was well spent: he completed the *Dead Model* painting and worked on *Man Watching Woman Walk Away*. On the 17th he returned to London, but for almost a week there is no mention of his mother. Most of the time he spends painting with Annie and Aury. 'Aury drove me to the East End and bought me £150 worth of best canvas'. 'Talked to old Mr Rich who studied Cabala [...] talked of Cordavero, Luzatto, Luria, Baal Shemtov, etc.' Annie drove him to events such as the movies *Z* and *Walkabout*, and 'the Nonsuch group displaying their Medieval/Tudor/Elizabethan cullings. Very charming and exciting costumery'. There were many visits to book dealers. He encountered Jacquetta who was again based in London and in contact with Annie, so the chances of such a meeting were not remote. But in a very long-odds coincidence 'as I loaded the canvasses from Aury's car to Annie's van who should drift like a strange vapour around the corner – Belle. I was heading for Plymouth immediately so said goodbye before I said hello. She seemed depressed' (Diary, 22 March 1977). It seems Robert had made no attempt to visit his mother during this visit, nor to discover how Belle happened to be on the same rather obscure London street as him.

He returned to Plymouth and completed several large works including Prete's Mural (Diary, 13 March 1977). Untroubled as Robert was by the impending death of Alice von Schlossberg, the people around him made adjustments. Bills were paid on his behalf, cheques appeared in the post, the women around him performed random acts of kindness: 'Myriam made tea. I finished, we separated – she went to my house. I went up to the main studio. Dr Gail came shortly. She had brought food. Had a very pleasant bed-picnic with yoghurt, oranges, cheeses, olives, milk, etc. Lively incident. No idea why. No use to her though. Talked of death/cancer/violence etc.' (Diary, 24 March 1977). Meanwhile in London, Alice von Schlossberg had seen her sons for the last time:

> Bernard and I had gone to visit her and she was relatively [...] not comatose, but she wasn't responsive at all. As we left I remember looking back into the ward and she was waving. That was the last I saw of her. She died in the early hours of the next morning. (Johnny Lenkiewicz, Interview, June 2019)

When Bernard phoned Robert he could not resist the joke:

> I said 'Robert, I've got some good news and some bad news. Which do you want first?' He said, give me the bad news first so I said, 'It is raining really heavily.' He said, 'So what's the good news?' and I said, 'Ma is dead.' (Bernard, Interview, March 2018)

Robert already knew. That morning he noted: 'Several "URGENT" messages. I realised straight away that mother was dead. So tiresome to be confronted by people's fear disguised as "empathy" and "bereavement" tactics' (Diary, 25 March 1977). So little planning had gone into the well-known fact of Ma's mortality that Robert had not even set aside the train fare to London: 'Decided to go to London [...] Decided to raise money: £2 from J. Nash for Taxis, £15 from Hans de Rijke [...] went to Myriam, asked her to phone various people [...] Took the train to London' (Diary, 25 March 1977). Johnny says this of Robert and Bernard's attitudes:

311

She was not an easy person. But I think I got the least of it. Bernard hated her because she was so [...] vile towards him, so negative, and destructive of his self-regard and all that stuff about him being 'backward' and so on, when he was so grown up so young. He was ahead of us by decades in that respect – we were not hippies exactly, but layabouts by comparison. Bernard had those reasons and wasn't shy about saying so. And Robert, because of the opposite. Because Ma was in love with him, and that was discomforting and suffocating [...] to say the very least. That was all to do with her father having died when she was so young, and he was a painter, and her attachment needs were very strong and Robert – ironically – became a father figure and romantic figure to her. Maybe I shouldn't call him a romantic figure for her, but an archetype, a very important figure. And he was also good looking, creative, charismatic, and unavailable. (Johnny, Interview, June 2019)

Arriving in London Robert went straight to Johnny's laboratory in University College where the brothers had a 'long talk about being robbed of death' (Diary, 25 March 1977). That night he slept with 'Annie, with ghosts'.

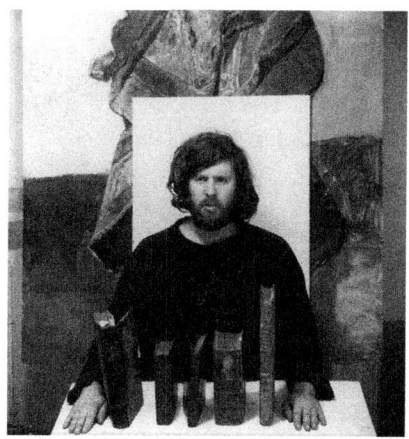

19.1 & 19.2 Robert photographed by Hans de Rijke in March 1977, with
 animal skeleton and antiquarian books, including Agrippa von
 Nettesheim's *Occulta Philosophia*, 1533 *(right)*.

19.3 Robert's daughter, Alice, at the mural on 4 July 1977.

19.4 Robert's sons, Reuben and Wolfe, at the studio on 16 July 1977.

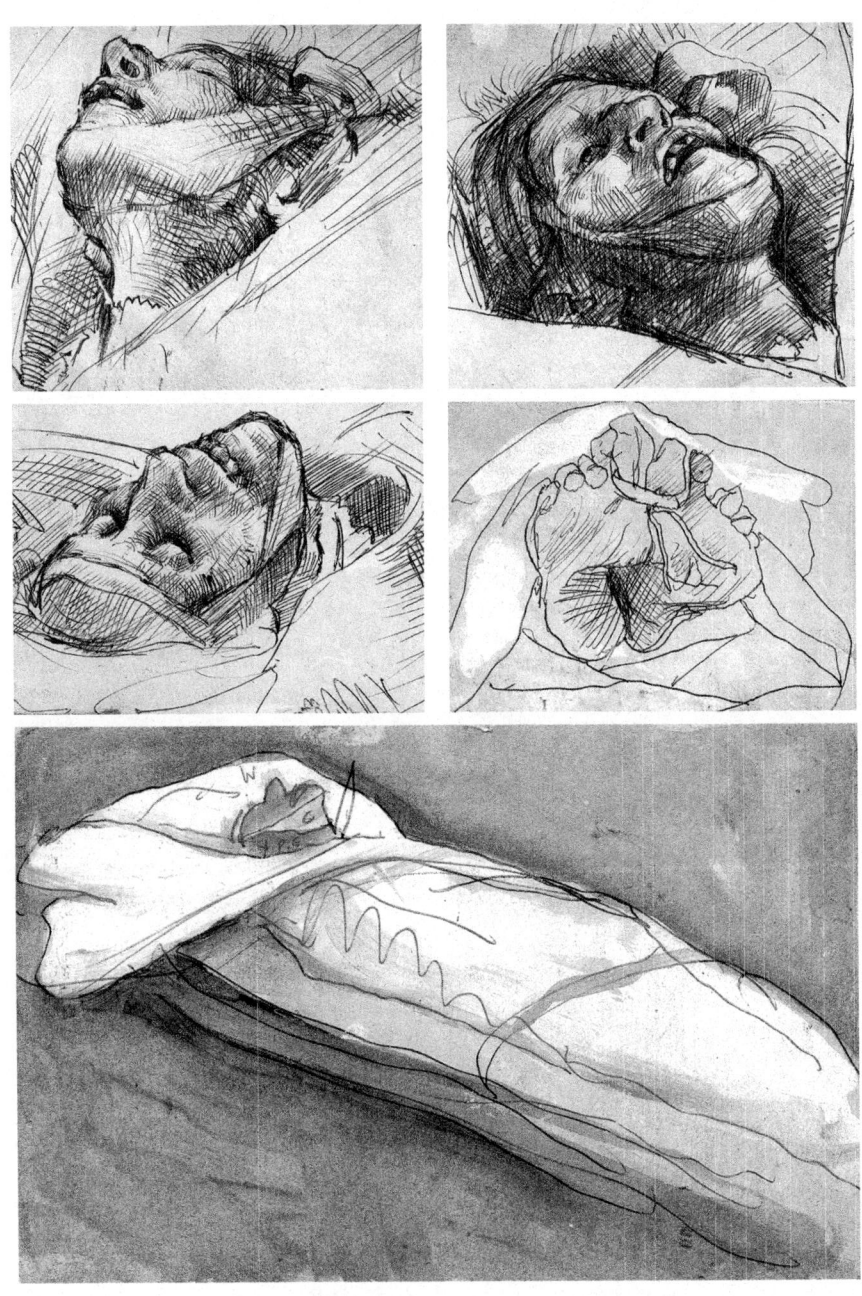

19.5 Sketches made by Robert at the mortuary of his mother's dead body wrapped in a shroud, her jaw secured by a bandage, March 1977.

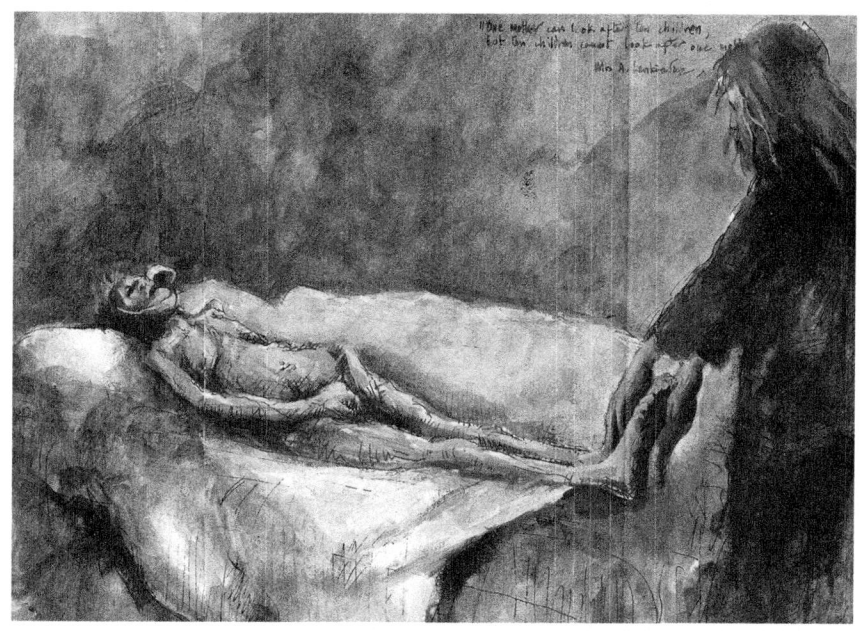

19.6 Illustration made from the mortuary sketches of Robert contemplating his mother's naked body. The work appears in the notebook *Self-Portrait/ Death Bed*.

The text reads: 'One mother can look after ten children, but ten children cannot look after one mother. Mrs A. Lenkiewicz.'

19.7 Robert photographed in his coffin by Hans de Rijke, 8 April 1977.

19

Burial of a Baroness – Paris with Doctor Gail – An Army of Lunatics

Robert's utter silence surrounding the death of his father is thrown into counterpoint by the many and serious reflections prompted by his mother's death:

> There is a most remarkable story in the Grimm Brothers' tales about a boy who set out on a journey in order to learn how to shudder, that is, to learn how to be afraid. The boy who cannot shudder is still living in an undifferentiated state of the world. He is a part of the world with no individual destiny of his own, so that like the animals he is an unthinking expression of life and existence: that is why he cannot experience fear. He is not horrified by the dead lying in the churchyard, nor the spectre in the church tower at midnight, because he has not become aware of 'the Other' as other than himself.
>
> This is why the boy is sent away from human beings into the unknown, without a name or any individuality. His father says, 'Do not tell anyone where you came from or who is your father – I am ashamed of you!'. His father, the sexton, the carter, the innkeeper, all agree that in order to become human one must be able to experience horror. And the boy agrees as well, since he has vague longings which drive him out to 'learn to shudder'. The horror which is constantly presented to him in a vain attempt to evoke fear is horror in its original and immediate form – the horror of death. (Diary, 25 March 1977)

This is Robert's first strong statement of an idea that will resonate in his work for years to come – the idea of a specially human experience of death, Death with a capital D, an annihilating but paradoxically co-creative force. The images and the ideas Robert pursues are, logically speaking, a rabble of walking abortions. It does not make rational sense to grant Death the powers Robert does – as both the cause and the outcome of 'the human condition'. But logic is not the judge here: we must remember that we are not dealing with the truth of propositions but rather an inchoate experience, and an 'uncanny' and 'untimely' one at that. Robert expands upon the death of the mother and the maternity of death:

> The image of Earth as a maternal being does not cancel out the other fearsome aspects, and the Mother Earth that bears and nourishes is the same as that which gapes open with threats of death: the Earth is a mother with the gaping jaws of a wolf. Earth becomes the symbol of the maternal and the mother becomes a symbol of Death, for the ambiguity of the Earth is shared by the Mother. In earliest childhood each individual has to suffer the experience of finding that his own mother, that which he has regarded as the most secure, supporting and embracing foundation of his life, could be unexpectedly and incomprehensibly transformed from the closest to the most alien, from the most secure to the most dangerous object angrily threatening death and destruction – while remaining always the mother whose womb offers hiding and refuge, and the highest bliss of rebirth into light.
>
> When the image of the Mother is struck by the rays emanating from the experience of death, or the image of death is touched by the glow of the maternal, then that which is nearest and that which is most alien, nourishing life and devouring death, are brought together in one image. (Diary, 25 March 1977)

> Curious night – but restful morning. Full of images of Ma's haggard visage with clattering jaws – peering over the armchairs and settees. The Pnoobs snooze on. Annie snoozes on. The world snoozes on. I snooze on. (Diary, 26 March 1977)

Robert met Johnny at Belsize Park station then on to the mortuary at the Royal Free Hospital 'to draw Ma'. Robert's account of the visit is as follows:

> We went in and saw her lying there. I did 3–4 drawings. We were there for 55 minutes. Mused, considered – looked – felt – studied – mused.
>
> She lay there yellowed – hard – with teeth protruding – left eye closed – right eye open. Cold – with a soft nose. She seemed like something from Auschwitz, or a rat-infested archway in the East End of the 19th century, or a floating cadaver from outer space – or an ex-baroness
> ...

I suggested to Johnny that he stay there for a minute on his own – I did likewise. We switched off the lights and left together. (Diary, 26 March 1977)

Johnny's account of the visit is somewhat different:

Robert and I went to see my mother's body at the hospital, we went to this 'lying in state' type of room, all clad in purple, and the body was on a kind of special table covered in purple cloth, and Robert very dramatically walked up to the corpse and pulled away the cloth like a magician – swoosh! My purpose in going was to make sure that she was dead. My last favour to her. To make sure she wasn't going to be buried alive. I'd seen a few Edgar Allen Poe films and Robert's purpose was to paint her, I suppose, but he always left it unclear as to what else he might have done. He asked me to leave him alone for maybe ten minutes or so. Which I did, and God only knows what he did in those ten minutes. He may just have done drawings of the feet with the toes tied together, but [...] I don't know what happened. I have thoughts [...] but [...] anyway. (Johnny, Interview, June 2019)

The body was fully shrouded except for the face when the sons entered the room: we have Robert's pencil and watercolour image of this. He also left us a series of studies with the corpse entirely naked, except for the binding cloth on her jaws. Alice's hands nest on her vulva, Robert's hands rest gently on her monstrously large feet, larger than those of any ancient Egyptian statue. Her mouth is bound. Even so, a tiny flame seems to escape the mouth and ascend – perhaps a reference to the transmigration of souls. In front of Robert's slightly bowed head he has written "'One mother can look after ten children, but ten children cannot look after one mother" – Mrs A Lenkiewicz'.

Taking final leave of Ma, Robert taxied to Primrose Hill to meet Belle. He 'watched her loom larger from a considerable distance [...] touched her with the same fingers that had just touched Ma. Went to restaurant. She seemed upset (at one point she broke into tears) but she was unwilling/ unable to explain her behaviour'. They separated after planning to meet the next day. Robert visited various galleries to 'snoop around the few sly techniques left'. When he first left his mother, Robert said he could find work anywhere, anytime, and in 1977 he was without a doubt one of the busiest and still one of the hungriest artists of his generation. The diary entry for the last day he would see his mother's face reads: 'enjoyed a work-man's meal'.

There was alarm and consternation on the morning of the funeral. The body had gone missing. The undertakers phoned Bernard to apologise and:

> The first thing we thought was ... *Robert!* What's he done with her? Because he has always said that he would take her body in a wheelchair around the National Gallery. We thought he'd done that. It turned out it was much less dramatic [...] the porters had left her body in the viewing room instead of taking it back to the mortuary, so when the undertakers went to collect her the mortuary drawer was empty. I remember asking them 'what did she look like?' and so forth, to make sure that it was the right person. They led me to believe that it was, but later I realised they wouldn't have known because the people I was asking were men and [in Judaism they] wouldn't have been allowed to deal with the body, it would be female people called *waschers*, who wash the body and prepare it for burial. So we none of us really know who is buried there. (Johnny, Interview, June 2019)

And so at noon on 27 March 1977, a coffin almost certainly but not indubitably containing the mortal remains of Alice von Schlossberg came first to Bernard's house then on to Bushey Jewish Cemetery. The three sons followed the coffin. Bernard had his clothes ritually cut. Robert thought it unnecessary because:

> I was in rags already. Went to the Bushey Chapel, same place that Aury's father went. Said Kaddish. Followed the coffin, arrived at the site where Ma used to visit when visiting our father's grave. She used to do a little dance on the spot she had bought for herself – I understand. (Diary, 27 March 1977)

Johnny says:

> She was buried near, but not next to my father, in the same grave-yard. The usual showboating from Robert, holding the prayer book upside down, he turned up wearing his duffle coat. Various people commented that they thought he was one of the gravediggers rather than a mourning son. He was certainly very energetic when it came to

shovelling the soil on top, as if he wanted to make sure she was well buried. (Johnny, Interview, June 2019)

Robert wrote:

> They lowered the coffin in with two ropes. The three sons than had to shovel three loads of earth each on to the coffin. After my turn I proceeded without stopping to cover the coffin with earth, until it could no longer be seen. Returned to Bernard's house. Sat on the Shiva chairs and other ritual activities. All so strange, the alleged business of being Jewish. (Diary, 27 March 1977)

Robert bailed out of one set of ritual activities to meet Belle at Primrose Hill to engage in another:

> Met Belle at the Hill. Walked around for a while surveying the world. Finally had a very pleasant meal in small restaurant [...] walked to the side of St Mary's Church and fucked in a damp recess to the rhythm of my mother's clattering jaws. Very pleasant incident. Drizzly, dark, and Gothic. Belle in curiously stressed mood. (Diary, 27 March 1977)

The day of the funeral was done. He spent the night with Annie, then next morning met Maria Ney-Hoch at the Victoria and Albert Museum where a 'pleasant situation developed in the Queen Anne section of furnishings. Quite strong incident. Another year's fidelity down the drain for her. She plans to come to Plymouth for a weekend: and then for six months' (Diary, 28 March 1977). In the afternoon he met with Aury and Myrna while Annie looked after their shop. The next day he and Annie breakfasted in Portobello market with Aury and Myrna and the poet Heathcote Williams. Robert returned to Plymouth on 29 March, untraumatized by the funeral and all its pleasures.

The first week of his return was spent mainly at Port Eliot where he worked on the 'Great Dragon' section of the mural. Robert received the bittersweet news that his lover Dr Gail Steadman was being promoted to Senior House Doctor at the Hospital for Tropical Diseases in London, so he would be seeing considerably less of her. In response to the impending separation Dr Gail planned a five-day tour of Paris for herself and Robert. The return to Plymouth from London in April 1977 marks the beginning of a sea-change in Robert's relationships with the dossers. Perhaps Robert had not changed much – he records the happy minutiae of Barbican life – 'a word with sweet old Joe Prete', his visits to Clements' bookshop, and is perfectly at ease in Priory Road: 'Went to my house – quiet – peaceful and familiar' (Diary, 7 April 1977). His sleep is sometimes troubled by dreams of his mother: 'Bad night, full of clattering jaws' (Diary, 9 April 1977) but never so badly that the word 'nightmare' is used. The dead mother was certainly less vexatious than the still-living Brother Blair, who wrote frequently from unspecified locations but was nowhere to be seen in Plymouth. Robert found some letters amusing, others menacing. He began to develop a sense – not entirely paranoid – that Brother Blair was engineering something terrible. The diaries record the arrival of strange new faces on the Barbican, some of them dossers, others more like regular mental patients. A few of them were making more than causal enquiries about Robert. There was no way of knowing what real or imaginary links these characters had to each other, to Brother Blair, or to each other. A known menace happens to reappear at this point:

> Two Cowboys called Jim and James turned up for a beg: took them to Joe's: Who should turn up as I was talking to them but 'Big Brummie [O'Connor]', looking madder than ever in a long brown coat. 'Ello Robert, Oi thought Oi'd pay moi respeks' ... followed by a vicious grin. Started babbling about how the hospitals were bending his mind, and the usual aggressive rubbish. 'No-one c'n 'elp' he said, 'Ya can't 'elp anover person.' (Diary, 8 April 1977)

Robert returned to 25 The Parade to continue work but the pressure was building horribly. Until now he had tolerated every level of violence from being spat on to being threatened with knives and being doused in petrol. But on the afternoon of 8 April 1977 he did something entirely new:

> I decided to leave – closed the shop and went to the police. The thug must have noticed I had gone very soon after. I saw him in the distance with a wrapped cider bottle cradled in his arms and an indefinable intent on his face. I went (very uncharacteristically) to the police – and was introduced to a Sergeant who already knew that O'Connor was in town, and had seen him 3 days running [...] he observed that any arrests would not be made by any less than two people.

Robert went home to Priory Road and met Hans de Rijke, who photographed him in the library in an open coffin. Myriam came 'looking very attractive [...] strange shouting at shadows night ... pleasant' (Diary, 8 April 1977).

The following morning, perhaps for psychological protection, Hans accompanied Robert to the Barbican and stayed with him for as long as his doctoring duties permitted. Going to the police was something new for Robert. So was working in a studio where the door was locked behind him:

It was shortly after [Hans left] that Brummie's loathsome form appeared. He grinned in his usual manner and indicated from behind the locked door that he wanted to see me. Considering it best to leave him in no doubt that I wanted no contact of any kind with him, and as my back was to him and the window as a result of sitting in the drawing chair, I mouthed that I did not want to see him with a gentle please leave me alone and go away look on my face. He grinned viciously and slunk away. I stayed another ½ hour but decided to go, as the atmosphere of his presence in the area was not conducive to my work or thoughts, and I am nervous of what the unpredictable thug might do with children and innocent public in my shop. I collected books to take with me and was in the process of locking the door and leaving when he swirled into sight with that hasty savage walk.

'Oi've written to six thousand psychopaths to come down and kill you Robert. I wrote to them all today. 'Cause Oi'v heard talk that you were responsible for getting two people hanged.'

'They abolished hanging several years ago Brummie,' I said and walked off quickly before he could decide his next move. I could sense his desire to lash out. I got to a taxi quickly and as Derek, the driver, turned the corner to take me to Compton I saw Brummie walking in the direction of where it must have looked that I went, craning his head to the left and the right in search of God knows what. I cannot help but feel some empathy for the total rejection that must necessarily be the lot of the brute. (Diary, 9 April 1977)

In the next weeks there were alarming developments, including a mysterious break-in at the studio (Diary, 20 April 1977) and on May 26 Robert:

Went to Clements' and purchased delightful book called 'Tales of Turkey' by Ramsay and McCulloch. With 50 pages of Mulla Nasrudin. Mr Clements related to me a foreboding description of an 'Italian' who was looking for me to kill me.

This tells you all you need to know about Mr Clements' relationship with Robert. A potential killer visits his shop specifically looking for Robert, but why bother to walk 60 yards to warn the target when you can wait until he comes in to buy something?

It seems to have been a month of paranoia. This man – he explained – seemed to feel that I was a chief warlock of a central witchcraft activity on the Barbican – 'the place' in the world for such indulgences. Mr Clements described him as 5' 8", medium build, well-dressed, with intense staring eyes. He appears to have made concentrated efforts to find me, going so far as to ask a 70-year-old lady in the street if 'she was one of my girlfriends'. I have been described, he said, in several different ways and he needed an accurate description, etc.

Perhaps Mr Clements had been reading Kant or George Washington, for he could not tell a lie. He provided this obviously deranged man with a brief but accurate description of Robert (Diary, 26 May 1977). The only precautions Robert seems to have taken were limiting his time on the Barbican for a few days while he prepared for his Paris trip with Dr Gail.

Warrants were issued for Robert's arrest that spring. Annie was working overtime as a Catcher in the Rye: 'Annie sent me £5. Told me she had paid the £93.34 into the courts for debts, etc. There should be no arrest' (Diary, 11 May 1977). Before Robert could leave the country, he began some business involving the Queen – or as he refers to her in the Diaries – 'Da Kveen!' This was the year of the Silver Jubilee celebrations, and for reasons at first obscure Robert's long-time collector and friend Mr Eddie 'I am a legitimate businessman' Kanter was ablaze with royalism. Clearly some scheme was afoot: urgent telegrams arrived at the Studio. On 21 April Robert rushed to London with a batch of paintings: the car broke down *en route* and had to be towed into Reading. The journey was completed by rail with Robert and Dr Gail carrying dozens of canvasses between them. These were then loaded into a van by Annie who met them at Paddington station. Taking temporary leave of Dr Gail, Robert rushed to the not inexpensive Court Hotel: '*Oy Gewalt!* Extraordinary dinner. All the news, etc. Long talk'. From the Love and Mediocrity series Eddie purchased 12 pieces including the *Thaïs and Athanael* canvas. He arranged to send £200 to cover monies due at The Fool Gallery in Plymouth, and gave Robert £60 in cash. So tangled are Robert's finances that even after these sales and a new, slightly ridiculous commission to paint a portrait of Da Kveen from a photograph, Robert notes 'Eddie is owed £110' (Diary, 21 April 1977).

On 24 April, Robert and Dr Gail left London for Paris travelling by train and hovercraft, which Robert did not enjoy at all. What he enjoyed immensely was staying in the Hôtel Du Brésil on the Rue le Goff, where Sigmund Freud had lived for a year. Picasso used to have a studio just around the corner. Any addict has invisible, highly selective antennae for finding their required fix and Robert's first observations on Paris were: 'Walked around the Rue de La Huchette. Cowboys by the dozen. Extraordinary little shop selling 16th and 17th century alchemical material [...] books and MS on alchemy and magic' (Diary, 24 April 1977).

The following four days were a whirl of galleries, bookshops, and late-night walks. At the Louvre he made 'a careful study of everything there from David to Courbet – '*The Oath of the Horatii, Raft of the Medusa, Massacre of Chois, Burial at Ornans, Baigneuse, Odalisque, M. Bertio.* Such a fascinating time-travel back into my youth-eyed heroes'. He made efforts to establish 'permanent contact' with booksellers such as The Emerald Tablet, specialists in 'Mystique, L'Alchimie, Sciences Occultes and Sociétés Secrètes'. He bought for 300 francs, or rather Dr Gail bought for him, Francis Rolt-Wheeler's astrological text *Systèmes Scientifique, Sélénologique et Cabbalistique* from a street bookstall near the Seine, and an alchemical study of Notre Dame. The building impressed him hugely: 'The Rose windows are like another Galaxy' (Diary, 26 April 1977).

Later he made watercolour studies of the important sights – the Rue Utrillo, Sacré-Coeur, Montmartre, the late evening cafés, and the nude Dr Gail. The next day was extremely full, taking in the Museum of Modern Art and the Museum of the City of Paris, 'an enormous amount of material I have never seen before', then to the Pompidou Centre for the Duchamp exhibition and a 'wonderful display of French/American contemporary work. Stayed there from 6pm until 10.15pm'. Somehow Robert and Dr Gail found time for the timeless, tattered magic of Paris to shine through all that culture: 'Returned to the street area of Huchette, had a meal. Dosser trouble – a player with a plaintive tune glides past. The police with guns'.

The 27th was the day of return, though they had an opportunity to visit the 'beautiful house where Rodin and Rilke lived. Exquisite taste. White/stripped greyed wood. Light and almost feminine context for Rodin's little tragedies'. They continued to Calais and with minutes to spare caught the last hovercraft back to Dover. He notes it was a more comfortable journey that the outward bound ride, but Dr Gail was all too aware of what time was taking away. And so, she wept.

> Gail drove non-stop from Dover to London. Seemed upset over this and that – but agreed generally that the four days were very loaded and rich, etc. Arrived back from Paris, Gail dropped me at Annie's. 10:10. Omnibus: Human Faces ['Portraits – Face to Face']. Missed it by ten minutes. (Diary, 28 April 1977)

The next few days were spent in London while Annie tried to put his finances in order. He painted a portrait of Barbara Collier, visited galleries, and noted the graffiti on the tube trains: 'NF! £ JEWS £ OUT! NF'. He and Annie met Eddie Kanter to talk projects and legitimate business with several of Eddie's friends who were some way advanced in lunchtime drinking: 'everything from slathering inanities to hearts on their sleeves bullshit. Annie did not seem to mind their behaviour so much – called me snobbish – maybe. Delicious meal' (Diary, 9 May 1977).

He returned to Plymouth on 5 May. For the rest of the month he was somewhat pestered by Eddie who sent copies of the Yousuf Karsh photographs of the Queen as a basis for a portrait. Robert was not entirely happy about this, but he made the painting. He did not want to sign it. This was an interruption to his project work which now included a venture into ceramics: 'Went to see [potter] John Pollex for advice re: my "Death Devouring Entrails" statuette. He was very helpful and will fire the piece for me in his kiln' (Diary, 6 May 1977). It was deemed 'very striking and effective' (Diary, 11 May 1977) and a larger clay piece was attempted. This collapsed before completion but was the seed for the seven-foot-tall red-and-white skeleton which would haunt Robert's studio for the following three decades. Alongside this and several other Death images, the Jealousy theme gathered pace. Monica called at Priory Road to tell him he had a new daughter – Sophie. Robert's response was 'I conceded the likelihood in my heart, but said to her these sole words: "I reserve my Judgement"' (Diary, 11 May 1977). Eddie's painting of Da Kveen came to a completion with a 'gentle row over the signing of the painting [...] all over, at last. Looks very effective in all its sickening style and technique'. On 31 May he went to London to hand the unsigned canvas to Eddie, who gave him £60, bringing Robert's total fee to £110. Later Robert heard: 'The Painting of the Queen was purchased by Lord Delfort for £4,000. He – it appears – intends presenting the rubbish to the Queen. There is talk of painting His Royal Highness the Prince of Wales: who is Prince Charles (I think)' (Diary, 3 June 1977). There is no indication of whether Robert believed the sum of money and story to be true, and no indication he felt exploited if it were. He would probably charge the same flat fee for whoever was buying, and refuse to sign it for any sum.

The first half of 1977 had been an exceptionally full and demanding time even by Robert's standards. Three strands of the Relationship Projects were running together. His travels with Dr Gail, the death of his mother, the visitation of the Rivera sisters, the situation with Belle, the rising danger from some of the vagrants: all of these had their costs in terms of mental and emotional energy. We can add to this the business pressure of a new opportunity. Until now, 25 The Parade meant a small window space for Robert, but that summer he was told the entire building, including its two upper floors, might become available: he would need money, and a plan. His head and heart were busy with all these considerations when a new relationship began. It became a monsterpiece of art, abnormal psychology, and erotic-philosophical research. It deserves its own chapter.

20.1 & 20.2 Gillian Pearce (Mary) at the studio in February 1977. Mary refused to sit for paintings, forcing Robert to work from photographs.

20.3 Two private language works featuring Mary's likeness from the Jealousy Project, 1977: *Man Watching Himself with Mary* and *Mary With Bed*.

20

Mary (1977–1982)

She was like water – and I with my fear of drowning. (Robert in the 'Mary Notebook', 2 April 1978)

Ultimately it is not the object of our desire, but our desires themselves that we love. (Nietzsche, *Beyond Good and Evil*)

As noted earlier Robert often but not always combined his sexual relationships with aesthetic research, compiling information in the books he and his partners made to chart the tides of their experiences. One of the most remarkable and certainly the most disturbing of these testaments is the Mary Notebook. Robert first met Mary via Yana Trevail who recalls:

[In 1975 Robert and I] became involved, and then I went off to London, to art college. He would come up and visit sometimes but the big thing was that he met Mary almost as soon as he met me. So I was [makes a pushing away gesture and laughs] ... well, he only had eyes for Mary then! I knew her as Gillian, Gillian Edwina Mary Pearce. He didn't like the associations of her given name because his twin brother was married to a woman called Gillian. And with 'Mary' there's the Virgin Mary connotation.

One day I was having a sitting at 25 The Parade and Mary came down to meet me, and ... that was it ... he was smitten! She was very, very private, and I wouldn't want to speak on her behalf, but ... she wasn't really interested in him. At all! I mean, he really had to struggle. She wasn't interested, but it's fascinating isn't it, somebody chasing you around, somebody surrounded by beautiful women but still wants to pursue you? There's an element of that 'look at all these other lovely ladies' and competitiveness. [Robert's term was 'hunting'] and that's what he did with Mary, he hunted her for four years. It was ruthless, because he thought that he could have anyone, and he was interested to find out what it was like to be with ... anybody! Well, not anybody, he did have limits, but ... [laughs]. He was interested in people, all people. (Yana Trevail, Interview, September 2018)

She felt she could not take it; I said I would post it to her time and again, time and again it would fall through her door. she could hardly destroy it or give it to someone else - not with her kind of behaviour. Eventually she took it - saying she would not look at it.

I took a skull that I had brought with me and set it beside the image of me as a boy.
She seemed almost to recoil - I have several death's heads - but this one's curiously grotesque with an atmosphere of corruption. She was not revolted but she did not like it.
I asked her about death. Her terror was the sense of 'not existing any more'. But I asked her whether she felt she existed now. Surely she did not feel 'here' now either? She agreed that the fear of death echoed the fear of life. etc.

Sensed a kind of wilting - a gentle subsidence within her and towards her left, as though she was repelled from and drawn towards the space around the death's head.
It lay - nestled by her frozen arm - ready to fall. She sat shifting waiting for me to remove it.
My photograph on the table.
It seemed as though the skull was surrounded with my 'red' - fed from across the table and that her cold wilting form was vanishing like a ghost by its merciless presence. The photograph of myself as a child still making a whitish line to her eye.
Her yellow surround seemed to disappear to her left as she slid down into air.
No sexual feelings - but captivated by her blue-greyness.

Sense of loss as I saw her off at the co-op staircase.
Addictive state serious.

20.4 Aesthetic note on Mary. 24 February 1978.

In Joe Prete's café Robert juxtaposes a *memento mori*, a human skull, with a photograph of himself as a young boy to investigate Mary's response to the pathos of the images.

20.5 Lenkiewicz records his physiological states using colour formula suggestive of synaesthesia.

'Day of pain. ... A sense of dull dark crimson heat in the front part of the diaphragm. The unique tearing sensation of rejection. Where as a child did it first happen?' Page from the Mary aesthetic notes dated 13 March 1978.

Robert's determined pursuit of his muse began in 1976. Mary, then eighteen years old, makes her first appearance in the painter's diaries on 27 December 1976, four days before his thirty-fifth birthday. She drives him to the stately home of his friend and patron, Lord Eliot, where Robert installs Mary's image high up on the vast Riddle Mural in the 12-metre diameter Round Room. As the artist later explained in the 1982 TV documentary *The Leaves Were Full of Children*, she represents 'the prime articulation of Heaven, as far as mortal man is concerned, Woman, in the form, in this case, of The Virgin Mary' – Lenkiewicz's private joke about his companion's lack of experience.

He notes in his diary a few days later:

> She is afraid and, of course, she is entitled to her fears. What she calls 'experience' and what I call 'innocence'. *Oy gevalt!* She agreed that authority in the situation was limited. I explained that the irreligious authority of her appearance was all she needed. Far more authority than I would ever have.

She is also unsettled by Robert's conviction that a constant awareness of darkness and death is the best way to sharpen our capacity to live a rich life. As Dr Ernest Becker puts it in *The Denial of Death* (1973), one of the key influences on Robert's thinking:

> I think that taking life seriously means something such as this: that whatever man does on this planet has to be done in the lived truth of the terror of creation, of the grotesque, of the rumble of panic underneath everything. Otherwise it is false. Whatever is achieved must be achieved with the full exercise of passion, of vision, of pain, of fear, and of sorrow. How do we know, that our part of the meaning of the universe might not be a rhythm in sorrow? [35]

The 'first date' at Lord Eliot's home ends with this:

> She is terrified of graveyards, so at midnight I took her to Ford Park Cemetery and philosophized – will see her soon. (Diary, 27 December 1976)

Mary would become 'a book' like no other. Many who experience 'love at first sight' can cite the date and time when the lightning struck. But few can stir a conscious conspiracy against themselves, throw reason over-board, and dare the storm to do its worst. Yet on 30 June 1977 Robert writes 'On this day I decided' ... to do that.

> I made notes in a huge book, on serviettes, on scraps of newspaper, on anything at all really, with tremendous energy, and there was no end to it. I wanted to record every tiny thing: the removing of a coat, the sitting on a chair, the washing of the face, some tiny erotic gesture, watching television, going to the cinema, the shadow on the pavement as one was walking. All of them were metaphors for the pathos of the situation. But it's heightened when you are old enough to know that everything passes. (Robert, *Paintings and Projects*, p. 15)

According to Robert's aesthetic theories these heightened experiences were self-inflicted, for 'the other person has nothing to do with it'. More em-phatically: 'When I tire, she dies. She lives solely in my aesthetic response. Without it she is a shadow in the world' (Mary Notebook, 25 February 1978). Robert was mature enough to assimilate this perspective, but Mary was not. Although highly intelligent she was inexperienced and flying without instruments. One need not be a moralising prude to feel very uncomfortable about a middle-aged man with encyclopaedic knowledge of sexual relationships pursuing an introverted girl in her teens.

She appears in the diaries in January 1977 under her proper name, Gil-lian. Robert was already optimistic about a sexual relationship. Something intervened. What this was he does not specify, but the temperature on Mary's side of the equation was close to zero when the Mary Notebook begins. Robert is already feverish with plans to adjust the situation. He notes, 'There is no doubt that my passive approach has brought about innuendos that my monstrously domineering and aggressive tactics of last year had patently failed to do' (Mary Notebook, 14 February 1978).

> So sad to see her skipping down the Co-Op [where Mary was working as a shop assistant] stairs with her sister and mother [...] They did not see me. What a psychopath I feel as I watch the trio on the Co-Op stairs. She looked irritatingly well – I should leave her alone. (Diary, 22 July 1977)

The published version of *The Mary Notebook* (1998) [36] suggests Robert had some sort of sexual contact with Mary in 1977. 'I asked her over a year ago' (Mary Notebook, 24 February 1978) and 'I had reference to the sexual incident a year ago' (Mary Notebook, 1 March 1978). 'Incidents' were indeed recorded in the notebook material in July and August 1977 but never published. But in the original quarto-sized folio – *'Mary: Aesthetic Notes'* – we find six small illustrations in which Robert records:

> She will never know the joys of handing herself over; but she will never know the misery of rejection. [...] La Belle et La Béte in my kitchen. [...] Talked at length re: her mouth. Really difficult for her to kiss. Came to agreements about various possibilities but time and again she winced away when approached. Talked of the kiss being the first fuck ... put my fingers in her mouth and hers in mine. [...] Sat her across my knee for some time. Arms behind her back. Beautiful. Astride like a horse. [...] (*Mary: Aesthetic Notes*, July 1977)

Robert's seduction technique did not produce the desired result and on 14 August he commits to a long siege. The prize will be worth the effort: 'Few things compare to an encounter with a professional virgin'. Two weeks later, he admits defeat:

> 'Talked in the kitchen. Savoured memories of 'past' relationships with 'her'. ... She understands that there are many relationships within the one relationship. ... Walked her to her home. Shook hands – goodbye. I will not trouble her again. It is all in her hands. Cunning beyond her years.' (Diary, 28 August 1977)

Early admissions of monstrosity and psychopathy did not prompt him to question if he should proceed at all. He readily acknowledges the sado-masochistic impulses at work in his pursuit of Mary. As contact resumes some months later he describes the situation as 'an erotically over-controlled conspiracy' (Mary Notebook, 6 February 1978) though his worldview demands that it is a conspiracy of one. The Mary Notebook records realities, desires, and fantasies which anyone more 'socialised' would abort, deny, or repress rather than diligently map. Musings on rape, dismemberment, and murder accompany his obsessional behaviour. If he worries how he might appear to his readers, or if there is any 'pose' at all in his meditations, it leans to the side of those 'dirty old men' of philosophy, de Sade and Bataille:

Went into Stephens café. Everything fine. The same table. I stared at the creature, thinking of Belle, and the extraordinary similarities and differences. I sat there feeling the taut skin around my mouth where some of Belle's vaginal fluids still hung in melancholy scent. And Mary slowly slid through the erotic prelude – all molly-coddled certitude of her, clean-fresh and guiltless as I watched her dangerous mouth and the cruel talons of her eyes. A longing for some permanence in her gestures – in a glance – some intangible silence – a desire for the menace I sense in her to scream out, to tear and threaten me for my assaults. But I sat opposite her in all gentleness, feeling alive enough to dismiss all realities. (Mary Notebook, 2 March 1978)

This is clearly not a book for everybody. Readers with quick moral reflexes will find only two things in it: episodes to condemn, and reasons to congratulate themselves on the wholesomeness of their own sexuality. Readers who consider themselves more broad-minded might discover in it 'valuable subjective insights' into the world of mental aberration, in the manner of therapists and academics decoding the writings of Hildegaard of Bingen, Daniel Paul Schreber, or Barbara O'Brien. But some may go further. Instead of seeing in The Mary Notebook a catalogue of prolonged, self-inflicted derangements, some might be prepared to travel the distance and take up the suggestion of Dr Nick Fox: Robert's experiences, though rare and raw, are those of a genuine mystic (Interview, February 2019).

The word 'mystic' is neither fashionable nor respectable. It is generally assumed that mystics are buried in the strata of history, and their experiences were the result of brain abnormalities brought on by extreme fasting, mind-bending fungi, or knocks on the head. Mechanistic biology dictates that 'mystical' experiences are hallucinations, and that hallucinations are not 'real' in any meaningful way. But if we journey with Robert and take seriously the implications of Nietzsche's claim that the so-called 'real world' has itself become a myth, then the doors open to all manner of interesting new interpretations of those experiences. The Mary Notebook is most fruitfully read with the spirit of openness and generosity which Robert had for topics like alchemy or extra-terrestrial life: which is to say by putting aside our presumed certainties about what might be 'real'.

Walked to Stephens [café]. How is it possible for such things to creep up on one? She stands by my side and something transforms. I accept her – perhaps not – as she is, nervous, devious, passionless – though difficult to believe – and I push on through the matter of familiarity. I push on with the last memories of her aesthetic effect leaping on my back like a demon. Whispering in my ear 'Seek me out! Seek me out! Look at her again and you'll see me!'. And I look, and I catch an angle of her head, the fast smile on her mouth – and the creature on my back leaps off and into her mouth and I am all attention – all attention. Like all addictions, irresistible as long as the drug remains available. And I think of the thought that I had as I first entered the doors – and now, as I re-emerge from them. And she merges with the thought of us walking down the road. Two parallel events – one no more real than the other. (Mary Notebook, 10 March 1978)

Perhaps more than any other of his relationships Robert used this one as a laboratory in which to work upon himself. Since the early 1970s he produced 'private language' paintings in which inner and outer perceptions were mingled. But in the Mary experiment he deliberately pushed himself further into synaesthesia. Johnny Lenkiewicz had significant clinical experience of unusual psychological states and his opinion was that Robert was already mildly synaesthesic (Interview, September 2018). Robert's emotional states came with associations of colours, and these associations were in some cases so strong that they bled over into actual perceptions, and vice versa. To say that they are 'not really real' is a dull prejudice. Sensations, emotions, affects are as real as anything you can stub your toe on, and lives are cut short by 'subjective' experiences such as loneliness, anxiety, or loss. Perhaps at first Robert was 'imagining' the colours and lines which grew like tropical plants around and inside his and Mary's bodies. But imagination is the driving force for making things actual. Imagination and desire, aided by experiment and work, puts murals on walls and launches astronauts into space. Robert was imagining and field testing the ways in which aesthetic forces leak from bodies, interact, and communicate. He was not just inventing a 'private language' of colours, he was closely observing his experiences in what appears to be an attempt to develop new sense organs.

The watercolours of the Mary Notebook contain elements inherited from alchemy, Cabala, and Sufism. Anyone a little way advanced in psychonautics will note resemblances to a mid-dose LSD experience. Colour traces leave the bodies they are ordinarily attached to, forming semi-objects with lives of their own until they 'vaporise like birds starting away into a white sky' (Mary Notebook, 15 February 1978). Auras and emanations break out of Mary's body like nerve-rashes: 'sections of her where [*sic*] combinations of red and silvery-grey. Pieces of "bad mood" floating in a slightly stagnant pond of complacency' (Mary Notebook, 15 March 1978). The psychedelic parallels are remarkable, but let us be absolutely clear that Robert could not be compelled to nibble so much as a crumb of hashish, let alone the dreaded 'acid'. Unless one entertains a delusion that someone was diligently spiking Robert shortly before every meeting with Mary, the conclusion is overwhelming: any chemicals involved in the visual carnival of the Mary Notebook were synthesised in the laboratory of Robert's own body. Feats of imagination and bio-chemical reactions worked together, and Robert began to perceive his body as a blue-grey 'corpse' shrouded in a red glow sending out exploratory tendrils.

In late April 1978 Robert absented himself from Mary and retired to Port Eliot for two weeks to test his 'withdrawal symptoms'. Like a heroin addict double-dipping on methadone he took the precaution of having Belle for company. In an aesthetic note that seems to relate to the Mary material (if Robert's tentative date 'Modbury 1977?' is reasonably accurate), he draws himself and Belle entwined in passion and expresses regret – and Robert regrets *nothing!* – at the missed opportunity in the early 1970s to discover the erotic philosopher's stone with Belle Pecorini that now presents itself as a second chance with Mary:

> Belle and the moon outside the window. Ah Belle! Such a loss – there never was a woman like you – I only ever had you in my sense of loss – All that we did was half a dream. You used Nature to lure me to your madness. It was Nature that cheated the town rat. The whole thing was a promise that could not be kept.
> We were both fools – you for troubling with me – and me for wasting you.
> Regrets – My bad work is at the top of the list – then – I think, it may be you.

The cocktail of human 'fixes' became even more complex when Ria Ney-Hoch announced a surprise visit as soon as Robert returned to Plymouth, which he saw as 'an opportunity for me to extend my absence from Mary – to take the edge off the withdrawal' (Mary Notebook, 8 May 1978). The plan fell apart within hours:

I take a bus which does not go direct to the viaduct; it fatally passes the Co-Op and without desire, without shaking anticipation, I step off and stand upstairs in the familiar spot. She darts out in blue, a shocked smile on her face [...] Old fears and inadequacies follow as though from habit rather than present necessity. Within minutes we are seated at Stephens' café with nervous, gentle, patient familiarity. (Mary Notebook, 8 May 1978)

It has appeared at least a dozen times already in the Mary Notebook, and by now Robert's use of the word 'familiar' is starting to whiff of both incest and witchcraft. On this day he makes what may be the first written reference to his love for Mary, though he seals the word in inverted commas. The mention of 'love' is immediately followed by a series of reflections on fantasy, punishment, murder, and self-hatred. It appears that he is using Mary – or in his terms, the bundle of aesthetic forces called 'Mary' – as a toolkit to take himself and/or her apart.

He muses darkly on 'the warrior being prepared to lie down as a human sacrifice on his/her own altar [...] The question is, who will be sacrificed?' (Mary Notebook, 3 June 1978). The disappearance of the 1975 diary is frustrating on this front. Robert was fascinated by the writer Yukio Mishima who in traditional Samurai fashion opened himself up on the altar of his own aesthetic commitments in that year. It is around this time that Robert began using the phrase 'A relationship can only be over when *both* participants are dead'. In November 1978, beneath a watercolour of Mary in the studio cradling him like a dead infant, he writes:

To 'consciously' prepare oneself for committed addiction. The peculiarities of such a venture. The pose took two years to organize and stage. The reader might view it as a commonplace. The reader might suspect that my companion was asleep. I must confess to similar suspicion on a number of occasions. We are both very much awake. (Mary Notebook, 24 November 1978)

This curious and moving image records some mysterious change in the elements. For the first time it appears that they are *both* conscious of what they were doing and what they were committing to. It would be too much to expect either to have known why. We do not know what passed between Robert and Mary on that night but it is hard not to suspect it was a commitment to something more than just a fuller physical sexuality. On Tuesday 12 December, as if he were recording conclusive proof of alien visitation or life-after-death, Robert writes: 'First Contact'. This work deploys long quotations about the transition from girlhood to womanhood from existentialist writer Simone de Beauvoir's *The Second Sex* (1949), one of the founding texts of feminism. And two lines of the diary are included in the work – 'peculiar anti-gravity sensation … cutting off the world and absorbing it simultaneously'. The full diary entry records the event; the number in brackets records that this is the 153rd meeting with Mary.

> 12 December 1978. 8pm MARY [153] Arrived in her brown rust coat. She asked questions about my paintings and the mechanics involved. Studied self-portrait a little. Went to the Wine Lodge. Spoke at great length upon our circumstance – so close and beautiful. Hands, etc. Same corner table. So strange the hints of 'exclusive' addiction – of cutting off the world and absorbing it simultaneously. Returned to my shop. I sat on the floor by the door – she came over. Sat down – so comfortable; beautifully held. Exquisite hour of contact. The first time we have really established a connection and only a beginning to a terrifying future. So beautiful, the whole timeless phenomena. Peculiar anti-gravitational sensation. To have her enclosed: a strange double-helix world of life and death. Such a haunting memorable event. She drove home to her parents at 11pm.

Lenkiewicz showed this aesthetic note to Mary soon after its completion. It remains an unequal arrangement of forces, with Mary passively being Mary – as she has every right to be – and Robert making immense efforts to move a vehicle with square wheels. He describes the development of the relationship as a series of 'jolts' (Mary Notebook, 11 January 1979), 'continuity limited, no flow', and 'things come and go in spasms' (Mary Notebook, 1 February 1979). These observations are sometimes linked to Mary's sexual reserve. Like many young lovers she was nervous about being put in the spotlight or under the microscope. As a primarily visual sensualist Robert was frustrated by this. Beneath a watercolour of himself, fully clothed, giving oral sex to the partly clothed Mary, he writes:

> Lay down. No expectations. Her unpredictability. I wanted to see, but it was dark. If I could have seen – just a little – she might have climaxed

– despite thoughts in her head. Sensed the possibility twice. Nerves, over-sensitivity. The fear of disgust. (Mary Notebook, 6 May 1979)

By this stage the problem of interpretation facing readers of the Mary Notebook is not whether Robert is describing sexual difficulties of a mechanical nature, or some psychological 'block' between him and Mary, or between Mary and herself. Or indeed, his own anxieties about his capabilities. Probably all those things, and much more besides. He is making the reader complicit in a conspiracy to undermine the walls of a 'separate self'. He had set out to dissolve the borders between inner and outer experience. As early as 17 March 1978 Robert is writing as if belief in separateness were itself a delusion: 'her laugh – meanders past the walls [...] secreting itself under the door to disperse into the "outside" world. Sections of her are breaking off like rain-weathered stone, floating and permeating iridescently – everywhere.'

The challenge is not whether we 'believe' Robert's testimony but rather to question our own aesthetic vulnerabilities, our own susceptibilities and resistances to the material he presents. The Notebook seduces us toward the dangerous question 'What if?'. What if objects, sensations, desires, and persons can wrench free from *being* and transform into *becoming*? Robert's views on that topic will be explored elsewhere: for now let us consider two related alchemical themes in the Mary Notebook.

Robert explicitly identifies his synaesthesic experiences with 'an alchemist's vision' (Mary Notebook, 9 March 1978). This much is obvious in his images of golden serpents climbing Mary's body, vaporous birds circling her, and red dragons of desire flitting from body to body. It is worth reminding ourselves that alchemy was a suspect *activity*, not a heretical set of beliefs. Depending on their moods, both state and Church subjected alchemy to phases of promotion and suppression, possibly because alchemy had no priesthood, no authority beyond results, no demands for allegiance, and no requirements that one believed in any creed. With no central organisation, *some* of these alchemists' sign systems partly overlapped with others but were frequently as idiosyncratic as Robert's 'private language'. What an image represented in one context may have little or nothing to do with 'the same image' in another. Thus and therefore alchemy is the bane of science historians and the joy of poets and artists. There are some broad thematic agreements in the imagery, two of which are undeniably present in Robert's seemingly 'private language' in the Mary Notebook. The first concerns the necessity of death and dissolution. The second is that of recombining separate elements into a new and more perfect whole. Together they are summed up in the alchemical motto *solve et coagula* – dissolve and coagulate, or separate and rejoin.

Throughout the first year of the relationship there is a riot of references to Robert falling to pieces, taking Mary to pieces, and the decay of their bodies. Mary walks beside him in a hooded coat 'like Death' (Mary Notebook, 2 March 1978). Robert is filled with 'a sense of putrefaction [...] I am carrion' (Mary Notebook, 6 March 1978). Meeting her in Stephens' café he brings a photograph of himself as a child and a human skull, as if his life is already over: 'I imagine my own decomposed corpse' (Diary, 24 February 1978). He refers to both his and her body as 'a corpse'.

If there were an ethics committee overseeing this experiment – or indeed any human being with a concern for Mary's welfare – then the project would have been called to a halt on 2 April 1978. He records walking with her past felled trees. 'She draws my attention to them. But I am already well aware. I say I do not wish to discuss them. Too depressing. Our shadows on the path.' Beneath this is a watercolour of her naked and butchered body. 'I see her hideously dismembered' he writes. A month earlier he had mapped out a fate no less horrible for himself:

> It is crashing with snow – late, cold, magnificent [...] I imagine that my footprints are patches of blood – though I do not look back [...] I feel a terrible disgust with myself. I feel the sludge and slime of iced snow beneath my feet and imagine it is my own decomposed corpse lain waste and trodden into the dirt. I pass across her footprints like an open sewer. I turn around to view, and as my jaw opens, I feel the iced wind blow through my empty sockets and mandible. (Mary Notebook, 18 February 1978)

Robert's reflections on – and perceptions of – death and decay resonate with the first phase of the alchemical transformation, the *nigredo* or blackening putrefaction: 'Putrefaction is the gate to the *conjunctio* and conception. It is the key to transmutation' (J.C. Barchusen, *Elementa Chemicae*, 1718). Images from Michael Maier's *Atalanta Fugiens* (1617) show wolves eating the corpse of the king and a crowned Saturn, god of dissolution, melancholy, and periodic regeneration, being slowly cooked in a coffin-like box. The accelerated decomposition of the raw material, the *prima materia*, is intended to free it from the 'black gall and Saturnine filth' which hinder its journey to a higher state. 'The process lasts until the skin breaks and a red colour appears' (quoted in Roob, *Alchemy and Mysticism*, p. 145). There are hundreds more examples of this preliminary corruption throughout the texts of European alchemy. The following passage draws on Maier and the 14th-century *Rosarium Philosophorum*. It resonates with Robert's early lesson concerning 'all colours in all colours' no less than alchemical death and rebirth:

> On top of the mountain where the *prima materia* is found, the philosopher's vulture sits screaming incessantly 'I am the Black of the White and the Red of the White and the Yellow of the Red [...] and know this, that the summit of the art is the Raven, who flies without wings in the blackness of night and the holiness of the day'. This refers to the phase of the *nigredo*, in which the solid components of the matter succumb to putrefaction. (Roob, *Alchemy and Mysticism*, p. 292)

Psychologists of a Jungian bent link this morbid imagery to a specific kind of mental breakdown, a 'functional crisis' which provides opportunities for psychic redevelopment and artistic breakthrough.[37] To speak by analogy, if the world is spherical then we can only fall apart so much before the pieces start falling back together again – if only there is enough energy to keep the fragments moving. Without the continuation of the process things fall apart and stay apart, and the voyager remains lost in madness. I do not know if Robert subscribed to such a view, but he was certainly impressed by the arguments of Fromm, Laing, Cooper, and Szasz. Broadly speaking these 'anti-psychiatrists' contended that rather than attempting to put the brakes on the processes of mental aberration it is healthier to consider madness as an opportunity to liberate the 'self' from a collectively crazed society. The 'cure' is not drugs or psychotherapy or lobotomy, which merely aim to bring the sufferer back to a 'normal decent self' fit only for 'normal decent' society. The anti-psychiatric 'cure' involves taking the visions and rogue emotions seriously, nurturing them, examining them, and accelerating them until a 'higher self' emerges. Judging from the diaries and Vagrancy notes, this approach broadly characterised Robert's dealings with Albert 'The Bishop' Fisher.

We wrote above that Robert repeatedly 'refers to both his and her body as a corpse'. The move from plural to singular is instructive. Death unites all things into nothing. 'His and her body' suggests a combining of the two and a transcendence of the 'one'. This leads us to the second of the great alchemical themes in the Mary Notebook: the *coagula* or *conjuntio*, a paradoxical union of things previously opposed. One of the key images for this concept is the Black Sun. This does not figure explicitly in the Mary Notebook although Robert makes occasional references to the solar union of opposites. When Mary describes him as 'sunny' – 'I speak of Apollo, riding his chariot [...] of the turning world of distant galaxies, lit by my brothers'. Mary says, 'Not that kind of sun, just sunny, you know cheerful, etc.'. Robert's response is to sing 'That lucky old Sun, ain't got nothing to do, but roll around heaven all day' – in 'dirge tones' (Mary Notebook, 9 May 1978). And interestingly, towards the end of the relationship, he paints a square sun framing the ellipse of a cosmic vulva, like a generative zero at the heart of the paradox (Mary Notebook, 23 October 1974). These solar references are few compared to the main image of alchemical conjunction in the Mary Notebook – the figure of the sacred hermaphrodite which appears in words more than visual images but nevertheless sparked some of Robert's finest painting of this period.

Hermes is the divine messenger, god of symbols and codes, of alchemy and transformation, cosmic trickster. Aphrodite is the Goddess of Love whose mortal lovers invariably come to a tragic end. The sacred hermaphrodite *is not* the happy or natural offspring of these two divinities. The story is far more impure. According to Greek myth, their inevitably gorgeous boy-child Hermaphroditus was bathing in a pool where the local water-spirit Salamancis – also inevitably – fell in lust with him. Like so many young men of his culture, Hermaphroditus was not much up for this heterosexual union. But 'inflamed with desire for his naked form' – Salamancis pounced. She set about him with violence, 'putting her hands beneath him, touching his unwilling breast, overwhelming the youth from this side and that [...] as ivy coils around a tree trunk, or as the cuttlefish holds the prey it has surprised underwater, wrapping its tentacles everywhere'. Ovid does not record which of the Greek gods granted Salamancis' mid-rape prayer to co-mingle her body with that of her victim forever: both Hermes and Aphrodite had many powerful enemies, so you can take your pick. But 'her prayer reached the Gods and their entwined bodies were merged together, and one form covered both [...] mated together, they were not two, but a two-fold form, so they could not be called male or female, and seemed neither or either'. The resultant creature was in no position to demand revenge upon the rapist who was now part of him/herself, so somewhat arbitrarily he/she asked Hermes and Aphrodite to make sure any man who entered the pool would suffer a similar fate. With exemplary irrationality 'this they did, and contaminated the pool with a damaging drug' which would effect this transformation' (Ovid, *Metamorphoses*, Book IV, 346–388).

I quote at length to head off the legions of pop-psychological self-help interpretations which draw the fangs of the original myth of the sacred hermaphrodite. 'Achieving the essence of wholeness' and so forth is all very well, but the terrible precondition of this wholeness is the rape of a teenage divinity by a backwater spirit. For one-half of the 'wholeness', it was not a willing union. The cruelty and monstrosity of the process is unflinchingly retained in the Mary Notebook.

In a separate tradition drawn from Plato's *Symposium* the hermaphrodite figures as the original and happy human condition. Jealous of mortals' happiness and seeing a quick way to double his worshippers, Zeus crippled us all by slicing us in half. This is very likely the reference point for Robert's image in The Mary Notebook of a knife bisecting a sphere which is dripping blood. A white line connects one-half of the sphere to a sun-like glow at the top of Robert's skull as he is mounted by Magdalena. This physical coupling is not characterised by two people failing to become one, but by a multiplication of personae which nevertheless leaves Robert isolated. The white line extends to touch the vulvas of a conjoined Mary–Magdalena. The bold coloration of this image – black, white, yellow, red – strongly hints at alchemical influences. So do most of the surrounding comments, though they are curiously contradictory of much he has recorded in the previous months:

> All complexities and subtleties return to the first point. Whether I am the point from which the word 'together' stems, or whether she is the point: the desire to 'make whole' cannot break the surface of our own bodies. There is always an inside and an outside [...] the separation of one image into two: how to divide? To assay the precise longitude and latitude of 'the individual'. The point at which either beginning or end might have reality as representing the 'other'. The 'not-me' aspect of a relationship. (Mary Notebook, 3 June 1978)

Robert's attempts at conjunction are maximally inclusive. Choose any five consecutive pages of The Mary Notebook and you will find attempts to reconcile gendered pairs of concepts: self and other, active and passive, conscious and unconscious, safety and threat, life and death, parts and wholes. The meeting of hands is an obvious emblem for separation giving way to unity, and throughout the Notebook this image is linked to androgyny or sexual transformation. Very early in the relationship he muses:

> I was again aware of my hands, particularly the finger sections – and my tendency to use them discretely and pliantly, particularly when holding a cup or a book. Unsure whether an attempt to feminise myself or desire to minimize masculinity and threatening image. Possibly part of me (top left?) is trying to be a young girl in order that the more masculine positive side of her can emerge. (Mary Notebook, 8 February 1978)
>
> She wore green – green jumper, scarf – seemed like some sort of plant. Exquisite quality of colour again – with her hair. I am constantly struck by the number of colours she agrees with. I asked her to raise her hands, and I rested mine against them to see what it feels like. Our hands are the same size. I slowly find her large hands erotic – tremendously evocative of a masculine tenderness. A wind seemed to be blowing through her and she seemed a tree against the sky. We seemed to laugh again, both of us travelling into each other's laugh like a run – like a race down a hill. Such a gentle crying pleasure to laugh with her. (Mary Notebook, 3 March 1978)

As Mary plays violin, he notes her 'taut neck tragically, lyrically balanced over a hand and shoulder – the head turned profile over a hopeless open palm. The erotic masculine hip sweeping through her awkward stance, so movingly evoking my own obsessional anxiety' (Mary Notebook, 16 March 1978). We have long since cancelled our subscriptions to the concept of 'normal perception' in this relationship, but Robert's focus on the few and slight 'masculine' features of Mary's body is a masterpiece of selective attention. Even more peculiar is his projection – an alchemical term long before it was a psychological one – of his own intentions and qualities upon the young woman. This tendency is sometimes so perverse it is both funny and painful to read: 'I speak of her pride and arrogance, her desire to mystify herself. The way in which I am being employed as an experimental relationship' (Mary Notebook, 1 February 1979).

'Oh woe; poor Robert!' – cries nobody except Robert, while he describes himself as a passive victim of Mary's 'devious' will (Mary Notebook, 10 March 1978). All the evidence suggests that initially and for a long time Mary's sexual interest in him was nil. He reads this 'sexual coldness' as an instrument directed against him, personally. He imagines Mary as a sly dominatrix, or an animal predator: 'I am sitting in front of a fay spider [...] There is nothing I can do – I talk like an obsolete fly' (Mary Notebook, 15 February 1978). 'I had to wait: she always seemed elusively one step ahead not cerebrally but intuitively, as though her inner state seemed cleaner – less greedy than my own. Not naïve, not just spidery and manipulative' (Mary Notebook, 20 February 1978).

At times he is aware of how twisted he has become. *Man in a Knot by the Straight Back of a Woman* (1980) found its way into the Suicide Project, but it captures a key aspect of the painter's situation with Mary. He moves but cannot move, and via a kind of self-enforced passivity and the delusion of his 'patient gentleness' he tries to find a physical form appropriate to his feelings. He writes in jolting language reminiscent of Samuel Beckett:

> The primary activity of man is waiting. Waiting for what may not or cannot happen. And when it happens, waiting again for what has happened not to happen. – or to happen more often, with more intensity/ the physiology of waiting. The moment life finds its form in the end of waiting. Moods are a residence for the uninvited guests of events. The invited rarely attend. When they do, the party is over or one's priorities are altered. I wait for the formless hollow creature of my psychosis. I turn it as I please, a chimera of the will of my will. All 'others' are simply the shape and disguise the ghost takes on. I am my own portable ghost; I invite myself to every party: one host, one guest. I walk over her, under her, through her – never 'into her' – If I could become my own Mobius strip instead of the amorphous circle. (Mary Notebook, 21 October 1979)

If we allow ourselves the reductive symbolism of masculine sexuality as phallic, projecting out, and of feminine sexuality as vaginal, folding within, then the Möbius strip is a perfect geometric cartoon of the androgynous 'conjunction'. In an undated aesthetic note Robert made a rough sketch of such an 'androgynous knot'. The 'inside' of the Möbius strip is continuous with its 'outside'. It is three dimensional, but has only one edge, only one surface. Its angular properties in relation to its 'centre' are infinite. It is the one, and the two, and the many. Several of the paintings from the Mary Project (full title: Project 14 – 'The Painter with Mary: A Study of Obsessional Behaviour') rank among the finest of Robert's career, and there is no doubt that Mary is their co-creator. The one which stands out as most gorgeous and mysterious and which unusually Robert himself rated as excellent is *The Painter and Mary in Magi-fool's Hats*. The roughly torn crowns resemble nothing so much as violently fashioned Möbius strips.

Known more often as 'Paper Crowns', it is a very small painting by Robert's standards, but its dimensions are dwarfed by its *mass*. It seems heavier than lead or gold. The paper crowns grant a disposable majesty to the lovers. The paint is as Robert said of Rembrandt's: 'almost ethical in its treatment of flesh'. The image fixes a moment which will be blown away with the next breath of time. It captures the glow of a tragic wisdom which has arrived precisely when the moment of its relevance is departing, a paradoxical conjunction of depression and triumph. The differences between the faces of the bearded older man and younger woman are evident. But Jim Pascoe, commenting on the painting during a gallery talk by artist Louise Courtnell at a posthumous exhibition in Plymouth, remarked, 'Don't you think it is uncanny how *similar* they look?' Not brother and sister or father and daughter but daemonic familiars who have sold their souls to each other. Or, to refashion that interpretation of the image in Robert's terms, sold their souls to their own aesthetic vulnerabilities. It is a conjunction of togetherness and profound isolation.

In November Robert is interviewed at his easel by local television with Mary sat upon his knee, modelling. He explains his 'aesthetic theory' of relationships as:

> An attempt to articulate human behaviour in terms of that which attracts and that which repels. An attempt to give shape to the notion that the gentlest impulse, the kiss and the caress, is a violent act – not in the 'drunk in the street' sense, but in a civilised, controlled and incredibly brutal way.

In the diary he crows triumphantly over 'the sly and endless delight of having placed her there before the South of England'.

Robert now feels himself to have gained the upper hand. He feels that Mary's addictive state may be serious enough for him to take the initiative: 'My power grows – hers wanes ... or so it appears and is intended – explained my avowed intention to cause her pain as well as pleasure – then to love all. To love what will be lost anyway'.

[125] I am capable of saying and doing anything. Constant desire to be that part of myself – no separation and beyond sex ... and there *is* a beyond. She does not know what is set off and what I will lose. Before the loss is the possession. Unable to stop with her once I start – clear indication of mutuality in the affair. Youth means experiment, so my indulgence lives under the cloud of a cut throat. She will see me tomorrow. (Diary, 16 November 1979)

We flash-forwards here to a kind of ending. Robert was well-informed about the likely psychological and physical effects he would suffer:

January 8 1981. Mary did not appear –
Mary did not appear – interesting to realise my isolation without her. Isolation in those special areas – the rest I live with all along. It will get much worse when I get older – much worse; must prepare. With no income things are difficult.
[...] Began first statement of large three chair still-life. Slept alone.

No-one can say whether Robert felt more pain at the departure of Mary than he felt when the 'Paper Crowns' painting was cut from its stretcher and stolen by gangsters. Mary left very slowly, almost imperceptibly. The painting went very quickly. Both events were expected. And according to Robert's philosophy it was all about himself. But as Robert said, 'An unrequited love is the life-blood of creativity' and he would use Mary's departure to create one of his finest works – *Still-Life: Three Chairs* – across a month of solitary painting.

The painter's notes on the still-life become filled with organic metaphors:

Worked until 3am on Still-Life/ Chairs – ... The glow of light on the yellow – white canvas/ brilliant convoluted entrails of canvas within the ribs of the chair. A great glowing heart in the body of the chair. [...]

It is the in the intense identification with the woman's form as an extension for one's own desire for a pure sense-less tangibility. Her 'fidelity' represents one's own potential cleansing of all that is insincere/ unreal. To keep her virginal; means that by 'being with her' – she cannot be with anyone else. Obsessional attention forces her 'fidelity' – when it is forced it dies. What is so intolerable about her lust is that it threatens the four walls within which the lover experiences it. That prison is shaped, a cell with two inhabitants. If the one prisoner breaks out, the other must soon follow; enter the strange air scented through the hole. The fragility of passion lies in the fact that the prison is so easily breached. When she goes elsewhere, you lose your innocence too. You too are driven out from the garden.

Worked until 3am on 'Three Chairs/ Still-Life. Beginning to develop strongly – but illustrational tendencies. Not yet 'painted through'. The objects have to be painted through. Not the ones on the canvas, but the 'real' ones before me. The eye has to dissolve them, and in that moment of mutability they may be 'ethically transformed'. All matter is a question of ethics … a 'matter of ethics'.

Then on 20 January Lenkiewicz makes a positive resolution: 'Thought much about 'Painter with Mary' project. Determined to do it notwithstanding. To make it powerful'. He makes numerous drawings in the notebook.

Worked hard on Still-Life/ Three Chairs. Much thought on situation. Clear in my mind that it is insensitive to see life negatively – anxieties are part of the creative process. To come to acceptance, however, necessarily kills the creative process. Can understand how 'Art' is born of pain or at the very least discomfort. A genetic imprint that demands ordering or re-ordering of everything stressful. Acceptance implies that some compromise, some peace has been made. The art dies. Order and chaos is intimately related and simultaneous. Absolutes are illusory. One 'goes through' all form. It is recorded in retrospect with a perception that witnessed but did not experience. 'Looking' itself is already a third remove. Worked until 2am. Slept alone. Difficult time. Held a ghost.

Five days later the painting is complete:

Worked hard on Three Chairs – Quiet morning. Had some egg on toast by the window – watched people/ couples/ walking by. A tremulous vulnerable fragility about everything.

Worked on 'Three Chairs' Still-Life. Worked and worked. Stopped working on 'Three Chairs' Still-Life. Will leave it now. Looks very rich. So fascinating to see what can be done with such a limited tonal range. Warm and cold whites. The white canvas like breathing entrails with the rib-cage of the chair. 17 days. Interesting.

Moved the big paintings – lowered 'Three Chairs' Still-Life out of window. Looks splendid in the window. Began to organize the rooms for 'Still Life' exhibition ad miscellanies. Much thought of Mary. Went for walk. Painful thoughts of Mary. I find it so insolubly beautiful. It seems that everything I do is in some obscure intangible way ... for her. Compassionately for her.

Then in February, Mary is sighted at the studio and he meets her on 14 February at Piermasters restaurant where vows are exchanged with respect to marriage ... and something more:

8pm. MARY [29] Piermasters. Incredible time. She came in silver velvet dress and black shawl. So intense and beautiful. She embraced, how she embraced! In the street turning; turning; such small movements and gestures, hurtling, deep with their power. Corner table at Piermasters/ Steve [the chef] very sweet – delicious hot vegetables. Talked of Taraneh, Yana etc. Her parents – the stress they were under re: the recent 'death' plan and then – the decision. Instinctive, primeval and certain.

How strange it all is. Tension of the highest quality and then ½ hr later some possibility of perception. Not to value the emotion as anything other than a means. We confirmed, confirmed and recognised. It is so interesting – so interesting. Rich time along the street – so erotic and disturbing. *The child* [author's emphasis], of course, will go with it – not one without the other.

Mary and Robert married in Plymouth Registry Office in March 1981. The wedding was the simplest possible, with only Mary's parents present as witnesses (Yana, Interview, September 2019). The groom wore white. The union would not result in a child.

Despite his usual disdain for social conventions Robert arranged a 'honeymoon'. The location was Rome, ground-zero of good mysticism turned bad, and the epicentre of European Fascism, if not the universal 'aesthetic fascism'. Rome's myth, its empire, its 'eternity' was the magnificent and politically filthy blueprint for the Nazi regime. Robert predicted that this honeymoon was the zenith of Mary's interest in him. She did not cut off, but year by year the feelings bled away into the past. Or so he claims. Other observers tell different stories which lie outside the scope of our work. We return now to the late 1970s to chart the rise of Robert's own empire.

21.1 Poster for Project 8, shown in August/September 1977 at The Fool.
21.2 The Bishop seated opposite the studio with Jeny Bremer, August 1977.
21.3 Diogenes with a print of the Barbican Mural, 23 August 1977.
21.4 Diogenes and Jon Cox, known as 'Diaghileff', managing the studio
      together, August 1977.

At the Barbican studio in the summer of 1977 with works from the Jealousy Project.

21.5 Robert holds up *You Offer Me a Dead Rose, May I Give You a Dead Rat?* (1976), a work from Love & Mediocrity.

21.6 Gillian Pearce (Mary) outside the Barbican studio, 30 July 1977.

21.7 Belle Pecorini with the tondo *Man Holding a Woman's Dress* (1977).

21.8 Belle Pecorini with *Man Watching Himself With Mary* (1977).

21.9 Ruti Cohen and Robert's daughter Laila on the Barbican in July 1977.

21.10 Laila on 20 July holding the painting *Man Holding a Woman's Dress Watching Her Walk Away* (1977).

21.11 Ria Ney-Hoch visiting on 8 August 1977.

21.12 Amelie Cachia visiting on 14 August 1977.

21.13 Robert strides past *The Night Watch* (1976) with posters for Project 8.

21.14 Robert holding *Woman Walking Away* (1977), painted in the artist's garden at Compton, based on the painting on the theme of jealousy *Apollo in the Forge of Vulcan* (1630), by Velázquez.

354

21.15 *The Last Supper* mural (81 x 345 cm), based on Leonardo's mural, in Joe Prete's ice cream parlour. The mural depicts the Prete family and Robert punned as 'Jesus holding a Mars Bar (interviewer's microphone)'. The blonde boy is Lenkiewicz's son, Sholem. To either side, making up the requisite thirteen attendees of The Last Supper, are various members of the Prete family. Behind Lenkiewicz John wears his Plymouth Argyll club blazer; Jim holds an ice cream seated to Joe's right; Joe's wife Margaret is to the left of the picture, behind grandson Dean holding the toys; rightmost is Sissy and to her right, John's wife Joyce.

21.16 Snowy, Robert's handyman Ian, and Cockney Jim, at the 1977 Christmas Day dinner.

21.17 2.4 x 5 metre canvas *Plymouth Building Its Future* (1977) [and detail].

The comissioned painting hung for many years in the basement cafeteria of Plymouth Guildhall before moving to Devonport Guildhall in 2014. It shows Plymouth's celebrated architects Isambard Kingdom Brunel, John Foulston, Sir Patrick Abercrombie, and post-war city planner J. Paton Watson, together with many of the city's most recognisable architectural landmarks.

To the right, a familiar cast of vagrants are grouped around Robert and Myriam: 'Wee Jock', Diogenes, Dave Helingoe, Eugene, Bill, 'Cockney Jim', and The Bishop.

21

Jealousy, Sickness, and Agony in Death House (1977–1980)

Early in the Mary relationship when Robert was still calling her Gillian, the studio space at 25 The Parade began to change. Peter and Joy Wanstall's hi-fi business occupied the upper floors of the building. For years Peter Wanstall had pressed the Barbican Association for Robert's eviction, but Robert was too charismatic and too lucky to be winkled out. The recession of the late 1970s ruined Wanstall's business. The diaries suggest a vile and vexatious neighbour, but Robert is not without sympathy: 'Wanstall appeared [...] rather white and greatly troubled. I felt very sorry that things went this way for him' (Diary, 14 June 1977). 'Wanstalls Hi-Fi have definitely closed up. In theory the upstairs is mine' (Diary, 19 June 1977).

Andrew Beaumont started negotiations with the owner, Mr Cornish, who was not enthusiastic, for he knew of Robert's close association with the Cowboys and the bailiffs. It was June before Robert received the keys to the entire building. It was considerably later that Andrew received his payment – a beautifully painted scene on his harpsichord lid showing Hercules beating his music teacher to death with his own lute (Diary, 15 June 1978). After years of struggling in the cramped ground floor window, Robert's new space must have seemed palatial – though it required work to make it suitable to hang paintings.

At street level the old 'shop window' became a display area for the best of his canvasses: also for books, academic journals and pamphlets, and related artefacts. Facing into the building, the right-hand doorway now became the main entrance. Behind this was a narrow hallway, made thinner by stacks of exhibition notes, catalogues, journals, and news clippings. This hallway led to the room which became Robert's in-studio library. Next to this was a steep and twisting staircase. Every step wobbled and had its own ominous noise. Ascending or descending was like voyaging through a clown's concertina. Robert frequently resorted to snapping stretchers to get a painting around its tight corners. There were two modest rooms on the first floor, another two on the second floor, with small north-facing windows set in flaky walls, bare floorboards, maritime damp, and rodents, all under a buckled roof which leaked in all weathers, and not a straight line in the building. When paintings were hung Robert had to decide which edge should roughly fall in line with the curved floor or bowed ceiling. Even vacant, 25 The Parade would have looked disorderly. With canvases stacked in serried ranks against the walls, easels, used palettes, and overflowing bookcases it may have been merely chaotic. But here were skulls, both animal and human: and there were fabrics and other props, rolls of scavenged sail-cloth, random timbers for stretchers, maul sticks and boxes of building tools, hundreds of brushes in dozens of tin cans, tubes of paint scattered and squirming like rainbowed caterpillars on every flat surface. It was primal matter which had developed its own spirit, and it was rioting.

Through this stage-set the human tides flowed. Local fishermen, students, shopkeepers, mariners, and tourist visitors from other nations. Voyagers from other mental states, regular dossers, and wandering Cowboys. Debt collectors, members of Her Majesty's Government, lords and ladies, thieves and vagabonds, the Chief of the Criminal Intelligence Division mooching for clues to unsolved murders (Diary, 12 January 1978). There were philosophers, musicians, medics, academics, and artists: many on these lists were also rare and beautiful women who were *almost* the most welcome of visitors, second only to book dealers bearing rare and beautiful books.

Alice von Schlossberg's death had not made Robert nostalgic or sentimental but his perversity of feeling became more nuanced: 'Conceived notion of a life-sized Pieta. Myself with my Mother over my lap – putrefying, with cloth around her jaw and my hand in her vagina' (Diary, 22 September 1977). With 'Ma' commuted from the land of the living to the land of imagination, Robert's visits to the capital became more frequent. Johnny, Bernard, Aury, Myrna, Ruti, Annie, and Eddie were regularly called on when he made his rounds of the galleries and bookshops.

For the most part the relationships were unchanged or they matured and became richer. There was one notable exception: Axel Ney-Hoch. When Robert saw Heathcote Williams's book *The Speakers* adapted for the stage at Plymouth's Abbey Hall on 15 October 1976, he seemed well disposed to Axel, at least in effigy: 'Very enjoyable nostalgic evening watching the play, to listen again to Axel and McGuiness. So strange to hear him call "Gladys!". Little Ria in bed'. But shortly thereafter news reached Robert that Axel had been hitting the drugs, and the bottle, and his wife and children with increasing regularity and force. Robert was still very much involved with Ria. His attitude to Axel changed somewhat: 'Myrna and Ruti took me to see Maria Ney's work on her judging day at the polytechnic. Met Axel and Gladys there after so many years. Strange to do the old battle of limited wits with Mr Hoch. He was unexpectedly friendly and agreeable' (Diary, 3 June 1977). The new distance implied by 'Mr Hoch' and the word 'unexpectedly' suggest Robert had information, most likely from Ria, about at least some of Axel's behaviour. His treatment of the women around him was bad enough for Stella to write: 'One of my ambitions was to see my father die [...] There was a time he had overdosed – again – and Ria said "Let's phone an ambulance" and I said – "Let's not!" We had an argument over it, a fight, but she phoned the ambulance and he lived' (Stella, Letter, March 2018).

Coincidence is magic in action, said Crowley. Robert's relationship with Mary – still mainly physically chaste in 1977 though psychologically filthy – reached an early point of intensity. This coincided with a new peak in the relationship with Belle. And at the same time Robert had what he refers to as 'one of those moments' – an insight profoundly sensual and intellectually encompassing. It connected several of his lovers and the relationship projects in new and unexpected ways. Too restless to sleep or work he set himself to night-wandering. Wandering is a no-time and a no-place, and often the best habitat for wild thoughts which come unbidden. On return to the Studio, next to a drawing of a pelvis and thighbones crowned with bright red, blue, and gold organs, he writes:

2.30am approx. One of those moments again. Have thought so much about Jealousy etc. Could not resolve anything of it apart from disparate relevances. Walking through Southside Street: suddenly – it all came together in the formula of entrails and all the hidden meanings of why I constantly return to viscera. The theme of pregnancy in direct relation to cannibalism where suffering (aesthetic withdrawal symptoms) are undergone became crystal clear.

Jealousy, murder, and ultimately suicide is all the withdrawal can lead to in terms of the 'enjoyment of misery' as another taste extension. Tremendous sense of joyousness when so much of what I have been thinking came together in this pathological image. (Diary, 1 August 1977)

Next to the image he writes: 'Entrails/Pregnancy/1/6/1977 Revelation' – and that last word has sacred overtones for Robert. His lifelong search for hidden meanings was a voyage not to the Old Gods or beyond the stars but further into the sacred mysteries of the body.

Hard work continued and the Jealousy paintings grew in number. At 11 a.m. on 10 August 1977 at The Fool, the 'Jealousy exhibition opened with a resounding – nothing. No queues, no knocks on the door. Not a single visitor. Monica came in and gave me back £5 I had loaned her. *Gewalt*. Worked in The Fool until 3pm. Painted skeleton white – Reuben helped. Went down to my derelict looking shop'. Two days later he writes: 'Nothing in the papers'. Although Robert frequently behaved like there was no such thing as bad publicity, the lack of journalistic attention may have been for the best. Paintings with titles such as *What Is the Difference Between His Penis and My Knife?* lend themselves to hysterical reactions. Some viewers might read the exhibition notes' exploration of the murderous habit of people 'owning each other' and 'belonging' in relationships, and engage with the ideas. Others might feel compelled to contact the police with accusations of incitement to violence as well as obscenity. The larger the audience, the larger the risk of Robert being entangled in legal proceedings. The first review came on 21 August in the *Sunday Independent* under the headline 'Horrors of Jealousy'.

> The public seems to have drawn the line at the latest horror exhibition by Plymouth artist Robert Lenkiewicz [...] nearly 100 paintings and models fill the gallery in Clifton Street. And most of them are grotesque distortions of the human body, especially the heart and genitalia. But sensational or not, the exhibition is flopping, in terms of people paying their 10p to go and see it.

In the same article Robert is reported as saying:

> I suppose there is a bit of a butcher's shop element [...] but it is a strong subject and I have presented my view of it in a strong manner. [...] You don't measure success in numbers. A lot of younger people have seen it and their reaction is intelligent and sensitive. There has been the other reaction of course. One man came in, paid his 10p, raced around and noted 100 paintings and left saying: 'Very interesting'. That, to me is failure [...] I would be quite happy if it is seen by a handful of people – and they have a strong and intelligent reaction to it.

The 'butcher's shop' feel was provided in large part by the centrepiece painting *Man Eating his Heart and Entrails/Still-Born Child in the Kitchen* (1977). In it, Robert sits in Annie Hill-Smith's living room, nude from the waist down, with his own viscera piled in his lap. He helps himself to a bite from the glistening mass of guts. Annie stands in the background holding their youngest son Jascha while Sholem is blissfully asleep on the sofa. Annie Hill-Smith explains that:

> ...after the piece was shown in Jealousy and the project was complete he cut the painting into two parts and then painted the so-called 'still-born' (which I would call 'abortion') image onto the smaller section (that part was put on in Plymouth). It was then hung in the Death project, so you see that the two parts are simultaneously conjoined and distinct. [38]

Annie described the motivation for the painting:

> He was exploring jealousy in that project using his so-called 'private language' paintings. That is, he was using his skills of 'painting things that look like things' to try to represent some of the very visceral stuff of jealousy. You know that visceral feeling (I'm sure you do) ... he thought that most people would recognize it and that the representation of the viscera pouring out of him would 'speak' to the viewer of those painful feelings. So this one was one of many in that project that all 'spoke' to you the viewer (he hoped) of the jealousy experience.
>
> So that painting arose. While it was being painted I was indeed having an affair, the raw material of jealousy ... so it's a fair bet that the piece is loosely inspired by my activities and while it was being painted we talked about the emotions of jealousy all the time. It was part of his research as you might say. [39]

Entrails made a second memorable appearance in what Robert's diary refers to as the 'Garden of Eden' painting but was formally titled *Woman Walking Away* (1977). Eden is the garden at 'Death House' in Compton in which Myriam walks away from a naked male figure drawn straight from Velázquez's jealousy-themed *Apollo in the Forge of Vulcan* (1630). Vulcan is the Roman equivalent to the Greek blacksmith god Hephaestus, who made the first woman, Pandora, from clay. In the Roman myth, told in Ovid's *Metamorphoses*, the god Apollo tells Vulcan that his wife,

Venus, has been unfaithful to him with the god of war, Mars. The extruded entrails snaking after Myriam (who is wearing her sister Magdalena's dress) exactly follow a sinuous line in Velázquez's composition. Myriam is the dominant model in the project. Her remarkable physical composure enabled her to sit motionless for long periods of time; the triangular relationship between her, Magdalena and Robert was a goldmine of jealous motivations.

But Robert's 'enjoyment of misery' epiphany on 1 August spelled the end of realistically painted viscera imagery, more or less. In resolving this metaphor, he was freed to explore a new 'private language' in the next project (on 'Orgasm'), the raw meat gave way to the *aesthetic note*, with its characteristic use of colour metaphors for the sensations experienced by human physiology in a state of crisis. Not entrails but coloured tendrils of 'aesthetic responses' to the object of desire would now emerge from the body. And a new, aggressive element began to appear in the work. Instead of the lover being the passive victim of his or her own evisceration, they began to be shown reaching into or through their partner's body:

> I was engrossed by the notion that when lovers embraced each other what they really wanted to do was to pass their arms through each other, not round each other; they wanted to make holes and get a good grip. And this was in order to compensate for the fact that no matter how much you press, say, your fingers together, they're separate – it doesn't matter how intense the embrace is, you're separate. [40]

Work on the next Project, 'Orgasm', was already underway. There were also the first stirrings of the Gossip on the Barbican Project. This began life as a series of 25 paintings commissioned by the local gallery owner Bill Hodges and Stan Goodman of the Barbican Association, to be called 'Work on the Barbican' (Diary, 20 September 1977). Robert saw gossip as the more laudable social activity, especially since much local 'work' was tied to tourists' historical sentimentality and selling vast quantities of booze. So much did Robert detest the pub trade that he later designed posters demanding that the Barbican become an alcohol-free zone. Alongside these projects he also completed the School of Night Mural for the Shakespeare pub on Union Street in late 1977.

The year 1977 brought a youth movement to Plymouth which went well beyond the raucous back-to-basics music called 'punk rock'. The punk movement was partly an offshoot of avant-garde political art. Its methods and energies would have been recognised by Kurt Schwitters, the Surrealists, or the Situationists. Much of the iconography was immediately hoovered up by record companies for mere shock value. Robert appreciated the energy and do-it-yourself creativity of the punk movement but he was less sure about its generalised iconoclasm. Razzing the establishment was amusing, but Robert saw something of enduring worth in the figure of the 'celebrity'.

Robert was very conservative in his music tastes. He loved opera and tolerated rock 'n' rollers only according to the quality of their voice. Roy Orbison he considered the better baritone than Elvis Presley, but The King remained the King. The drama of Elvis's birth during a thunderstorm, in a dirt-floored shotgun-shack, arriving hot on the heels of the dead first-born, appealed to Robert's sense of the mythic: from such beginnings there is a sense of destiny in the rise from abject poverty to global adoration. When Elvis died Robert paid one of the Barbican boys to buy up as many different newspapers as he could to harvest the public response. Many people have thought of Elvis as they laid with somebody else, but the nature of Robert's imaginings may have been a world first: 'My head between her legs as Presley putrefies in Memphis' (Diary, 17 August 1977). Celebrity, tragedy, and death are erotic materials of huge social importance. The death of Maria Callas only a month later prompted plans for a project on the relationship between the 'god-star' and their adoring acolytes from Dionysus and Orpheus onwards. Sadly this plan went the way of the prostitution, homosexuality, law, and pregnancy themes.

The main celebrity event of 1977 was the Queen's Silver Jubilee which Robert considered a trashy and booze-fuelled festival of hate: 'Fascist patriotism hangs in the air', he notes at the street party in North Hill (Diary, 7 June 1977). He enjoyed the party with Annie, Aury, 'Alice, Wolfie, Reuben and all the rest', but was happy when it was over. He knew how quickly nationalism converts to anti-Semitism. At the close of the celebrations he noted 'it looks like The Fool has escaped laceration. Pete Libby was drunk and although friendly to me, broiling for trouble. Saw Terry Bourne in the distance of a smoke filled bar, leering with a working class wisdom at something suitable for bombing – me, I think' (Diary, 7 June 1977).

Despite Annie's relentless efforts on his behalf Robert made harsh comments about her: 'Annie suddenly phoned: "There's something I want to talk about". Probably fucking pregnant or worse still – in love: Both possibilities destined for "abortive" consequences' (Diary, 27 June 1977). It seems likely that pregnancy was the reason for the call. In 1978 Annie gave birth to her third child by Robert, Kate. Speaking of the late 1970s Annie says:

> It was a very productive time [for Robert]. And it was hard work for the women he was most closely involved with: for me, and I'm thinking for all the people that were drawn into deep and serious relationships with Robert as well, we also needed to be emotionally and psychologically fit. And robust and resilient and able to face all directions. Robert inhabited a very unusual world. (Annie, Facebook, 20 May 2019)

The year 1977 was a watershed in terms of Robert's attitude to the Cowboys. Some of the worst types were wrecking the scene by begging or swindling Robert's studio helpers, sitters, companions – even his children. 'Ray John' conned Reuben out of a pound, mercilessly it seems. Robert was so outraged by this that his response was untypical and vengeful: 'Ray John came in, tried begging me again. Took out £1 note and ripped it up to shreds before him. He left somewhat upset' (Diary, 7 August 1977). This callousness was not generalised. The Diaries record that Robert was on the same day buying food for random 'third division' types who washed up at the studio. Depending on their performance, Cowboys could move up or down divisions, which Robert thought of as follows:

> The top division live on their wits manipulating the handouts the state provides. They have deep personal problems and usually develop a degree of alcoholism. They are socially incompetent, but capable of looking after themselves. They develop a stack of tricks to suck money or food out of people.
>
> Those in the second division feed on extremes of experience and live in the street and the pubs. They are on the increase.
>
> The minority are the third division, the no-hopers like Ivor, chronic alcoholics, middle aged, the types who usually drink cider and whatever they can find and have become crystallised in their way of life. They are usually in a psychotic state and usually never attract public attention [...] Very few of these people can be helped. (Robert, in *The Independent*, 24 April 1978)

Brother Blair continued to write regularly and menacingly. It seems that he and other malicious or unwise dossers were spreading word of Robert's helpfulness very indiscriminately: 'Extraordinary looking Cowboy known as Fagin tried a beg. Worked out that he'd been sent by "Wee Jock" in Torquay, the cunt' (Diary, 21 July 1977). Robert notes four of his regular vagrants outside 25 The Parade 'sitting on the wall, waiting like monkeys. Dangerous 3rd Division bum – "Monighay" in town. Cut off "Big Hughie's" ears a couple of years ago. Expect him to beg me. Mouth McCarthy also in town. Could be a lot of trouble those two' (Diary, 28 July 1977). Launching another of the dossers on his travels Robert 'bought him a meal, gave him £2. One [ticket] for the 6:10 bus to Exeter' and adds: 'Would I were rid of the lot of them' (Diary, 19 June 1977).

Robert always preferred to outwit the violent rather than match them. When a known 'knuckler' appeared on the Plymouth scene Robert tried to discover which strings to pull and what levers to push. For example: 'Big Frankie Carol is terrified of The Bishop – so I paid The Bishop 50p for acting the part of being thrown out of the shop by me' (Diary, 27 June 1977). Sometimes psychology was impossible. Very occasionally Robert threw punches. Unsurprisingly some were aimed at one of the unholy trinity of Brother Blair, Big Brummy, and Brighton. Robert admired control in matters of violence and pain. He writes of Myriam: '[She is] one of the few that has passed through much. Born with a talent for controlled self-murder' (Diary, 3 August 1977). And for a man who never studied martial arts Robert showed admirable restraint against Brighton. Strikes to an opponent's head are natural and rational moves for someone with Robert's height advantage, but he held back:

One of *those* days. Wanstall's fucking alarm went off. Brighton came, drunk, threw him out. Annie went to fetch the police for both. Noise intolerable. Everyone complaining. Pulled out all the wires but the thing still went on. Brighton came back again, more trouble. Hit him hard in the solar plexus and ribs. He fell down – got up and took a swing. Hit him in the stomach a few times, he fell against the van – difficult for him to breathe. Hit him again in the ribs and tummy, he ran off shouting 'Bastard!' (Diary, 14 August 1977)

For a while Brighton kept a distance from Robert on the Barbican. He began instead to visit The Fool gallery in Clifton Street, menacing monies out of people there (Diary, 13 October 1977). During this time Robert became somewhat more tolerant of Her Majesty's police force: 'C.I.D. Allison and colleague visited. Long pleasant chat about relationships theme.

So extraordinary to be discussing Love/sex/education etc with these police officers. Belle was there, with her hash in a bag under their noses' (Diary, 4 August 1977). In the same week Her Majesty the Queen came to Plymouth as part of her Silver Jubilee tour. Lord Eliot was invited to dinner on the Royal Yacht. Robert was not. It was estimated that a crowd of 15,000 people would be in town to see the Queen. Robert joked that it would be more like 50,000 if the right-wing politician Enoch Powell was visiting (Diary, 6 August 1977).

Released from jail in the autumn of 1977 Big Brummy redoubled his vileness, forcing Robert to avoid the Barbican at times: 'Horror of horrors, Big Brummy turned up. Won't leave me alone, smashing on the door, Threatening me as I write [...] Police utterly useless: ridiculously unaware of the danger of the situation' (Diary, 2 September 1977). Two days later 'he leered in, threatened me, talked gibberish, said he would not leave me alone as long as he remained in Plymouth' (Diary, 4 September 1977). Robert was so unnerved he went immediately to the police. They could do nothing but say they would patrol the area the next day. On the 6th, Brummy sent a message via Annie at The Fool Gallery that he would quit Plymouth if Robert paid his ticket. Foolishly, Robert agreed and even allowed himself the dangerous luxury of sympathy:

> We drove the poor animal to the station. I had twenty minutes to kill with him. Sat in compartment as he sweated it out. Made up his 'Jack' concoction in the toilet. Gave him cigarettes. He has been in every city in the country. Like a terrible Minotaur, unwanted everywhere – bricks through his brother's windows – smashed up his brother's car – constant violence against rejection. Impossible man to deal with. Something dark – Saturnine – archetypal power about his black hopelessness. I assume he will get off [the train] at Totnes – sell the ticket and be back in Plymouth in a day or so. He is no better off in Exeter. Terrible, hopeless business. (Diary, 6 August 1977)

The year 1977 saw one mural finished and another commissioned. Completed in March 1977, the mural in Joe Prete's café quotes the ceiling/backdrop of Leonardo's *The Last Supper*, which is shown in the open Phaidon art book which supports a menorah, the seven-lamped symbol of Judaism. Two other books are depicted: Foucault's *Madness and Civilization*, which Robert acquired in 1976 when the mural was begun, and Thomas Mann's *Death in Venice*. Lenkiewicz has punned himself 'painted as Jesus holding a Mars Bar (interviewer's microphone)'. The blonde boy is Lenk-iewicz's son, Sholem. To either side, making up the requisite 13 attend-ees of The Last Supper, are various members of the Prete family. Behind Lenkiewicz, John Prete wears his Plymouth Argyll club blazer; Jim holds an ice cream seated to Joe's right; Joe's wife Margaret is to the left of the picture, behind grandson Dean holding the toys; rightmost is Sissy, and to her right, John's wife Joyce. The work was removed from the building in 2014 when Prete's finally closed. As the mural had been painted onto canvas fixed to the wall with tallow it was relatively easy to remove and is therefore one of the few public murals to survive.

On 16 October 1977 the *Sunday Independent* reported on a second mu-ral on canvas in the city, commissioned by Paul and Chris U'ren, directors of the Michael Wing and Partners estate agency in Union Street. 'We think Robert is a very fine artist indeed and we asked him to represent Plymouth and its architects in any way he liked. We are tremendously pleased with the mural, which combines the city's landmarks, the men who built them, plus some of the local characters the artist knows'. The 8 ft x 16 ft work depicts Brunel (the Royal Albert Bridge), Abercrombie (post-World War II 'Plan for Plymouth'), Foulston (Union Street, and town hall, column, and library in Devonport), and city engineer and surveyor J. Paton Wat-son, who designed much of the rebuilt city in the post-war period. Other landmarks include the Derry's Cross clock, the Citadel gate, Smeaton's lighthouse, the then new Civic Centre, and Boehm's statue of Sir Francis Drake. The canvas includes a self-portrait by Robert next to Myriam Rive-ra, and behind them a cast of familiar characters – 'Wee Jock', Diogenes, Dave Helingoe, Eugene (a vagrant who was once an estate agent), Bill, 'Cockney Jim', and 'The Bishop'. For many years the painting hung in the basement canteen in Plymouth Guildhall. But in 2014 it was relocated with the kind permission of Pam U'ren and Plymouth City Museum and Art Gallery into the main room at the Devonport Town Hall. It was also given a formal title, *Plymouth Building Its Future*, a nod towards Robert's juxtaposition of the expensively suited gentlemen to the left, with their grand civic improvement plans, and the great unwashed to the right, who have somehow failed to be uplifted by these ambitious schemes.

The late 1970s also saw a change in Robert's distinctively 'hands-off' – and arguably 'mind-off and heart-off' style of parenting. The diaries record an increasing number of entries such as 'Went to see Mouse and the children. Atmosphere delightful' (Diary, 6 November 1977). Dorian remained almost entirely off-radar but Robert became better inclined to

Alice and Becky and Laila and Jimmy and Wolfe and Reuben and Sholem and Hayyam (Belle's daughter) – the whole mixed bag taken together, regardless of whose 'biological property' they might be. He was careful not to refer to them as 'his' children. There was an increase in cinema visits, bed-time stories, and shared mealtimes. Alice and Becky moved towards their teens and Robert records intellectual and aesthetic discussions with them while Wolfe and Reuben were enjoying happy hours pretending to be fighter planes attacking Robert in his role as King Kong.

From October to November of 1977 Robert visited France to spend time with Tunisian friend Amelie Cachia and explore the cultural wealth of the Marseille area. This was his longest time out of England. The Diaries list a pageant of pleasures – the great Cézanne exhibition at the Ville D'Aix-en-Provence; Picasso's house in Vauvenargues, now a gallery; a close viewing of Ingres's *Thetis and Jupiter* which moved him to deliver a long talk on the virtues of 'flash' art; listening to the music of the troubadours; several visits to Van Gogh's old haunts in Arles; visits to museums and picturesque villages; and beautiful nights with Amelie. He made watercolour studies of Van Gogh's old haunts, where the night café and yellow house stood. He visited Mont Sainte-Victoire. Amazed by its immensity he wrote of Cézanne's achievements and sorrows:

Went to Mont Sainte-Victoire – Cézanne's little 3,300ft still-life. Over 60 times he painted this little bit of Poussinesque majesty. Something durable. Impossible to articulate scale as we drove towards it – seemed to be moving away Time and Space – the old dog – never made it. Curious menace about the limestone ridge over little St Antonin. Poor sly Cézanne: 'Old age and failing health will see to it now that the dream of art I have spent my life pursuing will never come true'. Cézanne to Vollard: 'There is only one painter in the world: myself' [...] Sylvain took a photo of me and the mountain. So sad. Did a watercolour study. Drove to St Antonin. Left Cézanne's monolith in the dark. (Diary, 31 October 1977)

The next day was a local holiday in Aix-en-Provence: 'Delightful walk to the café under the bridge, then back. Sat on the pavement with coffee etc. Considered ants and mountains. Worked on nude portrait – painted the cat on her lap. Olympia miscellany. Walked past the graveyard – the dark street lined with hundreds of flowers for the Festival of the Dead' (Diary, 1 November 1977). On 3 November Robert said his goodbyes to Amelie: 'We talked, etc. Sad business. Everything is birth and death. She left. I considered for a while. Got up collected my things, and saying goodbye to the cats – leaving a note on her table and in her bed – left' (Diary, 3 November 1977).

The week of his return to Plymouth brought mixed news – relief that Brummy was again in jail, and woe that local bailiffs were pursuing him for fully £1,000 (Diary, 8 November 1977) and the repulsive discovery that his bed was infested with insect larvae (Diary, 6 November 1977). There they writhed for several more days, for Robert had to rush to catch the Manchester train to keep an appointment with another companion, Lizbeth. She showed him around the Whitworth and City Galleries where he was impressed by the 'marvellous Stubbs'. On his return to Plymouth he bought cleaning supplies and spent the day firstly cleaning out the Studio then 'went to my house by taxi with my final pound. Amazed to find my door open! Spent hours cleaning my bed, covering each mattress with polythene with meticulous care' (Diary, 14 November 1977).

As winter blew in, Priory Road was still very basic, with some of the windows still awaiting glass; 25 The Parade was improving, with the rear 'library room' in good condition by November 1977. There was decent shelving for the books and a single bed, though it was seldom occupied singly. The Parade Studio was now an address, and it claimed a capital letter. Robert was very proud that post from far lands arrived with the simple address 'Painter, Studio, Plymouth'. His other studio spaces on Southside Street and White Lane were less comfortable and still doubled as Cowboy's Holiday Inns. They leaked so badly that many canvasses were damaged or destroyed. But Robert needed space, ever more space for the projects. Single portraits or even a meaningful series like 'Work on the Barbican' were accepted as commissions but he often felt they were dead ends in terms of his artistic or intellectual development:

> Dirk Hansen. Started portrait. Pleasant man 32" x 24" canvas. Talked about [...] Architecture /Nazi Ideology (he is German) – Anti-Semitism – Nietzsche/ Hegel/ Hölderlin etc. Portrait so-so – cannot find anything in doing them. (Diary, 21 November 1977)

Even when Robert found an interesting visual detail his response was often 'academic' in the most sterile sense of the word:

Continued Stanley (fisherman) study. Painted the hands – nearly completed. Strange tensile light violet hands. The light seems iridescent on the surface like water: an attractive useless academic detail, like those absurd but competent veined glints on Ingres/Millais/Etty (at times) and Watts. Something to do with the white, alizarine crimson and ultramarine. They all got hooked on the 'scumble' trick. (Diary, 7 December 1977)

It was very different with group pieces, for which he retained great enthusiasm. Robert began work on '*Self-Portrait on Death Bed*' in the closing months of 1977. It was put aside entirely for many months and completed in 1978 in a flurry of activity. Part of the reason for the delay was the run of terrible luck Robert and several people close to him had with their relationships that winter. On 29 November 1977 the diary records 'Bad sleep. Extraordinary and disturbing dreams about Belle'. Belle enjoyed psychedelic drugs in a responsible manner and mainly handled her relationship with Robert well in situations which many other of the companions found difficult. I met Belle several times in the 1980s and she seemed as she does in the diaries – fundamentally strong and sane, though occasionally infuriated by Robert. Nevertheless it was inevitable that imperfectly balanced persons were also attracted to Robert. Therefore on 29 November Robert records:

Christiane Callow visited. *Oy Gewalt!* Wants to have me as a 'soul mate' – would I commit a murder with her? – and a variety of other satanic Hammer film juvenilia. But she is in a terrible state in her isolation with her mother and could snap and do something terrible. Cheered her up and [arranged to see] her on Friday.

On the same day Robert continued work on the '*Self-Portrait on Death Bed*' and carefully figured Monica as Georges de La Tour's Magdalena. The techniques which give life to de La Tour's repentant and contemplative figure are deeply indebted to those of Caravaggio, using the maximum tonal range while letting large areas of darkness to do much of the dramatic work. It is precisely what Robert would call 'flash' painting. His reflections on the sitting are:

Monca [variant on Monica]. Taxi to collect. Cont. painting. She was in a very nervous state. Took her to the wine lodge for a meal to cheer her up. Painted her but she posed badly. The atmosphere was agreeable but shot through with her desire to escape her present position at her house. Curiously courageous in a deluded sort of way. Told me she'll always 'love' me – always has and always will – etc. and observed ironically enough how the sexual situation was the best she'd had etc, etc. Taxi'd her home. Drove home myself. Considered. Slept alone. (Diary, 29 November 1977)

There were difficult situations that December. 'Brother Blair visited for more wargames' (Diary, 13 December 1977). Mouse was seemingly immune to self-pity or fatigue: she soldiered on to help to set up the 'Cowboy's Christmas Dinner' at the Bus Station. Food was donated by local business, cooked by Joe Prete's family, and distributed by the extended Lenkiewicz clan and friends. But Monica was not there. Concerned, Robert took a taxi to North Hill:

> She was flat – heavy and utterly miserable. Apart from Tony Bourne's boring drunken behaviour [...] Terry came in drunk and offensive: he had been thrown out by his Brother-In-Law, and on return seems to have behaved in an ugly manner with poor Monca. She wants to get out of there now and can only think of the battered wives' home. (Diary, 25 December 1977)

This dismal episode aside, Robert's Christmas was happy and energetic. He announced the start of the Orgasm Project. Ria Ney-Hoch arrived from London, to his great joy. Ria's time with him over the holiday season is marked by such notes as 'Sweet night, very rich incident – strange creature. Very affectionate in the morning – slightly Oy Gewalt' (Diary, 29 December 1977). Ria returned to London before the New Year, leaving Robert more time to navigate his labyrinthine relationship with Mary.

The year 1978 began with much thought on sociology and philosophy which helped to transform the 'Work on the Barbican' paintings into the 'Gossip' Project. Robert's friendship with Joe Prete may also have been a factor. As the years passed Robert and Joe developed a complex and semi-felonious set of routines. They played cards for small monies and snooker at the Drake Circus Club, an ingloriously atmospheric den which opened seven days a week from 10 a.m. until 4 a.m. This was an office for people with unusual trades and business hours, at its busiest when the ordinarily disreputable nightclubs had closed. There was an unwritten commandment that conversations be whispered. Joe resembled a jocular mafia boss, a keen observer and sometimes co-director of local narratives. Joe was not a criminal, but if you needed a used car or a live dolphin or at short notice he could put you in touch with the right people. Robert took great interest in the role of everyday storytelling, which contained similar 'hidden connections' to those of his more arcane studies. He notes how he: 'Listened to a charming study of "soap operas" – Coronation Street, Crossroads, The Archers – etc. "I believe that the great script-writer in the sky is constantly writing the soap opera of Earth" – said a producer' (Diary, 1 January 1978). Such reflections found a home in Robert's conclusions to the Gossip Project – that we are narrative creatures, addicted to joining dots however we can, and our sense of significance is far more important to us than lofty considerations of 'the truth'.

One story from the mid-1980s illustrates the point well. When the actors Dennis Waterman and his soon-to-be wife Rula Lenska were performing in Plymouth, Lenska paid a visit, perhaps two or three, to Robert's Studio. I worked at the theatre at that time and recall that a rumour spread that Robert was involved with Lenska, so out of sheer curiosity and no concern for people's welfare I had to ask him if this were true. Robert replied no, it was not true, though he would like it to be. Then he added: 'The far more important thing ... is that people *believe* it to be true'.

At times Robert's garrulous 'public character' seems straight out of an Oscar Wilde comedy: against it we should balance his equally sincere tendency to what Colin Wilson called 'Outsider-ism'. He was not so much a 'man of parts' as a man of fragments and facets, with simultaneous projects and loves and selves pointing in all directions:

> I am in one of my wise/bitter/isolated/indifferent/superior moods – they become more regular – and my patience with mediocrity becomes minuscule. Worse as I age. Anti-social – misanthropic etc. All so standardised and artistic ... but it seems a natural thing under the circumstances. What is coming to terms with painting other than coming to terms with defeat? (Diary, 3 January 1978)

Within hours the prevailing winds have changed, and far from feeling isolated he senses his part in a network of international, trans-temporal artistic explorers:

Listened to Björling and Pavarotti all morning [...] Started drawing re: Munch's 'Woman With Heart' – all so curious considering. Again and again I touch on themes and motifs only to discover afterwards there are precedents, always in connection with the Relationships theme [...] must look through my library and find prints of Saturn devouring his children/Rubens/Goya. Made myself comfortable and read a great deal – Strindberg – Munch – Swedenborg etc. (Diary, 4 January 1978)

Such is the lot of all creators: when the work goes well, the universe is divine in its perfection. The next hour brings some difficulty of composition, and the entire cosmos is a Schopenhauerian nightmare. The principle goes double or quadruple for lovers, as Robert records in several of the Relationship notebooks. Few provocations are as violent in this 'turning of the world upside down' as that of jealousy. Hence the violently visceral images such as *Woman Walking Away* (1977) with his entrails being drawn out after her. Whether or not such violent emotions can be put to creative use is an area of fascination for Robert. His reading throughout the winter of 1977–78 suggests he was examining the jealousies inspired by Lou Salomé, whose intellectual erotic presence connects Nietzsche, Rée, Freud, and several of the Surrealists.

Belle Pecorini was still a powerful if variable muse. Robert notes: 'Poor sleep. Curious dreams/images re: Belle. Such an odd issue with that woman. Wider swings of the pendulum than anyone' (Diary, 9 January 1978). The disturbed sleep continued throughout the month: 'Strange restless night. Terrible dreams – and more unmentionables' (Diary, 11 January 1978). Ruti arrived from London on the 12th. Her influence was ambivalent. She was calming and intelligently physical but she also brought a sense of demonic delights: 'She looks so beautiful by candlelight, so many dark associations!' (Diary, 12 January 1978). The day turned darker though not in a pleasant or sensual way when he taxied to the Studio.

Three years earlier he described the police as 'the only people truly worthy of contempt' but was by now entering into a waltz of mutual toleration:

Arrived at the shop. Chief of [Criminal Intelligence Division] waiting for me with cohort. Asked me to do a drawing from a 'secret' photograph of a man who poses as a doctor – gains entry into the houses of the elderly and drugs them. Then steals everything. Long history of violence. T.V. does not allow photographs [of 'persons of interest' in ongoing cases]. Would I do an 'artist's impression'? As it was a matter of physical violence I obliged. Strange business when I reflect upon my youth. (Diary, 12 January 1978)

The mysteries of Robert's finances deepened. He had several thousands of pounds of inheritance due to him, and Johnny and Aury had both made it very clear that he could pick up money from them when he needed. But Robert remained committed to primitive barter. He was still trading basic sign-writing jobs for credit at Prete's while scraping cash together for little treats such as theatre visits:

> Went to see the Faust study at Abbey Hall [...] Courageous attempt at the impossible sections of Marlowe's work related to 'alter-ego' formulas [...] Over the heads of an audience too young to register Faust's problems. I failed to catch the final words due to schlemiels coughing, so went backstage and found Mephistopheles who re-quoted it for me: Byron's Don Juan. I talked with him a little re: Goethe's admiration for Polidori's Vampire, etc. (Diary, 13 January 1978)

There was an incident with Ruti that night, not written of in detail but recorded as: 'an extraordinary circumstance. Quite unique behaviour – something like "possession". Demonic behaviour. Slightly frightening. Psychopathia sexualis one might say' (Diary, 14 January 1978). The episode did not spook Robert unduly. He spent the day taking photographs of Ruti and Laila and made a fine watercolour study of Laila with Victoria's cat before seeing them off to London. I will follow Robert's lead by using quote marks, but it is obvious that the man has progressed some way 'in love with Ruti'. He sleeps alone for the next two nights and 'crept into bed with definite withdrawal symptoms' (Diary, 16 January 1978).

The radio lectures of Isaiah Berlin and the physical company of Belle Pecorini rushed to fill the gap left by Ruti, and the rest of January was spent producing many interesting and grotesque images relating to both the Death and Orgasm themes. One of the most striking depicts a naked woman, pale of skin and dark of hair, engaged in an act which can only be described as a reverse-birth or skull-fuck with death (Aesthetic Note, 20 January 1978). This, like many of the images Robert produced towards the close of the 1970s would be difficult to exhibit to the public. Robert thought it was high time he featured in the national press: 'Parcel from

Richard Adams containing splendid facsimile of *Times* arts page article "on me" – highly amusing'. Despite this article being cut-and-pasted into existence and having nothing to do with *The Times*, Robert placed the cutting in the window of 25 The Parade. He was optimistic that the news – which is to say the gossip, true or false – would grow. And of course it did.

22.1 Edwin Mackenzie and Albert Fisher outside the studio, March 1978.

22.2 The vagrant Victor Jonson (b. 1905), known as 'Cockney Jim' or 'Sturmwaffer', with Reuben (aged 10) and Wolfe Lenkiewicz (aged 11), April 1978.

22

Enough Is Enough, Except When It Isn't

A visit to London provided Robert with a chance to catch up with Aury, Myrna, and their young son Nahem Shoa. It also provided an opportunity for him to precisely and elegantly frame his estimation of fascist Christianity, as contrasted with his respectful interest in the Christian mystics:

> Went to the [Victoria and Albert Museum]. Took them to three little-used rooms and showed them *memento mori* pieces and crucifixions, flagellations, stripping, murders, possessions, tearings, and rendings – all in the name of Jesus the Lamb. Talked about culture as a means of destruction and aggression. Pleasant time with them as usual. (Diary, 22 January 1978)

Reuben and Wolfe accompanied Robert to London – 'they were well-behaved, and good company'. They and all of Annie's 'Little Pnoobies' were taken to the Natural History Museum to enjoy the dinosaur skeletons. Robert spent time with Johnny, who was now blending his sexology studies with gerontology and methods for extending joy into old age. The visit seems to have prompted thoughts of his own mortality for on his return to Plymouth Robert notes:

> Spoke to Mouse and Monica [...]. Drove to my house. Everything well. Mary's light is on [across the valley]. How sad everything suddenly seemed. The dank night, a high moon. Excited children. All the transitory labour [...] the painting – so many years in my mother's flat – now in my house. And my house – soon all to pass – pass – pass. (Diary, 23 January 1978)

His efforts are Herculean, his productivity at its peak, but already in his late 30s he occasionally felt his energies fading. He is energised by the women, especially the mysterious powers of Mary, but sleeps alone more frequently and feels 'tired and getting older' (Diary, 29 January 1978). The next morning the Diary records: 'Terrible night. Monsters of all kinds ... particularly those' (Diary, 30 January 1978). A psychiatrist might have diagnosed Robert with mild psychosis had they known of his growing synaesthesia. Perhaps Robert no longer possessed the energy needed to repress his 'hallucinations'. They are certainly recorded with more intensity and regularity as middle age comes: 'Cannot express the pleasure of seeing [Mary] again [...] same clean, fay presence. Identical tendrils of attraction and gentleness exuding from me like an invisible plasma, enveloping the world' (Diary, 3 February 1978). Note that at this point the forces remain invisible – by the 1980s it was more common for Robert to report full 'manifestations'. The extent to which he could distinguish between what he imagined and what he saw is unclear but there were times he was disturbed by his own imagination, as when he 'saw' the dismembered body of Mary under the trees. It is worth restating that Robert never used street drugs and gave stern but kindly warnings to those of us who did. His 'visions' were induced by something more subtle. They seldom brought any knowledge. A typical episode might be: 'Curious half-hallucination of part of a bed on the floor. Some sort of gold-red quilt? Blanket beneath? Very much in a "left hand corner". May have been a figure on it' (Diary, 25 July 1977). They were mainly visions without insights.

His working imagination was far more symbolically inclined. On 8 February 1978 Robert made a small watercolour sketch in his diary. It is a motif he will repeat and refigure through several projects: two lovers crash towards each other, collide, and interpenetrate. Their union is paradoxically a 'dis-junction' of both bodies. The idea that what appears as mere carnage and biological wreckage is governed by some underlying aesthetic principles relates to Robert's broadly Pythagorean and Neo-Platonic sympathies. Whether looking at local reports of murder/suicides or photographs of corpse heaps in the Nazi death camps, Robert refuses the conclusion that violence is essentially chaotic. This may in part explain his life-long love of boxing. To the uninitiated the sport concerns barbarians punching each other into oblivion. To the cognoscenti it is 'the sweet science' governed by rules, skill, and art. Robert would stay awake until the early hours to catch live radio accounts of Ali's fights (Diary, 16 February 1978).

The need to find order even in what seems to be the most irrational butchery also explains why Robert surrounded himself with images of the most terrible atrocities. This was not without some risks for those around him. 'Reuben suddenly visited. Saw the unpleasant photos of corpses/ murdered and mutilated people I had strewn around the studio room. I had rather he had not seen them'. Perhaps not, but they were not hastily stowed. Instead 'we look[ed] at the anatomy dissection photographs – which he enjoyed. Also listened to my record of Van Gogh's letters and his suicide' (Diary, 26 February 1978).

Robert's collection of human artefacts grew steadily: it would be too crude to call them trophies, but they retained something of that. Earlier that month he had been delighted to find 'a human skull and three quarters of a skeleton in a London shop for £35. Amazingly cheap. I purchased it immediately, borrowing money from Aury', after making arrangements for the shop owner to 'contact Aury the moment any more "death" material came his way' (Diary, 18 February 1978).

For Robert these were legitimate research interests. They were not to be confused with the pathological activities of other painters, however much he admired their work: 'Aury drove to town first – I wanted to see the Lucian Freud collection at Anthony D'Offay's. Powerful and haunting studies of corpses, enchanting study of Jacquetta. What a demonic sly-minded swindling painter. He must be psychotic. Work highly sensitive and absorbing. Simply good painting' (Diary, 22 February 1978). It was a proficient diagnosis on all levels. As we shall soon relate, Robert worried about what information Jacquetta was passing to Mr Freud. He sensed trouble being stirred. The marriage between Perry and Jacquetta 'had never been a happy one' and they spent very little time together (Andrew Beaumont, Interview, February 2019). Jacquetta often tried contacting Robert via the telephones of his lovers in Plymouth and London. When that failed, she sent telegrams insisting he phoned her, but Robert would not comply with a summons from the Countess of St Germans: 'Did not phone Jacquetta' (Diary, 26 March 1978).

Robert returned to Plymouth on 22 February 1978, driven by Aury who stayed for several days. Aury is a man of fine manners and his thoughts on his lodgings went unspoken, but Priory Road was in a perilous state. The inside of 'Death House' was as cold and wet as the weather outdoors. The water supply was disconnected, and the rats so well-established Robert was naming them. One was called 'Faustus' (Diary, 24 February 1978). Despite an affected phobia in later life, rats were not the stuff of nightmares for Robert. Book theft was: 'Difficult sleep. Terrible dream – entered my library – all the shelves on my right – empty – bare – books gone' (Diary, 3 March 1978). Young Reuben's exposure to the horrific images of the previous week did not vex him to nightmares but rather coincided with a positive advance:

Reuben came back. The most curious thing developed. He started to ask about 'the origin of things', etc. He was unexpectedly sensitive to abstracts. Told him about Aristotle and prima causes and concepts of Nothing and definitions of the 'unique' and there he sat in my shop, discoursing like a little Platonist. (Diary, 3 March 1978)

The next day Robert records a strongly held view which he repeats until his dying day although it is not entirely true: 'I loathe the studio when the time comes for it to be a shop' (Diary, 4 March 1978). In the 1980s he would firmly correct people if they described 25 The Parade as a 'shop', usually with the formula 'It is not a shop. There is nothing for sale, especially not knowledge. I cause information to circulate, that is all'. There were in fact days when he was glad of its status as a shop. It was a life-line, with Monica seemingly on the verge of homelessness, and 'poor old Diogenes' truly homeless again (Diary, 18 March 1978), Priory Road not fit for habitation with its rodents and lethal heating arrangements: 'Nearly burned to death. Woke up to find the towel having fallen on the fire' (Diary, 23 March 1978). Cash was needed to secure the upper floors of 25 The Parade. Robert expresses no regrets about its commercial status when on 20 March Mr Rollason buys 11 pieces, mainly portraits, for £400. It was a day of mixed news – the police called in to discuss Brummy, who had been writing menacing letters from jail and was due for release. They admitted there was nothing they could do to protect Robert. On 2 April Mr Rollason returned to buy another 'eleven paintings for £350. Wanted to see other work at my house [...] pleasant *schmilosophical* talk with Mr Rollason. Said that if I needed money, contact him, and he will let me have it in lieu of work' (Diary, 22 April 1978).

Robert remained ambivalent about the public – he was interested in their opinions; he sought their attention and was perplexed or even hurt that the reactions to his projects were often so mean. But he also sought to vex them. He decided to place some of his most disturbing images in the 'shop window' – with rapid results: 'Many people offended by my Orgasm/Jealousy studies. Quite enjoyable day' (Diary, 26 March 1978).

In some ways Robert was living the life of a medieval king, with his amoral public presence, cashless access to food, ample supply of beautiful women, and surrounded by layers of 'high culture' which did nothing to cocoon him from the threat of a sudden and violent death. And yet so precarious was Robert's position that in other respects he was no better off than the dossers. At times he felt the great artistic and intellectual efforts of the Relationship Projects were already dust in the wind. As a favour to a friend he dashed off a back-drop for Plymouth's Country and Western Music Club. The local papers ran an article headlined 'Lenkiewicz Paints a Train'. He comments in the Diary: 'Embarrassing rubbish. All the work I put into the Projects over each year, and all they can do is blow up painting trains' (Diary, 14 March 1978). Twenty years later in televised interviews he would still be expressing this sense of exasperation. 'Project on this, Project on that, no response' (*Demon or Delight*, 1996).

As he moved to the end of his fourth decade, he was increasingly aware that some tasks had to be prioritised, and others set aside. A shifting sense of loss, anger, and deep sadness permeates the diaries during spring–summer 1978. There is more of a 'bereavement process' for the Cowboys than for his mother. Understandably so, for dozens upon dozens of long-term relationships were ending at or around the same time. Friendships with The Bishop and Diogenes and a few of the more capable types would continue, but Robert had to be seen as a 'dead road' for the Cowboys. It was necessary for his heart and soul to harden.

> Saw two men beating each other horribly in a street fight. I did nothing to stop it and passed by. 'Two dossers less, with a little luck' – I thought. (Diary, 20 February 1978)

> Visited by Paddy McKenna and Willy Bannen [...] close friend of 'The Singer' – seemed a remarkable chap. Told me he'd been knocked down, was in a bad way, and would not see me again. Wished me well, with a strange, wise kindliness. Don't see Cowboys like him much anymore. (Diary, 8 March 1978)

> Ivor Edmonds, Plymouth's one-time hard man found dead in toilet at the rear of Bath Street [Mission House]. His eyes had been eaten away – had been there a week. (Diary, 24 March 1978)
> 'Harry Harkness' 3rd division – in a bad way – tried a beg. Haven't seen someone in such a state for years. So sad, all so sad. Ridiculous ugly stupid waste. Told him to spread the word that I was no good. (Diary, 8 March 1978)

> Chic the Bam and a chancer called 'Bob' slimed into the shop. Very firm with the thugs. Explained that I wanted to be left alone. That I meant it, etc. I explained it was the last time. 'McCarthy's been fixed

up ... and Flannagan's been fixed up' and other boring bullshit. Told him I wasn't interested. (Diary, 24 March 1978)

Les Ryder came down for a beg. Knocked him back, and explained it was all finished. So sad really. The wrong ones suffer. (Diary, 24 March 1978)

Poor old Les Ryder came down for the 3rd time. He can't believe he's been refused. Knocked him back again. So sad, for the man has never done me any harm – and he's old. But he's lost control of his head and I can't slip him anything for fear of him telling all the 3rd division. So hard to see him hobble off. (Diary, 2 April 1978)

Throughout spring and summer Robert told every passing dosser to 'spread the bad news' that Lenkiewicz was 'no good' for a beg or a skipper (Diary, 12 May 1978). In a newspaper interview on the horrible death of Ivor Edmonds, Robert states plainly that the old-time tramps were almost extinct.

Barbican painter Robert Lenkiewicz spent years trying to provide shelter and help for tramps and wanderers [...] he set up hostels, had them staying in his home, and nursed them over 15 years. Today, the smelly, sick vagabonds are not even given the price of a cup of tea by Robert. He does not believe anyone can help the majority of people on the road. 'Vagrancy is not now a problem but a trade' he said. He believes there are no more than about half a dozen real tramps left – the men of the road who just travel around, bother no-one, are not violent or alcoholics. (*The Independent*, 24 April 1978)

During the interview Robert had been impatient with the reporter's sentimentality (Diary, 19 April 1978). He sensed a hypocritical, 'moral' refusal to acknowledge how much the new wave of 'unfortunates' were dangerous and loathsome types who could not be helped and were undeserving of help (Diary, 24 April 1978). Worst of all they were not interesting: one could learn nothing from them. Robert attended more closely to professional fools and literary psychopaths. He renewed his interest in Charlie Chaplin and the Marquis de Sade. He was especially impressed by the elderly but athletic and mentally sharp Max Wall at the Hoe Theatre that April: 'Max Wall – extraordinary. Endlessly skilful performance. Actually, really funny, really moving and sad – which is all humour is I suppose. Extraordinary sense of movements. Buster Keaton melancholies' (Diary, 14 April 1978). Written vertically in tiny letters next to these reflections: 'Annie's third child – a daughter [Kate] – was born to her at 10-14 pm this night'.

Perry was by now irritated by Robert's slow progress on the Round Room Mural and Robert was keen to smooth some lordly feathers. On 21 April Robert wrote 'PORT ELIOT: Work for 15 days!'. And so he did, almost without rest or interruption. Belle stayed with him most nights. There were interesting visitors, including the police on yet another murder case they thought Robert might help with. But some days are described in a dozen words, such as 'Woke early. Breakfast. Painted camelias all day. Lunch. Supper. Completed letter to Mary. Slept alone in four-poster'. By 5 May, a large arc of the mural was completed to the great satisfaction of Perry and Robert.

Work also began on the notebook for the Orgasm Project titled 'Orgasm/Attitudes/Affinities'. A shorter production with just 30 pages and around a dozen illustrations, almost the entire text consists of Robert's hand-written transcriptions of relevant texts from Georges Bataille, Philippe Ariès (*Centuries of Childhood*) and Norman O. Brown's *Love's Body*, first published in 1966, when Brown was 53 years old. Brown was an American professor of literature whose first publications were about classical texts. But in response to the publication of *Eros and Civilization* (1956) by fellow Marxist Herbert Marcuse, whom Brown had befriended during his wartime service in US Intelligence, he took a deep-dive into Freudian theory and produced his 1959 classic *Life Against Death: The Psychoanalytic Meaning of History*. The work portrayed human history as a story of neurotic repression of the erotic impulses closing off the path to human fulfilment. Robert would have admired in *Love's Body* the prodigious erudition spanning classical literature, philosophy, philology, psychoanalysis, history, and Marxism. Brown approaches his subject through collage and quotation, drawing together many wisdom traditions to find a path to 'The Resurrection of the Body' – that is, to attain the joys promised in the afterlife in the here and now.

It seems that Robert's commitment to 'provide information' for the visitor to the exhibition did not always demand original expression as an author when such rich philosophical resources were to hand. It is in these notes we encounter Brown's phrase 'murder is suicide with/through mistaken identity'[41], which Robert strips of its Freudian basis and inverts in the notes for the Suicide Project (1980). The notes continue: 'We identify with whatever we kill and then reactively venerate our victims. This identification hints at the hidden truth which makes peace: the identity of the killer and the victim'.

Brown, a neo-Freudian, naturally uses these metaphors of homicide in a psychological sense. Robert cannot interpret them other than as *physiological* in nature. It is in that mode that we should read the following 'aesthetic note' of a profound experience from March 1978, written after Jacquetta Eliot has just dropped him off at Death House. Robert is wishing he could: 'Put all the lights off and make everything black and take and take and kill and kill. And cry her hard lines away in the dark until only her softness was real'. Jacquetta's grey form is sketched at the wheel of her van; Robert, duffel-coated and booted, slides out of the passenger seat but as he leaves his enflamed entrails give him:

> the leering demonic stab of an old pain. Spiteful stabbing diagonally from my right shoulder through to my genitals opening some hidden scar near the stomach. I don't want to separate from her – she knows I don't. Yes! It is a smile on her face after all. A secret smile of victory. (Robert Lenkiewicz, Aesthetic Note, 30 March 1978)

Who is the 'killer' here and who the 'victim'? No matter – both die in the embrace; but only the more knowing partner gains new knowledge:

> a sense of irreparable loss. Of utter waste. ... Ah! But I gathered some insights in my little way. I gathered some choice little bits of information on this memorable evening. It must be worth the sacrifice. The inevitable crucifixion anticipates a resurrection. 'New knowledge for old!' the old lamp dealer cried. But how I would run my hands over those hard edges if they were here now. (Robert Lenkiewicz, Aesthetic Note, 30 March 1978)

Returning to Plymouth from Port Eliot Robert found The Bishop deeply and understandably very upset over his four-hour interrogation by the police. The murder of the Plymouth Brethren grandmother Mrs Soper was still unsolved. The Bishop had been hauled in because he occasionally drank on the street bench near her house in Alma Road (Diary, 7 May 1978). Even setting the murder investigations aside it was a strange summer with many nuances of menace. Ria and her son Danny visited again.

This was usually a source of great joy for Robert but their arrival coincided with a break-in at Death House which the superstitious might interpret as a break-*out*:

> Someone had climbed like a vampire up to the left-hand window, athletically negotiating the stone wall. The coffin had been opened, and other chests. One skull was missing. (Diary, 11 May 1978)

It was found the next day in the garden. There seem only two ridiculous possibilities. Either somebody had risked a dangerous climb and house invasion to throw a skull out of a window. Or possessed by some unquiet spirit the skull had flung itself out to get away from the damp and the rats. The following week Magdalena returned from her travels in Spain – Robert reports that he is 'strangely terrified' by the prospect of being visited by this gentle and beautiful 20-year-old woman (Diary, 18 May 1978). His sleep is troubled. There were further unexpected outbreaks of angst. After another visit to Mouse and the children he:

> returned to my dark, empty house – perhaps for the last time for a while. Sensed a strange threatening terrible pain and loss on the stairs as I snatched the future for less than a second. Did notes. Slept alone. Late, restless, anxious. What will I deserve? (Diary, 9 May 1978)

Since the long session at Port Eliot Robert felt creatively depleted. Magdalena's arrival was a tonic: 'Felt very much like painting – first time in a long time. Feel full of energy' (Diary, 21 May 1978). But he also senses danger in her presence. Some of this is rational for there is a very real possibility that the joys of Magdalena might drive 'the Mary Project' off course (Diary, 25 May 1978).

Robert was visited by friends of Ivorine who passed on the message that 'my son Dorian wants to come down and stay. The boy is nearing 18-years-old and playing chess for Wales. Extraordinary business' (Diary, 27 May 1978). These were happy days due to the erotics of Magdalena, surprise visits from Aury and Myrna, plus a surge in tourist portraiture so great that Robert sometimes had to ask people to come back next day (Diary, 5 July 1978). It seemed like the sinister atmosphere of that summer had finally passed. Then the pain started.

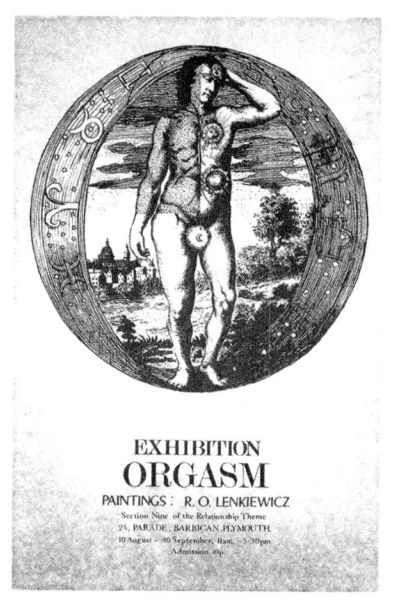

23.1 Poster for Project 9, 1978.

23.2 Edwin Mackenzie, or 'pigeon-structured Diogenes' in Robert's phrase, in a cast selling merchandise outside the Orgasm Project exhibition.

23.3 Belle Pecorini on the Barbican Quay, January 1978.

23.4 Gillian Pearce (Mary) with Robert's *Self-Portrait with Punch Magazine* (1957), which Robert hung in her flat in 1978.

23.5 Edwin Mackenzie with the canvas *Diogenes at Night in the Studio Window (1977).*

23.6 Eliza in the garden at the cottage in Compton, 1978.

23.7 Eliza outside the studio, late 1978.

23.8 *Left:* Robert with Mouse Mill's daughter Rebecca (aged 10).

23.9 Alice Lenkiewicz (aged 14) with Robert outside the Basket Ope flats on 25 November 1978.

23.10 The Bishop with Robert, Christmas Day, 1978.

23.11 '12 noon: "Cowboy" dinner at the bus station. Cockney Jim, The Bishop, Harmonica Jim, The Janner, Dave Helingoe, Snowy, Frank, Elvis Presley, Stranger, Corky, Les Ryder (he took food away for Andy Lynch who was rotting somewhere on the Hoe), Woman from Moorhaven. Hans de Rijke visited taking many photographs.' (Diary, Christmas Day, 1978).

23

Agony and the Orgasm Exhibition

For weeks Robert had been experiencing bad sleep and free-floating anxiety. In the early part of July, as he worked on the *Jesus and Mary Magdalene* painting for the Orgasm Project, his legs weakened. Some mornings he felt 'blissfully fatigued' by Magdalena (Diary, 5 July 1978) but this was more than sexual over-exercise. A terrible numbness and pain began to spread: 'Not feeling well. Elbow joints hurting' (Diary, 8 July 1978). Dr Hans de Rijke suggested Robert should have chest and leg X-rays but Robert claimed he was feeling better, possibly buoyed up by the arrival of the keys to a new paradise:

> ON THIS DAY I RECEIVED THE KEYS TO 25 PARADE – COMPLETE BUILDING – FROM PETER WANSTALL [...] Surveyed 'my' premises with a capitalist air: vaguely terrified of financial pressures incurred by aesthetic greed. (Diary, 9 June 1978)

At the point of triumph, the pain grew rapidly worse. Next morning, he writes: 'I am not well. Condition spreading to hands and feet. Difficult to move. Left foot and right hand stiffening'. On 11 June: 'UNABLE TO WALK'.

Crutches were brought to Death House, but even with these the slightest pressure on his feet was agony. The bathroom was upstairs and Robert so weakened that standing up was dangerous. Ian, Mouse, Jim, and Magdalena improvised a bed for him downstairs and made sure he was fed. News of his plight spread fast and far. Jeny Lelya Bremer arrived from Amsterdam with a splendid invalid blanket and, knowing Robert's awful dietary habits, a basket of healthy nutritional kindness:

> I was very into health food and brought all my herbs and bottles from the Netherlands. That night, Robert's mother attacked me in a dream. I knew she was dead, I knew she was dead and I was alive and I was stronger, but it was still scary ... because when I woke up, there she was again! I said to her 'Fuck off' and moved my arm and she disappeared. (Jeny Lelya Bremer, Letter, 9 July 2019)

The morning was a busy one. Ian visited: 'Kind and helpful: left me some money'. At Robert's prompting Magdalena 'read out passages on the theme of dying'. There were many well-wishers: 'the invalid's room is hectic' (Diary, 13 June 1978). Doctors Everett and Cowie came to prescribe anti-inflammatories and pentazocine. This is not a true opioid but a strong painkiller with highly variable side-effects. Robert was at best three-quarters prepared for vivid nightmares, delusions, hallucinations, and acute constipation. Against all advice Robert 'climbed upstairs quite well with crutches. Poo'd, washed etc. Magdalene affectionate but disturbed by circumstances. I asked her to divide time up here and there re: [Jeny] Lelya. She is so young and sweet, but she will go [...] Magdalena may decide to leave at very short notice through necessity' (Diary, 15 June 1978).

Doctor Cowie thought that Robert was suffering from 'very uncharacteristic sarcoid symptoms. Must get to hospital. Did not wish to go to hospital. Gave me another anti-inflammatory drug and painkiller to take, one every 4 hours. Asked Magdalena to get the drug immediately' (Diary, 16 June 1978). That night, possibly unbalanced by the drugs his squeaky-clean nervous system was trying to figure out, Robert:

Hobbled on crutches up the stairs to poo, against advice of Magdalena/Lelya. Teetered on the fourth step crashing twice on bad foot and floundering in obscene screaming heap on flagstones. Pain very severe and difficult to tolerate. The girls heaved me up after my noise had calmed down – I insisted on attacking the stairs again, for fear of being frightened of them.

He struggled to the toilet only to discover that the drugs had robbed him of the ability to unburden himself and so 'crawled back down the stairs in extreme pain', noting the 'interesting hysterical reactions' of his carers. We do not know if he was entirely serious or delirious, but he told Lelya he thought it was the ghost of his mother who had tried to push him to his doom. 'No sleep at all. Extreme pain. Poor Magdalena kind and patient on her last night'. When daylight arrives, he writes:

On this day Magdalena left my house. Sad in her red poncho and boots. The taxi driver carried her two bags and she went. Lelya is sitting outside in the sun like an extraordinary-looking Berber in her marvellous clothes. Magdalena left. I am lying in the bed smiling. So familiar with the gentle pains of people that come and go. Very tired. Magdalena stayed for 28 days.

Lelya came into bed. Sweet time. Very intense incidents. Something remarkable about her – but so sad. Rested with her most of the day. Beautiful body – such pleasure to see her. Became curiously mutually obsessed as the flies buzzed around and the wind blew through the open front door. I did little work of consequence with Magdalena. Never completed the large painting, etc. Aesthetic theory scribbles – never found a pattern.
Alice and Becky visited their sick father with a gift of two Kermits. Reuben and Wolfe likewise with amusing paraphernalia.
Letter from Monica.
Lelya went to town to buy food. What an odd sight she must be for the townsfolk. I rested. Feel a little better. I will start work. (Diary, 17 June 1978)

Lelya made a delicious meal. Shared it on the bed. How extraordinarily warm and solicitous she has been. Patient, intelligent, and practical [...] Very gentle erotic incidents – and sleep. She is sad to go. (Diary, 19 June 1978)

Very sweet night. Have never known her so warm. [...] Taxi came at 11.30am. Took her to the station. Old familiar partings. She returns to Amsterdam. Close incident as she left. Her extraordinary white Tibetan coat, her black hair and green eyes. Another look – and she's gone. (Diary, 20 June 1978)

To the poignancy of her departure Robert added a tragi-comic coda:

The sun shines, the birds chirrup. Tried to walk but not possible. The door is ajar. I see bits of green and hear the world outside [...] Must try and work. The day is so quiet.

Tried idea for landscape but couldn't do it. Also, one-legged attempt on large 'putrefying corpses' – but no use. Hurt too much and standing on one leg somewhat fatiguing. (Diary, 20 June 1978)

Robert remained hobbled well into the next month but was surrounded by well-wishers. These included Ruti, who made a surprise extended visit starting on 21 June. There was more good news from London: Aury understood how costly Robert's condition was in cash terms and sent a letter with a get-well gift of £120 (Diary, 22 June 1978). Lelya sent a large parcel from Holland – 'ten different kinds of health-teas and a variety of other herbal curiosities, a wooden Buddha, and an Indian death-card' (Diary, 30 June 1978) and next month when Robert was walking again she sent a beautiful pair of hand-made leather boots. Despite all these kindnesses the summer continued in its sinister and threatening aspects. Nightmare and delirium were common side-effects of Robert's pain killers, and may in part explain notes such as: 'Woke early – Strange dreams' (Diary, 13 July 1978) and 'Extraordinary horrific dream re: a black cat and my house' (Diary, 30 June 1978). His sense of humour was not diminished. He phoned Mary and asked: 'Would you like to meet a Jewish cripple?' And he retained his merciless intellectual honesty:

> 'Mad Steve' dropped in. Did I require company? 'No' I replied. He expressed the dilemma he was in regarding the necessity for heavier doses of tranquilizers. I lay on the bed gently listening, savouring how little I cared, side-tracked from his mumblings by the thought of Elizabeth's arse. (Diary, 2 July 1978)

Throughout the month he recuperated under the healing influences of Belle Pecorini with her 'extraordinary talents for pleasure' (Diary, 6 July 1978). There was good company to be had from Jim Pascoe reading his 'clever, enchanting poems' (Diary, 7 July 1978). Impatient to get back to the business of painting, Robert was well enough to visit the Barbican on 6 July. Almost immediately he was approached by the pestiferous Brighton who had to be chased away, with Robert brandishing his crutch as a weapon. Robert's appearance attracted the obvious comments from all and sundry – 'Ahoy matey!' and 'Where's your parrot?' Robert was amused by this as he was amused by the destruction of his Harlequinade Mural. The newspaper reports did not do full justice to the interview he gave on the topic:

> Reporter from Western Morning News [visited]. The mural at the Hoe Theatre has been covered by paint and wallpaper by the manager – what did I think, etc. I observed that I had no objections – considered the work mediocre rubbish – thought their decision a surprising evidence of good taste – and would be happy to advise them on wallpaper decor. (Diary, 30 June 1978)

From taxi-drivers to City Councillors, many Plymothians spoke up for the value of Robert's work and were angered on his behalf. Robert was 'amused by it all' (Diary, 5 July 1978). He was emerging from the illness and coming back to his senses. A convalescent has the entire world as a mirror:

> Sat in the garden having washed. Utterly delighted in the different species of birds. One bird seemed familiar to a disturbing degree, sitting by my side staring balefully at my silent white-clad corpse. I do not recollect a time that I have seen things emanate the rich verdant saturations of growth and green force – as this summer. (Diary, 5 July 1978)

Still in pain but mobile at last, Robert spent more time on the Barbican. The summer trade in tourist portraits again boomed: 'A good day tradewise: have not had a run like this for 3½ years' (Diary, 11 July 1978). There were pleasant talks with Hans and Annie and Jim on the implications of the Jealousy and Orgasm themes. His research notes had grown healthily while he had been unable to paint, partly through conversations with Johnny and Hans on neurophysiology (Diary, 15 July 1978); 25 The Parade was 'face-lifted' by 'Plasterer George and Peter the Painter'. The illness and those who nursed him through it improved his eating habits for a while – the diaries record more salads and fewer Mars Bars. Robert was even somewhat reconciled to family life, of a limited kind: 'Taxi'd to Mouse's house to watch "Our Mutual Friend". Pleasant time with the children. Becky is writing a study of Rembrandt. Promised to leave her some books in the morning. Precocious thing at nine' (Diary, 11 July 1978).

As if to underscore the end of an era for the true Cowboys, Robert called in favours and 'cajoled from the Council' a permanent abode for Diogenes (Diary, 16 July 1978). He *schmilosophised* endlessly about 'the self-interest in caring for others' and how much he deplored 'sentimentality' and so forth: but Robert loved the old geezer and would not forsake him when the Cowboys' Holiday Inns closed. Diogenes was 'in a semisenile state of excitement' when he moved 'into his own flat. The first time in 25 years' (Diary, 17 July 1978). The summer's run of ill luck continued. Within two weeks: 'Diogenes turned up looking terrible. Can't move his arm. Fortunately, Hans de Rijke was there – took him to casualty'. Robert sketched Diogenes on his return: 'Poor Pigeon-structured Diogenes in a sling. Hospital put him in plaster – washed him – trimmed his beard. He looks terribly shattered, frail and touching' (Diary, 29 July 1978).

The relationship with Mary proceeded at a glacial pace and under constant threat of 'going nowhere' – although it was generating copious notes and 'empirical evidence' for the aesthetic theory which Robert was constantly talking over with Hans de Rijke (Diary, 5 August 1978). Relationships with Yana and Eliza and Mary were in excellent health despite the pressures of time and conflicts of interest. The Jacquetta situation was unresolved and increasingly awkward as she tried to lead or press Robert in directions he did not want to go.

Two of the unholy trinity – Big Brummie and Brother Blair – were happily absent from the scene that autumn but Brighton haunted the Barbican. Robert's newly hardened heart was partly achieving the desired results. Some of the worst Cowboys – Brighton among them – worried that the gentle giant might have been pushed too far and they scarpered when they saw him (Diary, 1 September 1978). The police were by now well used to Robert and would doubtless take his side if ever he defended himself by busting a chair over a drunk's head. Awareness of that fact would deter Brighton and Brother Blair, but Big Brummy was too crazed to care. The police could do nothing unless Robert was attacked, and so were in the main genuinely but uselessly sympathetic. And they favoured 'softly-softly' community policing tactics for his upcoming exhibition – 'Orgasm'. The title alone meant they were duty-bound to be proactive in protecting public sensibilities. Robert notes:

> Visited by Mr Leonard and Mr Allison, the Chief and Head of the C.I.D. for Plymouth. Very pleasant – but warned about 'Orgasm' exhibition. They took me upstairs and we had a 'reasonable' long talk on the problems involved – public complaints – obscenity laws etc., etc. I finally agreed to move some of the paintings on the weekend from the downstairs to upstairs but will not change the collection. Allison has already bought 3 of my paintings. The Head wants to buy a seascape. (Diary, 1 August 1978)

The opening of the exhibition at the expanded Parade Studio was a muted affair. The local press tried to suggest a stand-off between the repressive forces of Law and the expansive forces of Art, but they were scraping the barrel. Detective Inspector Allison was very deflationary – 'It is just an ordinary exhibition. As far as I know we are doing nothing about it.

No-one is going to be down there' (Diary, unsourced news clipping, 10 August 1978). By which he meant no police, for he was well aware how crowds are drawn to such sights. Over 300 people arrived on the opening day, and on the Saturday '400 people visited the exhibition today' (Diary, 12 August 1978).

Here we approach a most important issue in Robert's work. He was interested in what it was to be human, and this involved exploring the limits of the human. One experience we almost all encounter is orgasm, and apart from sleep this is perhaps the most common of occasions for the breakdown of a coherent 'self' or 'conscious ego'. Orgasm dissolves boundaries, but paradoxically we are to a ridiculous degree defined by the 'who' and 'how' and 'what' rigmarole that takes us to our happy place. Subjectivity is summoned by 'what makes you come'. As the rise of sexual-identity politics has since proven beyond doubt, the causes and rituals of one's orgasms are seen as the deepest evidence of 'what one really is'. Perhaps this is a defensive measure rather than a sign of liberation, for the 'happy place' is threaded with dark and sinister elements. Robert's thinking about the pleasure, vertigo, and anxiety around orgasm is consonant with that of Georges Bataille's sinister religious atheism. Robert was himself aware of this similarity and considered it a confirmation of his aesthetic theories. A year earlier he wrote: 'READ G. BATAILLE AGAIN. Extraordinary how close my ideas are to his without my having any familiarity with his work' (Diary, 22 August 1977). The dissolution of orgasm is linked to laughter and to Death, which have similar convulsive effects. Drawing on themes first developed in Death and the Maiden, the Orgasm Exhibition notes explore the interplay of physiological forces which 'plunge us into a violent and possibly beautiful world' (Orgasm Exhibition Notes, p. 10).

The human body is an energy system – never a complete structure: never static: it is in perpetual inner self-construction and self-destruction: we destroy in order to make new. Destroy this temple, and in three days I will raise it up. Reality does not consist of substances, solidity, and stolidity each in its own place: but in events, activity: activity which crosses the boundary.

'It is certain that all bodies whatsoever, though they have no sense, yet they have perception' – Francis Bacon [1561–1626]. In the deepest level of the unconscious we find not fantasies, but telepathy. (Orgasm Exhibition Notes, p. 8)

This beautiful thought is written above a watercolour of two golden heads recirculating rays of sensual energy through their eyes and mouths. But why live in an interesting world of sensual intelligence when it takes so little effort to make it dull and ugly? And so the newspaper headline was printed – 'Rob's Randy Frame-Up':

> Artist Robert Lenkiewicz is a dab hand at loving. Now the master of the tender stroke has painted intimate scenes from his sexy frolics – and put them on public view. The paintings, of romps with twenty different girls, include detailed notes [...] Roberts [*sic*] said 'I keep detailed notes to help me'. He even asked some girls to write down their thoughts after love-making. But Robert insists the exhibition is part of a serious study of relationships. (*Daily Mirror*, 11 August 1978)

Robert notes: 'Really stupid, vulgar review – amusing'.

The exhibition poster showed a naked and somewhat androgynous man inside the wheel of the Zodiac. An image of the Sun covers his heart, the Moon his genitals. Much of the exhibition continues the broadly Hermetic theme: to be human is to be influenced and transformed by extra-human forces. The serpentine bodies depicted in the painting *Lovers* flow like waves, and the blue flesh of the male figure hints at a truly alien life form. Bodies do not so much collide as move through each other in dissolution. One study shows a dislocated female form, arms raised and legs wide, a plume of white light rising from her mouth like an erupting soul. There are a greater number of watercolours and works on paper than in previous projects. The scale is not 'epic'. But the overall feel of the material is a hugely disquieting interplay of weightiness, pressure, fluidity, and liberation. It is anything but the 'easy viewing' one might associate with pornography, and more exciting because it provokes a sexualised consideration of how our thoughts and sensations are related.

Robert steered by Warhol's principle: 'Let everyone else decide if it's good or bad, whether they love it or hate it. While they are deciding, make even more art'. Robert's pattern of work did not just repeat, it quickened. In summer 1978 he was partly advanced on at least two more projects – Self-Portrait and Old Age – and was musing on perhaps half a dozen more. The Orgasm Exhibition closed on the last day of September. The Self-Portrait Exhibition opened less than a hundred days later, at the end of December. During those days there were further intensifications of his relationships with Mary, Yana, and Eliza. These three were in the central cadre of companions which included but was not limited to Belle, Jeny Lelya Bremer, Myriam and Magdalena Rivera, Ria Ney-Hoch, Elizabeth, Ruti, Annie, Amelie, Gail, and Francesca. Whatever the jealousies or competing demands might have been, these women were mainly well-behaved towards each other when their paths crossed. There were presumably more women 'off the books', but like the cosmologists' 'dark matter' these are for us so theoretical we can say nothing about them or how they behaved. Anonymous hate mail arriving at 25 The Parade might have come from any number of persons. But the real mystery in the tangle of relationships was Jacquetta Eliot. Her name is very visible in the diaries but her status as lover, friend, enemy, or all three seems undecidable:

> Jacquetta was in the exhibition room on my return. Looked around for some time reading notes, etc. So strange. Eliza watching. Went for tea at Pilgrims' Rest with Jacquetta – her haunting battered used vicious face hiding behind 'the thickets of the law' of her clenched fists. I spoke and spoke of what I thought – she thought and thought of what I spoke. Became withdrawn and sorry for herself after my 'attack'. I left her at her van after she agreed to take photos of me. Returned to close exhibition. Eliza in gentle grump. Jacquetta came back, asked to continue seeing exhibition. Eliza coolly observed that the film we'd arranged to see would be starting soon. So amusing. Rushed off to the Belgrade – leaving Jacquetta with the key, showing her light switches etc. All so strange. (Diary, 23 August 1978)

Next morning Robert finds a note in his Studio: 'If we can meet tomorrow night please ring me. It doesn't matter if we can't.' He writes: 'Note from Jacquetta. Presumptive inadequate vampire. Did not contact her' (Diary, 24 August 1978). Yet the diaries never record any decisive action to rid himself of her company.

Robert's summer of murder, menace, and pain faded to a dark autumn. People he wanted to spend time with were inflected with shadows. Ria was suffering terrible depression due to Axel's drug use, which had been passed on to her like a bad chromosome. Axel's physical and psychological cruelty was now monstrous (Stella Ney-Hoch, Interview, May 2018). Robert's relationships with Mary and Yana became not just heavy but doomy: 'Yana visited [...] all so sweet and sad. How will it end? Other than dead memories and dead people?' (Diary, 25 August 1978). The sense of impending doom was perfected with a revisitation from Brummy and Brighton. Brummy had no fear of being reimprisoned. His first contact with Robert in almost a year accelerated from verbal abuse to a police incident in minutes. Eliza and Diogenes were present when the lunacy erupted. Eliza called the police, who moved the thugs on. They returned within the hour: 'hideously violent, smashing against the door and windows. Police were called again. Sent them off a second time. [Brummy] bent on revenge' (Diary, 15 September 1978).

As preparations were made for the Self-Portrait Exhibition in the late autumn, Robert tolerated some of the older dossers visiting the Studio but he took little interest in their inner worlds. A decade earlier he thought their psychoses might provide a port of entry into some other reality – but now he notes their delusions like a doctor ticking boxes on his clipboard for a ward of untreatables. Beneath one fine watercolour illustration he writes: 'Harmonica Jim playing hysterical tune after tune. Droning on about "The Atom People" and "The Muck Inside"' (Diary, 11 November 1978). Even The Bishop's alco-mysticism has lost its charm. Time is cruel: 'Poor old Cockney Jim looks likely to lose his hands to gangrene' (Diary, 24 December 1978). The dossers are dying like flies in the hot summer-time.

Death struck at the Ney-Hoch family too, with violence both self-inflicted and cruelly driven. Remembered by all as a gentle and beautiful person, Gladys was utterly broken by Axel's ill-treatment. He had threatened to kill her, the children, and her parents if she tried to leave him (Stella, Letter, 14 April 2019). Gladys's body was found on the bench of a playing fields at Crouch End by an early morning runner. She had walked out the night before with a brandy bottle and a bag of Axel's drugs. With her body was found a brief note requesting her daughters' forgiveness and instructions to look after the cat (Stella, Letter, 14 April 2019). On 11 October 1978 Robert records: 'Letter from Ria, speaking of her mother's death, Axel's behaviour, etc. All so very strange. The haunting meaninglessness of "significant events" – some too large in "pseudo-expectation" to relate to. Fear as essential basis versus events as distraction'.

For a man who studied relationships as Robert did, there is something odd about the idea of 'significant events too large to relate to'. With no relation to them, how are they 'events'? Robert knew of some but not all of Axel's behaviour inside the family. The phrase 'pseudo-expectation' suggests Robert could only 'foresee' the suicide when after the event it assumed the inevitability of Greek tragedy. Ria came from London to stay at Priory Road on the 22nd of the month. She told Robert the details of her mother's death, but Robert was much preoccupied with thoughts of Mary. Nevertheless, it is plausible that Gladys's fate was a stimulus to Project 13, Suicide, which gets its first mention very soon thereafter (Diary, 18 December 1978).

Robert began to consider the practicalities of his own death. In his discussions with Perry Eliot we hear first mention of 'the position re: my library and how it should be organised. Annie/Aury and Johnny as trustees, etc. My library and aesthetic notes to the Round Room'. Robert does not write 'in the event of my death', but he was on that very day working on his *Self-Portrait on Death-Bed*, which shortly acquired the longer name below.

Robert's thoughts and feelings on the parameters of a 'good death' were explored in *The Dead Painter Surrounded by His Children and Companions*, 'a parody of the death of his own mother and a drawing by André Slom of Courbet on his deathbed' painted in late 1978. It is a bold group painting and bears close analysis not least because it points forwards to many of his paintings of the 1980s. The interplay of presence and non-presence is complex. The interplay of multiple light sources from the many candles is complex. The emotional tone is complex too, with some companions mournful and others impassive, some watchful while others sleep beneath Robert's almost comedically tied big toes. And yet there is an almost painful simplicity to the painting taken as a whole: a man has died, nothing more, nothing less. The references to other paintings are numerous: an entire notebook was created to accompany the painting in order to explain the allusions and influences. The overarching theme is summed up in the phrase *Et in Arcadia ego*, Death's announcement that 'even in Arcadia (a pastoral Utopia), am I'. It is also a reference to Nicolas Poussin's 17th century painting of the same name which featured in some wild speculations about the Priory of Sion and the Holy Grail which Robert had been following since at least 1972.

The sitters for *The Dead Painter* included several of the children, Liza Gunning, and the somewhat mysterious Tunisian woman Amelie. Robert disliked painting from photographs – 'all the important decisions have already been made', he once told me. Thus the inclusion of people who could not sit for the painting – Jeny Lelya Bremer and Amelie, both painted from photographs – suggests a desire for their presence at his deathbed. His brothers were not included, though he had several photographs of them. Mouse, who he still cared for deeply, is not there. His eldest son Reuben is also absent. The themes of the Self-Portrait Project swept over into the next Project on Old Age. It was during preparations for the Old Age Project that Robert 'conceived notion of a painting of myself on my deathbed, for Self-Portrait Project' (Diary, 12 October 1978). In the Self-Portrait Exhibition notes, Robert writes: 'The painter paints this look that summons him, he stares at it. He compels it to appear before him' rather like a sorcerer summoning a planetary daemon or dead soul. Several notes might be connected to themes he raised in the early works from the Hotel Shemtov such as *Self-Portrait in Room Number Three*:

This painted look is no vacant stare, it isn't the look of waiting that a pose held so often puts on a sitter's face [...] it is the look that only moments before was searching the mirror. On the easel the portrait is finished. [...] the portrait is a record of the mirror, ephemeral and mobile, the reflection is frozen. The portrait looks at the painter. Painted in what was present time, the portrait watches the painter grow older, the portrait watches the face it once was become wrinkled with age. Indifferent, the portrait watches time, which from day to day discovers death. (Self-Portrait Exhibition Notes, p. 2)

In December 1978 Robert spent three days at Port Eliot progressing with the Round Room Mural. Perry drove him back to Plymouth where they had a 'long talk on domestic stresses – J – etc. Poor *schlemiel*' (Diary, 5 December 1978). Later in the week Robert returned to Port Eliot to deliver a lecture: 'Alchemical Discourse on the Dazing and Amazing Mural in Progress, by the artist ROBERT LENKIEWICZ'. This is one of the few times he refers to himself as an artist rather than a painter.

Arrived by taxi, organised things as required [...] Many people came. Stood there and *spieled*. Jacquetta sat there black and deathly. I did an 'average' performance – several Jewish jokes etc. Did not go down too well when in reply to a question I suggested that mystics abstained because they had the clap. Jacquetta awkward and pressing for some devilish pointless reason. Tried to make me stay for a meal etc. I left immediately with Eliza [...] met up with Aury/Myrna/Ruti/Annie/Charles at Yankeeburger. (Diary, 8 December 1978)

December passed with intense, almost daily encounters with Mary. She was a fuel, no doubt, and he was making up for time lost to illness. Robert 'worked like a maniac ... completely non-stop all day' (Diary, 21 December 1978). The Self-Portrait Exhibition was due to open on the next day. Eliza toiled with him day and night: 'Re-mounted/stretched and re-framed everything necessary. Can't do all this as I used to. Eliza heroic in her work. Stayed up with me all night – at one point while painting the slats for a frame she fell asleep on the brush' (Diary, 22 December 1978). Typically, on the day of the exhibition, he writes: 'So many ideas for my next Project'. He makes very few notes about the opening of the exhibition or its reception by the public. He is by now too familiar with the process to be greatly excited by it.

For reasons unknown a list of works, a price list, or a gallery handout for Project 10: Self-Portrait has never been found. Perhaps the obvious reason is that the subject matter did not lend itself to distinct titles. Perhaps a unique in-gallery price list will turn up, likely written in Eliza's hand, as was the Old Age Project list.

By now, Robert could stake a claim to being an extraordinarily varied and accomplished self-portraitist. He was an enthusiastic collector of his self-portraits and reluctant to part with the better examples, except to more discerning patrons. Early works dating from the Hotel Shemtov and London studios remained cherished possessions throughout his life, including the *Self-Portrait with Punch Magazine* (1957). It was a significant gesture when Robert hung this painting in Mary's flat, impressing her with the fact it had been painted when he was just 16 years old. *Mr R. Lenkiewicz*, shown with 1973's Vagrancy work, is workmanlike, but *You Offer Me a Dead Rose, May I Give You a Dead Rat?* (1976) from the Love and Mediocrity Project is one of the ironic peaks. Nahem Shoa said it reminded him 'of the great nineteenth-century animal painter Edwin Landseer and his paintings of a dog bringing in a dead-animal offering to its master, which it has just gleefully killed. Lenkiewicz's self-portrait has the same sheepish stare, a mixture between vulnerability and brute strength' (*Self-Portraits* (2016), p. 40, White Lane Press). More significant again is *Self-Portrait (after Franz Xaver Messerschmidt)* (1976). Messerschmidt (1736–1783) was a German–Austrian sculptor who had produced a series of startling busts with contorted faces and extreme expressions: he called them 'character heads'. Messerschmidt's work would have been known to a mere handful of art historians in the mid-1970s, and books on his work would have been rare. However, Robert had in his library the book by Ernst Kris *Psychoanalytic Explorations in Art* (1952) which contained an influential essay on Messerschmidt called 'A Psychotic Sculptor of the Eighteenth Century'.

Marking a costume change characteristic of Project 10, the double-mirror *Self-Portrait with Mephistopheles* shows the painter in a white smock and blue trousers. A red devil-doll, Faust's Mephistopheles, is fixed to a chipped, pale blue chair, both still-life objects appearing tripled in the canvas from the dual reflections in two mirrors. It is worth emphasising for non-artists that the painting of a self-portrait requires the use of a mirror. This simple fact explains why the portrait the viewer sees on the canvas is laterally reversed: when the right-handed artist paints the hand holding the brush, he or she will appear left-handed. Two examples of this were painted shortly after the exhibition ended. *Self-Portrait With Mary With Newspaper in Her Hair* (1980) contains no less than six self-portraits of Robert, and the Suicide Project *Self-Portrait* (1979) shows the painter holding a red-tipped brush that has just been used to slash his own wrist, against a swirling blue background, as if the painter is being haunted by his own ghost.

However, two other self-portraits use a previous wardrobe and previous style. Nahem Shoa states:

> In 1978 he painted two mesmerising self-portraits, directly inspired by Dürer's famous self-portrait as Christ. Like Dürer, the modelling of form in both these heads is rendered in microscopic detail. [...] This self-portrait is painted at the tail end of what I've always seen as Lenkiewicz's 'Frans Hals period' of the early to middle 1970s – paintings defined by swashbuckling brushstrokes, driven around the canvas at breakneck speed, but all held together by his sharpness of eye, scrupulously exact tones and dynamic draughtsmanship. During this period Lenkiewicz would often paint two of three portraits in one session in some manic competition with himself and the great painters of the past. Often he utilised a seventeenth-century Dutch palette of reddish-brown warm shadow tones, cooled a little by terre verte green and black, adding orange-brown in the mid-tones and yellow highlights. (*Self-Portraits* (2008), p. 40, White Lane Press)

With the Self-Portrait show running over Christmas and the New Year, Robert elected to avoid the bustle with a quiet Christmas dinner with Eliza at the Pilgrim's Rest. He gave £5 to a passing old-timer – 'Cockney Jim, in a gangrenous state, almost certainly lost his hand through the ring' on which he had cut the flesh to save it from thieves (Diary, 24 December 1978). Eliza was a skilled costumier and make-up artist. She took Robert to her flat where he was:

Dressed up and made up as – FATHER CHRISTMAS! Completed transformation. Annie came down. Final details re: my night rounds. Highly successful conversion. Nobody recognised me as I hobbled along the Barbican/Clifton Street/Whitleigh Council Estate/Mannamead, etc. with my red sack. Children in arms were taken from their beds to view me as I passed over pavements and hills. Finally came to rest at Mouse's, much to the amusement of Alice, Becky and Wolfe. Eliza went to her parents. Stayed at my house. Slept alone. (Diary, 24 December 1978)

He woke early to prepare for the Christmas dinner at the bus station at which some new and nameless faces appeared. He notes 'Stranger' and a 'Woman from Moorhaven [asylum]' alongside the characters who set the industry standard for dossing: Cockney Jim, The Janner, The Bishop, Corky, Snowy, Harmonica Jim, and Les Ryder who 'took food away for Andy Lynch who was rotting somewhere on the Hoe'. The festivities did not much interrupt Robert's flow of work. The next day he 'opened the gallery and studio. Quite a number of people visited, but no intelligent interest, however. Completed more notes for Death/Self-Portrait book. Closed the shop past midnight. Eliza came with delicious food' (Diary, 26 December 1978). On the 28th:

As I came up to the studio, I noticed the posters had been ripped down and cast aside. On one was written the words: 'WHORE MASTER – S 14 C'. I immediately checked the mural to see if it had incurred damage. Sure enough, for the first time in seven and a half years, it had been severely vandalised – but only the portrait of me section. The face had been slashed across, and the eyes gouged out deep into the cement.

24.1 Poster for Project 11: Old Age, featuring Snowy.

24.2 Myriam Rivera, Annie Hill-Smith and Robert's children, Jascha, Sholem, and infant Kate on April Fools Day 1979 at the cottage.

24.3 View of the studio, 1979, with *The Dead Painter* canvas *(left)* and *Self-Portrait with Mephistopheles* behind the easel *(right)*.

24.4 Robert and Eliza seated in front of *The Dead Painter Surrounded by His Children and Companions*, from the Self-Portrait Project, Barbican studio, 1979. Robert is holding the notebook to the Old Age Project.

24.5 Robert and Eliza outside the studio in early 1979.

24.6 Christmas Day Dinner, 1979.

'Snowy, Cockney Jim, Archie (new), Bishop, Big Paddy (new),
Bearded John (new), Corky, W.W. Pearce (new), Reg Hawke, Vic.
Hans de Rijke, Eliza, myself.'

24

The Coming of Age

All years change the living forever but 1978 saw large alterations in Robert's character. He was better disposed to his children and the law, and he acknowledged that his work was largely ignored no matter how much energy he put into it. He made a rough peace with the fact that the Cowboys' Holiday Inns had achieved very little, almost nothing. He had in some ways 'grown up'. Even Joe Prete jokingly referred to him as 'Old Man Lenkiewicz' (Diary, 3 January 1979). He became more nuanced and broader in his emotional range, gentler in some respects, and more ruthlessly determined in others. We mentioned earlier how even the mildest of vagrants were genuine threats to the forces of authority. Whether the dossers intended it or not their laughter, their disobedience, even their apathy was a form of violence against society. Something similar applies to Robert.

Robert's violence is worth exploring, for it is of a sharply refined type and open to several levels of interpretation. Alex Donoghue noted that despite Robert's mobility and brawn he seemed incapable of throwing a full-on punch. He was the proverbial 'gentle giant' in the realm of hand-to-hand fighting. But his mind and his passions were another matter entirely. A 'provocation to thought' usually involves a brawl with 'normal decent morality'. His thought processes and his loves often extend beyond fierceness and into a wild zone where no social or moral rules applied. It is no coincidence Robert rated Brontë's *Wuthering Heights* as one of the greatest works in English literature. Here is Bataille's analysis of the novel in *Literature and Evil* (1957):

> The lesson of *Wuthering Heights*, of Greek tragedy, and ultimately of all religions is that there is an instinctive tendency towards divine intoxication which the rational world of calculation cannot bear. This tendency is the opposite of Good. [...] What comes to light in Emily Brontë's attitude, by means of an intangible moral solidity, is the dream of a sacred violence which no settlement with organised society can attenuate. (pp. 22–24)

Robert habitually steered his relationships by the star of destruction, invoking 'the passion that breaks reason in two' and this, possibly – we can say no more than 'possibly' – with the aim of re-uniting the parts into a new unity. The alchemical dictum *solve et coagula* suggests a deliberate breakdown of base elements to build a higher and 'more spiritual' creation. Robert frequently splintered himself and his lovers in ways which appear childish, irrational, or even sadistic compared to the social notion of 'building a strong relationship'. The Mary relationship is the best documented example but by no means the only one:

> I want actions, not explanations [...] and then to watch it die. She wanted to go upstairs and lie down: this was an impulse that could be perfectly employed for what I was looking for – only after some considerable time did she become aware that I had other plans for the night – Eliza and so on. She said she felt like she had been tricked etc. Said too much. So moving to see her leave in the taxi. Any pain or withdrawal she felt became a pleasure for me that can only draw me closer. There would be no end to my pleasure in her suffering, and vice-versa. This is traditionally so counter-productive. But little do the non-creative analysts know – where it really leads. (Diary, 16 November 1979)

> One of those lacerating times again. Intense and impossible. Must come to understand 'socially conditioned destruction' etc., more carefully. She tried to ask so many questions – I lay in her bed – atmosphere of Mephistophelean defilement. References to Taraneh. Yana returns on Friday. She says at times 'I hate you – I really do!'. She hates me so much. Better the cruel hard contact of pain than the grey familiarity of sin. (Diary, 10 December 1979)

An undated note reads: 'Beautifully hopeless – always the best combination.'

If we focus only upon Robert's worst actions and the aspects of his self-analysis which paint his soul lamp-black, then we will misunderstand him. His contrasts were many and extreme. For all the Mephistophelean self-styling he was more imp than arch-demon, and most of our interviewees stress his wicked humour. I certainly recall plenty of song, laughter, and light-hearted foolery in the Studio and on the scaffold. He could be magnificently considerate. Some close friends and lovers did not see any violence in him at all:

He had some lovely tender moments with his children and families. The best thing was his interest in people. He was always compassionate, and kind, and fun. (Nina Calder, Interview, February 2019)

People used to ask me – you know Robert, what's his secret? Well I said it's no secret really, it's just he lets people take their time, he listens and takes an interest, he doesn't smoke or drink, he's polite, and generous, and kind. He's a gentle giant; it's like a helter-skelter, it's not just one thing, it's a lot of simple things turning around the middle. I remember when Patti had the diary, there were probably twenty women waiting for sittings with him, plenty of people coming through the studio, and the fact was that he made women feel comfortable with him. He was in no rush to get anybody's clothes off. A painter and their models [...] there's always going to be some electricity and buzz, always something going on, even if it's not directly sexual. It's always going to give people a kind of intimacy. [...] And he liked women he could talk to and get to know. (John Pollex, Interview, February 2019)

He took the trouble to know me. Never to judge, or criticize, never to be violent. He was remarkably calm – a strange man. The only thing he did do that I had to tolerate was put up with the ten thousand others and of course because of this, his time was precious. (Stella Ney-Hoch, Letter, January 2019)

On Robert's first meeting with actor and broadcaster Jojo Moreschi, the youth's self-consciousness was as plain as the nose on his face. Robert straight away introduced Jojo to the hero he needed: Cyrano de Bergerac. After dramatically relating the life of the duellist and romantic poet to Jojo, Robert lent him a copy of Rostand's book: 'How kind is that? How [...] humane. He didn't know me, I was just this bloke who walked in off the street and he immediately found a way to make me feel better about myself' (Jojo, Interview, May 2018). It is up to the reader to weigh the obvious cruelty in some of Robert's relationships with the saintlier aspects of his character.

As the Old Age Exhibition at the Studio closed at 7 p.m. on Sunday 30 September 1979 after a three-month run, Robert noted in the narrow feint record book: 'It looks as though inclusive of Old Age/Self-Portrait, also drawings, I made approx. £6,000, which somewhat amazes me.' To put this amount in perspective, £6,000 was an average annual income for the time. Robert had never had it so good in terms of the earning potential of his own work.

And yet on the eve of the opening of the exhibition his diary notes state: 'I am unexpectedly muted by the Old Age Project. Once set up and hung it looks singularly uninteresting ... to me. The bound book of notes of some value'.

For these notes, Robert again made use of the abundant chip-shop paper purchased for the Mary material, then bound almost 300 A3 sheets between plywood, finished off with a cover made from the exhibition poster, with its image of Old Snowy. As with the 'Orgasm Project Notebook', the written material drew heavily upon a 'cross-referential' publication he much admired, in this case the classic study of old age and gender, *The Coming of Age* (1970), by author Simone de Beauvoir, who was 62 at the time of its publication.

As Kathleen Woodward explains,

> She surveyed and synthesized what she had found in multiple domains, including biology, anthropology, philosophy, and the historical and cultural record, drawing it all together to argue with no holds barred that the elderly are not only marginalized in contemporary capitalist societies, they are dehumanized. [42]

Robert used de Beauvoir's work as the skeletal structure for his illustrated notes. To her selection of ageing French intellectuals and historical figures he added illustrations drawn from contemporary portraits or photographs to put a face to the quotations. He then vastly expanded the range of material relating to the ageing experience of famous painters, such as Michelangelo, Goya, Cézanne, and William Blake.

> Lenkiewicz was especially interested in her observation of the 'passive attitude of renunciation' that age and physical weariness could bring. De Beauvoir writes: 'A consequence of biological decay is the impossibility of surpassing oneself and of becoming passionately interested with anything; it kills all projects.' This warning resonated with the lessons learned by the young painter at the Hotel Shemtov, but he had taken a radical step further: Lenkiewicz concluded that this renunciation of life could affect people at any age. He would explore this theme in the next Project, on Suicide, developing the idea that the routines

and compromises of modern life in service to 'commerce' so stifled the creative impulses that whole populations had rendered themselves 'dead, whilst still alive'. ('The Coming of Age', Exhibition Notes, p. 3, Plymouth Art Weekender 2019, St Saviours Hall, Plymouth)

The notes begin with Albert Einstein's reflections on death from 1954: 'To think with fear of the end of one's life is pretty general with human beings. It is one of the means nature uses to preserve the species. Approached rationally, that fear is the most unjustified of all fears. For there is no risk of any accidents to one who is dead' (Old Age Notebook, p. 97). This acceptance of death differs from but merges with the 'death-welcoming' attitude which in turn differs from but merges with the topic of suicide: 'All my life I have done nothing but work. And really, when you come to think of it, why? If I let my thoughts wander, I find nobody. Death is best, after all' (Lou Andreas Salome, quoted in Old Age Notebook, p. 99). Terror is not compulsory.

But lest we think that all that is required for a happy old age is a life of meaningful work, Robert catalogues many examples of creative and socially celebrated people who are not at all pleased with the inevitable result of living so long: Sigmund Freud, Simone De Beauvoir herself, and composer Antonio Vivaldi expressed some particularly grim evaluations of their lot. Robert also felt a certain discomfort and could not remain a neutral observer. He was sometimes ungenerous to the subjects of his investigations. Old age had invaded his places of memory and he was not happy about it:

Drove to the Old Age home at No.1 Keppel Terrace. So strange to sit and paint old folk eating in the very room where I had lived with Monica when she was pregnant with Reuben. [...] To my left and behind [is] where the bed had been – to the right, the bookshelves. In the centre, the massive papier mâché unicorn – all around, large paintings etc. Did a study of them all eating – silent chewing munching – toothless wet grindings – like maggots in their graves. Eliza crouched in the corner – where Monica used to undress – stand with her white skin and round tummy. Eliza studied a Morris 1000 manual while I painted surly 80-year-old children. (Diary, 26 March 1979)

Robert began recruiting elderly sitters in the autumn of 1978. The local branch of the charity Age Concern was helpful. As was Sheree Dodd, a rare sober and sympathetic journalist: 'Controversial artist Robert Lenk-iewicz is scouring the West Country to find two models for the central painting of a new exhibition. No previous modelling experience is necessary but the models must have one important quality – they have to be the oldest man and woman in the South West'. To counteract the scandal mongering which might scare such models away Ms Dodd gave space to Robert's view that 'a lot of nonsense has been said about [the Orgasm Exhibition]. Anyone who takes the trouble to study the exhibition without scampering through looking for nudes is very conscious of the aesthetic theory behind the paintings' (news clipping, Diary, 17 September 1978). Whilst sitting for her portrait, Mrs Kathleen Binns, who was 95, confided in Lenkiewicz: 'They selected me as an example of a woman who enjoys old age, but it's not true … I don't! You can enjoy *life*, but not old age – too many frustrations!' (note of a conversation between artist and sitter, 1979).

Some of the elders were equally delightful: Rusty was charming and lusty, Frank was good company and a great sitter. Others were not so. In his diary on 5 October 1978 Robert notes 'Old Ken. Impossible model. Kept falling asleep. Finally destroyed the painting and re-started one of him snoring'. What jumps from the pages of the diaries is how the borders of 'old age' have changed since the 1970s. Cyril was a mere 67. Several vagrants were probably younger but with ages impossible to guess. Vagrants or not, most of the sitters had hard lives and it is possible that several did not know their age. Some could neither read nor write (Diary, 17 September 1978). Others were properly documented though almost unbelievably old, such as Mrs Lilian Williams, aged 110. She was born almost 50 years before the planet Pluto was discovered and could remember newspaper reports of Jack the Ripper terrorising Whitechapel.

The Old Age paintings are diverse in both style and quality. Robert was by now entirely committed to a strategy of pursuing ideas by any means necessary: it is as if he suspected any 'unity of artistic style' would limit the project. There are fewer oil paintings than in previous projects: only 57 are listed in his project notebook. He was working at a smaller scale (the study of Snowy is life-size), occasionally with composite groups of sitters such as the Almshouse paintings (which needed canvases 2 metres wide), but there are no huge canvases such as we saw in the Vagrancy Project. There are numerous watercolour studies of old people. The best of these are truly outstanding and the worst competent but merely documentary. Part of the reason for this may be financial – he was at times so poor that Eliza had to buy paints for him (Diary, 15 November 1978). On 26 November he notes: 'No money. Must stop electricity being cut off – and the bailiffs – somehow'. Also, he needed to be mobile: many of his sitters were not and setting up easels and large canvases in care homes and hospitals was impractical. Even if the sitters could come to the studio there were dire risks from other visitors who were incompatible with a tranquil old age. 'Psycho-knife Tim visited me, after 5 years in Dartmoor', Robert notes in his diary (26 November 1978). Small watercolour studies in quiet settings enabled the South West's oldest people to keep their titles a little longer.

Of the works on canvas the largest two are painted in the manner of the Dutch master Frans Hals (1582–1666). Two of the smaller oil paintings are of outstanding quality – the *Study of Rusty* quoting Edvard Munch (1863–1944), and the small but almost overwhelmingly powerful portrait of double-amputee Snowy. This latter is influenced by Rembrandt's and Rubens' portraiture with variations of cool half-tones, then warm lighter tones, and cool highlights applied in a rugged but highly controlled manner. I am thinking of Rembrandt's *Old Woman Reading* (1655) and Rubens' vigorous *Study of an Old Woman* from the series of studies painted around 1615–1620. Robert's portrait of Snowy is humane but almost scientific in its account of what happens to human flesh when gravity and time have done their work. The direct stare of the sitter echoes the thoughts of many writers in the project notebook, but especially Voltaire's doleful words: 'The heart does not grow old, but it is sad to live among ruins'. Robert wrote a rare commentary on the work in progress: 'Getting stronger and stronger. To wrap one's mental eye around the illusion of form like a lover; Pull the string bag of one's bright idea tight … and, nothing there as ever! The true magic trick all experienced painters know.' He added a caveat: 'Strong inch by inch – weak 3 inch by 3 inch'.

At 225 illustrated pages the notebook for this project is immense and gorgeous. It is amazing that he could produce work of such quality and sheer quantity while he was also compiling the huge 'Mary Notebook'. Many watercolours in the Old Age Notebook were of necessity painted from photographs. Most are unsentimental but moving and lively despite Robert's dislike of using photographs, but there is solemnity and warmth in his small works such as 'Augustus John, dead – last photograph, 1961' (Old Age Notebook, p. 40). The one of Einstein is taken from the classic Princeton photographs of the 1940s in which Einstein had become an iconic representation of a contemporary sage. This same portrait later informed the Old Age Mural at Age Concern in 1982.

Of the many fears attendant upon old age some are entirely rational and worth exploring. Due to his researches on Gurdjieff and Sufism Robert had a robust framework for thinking about how much of our life is spent 'sleepwalking' towards old age. He also studied folk tales and myths in which time passes over the central characters who are living, but unconscious. His notes include accounts of the Seven Sleepers of Ephesus and Rip Van Winkle (Old Age Notebook, p. 123). To live a long time but to have little by way of experience is a nightmare which Robert explored at length and in detail through a variety of stories: Swift's Luggnaggians from *Gulliver's Travels*, the story of the Wandering Jew, and the Book of Job. For all of these, the extension of life is much more a curse than a blessing. These are myths and parables, but Robert approaches the very real horror of ageing-without-living in his notes on the epidemic of encephalitis lethargica, the dreadful sleeping sickness which appeared in 1916. With grim fascination Robert hand-copied long sections of Oliver Sacks's *Awakenings* (1973). He closes this section of the Old Age notes with a haunting watercolour image of a presumably unconscious patient emitting a silent scream. Above the image is a quote from Sacks: 'and yet some lived on, in diminishing numbers, getting older and frailer (though usually looking younger than their age), inmates of institutions, profoundly isolated, deprived of experience, half forgetting, half dreaming of the world they once lived in' (Old Age Notebook, p. 139).

Other images of extreme old age are less depressing. Robert explores the culturally and psychologically important figure of that great anti-hero of longevity, the vampire. 'The archetypal allegory in the popular mind re: immortality – centres around the character of DRACULA. Since 1897 when it was written, it has interjected into Western culture the image of a creature of such symbolic force that though duty bound to hate him, we are impelled also to admiration. Elegant, graceful, strong, lonely, wise, deadly, and erotic' (Old Age Notebook, p. 217). As templates for ageing go one could do a lot worse, and Robert devotes hundreds of words and several fine watercolours to the various iterations of the vampire. He goes on to make the case that the elegance, wisdom, and eroticism of the old is drastically under-played in our culture.

Robert notes with approval the activities of Victor Hugo, aged 70, who pursued and was pursued by some of the greatest beauties of Europe. Sarah Bernhardt and Judith Gaultier were among his mistresses, although his energies were not unlimited. He complained that it was now difficult to make public speeches because 'talking tires me, as much as making love three times'. After a moment's thought he corrected himself: 'Even four' (Old Age Notebook, p. 106). In his sonnet 'Those Who Are about to Die Salute You' – dedicated to Judith Gaultier, 50 years his junior – Hugo wrote: 'We are both of us near to heaven, Madame, Since you are beautiful, and I am old.' In Hugo's view 'old age was by no means a blemish, but rather an honour, it brought us nearer to God, and it brought us into harmony with everything – that it is sublime, with beauty, and innocence' (Old Age Notebook, p. 406). Robert catalogues many other examples of joyful and triumphant old age such as Miss Plunkett, 111 years old and still in charge of all her own affairs (Old Age Notebook, p. 156).

Of course, Robert did not ignore the views of the sitters themselves. In a typical example, Cockney Jim's 'thoughts on growing old and impotence' are fixed to the back of a small watercolour and gouache study:

'Cockney Jim', 74yrs. Plymouth tramp etc.
'Nature decides to call a halt at 73: and quite right too. I could lie on top all night and nothin' would 'appen. I would get all the thrills as I did when a young man – but a young man's inclined to take things for granted.'
'Sometimes I feel I'm up against an insurmountable wall – I fight against it with cheap wine; but afterwards I'm covered with the same regrets of losing my youth. Artificial pleasure – 'Plonk' – blue films.'
'You and women are poles apart; you're a cork on the ocean. Sometimes you wish the earth would open and swallow you; other times you get thoughts of spring and youth comes back in spasms.'
'Age may bring wisdom but by that time you can't do much with it: wisdom and impotence.' (Painting notes, verso on *Study of Cockney Jim*, 1979)

The mass of evidence indicates that while bad luck, ill health, and poverty may well torment some of us in old age, those ills are just as likely to vex us at any age: and since the old have had time to develop strategies for such troubles the prospect of old age is not in itself cause for fear or depression. Like all changes it can be navigated with more or less skill. Such is the implication of his painting of Rusty, modelled upon Munch's *Puberty* (1894–1895). Like puberty, senescence is a time where fear and irreversible change feed off each other. But like the 'nigredo' or blackening

417

phase in alchemy this process is a degeneration necessary to new forms of maturity. It is not unreasonable to hope that something rare and valuable will emerge.

Which is why the lecture performance of Professor Jeremy Jacobson is so puzzling. The background to this is obscure but possibly has its roots in Eliza transforming Robert into a very credible Father Christmas in the previous December. The idea came to him very late in the project. On the final day of the exhibition Robert noted in his Dairy, 'Lunch with Johnny and Tova. More discussions on the Gerontological thesis' (undated diary page, but almost certainly Sunday 30 September 1979). Johnny, a scientific researcher specialising in the neurology and psychology of ageing, was profoundly impressed by the depth and breadth of the project. In an interview in 2018 he said:

> There's always critics and cynics and some people thought – and they said it – 'Well this [Robert] seems to think he's an expert on everything, jealously, sex, old age, everything' [...] There's a real hostility to intellectuals. Very British. I don't think other countries [have an equivalent to the] British expression 'He's too clever by half!'. He was a great self-publicist and that went against him but he was never a dilettante. He really knew what he was talking about. The research was solid. (Johnny, Interview, September 2018)

This tension between Robert's intellectual work and his showmanship was almost a self-sabotaging reflex. Johnny confirmed the sociological and scientific credentials of the project but there would also be this:

> [...] Suddenly conceived a plan for my talk on Old Age/Geriatrics versus Gerontology. I will dress and disguise myself as an old man in a drab suit and scarf. As I stand on the rostrum I shall start removing these clothes – jacket, then a T shirt with the inscription DIRTY OLD MEN NEED LOVE – then down to my smock and trousers – rejuvenating to a 37 year old – then spiel. (Undated diary page, but almost certainly Sunday 30 September 1979)

He also notes: 'The last day saw 207 visitors. The whole Project received 10,507 visitors'. The figure is plausible. Eliza and Myriam were often recording close to 200 visitors a day (Diary, 21 August 1979). In terms of public interest Robert did not need this fancy dress stunt. Much less did he need it in terms of making the art critics or academics sympathetic to his output. But 'The Imp of The Perverse' had whispered in his ear, and Robert chuckled as he listened, and was defenceless.

The initial date Robert placed in his diary for the 'Geriatrics versus Gerontology' (coping with age versus postponing old age) talk is 17 November 1979. It was in fact on the 15th. Robert was approached by Mrs Elspeth Sitters of Age Concern (now Age UK), which had a day centre on Notte Street no more than two minutes' walk from the Studio. She was not at first a likely helper but grew to like him as she began to appreciate the seriousness of his work. He records:

> Mrs Sitters visited the exhibition with health visitor. They seemed much impressed. She told me that Dr David Mercer had expressed interest in my attending a conference on Old Age at the medical centre this November. They hoped I could round off the lectures with observations as I wished, etc. Ironic development considering her original attitude. The whole event could be very interesting. (Undated, but almost certainly Tues 21 August 1979)

Whatever the initial clash with Mrs Sitters was about it was not due to any conservatism on her part. She soon proved herself to be a strong and even provocative ally. The conference was announced in the *Western Evening Herald* on Tuesday 6 November. For the first time in a long time, the name Lenkiewicz was not wrapped in shock-horror journalism.

> Barbican artist Robert Lenkiewicz is to present theories of Old Age at a Plymouth conference this month. [...] Lenkiewicz is the only amateur on a programme which includes a geriatrician, a consultant surgeon, social service workers and a retired health visitor. Mrs Cherry Martin of Age Concern said: 'We have got all these specialists, and we asked Mr Lenkiewicz to come because he is a theorist. He has made a year-long study of old age, its history and future, and his exhibition on the subject at his Barbican gallery has just closed'. [...] Lenkiewicz said 'Gerontology is an inevitable development in the medical world. It involves the philosophical framework for the geriatrics of the future.' Lenkiewicz has a brother who works as a gerontologist in London, specialising in the brain.

There is no mention of the esteemed Professor Jacobson speaking at the event, for Robert had not finished inventing him. Eliza was working hard to gather the necessary clothes and props and make-up. Hans de Rijke read through Robert's lecture notes and 'corrected a number of technical issues [...] Hans felt that the thesis was excellent and useful' (Diary, 13 November 1979). Throughout this project Robert regularly recorded a feeling that the painting was not enough. Earlier in the year he notes:

Worked non-stop from 10pm to 1am – on large self-portrait – full figure adequately resolved, nicely stained etc, subtle, altogether – but unsatisfying. (Diary, 21 August 1979)

Worked hard on portrait [of Mac] an extraordinary fellow. Told me about being torpedoed in the war – 400 drowned. He survived. Worked hard on portrait – slightly losing it now – depressing – I so rarely hold onto the form for long. (Diary, 8 November 1979)

He was still capable of feats of strength and nowhere near as ill as he had been during his attack of tubercular palsy. But he was feeling more than his age and often recorded minor but worrying episodes such as: 'suddenly started feeling shaky and embarrassingly feeble – as though I was seventy – Had carried a two-hundredweight washing machine down the stairs for Annie this morning and felt fine – most peculiar. Hands shaking, etc' (Diary, 9 November 1979). Awful though the experience was, feeling so ancient provided him with practice for the role he was about to assume. Eliza explains the transformation which took place on 15 November:

I bought him an outfit from charity shops: beige trousers, tweedy jacket, a shirt and tie, brown leather shoes, a walking cane [...] an actor friend of mine gave advice on make-up and somehow, with the help of a woolly scarf, we managed to disguise his hair, tucking it into his collar and winding the scarf around his neck. All that afternoon we spent at Annie's house on Clifton Street while I fiddled with his face. Stage make-up is fine when you are on stage, but Robert would be under close scrutiny so I had to be as subtle as I could manage. I had [my own] costume too: from somewhere I had procured a nurse's uniform and a wheelchair. (From *Remembering Robert*, Jojo Moreschi, University of Plymouth Press)

Robert writes:

Ready by 7.00pm. I stood up once the disguise was complete – and with wavering voice asked Pnoobie his name – 'Where's Robert?' he asked [...]. The effect really rather successful. Finally hobbled down with Eliza […] As we entered the Centre the wheelchair began to fall to bits just like those exploding circus cars – in order not to attract attention we ditched it. An old man of 73 helped into the lecture hall, I sat in the seat proscribed for Professor Jeremy Jacobson, shaking in palsied fashion with a rug over my legs. After an hour Johnny stood up and delivered a brief talk on gerontology from a slightly technical point of view. He then apologised for the absence of Mr Robert Lenkiewicz and introduced Prof Jacobson – an authority on this and that aspect of gerontology. I hobbled up and delivered my talk. The reaction was silently dramatic and highly amusing. A number of people that I knew – Jim Pascoe, Lord Eliot, Dr Pollard, John Nash, Hans de Rijke etc had come as well [...] Perhaps the most haunting aspect was the sensation of the Lenkiewicz duo. It appeared to me that despite a relatively dull-minded and immature audience the whole sequence was highly successful. How much of the philosophic-practical implication of the thesis came over is debatable, In my view very little. Successful as entertainment and eccentric philosophic humour – unsuccessful in terms of presenting information. A lot of affectionate attention afterwards. The press wanted a copy of my lecture to print in the paper, a health-authority asked for a copy, etc, etc. As I came out on the foyer, nervous confusion and excitement everywhere. Warm, light-hearted – amusing. So many innuendoes. (Diary, 15 November 1979)

Eliza recalls: 'People were completely taken in by it, completely. He was a marvellous actor, an incredible actor' (Interview, September 2019). Many listeners remember Professor Jacobson's acidic quotes on the miseries of old age. This seems peculiar and one-sided considering the guarded optimism of Robert's research findings. Johnny sees this as possibly another experiment: 'I think he wanted to see who would disagree with him. And nobody did. Which most likely says more about obedience to authority than anyone's real attitude' (Eliza Gunning, Interview, September 2018). Robert was clearly having fun, but as ever the foolery had a serious point which few people had contemplated in the 1970s. We noted how many of Robert's sitters were a mere 60 or so years of age. For working men born in 1921, fifty-five and a half years was the average span. For those born in 1930, it was still well under 60. The average expectancy for those born in 2010 has climbed to 80 years and reaching 100 is not unusual. When Robert gave his talk few people appreciated the steepness of the ageing trajectory. Fewer had any idea what it implied, or how we might deal with it. The *Western Evening Herald* reported:

> When he straightened up at the end of his talk, a gasp of amazement went up from his audience, who rubbed their eyes with disbelief. Mr Lenkiewicz said evidence today suggested that deterioration with age could be suppressed by science 'There is a good chance of delaying all of the ageing causes. What it is important to realise is that the period of senility would not be prolonged. In other words, you would become old later, you would not be old for longer: to prolong the quality of life so that it takes 80 years to get to be 60'. Mr Lenkiewicz said we should prepare ourselves where we can as a result. (News clipping, Diary, 16 November 1979)

Which, of course, we didn't. Robert was not a saint or a prophet but he was one of the most acute social observers of his time. He had the great advantage of being untethered to a university post or political party – or indeed, money. Nobody was paying the piper so nobody was calling the tune. Thus the Old Age Project is perhaps the best independent philosophical, sociological, and artistic inquiry we have on the topic for 20th-century England.

Other projects simmered concurrently. The 'Mary Notebook' was progressing well and the Suicide Project gained momentum from late summer onwards. The progress of the Gossip on the Barbican Project was hobbled by the fact that throughout that year Robert became increasingly wary of spending time in the area:

> Robert was terrified of [Big Brummie]. Truly terrified. We always had to hide in doorways when we saw him. Robert was always on the lookout, always scanning the horizon, he'd be [mimes fast, anxious head and eye movements] all the time. All the time, checking everywhere to see if this big dark figure was lurking. I think [Brummie] just went away someday and never came back, possibly just disappeared into the prison system I guess. That period was coming to a close when I first knew Robert, the whole Vagrancy thing. I think Robert was finding he

had to withdraw. It got too much, it took too much out of him [...] it was too dangerous. (Eliza Gunning, Interview, September 2019)

His instincts about the dangers from the dossers were well founded. He notes on Tuesday 21 August:

Mike Ryan – the lunatic that tried to kill me with the 7-inch butcher's knife some six years ago – suddenly turned up – sat grinning on the wall. How like 'Brummy' his face is. Interesting association. The wide boxer's nose, the brutalized small mouth, etc. I prepared for him becoming a nuisance – determined to discourage him without inhibition – but he made no attempt to come in. It is strange that Robert makes the link from Ryan to Brummie but does not note that the reappearance of both villains might have something to do with the recent reappearance of the manipulative 'Brighton'. (Diary, 21 August 1979)

Despite turning away from the world of the dossers there was another underworld which Robert was still very interested in. Its denizens were more than welcome in Robert's studio: 'Dougy – Douglas Edwin Cox. Scrap Metal Dealer. Good start. Lively hyper-active sensitive thug. Will paint him with his "persuader" (sledgehammer). Could be very dramatic study of the Cox gang' (Diary, 8 November 1979).

Robert enjoyed such raw villains boasting how they were 'lucky to be in one piece as a result of incident on Saturday' (Diary, 12 November 1979) and always asked for details. They obliged, for once a rough-neck is convinced the listener is not a 'grass' they love a lightly terrorised audience. It is plausible that their brutally physical and financially motivated violence formed a strange counterpoint to the violence of Robert's inner world.

Robert had already started paintings for the Suicide Project by September (Diary, 9 September 1979). The reading and thinking preceded that date by several months. From classical 'philosophical' suicides such as the deaths of Socrates, Seneca, and arguably Jesus, Robert moved though Dante to John Donne's 1644 'Biathanatos', to Madame de Staël and the pamphleteers of the 1700s to the modern sociology of Durkheim. The most influential single book was Al Alvarez's *The Savage God* (1972), the first study to place the human capacity for self-destruction in a wider historical and cultural context.

Although Robert often said he was a stranger to depression there are several episodes suggesting more than a temporary low mood. He habitually makes negative comments about his work: '[Studio roof] still leaking – but I don't care – damp and mould will make useful contributions to my rubbish' (Diary, 22 July 1979). He is uncharacteristically weary or, at the very least, supremely unconcerned about the opening of the exhibition (Diary, 26 July 1979).

The Suicide Project was going to test many of the sitters almost to destruction. Some, such as Heroin Geoff and his girlfriend, were already high-risk self-harmers sailing close to the edge of the world. Others were presently stable and tough, such as Annie, who 'agreed to pose in "suicide with dead children" theme at her house' (Diary, 26 October 1979). Robert started slashed-wrist studies and a large painting of Lelya – who had impulsively flown in from Holland – in which he encouraged a kind of method acting. She recalls, 'He would command me when he was painting "Be dead. Be dead!"' (Interview, May 2018). It is almost as if Robert's role as painter crossed over to that of a director coaxing the best possible performance from his cast.

Robert worked on the Gossip on the Barbican Project in tandem with Suicide, moving effortlessly between different styles of thought and painting. It recalls the legendary Barbican strongman 'Blind-A-Pig'. There may have been exaggerations, but he was real enough, for on 23 November 1979 a local woman called Flo brought Blind-A-Pig's daughter to visit Robert. He noted: 'She is 73 and rather extraordinary – smells offensively – but tolerable'. It seems Robert 'cut himself' in and out of character, in and out of widely different scenes, without any great mishap. The barely controlled synaesthesia he develops in the 'Mary Notebook' is almost entirely absent from the Old Age notes which he worked on at the same time. The mad and violent passions of the Mary relationship seem to take place in an entirely different world to that of Eliza:

I really think he protected me from his worst excesses; he was pretty gentle with me. I remember Annie saying that too, saying, 'He's got a real soft spot for you, he protects you from a lot of the stuff that goes on.' [Compared to the ferocity of the Mary relationship] he was quite protective to me. I mean, where is Mary now? I think she's going to make quite sure that she is never found I should imagine, and that speaks volumes.

He didn't like rats or *buttons*, but it was weird [...] I remember wearing a dress with buttons and he completely freaked about it – *'Never wear that again!'* – but with other people it wasn't an issue. It was obviously something to do with buttons and sex. But to come back to his life as a performer, he was very good at splitting himself into parts; he would switch from one 'Robert' to another effortlessly: the Robert who was very gentle and good with little old ladies and the Robert who was dealing with aggressive dossers and telling them to fuck off. A myriad of different Roberts. And he was in complete control of all of them. Which could be quite confusing, even for those of us close to him. (Eliza, Interview, October 2019)

At the end of the 1970s Robert's mental health was good considering the immense strain he worked under. His physical health had been precarious for several years but his strength remained impressive. He was still single -handedly hoisting huge canvases around the Barbican, often heaving them on ropes from the street to the upper floors. On 28 November he helped carry John Nash's piano up five flights of stairs. He still refused to divide children into 'his' and 'not-his', considering such ideas of owner-ship as fascistic, but he took more interest in the extended family than in previous years. The children's upsurge of strength and beauty interested him: 'Becky visited – sweet to see her intelligent face. She looks attractive too' (Diary, 1 December 1979). Their worries worried him: 'Reuben came down. Sad interesting talk with him about school life and bullies' (Diary, 6 December 1979). Sometimes their youth became for Robert another version of the *memento mori*: 'Mouse's [house]. See Wolfe (peculiar be-haviour problems etc). Pleasant time. Usual competitive element – but clean aggressive fun. Ended up with a ten round wrestling match. I won all rounds. But not long to go now' (Diary, 29 November 1979).

And the decade brought rays from that distant star called 'economic reality'. Whereas in the 1960s Robert had squashed opportunities from the likes of Douglas Fairbanks Jr, the necessity of paying at least some bills now led him to compromise – though never fully: 'Mrs Weller. Study of Pekinese bitch. Oil on canvas £35. Did the intolerable thing. She only paid £30 but I didn't have the heart to correct her' (Diary, 5 December 1979).

Throughout the late 1970s Robert read more European philosophy, with Foucault, Bataille, and Herbert Marcuse's *Art and Revolution* proving interesting enough to re-read (Diary, 9 December 1979). Nietzsche endures as an intellectual mainstay, though he remained far from academic respectability in the late 1970s: 'Listened to Robert Stevens' Nietzsche study on the radio – Interesting. So strange to hear him discussed' (Diary, 11 December 1979).

One of the largest changes of the decade was Robert's relationships with the dossers. His relationships with sexual companions had also became more dangerous, though he showed less will or ability to make safe his behaviour on this front. Quite the converse. The Mary relationship was the most reckless of experiments, not least because it ran concurrently with several profound involvements where jealousy, emotional and physical self-harm, and suicide should have been foreseen. Either Robert foolishly assumed that his extreme compartmentalisation of emotions would magically rub off on his companions, or he was following George Gurdjieff's maxim that human knowledge required the use of 'freely moving Guinea Pigs allotted to me by destiny for my experiments' (Gurdjieff, *Herald*, p. 22).

Let us reiterate that Robert was not merely pursuing his sexual jollies. A 'relationship notebook' is never a simple pleasure discourse. In poorly dated notes several months apart he writes: 'Met a girl called Helen – she was going to Spain tomorrow – had come via Plymouth to see me and stay overnight. I explained I was otherwise engaged. Not attracted to her physically – but would like to sleep with her for other reasons. She said she would contact me from Spain in a few weeks'. And more emphatically, a note possibly from late autumn 1979 records an approach by a woman who signalled her availability but for whom he had no sexual desire whatsoever. He takes her contact details and beneath these writes 'DO THE EXPERIMENT'. There are many more examples in the diaries. Even with Mary he is engineering situations which pain him. He craves Mary, truly craves her, but he puts fractures in the relationship to see how it feels:

'Are you really just too tired of it all?' she asks. I smiled [and said] 'Yes' [*this was a lie for the sake of the 'experiment'*]. We separated on the corner of Southside Street. She went to see Yana as arranged. 'I will see you again' she said. I must study myself carefully on this one – really carefully. (Diary, November/December 1979)

He then counts the days of this separation he has unilaterally planned until he records: 'No sign of Mary: exactly one month' (undated, late December 1979).

Robert was now seeing his 'research' in almost scientific terms. The early 'Relationship Series: Attitudes Towards Love' had officially been recast as 'sociological and philosophical enquiries by visual means', now termed 'Projects', examining human physiology (the functioning of the body) in a state of crisis. These were connected by his radical theory of 'aesthetic fascism' which proposed that all human behaviour was essentially *physiological* (not psychological) and addictive in nature. However, there were already clear signs that the next decade would see the line between doctor and patient increasingly blurred.

Further Reading

Callow, John. (2018) 'The Witch on The Barbican' in *Embracing the Darkness: A Cultural History of Witchcraft*. London: I.B. Tauris.

Jojo. (2010) *Remembering Robert: R. O. Lenkiewicz as Told by His Sitters.* Plymouth: University of Plymouth Press.

Lenkiewicz, Alice. (2019) *When Robert Met Mouse: A Memoir.*

Lenkiewicz, R. O. (1973) 'Melancholy, the Dance of Death and Fool Symbolism in relation to Vagrancy' in Observations on Local Vagrancy.

Lenkiewicz, R. O. (1974) Notes on Death and the Maiden.

Lenkiewicz, R. O. (1982) 'The Changing Pattern of Dying', *The Western Evening Herald*, 11 February.

Lenkiewicz, R. O., Mallett, F. and Penwill, M. (1997a) Interviews with Robert Lenkiewicz, published in edited form as *R.O. Lenkiewicz*, Plymouth: White Lane Press.

Lenkiewicz, R. O. (1997b) 'Retrospective' exhibition brochure, Plymouth: Plymouth City Museum and Art Gallery.

Lenkiewicz, R. O., Mallett, F. (ed.) and Penwill, M. (ed.) (1998) *The Mary Notebook*, Plymouth: White Lane Press.

Mallett, F. (ed.) (2006) *Robert Lenkiewicz: Paintings and Projects*, Plymouth: White Lane Press.

Mallett, F. and Penwill, M. (eds.) (2005) *A Portrait of Robert Lenkiewicz: Photographs by Dr Philip Stokes*, Plymouth: White Lane Press.

Mallett, F. (2011) *The Painter with Women: The Evolution of a Project.* Plymouth: White Lane Press.

Mallett, F. and Penwill, M. (eds.) (2008) *Robert Lenkiewicz: Self-Portraits*, Plymouth: White Lane Press.

'Memento mori in the Work of Robert Lenkiewicz' (1941–2002), Penwill, M. 'Still Lives' exhibition booklet (Royal West of England Academy 17 April–31 May) (2011). Plymouth: White Lane Press.

'Human, All Too Human', Catalogue, Spinnerei, Leipzig, 23 June–21 July 2013. Plymouth: The Lenkiewicz Archive; also available in German as 'Menschliches, Allzumenschliches.

Stokes, Philip (1984) *Robert Lenkiewicz: Notes and Transcriptions*, 5 vols, Nottingham: Philip Stokes.

Notes

1   Tracey Rich, Judaism 101 Genealogy.

2   Freddy Godshaw, article ID A3332611, 26 November 2004. (www.bbc.co.uk/history/ww2peopleswar/stories/11/a3332611.shtml)

3   Freddy Godshaw, op. cit.

4   Kurt Vonnegut, in the *Michigan Quarterly Review*, Winter 2010.

5   Robert Lenkiewicz in conversation with F. Mallett and M.A. Penwill, *R. O. Lenkiewicz*, White Lane Press, 1997.

6   *Robert Lenkiewicz, Self-Portraits*, White Lane Press, 2008. pp. 16–17.

7   *Robert Lenkiewicz, Self-Portraits*, White Lane Press, 2008. pp. 16–17.

8   Heathcote Williams, *The Speakers* (1964), p. 79.

9   Robert Lenkiewicz, 'Essay on Velázquez', pamphlet notes with illustrations, 1950s.

10 Robert Lenkiewicz in conversation with F. Mallett and M.A. Penwill, *R.O. Lenkiewicz*, White Lane Press, 1997.

11 (Manuscript version in *R. O. Lenkiewicz*, 1997).

12 Nietzsche, Ecce Homo, 'Why I am so Wise', 1888.

13 *Robert Lenkiewicz, Self-Portraits*, White Lane Press, 2008. p. 18.

14 Nietzsche, Beyond Good and Evil, 205.

15 Philip Stokes, *A Portrait of Robert Lenkiewicz*, Introduction, p. x.

16 Robert, in *Paintings and Projects,* 2006, p. 13.

17 Philip Stokes, *A Portrait of Robert Lenkiewicz*, Introduction, p. x.

18 Robert's affectionate term for younger offspring. Pnoob was Robert's Fool-like innocent alter-ego, and hence always entirely blameless whatever his faults.

19 Terence McKenna, *Magic and the Hermetic Tradition* (2016).

20 Terence McKenna, *Magic and the Hermetic Tradition* (2016).

21 T. E. Lawrence, *Seven Pillars of Wisdom* (1922), Introduction.

22 *Robert Lenkiewicz, Self-Portraits*, p. 30.

23 *Robert Lenkiewicz, Self-Portraits*, p. 30.

24 Büchlien vom Stein der Weisen, 1778.

25 Lenkiewicz, Vagrancy Project Notes, 1973.

26 Anna Cafolla, dazeddigital.comartsandculture/article/32864/1, 2017.

27 Anna Cafolla, op. cit.

28 Leon Battista Alberti (1407–1472), Ten Books of Architecture, in Siglind Bruhn, The Musical Order of the World, p. 196.

29 In Philip Stokes, *A Portrait of Robert Lenkiewicz*, p. xi.

30 www.robertlenkiewicz.org, Project 2.

31 Nietzsche, 'The Vision and the Riddle', Thus Spake Zarathustra.

33 Sigmund Freud, *On Beginning the Treatment*, 1913/1958, p. 131.

34 Tom Braden quoted by Frances Stonor Saunders, in The Independent, 22 October 1995.

35 Dr Ernest Becker, *The Denial of Death* (1973).

36 Published by White Lane Press as a limited edition in 1998 and by Harper Collins The Book Project in 2013.

37 See Stanton Marlan's book *The Black Sun: The Alchemy and Art of Darkness*, 2005.

38 Annie Hill-Smith review of the exhibition 'Robert Lenkiewicz: Still Lives' at the Royal West of England Academy, Bristol in 2011.

39 Op. cit.

40 *R. O. Lenkiewicz* (1997), White Lane Press.

41 'Murder is misdirected suicide, to destroy part of oneself; murder is suicide with mistaken identity. And suicide is also a case of mistaken identity, an attack on the (introjected) other.' *Love's Body*, reissue of 1966 Edition, by Norman O. Brown, University of California Press, 1996, pp. 162–175.

42 'Rereading Simone de Beauvoir's The Coming of Age', Age Culture Humanities, Issue 3, 2016.

List of illustrations and credits

The author and publishers would like to thank the following for permission to use photographs: The Lenkiewicz Foundation Trust (TLF), John Lenkiewicz (d. 2019), Stella Ney-Hoch, Celia Mills, Monica Quirk, Tarun Bedi, Hans de Rijke (d. 2012), Jeny Bremer, Annie Hill-Smith, Denzil Bath, Philip Stokes (d. 2003), Chris Robinson.

Front cover: Nick Rogers/Shutterstock.
Back cover: Courtesy of Chris Robinson.
Foreword: Courtesy of E. Kanter.

18.1 TLF; 18.2 Hans de Rijke; 18.3–18.7 Annie Hill-Smith;
18.8–18.9 TLF

19.1–19.4 Hans de Rijke; 19.5–19.6 TLF; 19.7 Hans de Rijke

20.1–20.5 TLF

21.1–21.17 TLF

22.1–22.2 TLF

23.1–23.3 TLF; 23.4 Philip Stokes; 23.5–23.9 TLF;
23.10–23.11 Hans de Rijke

24.1 TLF; 24.2 TLF; 24.3–24.5 Philip Stokes; 24.6 Annie Hill-Smith

About the Author

Mark D. Price lectured in philosophy at several UK universities before becoming an independent researcher in arts and humanities. His two PhD doctorates were inspired and encouraged by his conversations with Robert Lenkiewicz.

Printed in Great Britain
by Amazon